A Nation Like All Nations
Towards the Establishment of an Israeli Republic

MOSHE BERENT

©2015

A Nation Like All Nations
Towards the Establishment of an Israeli Republic

By Moshe Berent

This research was supported by
The Open University of Israel's Research Fund
(grant no. 43035)

Published by **ISRAEL ACADEMIC PRESS**

(A subsidiary of MultiEducator, Inc.)

553 North Avenue • New Rochelle, NY 10801

Email: nhkobrin@Israelacademicpress.com

ISBN # 978-1-885881-39-7

© 2015 Israel Academic Press

DEDICATION

To Iris, my beloved wife,

who made this book possible.

Table of Contents

ℭℛ ◇ ℬℴ

Preface

Hillel Kook and Joseph Agassi

More than thirty years have passed since the publication of Joseph Agassi's book, *Between Faith and Nationality* (Hebrew Edition, 1984). The book identified the inability of Israel to solve its fundamental problems with the prevalent fusion of faith and nationality, or with the idea that Judaism is both a nationality and a religion, from which stemmed the notion of Israel as the State of the entire "Jewish People". Following Hillel Kook, the book called for the establishment of an Israeli secular republic, or for the separation between nationality and religion and the recognition of Israel as the state of the Israeli nation without the distinction of religion, race or sex. The reader of the present book will notice that this work has much in common with Agassi's book. Indeed, the worldview presented in my book draws from Agassi's findings and from long conversations, conducted with both Agassi and Kook. In the introduction to his book Agassi wrote, *"[I]ts immediate target is to open a wide public debate, in Israel and abroad, and its final aim is to create an overall political change, according to a comprehensive political program"*. In this regard, the success of Agassi's book was partial, as the situation has been somewhat improved from what had been before Agassi's book was published.

Hillel Kook's plan remains unknown to the Israeli public. In the intervening years, I have found myself wondering why Kook's ideas were ignored – especially among the Israeli intellectual elite in general, and the Israeli academic community in particular. Indeed, Kook's ideas were innovative in as much as the Israeli experience was concerned. Nevertheless, the model he was offering for Israel, that of the "nation-state" was thought to be the conventional one, at least in the West, and is considered a starting point for any debate on nationalism.

Hillel Kook (1915 – 2001) has usually been identified with the Israeli right wing. He had come from Revisionist stock, admired Jabotinsky and to a large extent considered himself a disciple. He was a member of the *Irgun* and its envoy to the United States during World War II and a member of the Constituent Assembly on behalf of the *Herut* party until he stepped down. Therefore, it is possible that his ideas were perceived as representing the Israeli right and that this was a main cause for his marginalization. Yet, even those who have considered themselves followers of Jabotinsky after statehood was achieved had good reasons to ignore Kook, as his ideas had been far beyond the Israeli political right. Kook described himself as more leftist than the Israeli left and more rightist than the Israeli right.

Indeed, the marginalization of Kook's ideas seems to be an expression of the intensity of the struggle between faith and nationality in the Israeli experience. There is in this identity an ultimate expression of a "Jewish" worldview, created over the course of thousands of years of a being a persecuted and isolated minority. This basic premise of the Israeli experience is shared by all: left and right, secular and religious, "Zionists" and "Post-Zionists", intellectuals and the common people. To a large extent the Zionist revolution – at least at its beginning – rejected this premise, as it had rejected many aspects of Jewish Diaspora life. In many areas the revolution had been successful, yet here it had dramatically failed. The Zionist revolution succeeded in getting the Jew out of the ghetto, by creating a modern nation, but it failed in getting the ghetto out of the Jew. It had created a Hebrew farmer, a Hebrew soldier and a Hebrew worker and industrialist, but it had failed to create a Hebrew citizen; a member of the Hebrew nation who had remained a "Jew."

Inasmuch as the present book draws upon Agassi's work, there are still some differences. Agassi's book provided a philosophical background to Kook's programs by introducing a theory of liberal nationalism. My approach is different, as it puts more emphasis on comparative politics. In the 1980s, the introduction of a philosophy of liberal nationalism was an innovation. Until then, liberal thought tended to ignore the national character of the liberal state and considered nationalism and liberalism as being opposed to one another. In this sense, Agassi's book was groundbreaking. Indeed, the 1980s had witnessed a revolution as far as nationalism research was concerned. Perhaps the most distinctive book was Ernest Gellner's *Nations and Nationalism* (1983) published a year before Agassi's, which dealt with the relationship between the modern state and nationalism from sociological perspectives. Though Gellner's book did not discuss democracy directly, its conclusions were far reaching for the liberal democratic theory. According to Gellner, industrial society must be national. Therefore, as liberal democracy is committed to modernization, industrialization and common growth, nationalism is also a precondition for liberal democracy. Another important book published in the same year was Benedict Anderson's *Imagined Communities* (1983). These books were an expression of the growing debate on the relationship between liberal democracy and nationalism. The collapse of the Communist regimes in Eastern Europe and the reawakening of nationalism there, especially in countries characterized by cultural and ethnic pluralism, raised the question of the extent to which a liberal democracy could be established in multinational or multiethnic societies.

Western democracies had also undergone changes in their ethnic composition because of immigration enhanced by globalization. Until recently, the accepted approach in the west towards immigration had been the French republican model (or the American "melting pot"), which maintained that the immigrant should be assimilated. Yet, immigration in the second half of the twentieth century had been different as a result of the fact that the immigrants differed in both religion and race from the absorbing nations, making assimilation more difficult. Further, globalization and the improvement of the means of transportation and communication enabled the newcomers to keep in touch with their country of origin. Consequently, the novel question introduced by Agassi's book in the 1980s became one of the burning questions in contemporary social sciences.

The present book examines nationalism from the perspective of comparative politics. It assumes that nationalism does not need an introduction, and that Israelis are "nationalists" in the sense that they share the desire for national identity, as nationalism is a pre-condition for the modern man. This sentiment is embodied in the saying, "The universal man is the dead man". The blurring of nationality and religion has deprived Israelis of their right to one unified national identity and caused the emergence of twisted national identities. Furthermore, I have also assumed that Israelis share the desire for normalization, to become "a nation like all nations". This was the original vision of the founders of the Zionist movement, who rebelled against the notion of "uniqueness". According to the founders, the Jewish collective had no "vocation" and its aim was not to establish a "Kingdom of Priests and a Holy Nation"; not in the image of the "State governed by *halacha*"; but also not in the image of a "Perfect Society" based upon the morality of the prophets. In the words of one of the early Zionist, Moshe Leib Lilienblum: *"the essence of Zionism is that the People of Israel live and want to live for life itself, and not for any purpose which is transcendental to life"*.

There is another important difference between Agassi's book and mine – Agassi concentrates on the impact of the fusion of religion and nationality on the creation of Jewish chauvinism, ethnocentrism and messianism. He emphasizes the dynamic tension between an identity comprised of nationality and religion on one hand, and romanticist nationalism on the other; and how these elements are expressed by "ultra-nationalist" trends within the Israeli society. Agassi considered this romanticist nationalism to be a prime obstacle to the emergence of liberal nationalism. I do not deny the fact that the fusion of faith and nationality has led to dangerous and undemocratic chauvinism. However, I believe that Agassi does not sufficiently emphasize the fact that this identity was also a source of contradictory "universal" and "moral" ideas, which were anti-nationalist and served as an obstacle for the emergence of Israeli nationalism as well. Indeed, Agassi points out how universal ideas originating in the Enlightenment hindered the appearance of Israeli liberal nationalism. However, he fails to show that such ideas stem also from the fusion of faith and nationality. This book emphasizes this point, as I believe it characterizes the Israeli intellectual elite. It is possible this elite, which identifies religion and nationality is not "ultranationalist", yet it is also not "nationalist"and to a certain extent it is anti-nationalist.

In this book these anti-nationalist trends of the Israeli elite are emphasized by discussing two trends – one contemporary and the other, as old as the Zionist movement itself: namely, "post-Zionism" and "Spiritual Zionism". I have tried to show that these two trends aspired, and are still aspiring, to create a non-national state, the first and only one in modern times: a "Kingdom of Priests and a Holy Nation". There is no need to expand upon why Agassi's book did not discuss post-Zionist ideas, as those theories were scarce or at least marginal when the book was published. Yet, the case is different regarding "Spiritual Zionism". In his analysis of the history of Zionism, Agassi belittles the importance of the spiritual nationalism of the school of Ahad Ha'am and Martin Buber. In this approach Agassi followed a somewhat traditional conception, which considered this school as marginal when compared with the other two schools of Zionist thought: Political Zionism and Practical Zionism. However, I think that the dominance of what Agassi called "The New Zionist Myth" could not be understood without the influence of Spiritual Zionism. It was the latter which introduced the fusion of faith and nationality along with the notion of Jewish vocation into the Zionist movement. The purpose of Zionism, according to this school, was not normalization, but rather the realization of a Jewish vocation, identified by the ideas of the prophets, through a cultural center established in Palestine. According to spiritual nationalism, the realization of these ideas comes before the welfare and survival of the nation. This approach was anti-nationalist in its essence, as it considered nationalism and its characteristics something unworthy of Judaism. Thus, although perhaps marginal in the history of pre-independent Israel, the adoption of the fusion of religion and nationality and the emergence of the "Jewish State" marked the victory of Spiritual Zionism's school of thought. It would be almost impossible to overestimate its importance and influence. Not long ago, in a debate concerning Avraham Burg's book *The Holocaust is Over*, the author stated that the last century was that of Herzl and he wishes that the next would be the century of Ahad Ha'am. My interpretation of Israeli history is diametrically opposite: the last century – or a least the sixty-five years following Israel's independence – has been that of Ahad Ha'am, and let us hope that the next century will be that of Herzl.

It is easy to give Agassi credit for his ideas that appear in my book, mainly through references to his book. It is more difficult in the case of Hillel Kook. Though there is another difference between Agassi's book and mine: Agassi's book introduced Hillel Kook's plan, but also contained a biography of Kook. In contrast, while my book is influenced by Kook's ideas, it does not deal with Kook himself. Hillel Kook was not a "thinker" in the traditional sense. He did not leave a written legacy that could be referred to regarding his ideas. Another reason for the scarcity of references to Kook in my book is that the material concerned is not easily accessible. Over recent decades the volumes of literature about Hillel Kook have increased dramatically, especially in the United States. The newer literature highlights his activities in the United States during World War II, saving the Jews in Europe, rather than focusing on his notion of the Hebrew nation.[1]

The influence of Hillel Kook on this present book is less through what he wrote or what had been written about him, but rather through extensive personal conversations. Agassi introduced me to Hillel Kook on the eve of the publication of Agassi's book. I remember well that when I expressed my amazement about the connection between a well-known philosopher like him and the ideas of a layman like Kook, Agassi replied: "More than Hillel Kook needs Moshe Berent, it is Moshe Berent who needs Hillel Kook". Indeed, it is Agassi who should be credited for listening to Hillel Kook. His book constituted a rare case in which a well-known philosopher listened and based a political theory on the ideas of a layman. The doubts I had concerning the relations between them were a more genuine expression of the prevailing attitude in the Academy towards the layman, rather than the rare attitude expressed by Agassi.

The years to come corroborated Agassi's prediction. For me, Agassi's book created the philosophical background necessary for the acceptance of the nationalist idea in general, and the Israeli nationalist idea in specific. My conversations with Kook turned me into an Israeli patriot. Hillel Kook was perhaps the last voice of the school of Political Zionism. These included Herzl, Pinsker, Nordau, Zangwill, Jabotinsky, and others. I remember that when I first read *The Federalist Papers* by James Madison, Alexander Hamilton, and John Jay, I envied the Americans for having such prominent founding fathers. Today I think differently. Israel had formible founding fathers, and they were as noteworthy as those of the American nation. The Political Zionists were imbued with the idea of a coming catastrophe (though its magnitude could not have been foreseen by any human being) and their purpose was to prevent this catastrophe by forging a national revival. Against a background of terrible Jewish deprivation at the end of the 19th century, a new and radical nationalism developed. Inasmuch as it had contained 19th century romanticist ideas, its message was clear: Nationalism is for the sake of life.

Occasionally the question is raised: "If Herzl came back to life would he consider the Zionist movement successful?" There are those who would think, correctly so, that in as much as the construction of an Israeli Hebrew nation is concerned, Herzl would have considered the Zionist movement a success. Others would claim, also correctly, that the status of religion and that of non-Jewish minorities in the state would have disappointed Herzl. Yet it is likely that all these conjectures would have been meaningless, had Herzl known about the Holocaust. If Herzl could have known that Israel had been established over the ruins of its nation, he would have wished to return to his grave. As for him and for the Political Zionists, nationalism and nation building were for life; for the people, not for Judaism per se, and not for what is referred to today as a "Jewish State". Yet, the Zionist movement became a movement for national self-determination, perhaps the only one in history, that lost its nation on the road to independence. Those who knew Hillel Kook knew of his duality: on one hand a recognition of the great success of the creation of a modern Israeli nation (accompanied by criticism bordering with despair because of the fact that the members of this nation were not aware if its existence), and on the other hand a sense of a bitter failure to save the Jews of Europe, which he considered to be a failure of the Zionist movement as well as his own (even though by his actions he could be credited with saving more Jewish lives more than anyone else).

In the historiography of the Zionist movement, Political Zionism was marginalized by Practical Zionism, which was dominated by the Labor movement, and also by the "spirituals". The radical approach that considered politics an instrument for the solution of fundamental problems had been replaced by the "pragmatic" approach, according to which politics is nothing but "foam on the water" destined to put out fires, while bypassing fundamental problems; and the "spiritual" anti-political approach which stays away from the characteristics of modern politics: state, nation and sovereignty. We should go back and read the writings of Political Zionism – as they could tell us of the original purposes of Zionism. While their ideas do not oblige us, they might change us. My long talks with Hillel Kook were a rare opportunity for me to touch the last link of the chain of Political Zionism started by Herzl. And I am thankful also for that.

◆◆◆

It took me almost a decade to write the Hebrew version of this book (2009). During these years I have been lecturing about my ideas to different audiences, whose reactions encouraged me to write the book. Among them were my students at the Open University of Israel, especially those of the MA Program in Democracy Studies. I would like also to thank my colleagues at the Department of Sociology, Political Science and Communication at the Open University who, though not always agreed with the ideas presented in this book, still appreciated and encouraged me to publish them. I owe a special debt to the late Professor Gideon Doron, the editor of the series, that published the Hebrew version of this book, who fully trusted me and did all that was needed to publish the book. I say without reservations that he made the book possible. I also wish to thank Professor Yitzhak Reiter, the Chief Editor of Israel Academic Press, whose complimentary opinion of the Hebrew edition of this book was important to the publication of this English Edition.

Finally, I wish to thank my beloved wife Iris, who for many years "followed me through the (academic) wilderness, through a land not sown". Her support and determination were essential for the appearance of this book, which is dedicated to her.

Tel Aviv Winter 2015   Moshe Berent

જી ◇ ଓ

Introduction
Towards Normalization of Jewish Existence

Nation-States

The purpose of the Zionist Movement was the normalization of Jewish life, "to become a nation like all nations", which meant to become a nation that owns a state. The model of nations that own a state is called a **Nation-State**. The nation-state is both a nation and a state and its political borders overlap its national borders. It is considered as belonging to its territorial nation and as expressing its right for self-determination. The overlap between the nation and the state is expressed by the fusion of nationality and citizenship: every citizen is a member of the nation and vice versa. Thus, France is a nation-state. Consequently every French citizen is a member of the French nation, on one hand, while every Frenchmen or Frenchwomen is also a citizen of the French state, on the other hand.

Israel, contrary to the original purpose of Zionism, is not 'a nation like all nations', that is, it is not a nation-state. It does not recognize the existence of an Israeli nation. According to the formal national ethos, 'Zionist' Israel belongs to the entire "Jewish People" and not to its territorial nation. Israel's nation is not 'a nation like all nations', because while it outgrows Israel's political borders, it does not include considerable constituencies within its borders. In a normal nation-state there is a merger between nationality and citizenship; while in Israel there is a fusion of religion and nationality, or between faith and nationality. Israelis recognized by the state as Jews are also recognized as members of the Jewish nation. Though the so-called "Jewish people" is not a concrete political entity, as its sons and daughters (at least those who live in western countries), also remain equal members of their local nations. At the same time, many Israeli citizens of Arab origin, or those whose mother-tongue is Arabic, are considered members of the Arab nation, a nation which does not exist as well. Additionally, this means that Israel is a bi-national state: a country in which at least two national communities, Jewish and Arab, live. The Jewish national community is the dominant one and 'owns' the state, while the Arab national community is secondary, and at least formally, have no share in the state.[2]

The principle of national self-determination has become essential in the legitimization of the modern state. This is demonstrated by the name of the 'United Nations'. The international community is composed of independent nations, and membership in this community is given only to states expressing the will of these free nations.

Yet, in as much as the model of the nation-state constitutes the norm, many members of the United Nations are not nations, but rather states or regimes. In those countries it is impossible to trace the same cultural homogeneity and political unity usually characterizing the nation-state in the west. Thus, in many countries the ruling elites are preoccupied with "nation building", even though the socio-economic conditions in these countries sometimes make it impossible and undesirable to reach political and cultural homogeneity that characterizes the western nation-state. While the nation-state has become a fact in the west and in parts of Central and Eastern Europe, it has also become a model for imitation for the rest of the world (Deutsch & Foltz 1966; Smith G. et al, 1998; Fukuyama 2006).

In Western Europe and the Americas, there are countries such as Switzerland, Belgium, Spain, and Canada, which also seem to diverge from the model of the classical nation-state and are sometimes described as multinational countries. These countries will be extensively discussed (see below, pp. 130-137). At this stage it is suffice to say that even in these countries, besides specific national identities, there is an inclusive civic national identity or an attempt to create one.

In Israel, the nation-state is not set as a model for imitation: formally, the existence of an Israeli nation is not recognized and it seems unlikely that Israel is aspiring to build a territorial Israeli nation (Smooha, 2000, p. 572; Yakobson and Rubinstein, 2003, p. 371).

The nation-state aspires to the convergence of national or cultural borders, on one hand, and political borders, on the other. It does so by identifying membership in the nation with citizenship. Consequently, it aspires not only for cultural homogeneity but also for a political one, which means political consensus and civic equality. Thus, republicanism and nationalism are complementary, and most of the nation-states, which have become independent since the French Revolution, have also declared themselves republics. Traditionally, the republic had been considered the negation of, or the opposition to, the monarchy. Niccolò Machiavelli, one of the founders of modern republicanism, says in the opening of *The Prince* that, "All the states and governments, that have had, and have at present, dominion over men, have been and are either republics or principalities." (Machiavelli, 1965, p. 1).

The notion of free community is at the heart of republicanism, which is identified with a body of free citizens and with self-rule (Pettit, 1999, pp. 31-35). The traditional monarchs personally ruled their subjects, and their kingdoms were considered their personal properties. While in the republic, the government is the common interest (*res publica*) of the citizens who run it for the benefit of the common good. Republicanism means popular sovereignty, that the state belongs to its citizens and that its duty is to serve them. Republicanism is also a political disposition: the republican spirit emphasizes patriotism, the need to identify with the common good and the state, equality, democracy, and political participation. It is important to note that while republicanism considers the citizen body of the republic "a people", it does not necessarily consider the citizen body "a nation". The republican people are "political people" who draw their solidarity and patriotism from the civic equality and from the consensus about the political system and its targets while the nation has also a cultural dimension. Yet, while republicanism does not mean that "the people" necessarily constitute a nation, in the nation-state, where there is a fusion of nationality and citizenship, the civic people converges with the cultural nation. Thus, the French republic is also the state of the French nation. Consequently there are no "civic peoples", meaning people who lack cultural features. Alternatively, in as much as the national state emphasizes the cultural or ethnic features of its nation, being a republic (or the fusion of nationality and citizenship) defines in it also a "civic people". As Anthony Smith says, "the nation is a symbiosis, not always peaceful, but necessary, of ethnic and civic components" (Smith, 1996c, pp. 100-1).

Israel is not a republic and has never been declared as one. The citizens of Israel are formally divided into at least two nations: Jewish and Arab. These two nations are perceived as different, not only in culture, but also in oppoing political aspirations. Therefore, Israeli citizens are not recognized as "people" in the republican sense. Israel lacks equality of rights and duties, as the rights and duties are not derived only from citizenship, but also from religious or ethnic background. Furthermore, there is not an expectation that the Israeli citizens will form a citizen body characterized by patriotism and solidarity.

Republicanism has become a main source for political legitimization. Besides real republics such as the United States, France, and Ireland, there are many countries that are republics only by name. Iraq of Sadam Hussein's period titled itself as a republic as is contemporary Syria. Eastern European communist dictatorships were called "People's Republics". The regime of the Ayatollahs in Iran is called 'The Islamic Republic of Iran'. Thus, many countries that are not republics use the title. This stems from a desire to legitimize their undemocratic nature, or from the desire to reach a republican government in the future. In Israel there is no attempt to use the title republic, as in "the Israeli Republic". The official title of Israel is "state", as in the "State of Israel".

The so-called "Declaration of Independence" which Ben Gurion read on May 14th, 1948 and which appeared in the *Official Gazette* of the Provisional Government was titled: 'The Declaration of the Establishment of the State of Israel' (Shachar, 1991, p. 543). Although the document contains republican elements (as will be seen), it does not declare the establishment of a republic, but of "a state." While the word "state" could be used as a synonym for the word "republic", it is normally used to describe the ruling apparatus rather than the official title of the political entity. Therefore, France is not referred to as the "State of France", but rather the "French Republic". The United States is not referred to as the "State of the United States', but the "United States", and its government is called "a federal republic". Great Britain is not referred to as the "State of Britain", but "Great Britain" or the "United Kingdom", since Britain is a monarchy. The title the "State of Israel" is meaningless and proclaims Israel to be an administrative apparatus only, or a political entity whose constitutional and national character has not yet been decided.

This book argues that the fusion of faith and nationality, (that is, the perception of Judaism as both a religion and nationality,) and the absence of an Israeli nation-state, or an Israeli republic, is the principal cause of Israel's fundamental problems and its inability to solve these specific problems. These problems include the status of the religion in the State, the relations between secular and religious people, the status of non-Jews – especially of Arabs, the inability to draft a constitution, the inability to reach an agreement about Israel's borders and the inability to reach decisions concerning war and peace. A necessary condition for the solution of all these problems is the separation of nationality and religion, the recognition of the existence of an Israeli nation without distinction of religion, race and gender, and the establishment of Israel as a republic, that is, a state of the Israeli nation. Now, we encounter several questions: Is there an Israeli nation? How is it related to the historical Jewish people? How is it related to Zionism? Under what conditions can non-Jews become equal members of this nation? These questions stand at the core of this book.

Republicanism in Israel

The roots of republicanism are usually traced to the Roman republic (Skinner, 2002, p. 12), but the idea of the free community could be found in classical Greece. After hundreds of years of marginalization of republicanism by the Christian monarchy, it was revived in the late Middle Ages during the Renaissance (and thus under the influence of the classical world) especially in the city-states of northern Italy. In the 17th century, also under the influence of the classical world, it appeared in the English civil war as part of the struggle against the monarchy, and reached its heights in the American and French revolutions at the end of the 18th century. In the 19th century republicanism remained an ideal to fight for against the traditional monarchies and also became an important component of the emerging nationalism. The republican emphasis on the free community, on the attachment to the fatherland and on patriotism was also shared with nationalism. Consequently, since the French Revolution, most of the movements for national self-determination aspired to establish republics (Skinner, 1988; Pettit, 1999; Canovan, 1991).

Republican governing has remained the conventional form of government, though in the 20th century republicanism disappeared as a discourse from the political agenda. There were several reasons for this:

> (a) the classical distinction between monarchies and republics had been blurred as monarchies of democratic countries had become constitutional. Being nation-states, these monarchies

had defined a 'civic people' by the identity, which the nation-state drew between nationality and citizenship. Thus, already in the 18th Century Montesquieu described England as a republic concealed under the form of a monarchy (Pettit, 1999, p. 20).

(b) Some claim that the nationalist discourse, or the discourse that characterized movements for national self determination, had lost some of its republican elements at the end of the 19th and the beginning of the 20th Century as nationalism in Europe had become essentially 'eastern' (that is, from Eastern Europe). It had been more ethnic or collectivistic than the nationalism of the first half of the 19th Century, which tended to be more civic (Viroli, 1995; Benner, 1997).

(c) The relation between republican theory, on one hand, and liberal theory, on the other. The republican spirit, or the republican *virtu*, demanded of the citizen to prefer the public interest over private interests and also emphasized the individual's duties towards the communities as well as their rights. This seemed to contradict the basic ideas of capitalism and liberalism that had become dominant in the American political tradition (Pettit, 1999, ch.1).

(d) At the same time, republicanism was also attacked by multiculturalists. Their claim was that the republican demand for solidarity within the citizen body has turned into a demand for cultural monism and has been expressed by the idea of the "melting pot".

Lately republicanism reappeared on the political agenda mainly because what seems to be the crisis of liberal democracy. It has been claimed that classical liberalism's notion of the political community, which sees it primarily as an arena for the promotion of rights, cannot serve as the basis of the modern state, which should be equally based upon the duties of the citizens. The conguency which republicanism draws between the free citizen and the free community could become a middle way between extreme individualism, on one hand, and nationalist collectivist approaches which curtail human rights, on the other (Mautner, 2012). Furthermore, multiculturalism seems to have lost the popularity it had in the last decades in favor of theories, which stress the need for "moderate assimilation" (Brubaker, 2001).

Notwithstanding these qualifications, republicanism still remains essential for political legitimization, and consequently most of the countries, which have gained independence since the French Revolution (except for those which were constitutional monarchies) had declared themselves as republics. Therefore, even Eastern European nationalism, which has traditionally been classified as 'ethnic', aspired to establish republics and the new states which had emerged after the collapse of the Soviet Union and which had been classified by some researchers as 'ethnic states' had been declared republics. As a result, in these countries alongside the notion of the 'ethnic' nation exists also the notion of the "civic" nation (see below, pp. 138-155).

Republicanism has been a cornerstone of many, if not all, movements for national self-determination, and it could be expected that its place would not be missing in the Zionist movement. Indeed, on the eve of Independence there were indications that Israel would be established as a republic (see Chapter 5 below). The Zionist leadership, which convened at the Biltmore Hotel in New York on May 1942, pronounced what has been known as "the Biltmore Program" according to which the goal of Zionism was the establishment of a "Jewish Commonwealth"; the term "commonwealth" is the accepted translation in both America and Britain to the term "republic". Also the *Hebrew Committee for National Liberation,* founded in the United States by Hillel Kook, demanded the establishment of "The Hebrew Republic of Palestine" (Agassi, 1993, p. 183). To a large extent, the United Nations' 1947 Partition Plan for Palestine dictated the framework of the political and constitutional discourse on the eve of Independence, which practically imposed a republican government on the Jewish State (even though the term 'republic' did not appear in the resolution). Consequently on the table of the Provisional State Council laid a proposal of a constitution which proclaimed that "Israel is a sovereign, independent and democratic republic" alongside the declaration that "Israel was chosen to become a national home for the Jewish people" (Kohn, 1949). There were other proposals, which declared Israel as a republic. For instance, a proposal by Yochanan Bader, a member of the Constituent Assembly and the First Knesset from the opposition Herut Party, repeated Kohn's words that "the state of Israel is a democratic independent sovereign republic". There was also a proposal by MAPAI, (the ruling party), which was prepared by a committee headed by Zvi Berenzon (see discussion below, pp. 298-306).

Even though the Declaration of Independence did not mention the establishment of a republic, it is possible to trace clear republican elements in this declaration, especially its operative part, which laid the basis for the election of a Constituent Assembly whose task was to draw a Constitution. Also the programs of some of the parties, which were published on the eve of the elections for the Constituent Assembly proclaimed Israel as a republic. This republican discourse vanished to a great extent with the abolishment of the Constituent Assembly when it had been turned over into the First Knesset. It is important to see how this event contradicted the essence of republicanism. The body elected by the people on January 1949 was a Constituent Assembly and not a ruler. This body had turned itself into a legislative body, which, in the absence of a constitution was unlimited – without receiving any mandate to rule from the people.

The Israelis, in as much as they are not aware of the ideas of republicanism in general, are not aware of this event and its significance in Israel's constitutional history in particular. The fact that these moves had received an *a posteriori* legitimization by senior jurists, among them the former Supreme Court Chief Justice Aharon Barak (Rubinstein, 1996, p. 49), testifies to the general lack of sensitivity towards the meaning of popular sovereignty (see below, pp. 325-334). Even though, on the seventh meeting of the First Knesset on August 3rd, 1949, Ben Gurion announced the composition of his government and declared that, "the law which will establish the republican and democratic regime in the state of Israel will secure a complete equality of rights and duties to all its citizens without distinction of religion, race and nationality." He did not fulfill this promise.

Since 1948 the question of the establishment of an Israeli republic has been removed from the agenda, even though in 1965 professor Benjamin Akzin, who had participated in the constitutional debate on the eve of Independence, published a draft for a constitution which defined Israel as "a sovereign and democratic republic" (Akzin, 1996b). In 1975 Hillel Kook and Shmuel Merlin published a manifest in which they called again to separate religion from nationality and to establish Israel as a "secular republic" which will be Jewish as America is Christian and as France is Catholic. In the eighties Joseph Agassi published his book, which was dedicated to ideas of Hillel Kook and in which he repeated Kook's proposal to establish an Israeli Republic. Another important source for Israeli republicanism was centered in the otherwise marginal group of the Canaanites, which will be discussed. A year before the Hebrew edition of the present book was released, Shlomo Sand published *The Invention of the Jewish People*, (2008; 2009) which also called for the establishment of an Israeli republic.

Except for isolated incidents it is not easy to discern a republican element in the constitutional discourse in Israel. In the constitutional draft

(*"Huka LeYisrael"* – "Constitution for Israel") published in the 1980's by a group of law professors headed by professor Uriel Reichman, the term 'republic' was not mentioned at all. Also the constitution draft recently published (2005) by the Israeli Democracy Institute (*"Huka Behaskama"* – Constitution by Consensus) did not define Israel as a republic (see below, pp. 298-306). The drafters of the "Constitution for Israel" went to the United States (Prof. Baruch Bracha) and to Germany (Prof. Uriel Reichman) to be helped by the constitutional experience of those countries (Bechor, 1996, pp. 47-50). Both Germany and the United State are clearly republics and both express it in their constitutions. Nevertheless, the term "republic" does not appear in the draft of "Constitution for Israel", and it is obvious that the reason for this omission is not ignorance, since it was written by senior law professors. Yet, an explanation for this omission is still required.

Academics and jurists ignore the fact that Israel is not officially defined as a republic. A good example for this is Yakobson and Rubinstein's important book, *Israel and the Family of Nations* (2009). According to the authors, when compared to other countries, Israel is not unique in its national identity, nor in relations with its Diaspora. Yet, in all comparisons drawn, there is no mention of the fact that most of the countries Israel is compared to are republics. They are countries, which, at least formally, belong to their citizens without distinction of religion, race or sex. Perhaps the authors assume that it is only a question of a title, and in practice Israel is not different from other countries. I will try to show that this is a false assumption and that the declaration of a country as a republic could have implications on both its national identity and on its attitude towards what it considers as its Diaspora nation (if it considers itself as having one). In any case, an explanation is necessary. If the accepted norm is to declare a new state a republic, why Israel when according to Yakobson and Rubinstein is, "a nation like all nations", had not been declared one? Overlooking this question by the authors becomes more conspicuous as we notice that one of them, Amnon Rubinstein, is a constitutional jurist who had written the most comprehensive and popular source book on Israeli law (Rubinstein, 1996). Even if the absence of the title 'republic' from the official name of Israel is a semantic or formalistic issue, it is still a legal-constitutional one. Perhaps the disregard displayed by Yakobson and Rubinstein to the fact that Israel is not defined as a republic is not so surprising given the fact that in this source book, Rubinstein does not mention this fact as well.

A unique way of overlooking the uniqueness of Israel is provided by Asher Arian in his book, *The Second Israeli Republic: Politics and Government towards the 21th Century* (1997). Here Arian refers to Israel as a republic and to his credit it could be said that, unlike Yakobson and Rubinstein, he sees the connection between normalcy and the existence of a republic. Nevertheless, Arian does not give any explanation to his reference to Israel as a republic, and this also strange. As noted above, the term 'republic' is not included in the official title of Israel and, as far as I can tell, Arian was the first, if not the only one, in the academic or legalist establishments, who uses this term to describe the Israeli regime. Thus, an explanation for this innovation is wanted but not given.

Peled and Shafir, who think that that there is republican discourse in Israel, use another approach to discuss of the question of republicanism in Israel (Peled, 1993; Peled & Shafir, 2005). They claim that the civic discourse in Israel is a mixture of three discourses: 'a liberal discourse', which emphasizes individual's rights; 'a republican discourse', which emphasizes the public good; and 'an ethno-nationalist' discourse, which emphasizes the Jewish ethnic group. For many years the republican discourse was dominant, but it has declined in recent years – as both the liberal and the ethno-national discourses have increased (Peled, 1993, p. 21; Peled & Shafir, 2005, pp. 37-50). Similarly, Mautner (2012) speaks about the "crisis of republicanism in Israel".

Like Peled and Shafir, he thinks that Israel was characterized in the past by a mature republican tradition. Yet in the recent decades, with the decline of the hegemony of the labor movement, Israel is in a "republicanism's crisis." The boldest statement on this matter had been made by Nir Kedar (2009), who describes Ben Gurion as a full fledged republican and his policies during the 1950's what had been know as "*mamlakhtiyut*", as full fledged republicanism (Bareli & Kedar, 2011). This stand raises a general question – to what extent it is possible to have a republican discourse, or to what extent it is possible to practically have a republic, in countries, which are not republican by declaration? As noted above, in constitutional monarchies, though officially they are not republics, the fusion of nationality and citizenship defines a "civic people." Thus, it is possible to have republican discourse even in countries that are not officially republics.

While there was indeed a short "republican moment" on the eve of independence (cf. chapter 5), to the extent that it is possible to speak about "republican discourse" in Israel, it has been unique in the sense that from its inception it wanted essential elements which had characterized it elsewhere. Thus, this discourse did not put *the citizen* at its center, but rather the Jew, and in as much as it emphasized the collective, the borders of the collective were not clear. It was not identified with the citizen-body, but rather with a Jewish-Israeli collective. This discourse dictated what Peled and Shafir call "the republican virtu." It also demanded from non-Jews in general and from Arabs in particular to acknowledge it. Yet it had never demanded, nor thought, that they could share it or contribute to it. Nir Kedar maintains that "Ben Gurion's civic *mamlakhtiyut* affinity was in fact based on Jewish national and cultural bonds, and as such tolerated the Arab citizens of Israel as equal citizens, however did not see them as genuine partners in the Israeli *res publica*" (Kedar, 2007). It is not surprising, as Peled and Shafir observe, that this discourse originated in the pre-independence *Yishuv*. This is where "the Labor movement was formed from its beginning as a republican virtue project" (Peled & Shafir, 2005, p. 37). The absence of sovereignty enabled the emergence of discourse that could emphasize the general good, while ignoring the citizen. Another essential republican element, which was missing in both the practice and the discourse of the regime, was that of a constitution (Mautner, 2012). Since Ben Gurion had a crucial role in the constitutional fiasco that had led to the abolishment of the Constituent Assembly in 1949, it seems very problematic to describe his worldview as republican. Eventually *mamlakhtiyut* considered the state, rather than "the people", sovereign. Thus, Ben Gurion's *mamlakhyiut* had been more of etatism or collectivism rather than republicanism (see below, pp. 344-345; pp. 349-354).

Zionism and "A Jewish State"

The non-recognition in an Israeli nation and the fact that Israel was not established as a republic has been complemented by the continued existence of the Zionist Movement. The latter, as a movement for national self-determination, should had been disestablished in 1948 after reaching its goal – independence, while delivering its powers to the new republic. However, the founding fathers preferred to postpone the establishment of the republic and instead adopted the fusion of faith and nationality, which sees Israel as the state of the historical Jewish people, *Am Yisrael*, and its goals to preserve and promote Jewish values and interests, above all "the ingathering of the exiles." The continued existence of "Zionism" and Zionist institutions was explained by the need to bring the Jews, wherever they are, to Israel. Agassi called this "national ethos", which was nothing but a secular version of the biblical salvation prophesies, "the New Zionist Myth", to distinguish it from classical pre-independence Zionism (Agassi, 1993, pp. 253-7).

As we will see, contrary to what many Israelis think, this ethos had never been dominant in Zionism, and paradoxically, became dominant in post-independence Israel. To the extent that pre-independence Zionism considered the Jews to be a nation, it did not postulate 'the return of the exiles' for all the Jews, but rather for only a portion of the historical *Am Yisrael*. In as much as the Zionist movement as a movement for national self-determination addressed all Jews, it also entertained traits of distinction between the "Jewish nation", which was identified with the "Hebrew nation", which it represented, on one hand, and the mythical *"Am Yisrael"*, which was supposed to be saved in the End of Days, on the other. This distinction rested upon two principal elements: will and culture. The "will" element meant that only the Jews who wanted to join the nation and immigrate to *Eretz Yisarel* would eventually form the "Jewish nation". Most of the Zionist thinkers, if not all of them, assumed that parts of the historical *Am Yisrael*, especially those who were living in the West, would assimilate (either nationally, or religiously or both). In this sense Zionism mainly addressed the distressed Jews (*yahadut hamtsuka*) of Eastern Europe. But the "Jewish nation" identified almost from the start as the "Hebrew nation", and as such it was distinguished from the historical Jewish people in its culture, which was both Hebrew and modern. Thus by being modern, it was different from the culture or various popular cultures of *"Am Yisrael"*, and by being Hebrew, it was different also from the modern cultures of the Jews who preferred to settle in their local nations.

With the endorsement of inextricable fusing of religion and nationality, Israel had become a "Jewish State" in a sense that would have been strange to many of the Zionist forefathers. The term "Jewish State", as it was used on the eve of independence, meant a state which is established by Jews (as the complement concept, "Arab State," meant a State which is established by Arabs), rather than a state which reflects a given Jewish content or culture. As Benzion Netanyahu remarks, the forefathers of Zionism (who constituted what is usually called "Political Zionism") wished to concentrate on solving the general national problem, but they left the decisions about the social and cultural form to the inhabitants of the future state. Only the recognition of Hebrew as the national language was accepted as a fact acompli following the enrooting of Hebrew and the increased influence of the Hebrew literature (Netanyahu, 2003, p. 9). It is important to stress that as much as the choice of the Hebrew had been a cultural choice, it still had left the contents of the Hebrew culture open.

In other words, the "Jewish State" was not conceived as a state, which should necessarily reflect a given Jewish content. "Practical Zionism", which had become dominant after Herzl's death, and which had been dominated by the labor movement, also would have considered today's notion of the Jewish State bizarre. The latter did not share the cultural openness and tolerance of Political Zionism and usually advocated cultural activism. But the Hebrew culture, which they envisage was a rebellion against the Jewish culture, and the "New Jew" was antithetical to the "Old Jew" (Shapira, 1997). The only section within the Zionist Movement, which adopted the fusion of faith and nationality and demanded that the Jewish State reflect Jewish values was the "Spiritual Zionism" of the school of Ahad Ha'am and Martin Buber. This current, which is sometimes described mistakenly as marginal in the history of Zionism, had been demonstratively non-territorial and non-republican. The notion of the Jewish State adopted after independence signifies the victory of this school.

Contrary to what is usually assumed, the adoption of the fusion of faith and nationality that originated after independence was not self-evident. In a key speech in the 22th Zionist Congress held in Basel immediately after the Second World War, Ben Gurion expressed objection to both, a unique State for the Jews which he had identified with theocracy, and a state "that all the Jews of the world are its citizens" (Agassi, 1993, p. 169). The fact that the fusion of faith and nationality has become so popular in Israel could be related to its proximity to the traditional concept of "*Am Yisrael*". Yet the adoption of the fusion of faith and nationality signified a reaction to the Zionist revolution and the victory of the somewhat traditional religious image, which the secular elites had adopted precisely at the moment when the Zionist movement has reached its goal – independence for the nation.

The fusion of religion and nationality has turned Israel into a religious state. Jewish secular identity (which is completely disconnected from religion) is rare among Jews (Liebman, 1997a, pp. 101-4). In the West, and especially in the United States, Jewish public identity has become more and more identified with religion (Gorni, 1999, p. 20). The need to supply a common denominator to Jews wherever they are, means that Israel has adopted a "civil religion", which is a "new interpretation" of traditional religion (Liebman & Don Yehiya, 1983). The need to adopt a civil religion which is a revised version of Judaism, has made the separation of religion from the State, one of the most important pillars of modern democracy, impossible. At the same time the fusion of nationality and religion has turned Israeli politics into an arena of cultural or religious wars in which the various groups try to impose their version of Judaism on the State.

Indeed, as Charles Liebman pointed out, it had become commonplace to describe the conflict between the religious and the secular Israeli Jews as a "culture conflict". Liebman refers to culture as "the total way of life of a discrete society, its traditions, habits, beliefs and in the systematic body of learned behavior which is transmitted from parents to children" (Liebman, 1997b, pp. 172- 174). It is obvious, then, why cultural or religious conflicts are so hard, if not impossible, to resolve. Indeed, it seems that liberal democracy is not equipped to deal with cultural or religious conflict. Conflicts in liberal democracy are usually described as conflicts between interests rather than between cultures. It might be claimed that even though culture conflicts are not desired sometimes, as in the Israeli case, they are unescapable. Nevertheless, while according to the "New Zionist Myth" religion was supposed to unite the nation, in fact it has turned into a prime source of disunity and divisions within the nation.

Another expression of the adoption of the "New Civil Religion" was the emergence of Jewish chauvinism and a Jewish ethnocentrism enhanced by the politicization of concepts, which were taken from traditional or religious discourse used to describe the relations between the Jews and the gentiles (Liebman & Don Yehiya, 1983). The fusion of nationality and religion caused the penetration of theological and messianic motives in Israeli politics. The notion of the Jewish State was not limited to realizing and expressing Jewish values, but also to reach or fulfill goals or visions that were considered as "Jewish." An important component of the "New Zionist Myth" and a prime source for the formation of the vision of the Jewish State was the vision of the End of Days as it was set by the biblical prophets and which included various utopian components such as the total "Ingathering of the Exiles", salvation and the creation of a utopian perfect society (*chevrat mofet*). It is commonplace to relate the emergence of (religious) messianism in Israel to groups from the religious right. Indeed, these ideas had sources in the development of what has known as "Religious Zionism", especially in the teachings of Rabbi Avraham Itzhak Hachohen Kook and his son Rabbi Tzvi Yehuda Hacohen Kook (Ravitzky 1996 and see below, pp. 354-363).

Yet, the adoption of salvation and redemption as the goals of Zionism originated in the secular circles of "Spiritual Zionism" and was central to the ideas of Ahad Ha'am. The latter considered Zionism to be a reformed Judaism and his Zionist's messianic perception was a product of the fusion of faith and nationality, on one hand, and the romanticist idea that every nation has a vocation (*tehuda*), which it must fulfill, on the other. The idea of *tehuda*, which was used by Ahad Ha'am was also a continuation of the debate concerning the role of Judaism in the Diaspora in general, and in the new era in particular. Consequently it had sources also in the Jewish Enlightenment which faced the question why the enlighten Jew should not forsake his religion altogether. One of the answers that the Enlightenment gave to this question was that the Jews had a "mission" which was mainly to spread morality (that is the universal ideas of the prophets) among the gentiles. This, in a sense, was similar to one of the traditional explanations for the Jewish Diaspora, that God meant the Jews to spread monotheism. Yet, both the Enlightenment and traditional Judaism considered this mission to be personal, while for Ahad Ha'am it was a collective mission of Judaism identified with Zionism (see below, pp. 278-283). Even today, Eisenstadt, an internationally prominent Israeli sociologist, declares that the purpose of Zionism was "the fulfillment of the Jewish civilizationist vision" (Eisenstadt, 2002, p. 163) and describes the Israeli society as a society whose "object is to carry the burden of a certain completion" of this vision (ibid. p. 378).

The adoption of the idea of *tehuda* by the secular elites was no doubt connected also to its proximity to socialist utopias. It strengthened the notion of Israel as a unique abnormal entity, which is governed by different rules than other nations. Israeli political messianism considers Israel a community which is governed by a moral code – *chevrat mofet* ("Perfect Society"), *or lagoim* (A Light to all Nations), *mamlechet cohanim vegoi kadosh* ("A kingdom of priests and a holy nation"), and consequently Israel is conceived of as a religious-moral entity, while the "religious" and the "moralists" are debating what values it should adopt.

Borders

The absence of agreed borders, which is directly connected to the fusion of religion and nationality and the absence of recognition of an Israeli nation, is another manifestation of Israel's departure of Nation-State norms. Israel's borders are not only disputed by the international community, but by the Israelis themselves. As noted above, the "Nation-State" is both a nation and a state – the borders of the nation overlap with the borders of the state. The political borders of the state set the cultural borders of the nation and vice versa. If the claim of the nation-state to its territory is directly related to the notion that this territory is inhabited by members of its nation, the Israeli claim to any territory which is settled by non Jews is doubted. Consequently in Israel there is a contradiction between the aspiration of the nation-state to create a congruency between the nation and the state, on one hand, and the fusion of religion and nationality, on the other, as the territorial mixture of Jews and Arabs makes any pursuit after correlation between the borders of the nation and endurable state borders hopeless. Until relatively recently, Israel tried to solve the dilemma by the "Judaization" of the territories under its control (as it was called within the Green Line's borders), or "resettlement" in these territories (as it was called beyond the Green Line's borders), that is to diffuse individuals who were considered to be Jews in the Israeli territorial space to strengthen Israeli sovereignty (Yiftachel, 1999).

Yet, these actions could not bring about the desired overlap between nation and state, therefore demands have been raised for the transfer of either Arabs or Jews or both ("disengagement" or "convergence" plans are nothing but plans for the transfer of Jews). The uncertainty and disagreement among Israelis concerning Israeli borders is not limited to the territories conquered in the Six Days War, hence the suggestions for swapping with the future Palestinian state territories within the Green Line which are inhabited by Arabs with territories beyond the Green Line inhabited by Jews. This means that even what has been known as "proper Israel" is no longer agreed upon. Perhaps the most striking demonstration of the disagreement about the national borders is the debated status of Jerusalem: while the Israelis seem to agree that Jerusalem is the capital of Israel, there is no agreement about what is "Jerusalem", that is whether or not it includes the Arab neighborhoods of east Jerusalem. As such, we have here a rather paradoxical situation where there is no agreement among the Israelis about what they consider to be their own capital city.

The attempt to achieve an identity that fuses both state and nation contradicts not only "messianic" controversial aspirations, but also Israel's legitimate demand for endurable and secured borders. The separation of nationality from religion and the recognition in the existence of an Israeli Nation will increase the options facing Israel to achieve securable and endurable borders. This would create an option for equality and integration for non-Jews, and especially for Arabs. Thus, Israel could appear in territories inhabited by Arabs not only as a conquering or discriminating power but also as a liberating one. It would then be possible to interpret Israel's demand for a change in its borders not as an attempt of an apartheid state to impose second or third rate citizenship on non-Jews, but as an attempt of a sovereign nation to create securable borders, while reaching out for the those who are added to its territory to become equal members of its nation.

Constitution and the Rule of Law

The existence of a Constitution and the Rule of Law are considered as necessary conditions for a republic (Pettit, 1999, pp. 35-41; Mautner, 2012). The absence of a constitution in Israel stems from the fusion of religion and nationality and the absence of recognition of the existence of an Israeli nation. Many Israelis attribute the inability to draft a constitution to the objection of religious sectors. Indeed, the inability to draft a constitution stems from the status of religion in Israel, yet it has nothing to do with one or another political constellation, or with any occasional coalitionist pressures (Kimmerling, 1994, p. 128). The cause of this inability is the fusion of religion and nationality, which is accepted by both religious and secular Israelis. In other words, a "Jewish State" cannot have a constitution, and that a 'Jewish and Democratic' state is an oxymoron, at least according to the accepted model of liberal democracy.

One important reason is that the fusion of religion and nationality makes it impossible to separate the religion from the state, a fundamental principle in liberal democracy. As the nation-state is both a nation and a state, the separation between religion and nationality complements the separation between religion and state, and vice versa. Where there is no separation between religion and nationality there will be no separation between religion and state. The principle of the separation between state and religion as accepted in western liberal democracy does not necessarily mean institutional separation (what is known as separation between State and Church) as in the United State and France, since in certain democracies (like Britain, Norway or Sweden (until 2002) there is an official church (Stepan, 2000). Neither does it necessarily mean that an "ideological separation" between religion and politics. That is the idea that politics should be devoid of any religious dimension (Bellah, 1970). It is possible to carefully draw at least four essential pillars of the notion of the separation between state and religion: (a) Equality of rights of all citizens irrespective of religious affiliation. (b) Freedom of worship. (c) Non-intervention of the state in religious doctrines. (d) The inability of religion institutions to veto or obstruct democratically accepted decisions.

It is easy to show how at least three of these four elements do not exist in Israel because of the fusion of religion and nationality. In Israel there is no civic equality; that is the rights and duties of the Israelis are not derived from their citizenship but rather from their religious or ethnic background. In addition, freedom of worship does not exist in Israel, as each and every Israeli citizen must belong to a religious community recognized by the state while the religious family law is imposed upon the Israelis without any regard to their consent. Thus, all those who are identified by the state as Jews are subjected to Orthodox rabbinical courts. Similarly all those who are considered by the state as Muslims are subjugated to sharia courts without any regard to their wishes. Many Israelis think that this situation originated in coalitionist pressures of the religious parties, or from the existence of a certain balance of powers in Israeli politics. In reality it is the fusion of religion and nationality that has caused this. Traditional Judaism, as it had existed in the Diaspora for thousands of years, had not been hierarchal, since it was a collection of autonomous communities. This pluralistic character of Judaism does not prevail in Israel because the fusion of faith and nationality has imposed the unification of Judaism into one religious national community. The balance of powers in Israeli politics could explain perhaps the victory of what is known in Israel as "Orthodoxy", but it cannot explain the attempts by the state to unify all the Jews into one religious community.

It is commonplace in "liberal" and "secular" circles to refer to their attempts to abolish the subjugation of the Israelis to religious courts as attempts to separate religion from the state. Even if the rabbinical courts were abolished, there would be no separation of religion and state as it is understood in liberal democracies. The Israeli state, as a Jewish State, is forced to constantly intervene in controversial religious doctrines. One example is the question "Who is a Jew?" This intervention is essential to the Jewish State, since every state has to decide what is required to become a member of its nation. The fusion of religion and nationality, accepted by both religious and secular, does not enable the separation of religion and state and as a result it is impossible to draw up a Constitution for Israel.

The idea that Israel does not have a constitution, which was commonplace, has been challenged in the recent decades. Not long ago Aharon Barak, then the Chief Justice of the Israeli Supreme Court, declared, that the two Basic Laws: "Basic Law: Human Dignity and Freedom" and "Basic Law: Freedom of Occupation" were the beginning of a "Constitutional Revolution" and that consequently Israel has a constitution (Rubinstein, 1996, p. 15). The

Basic Law: Human Dignity and Freedom contains a paragraph, which states that this law cannot annul any former legislation. Thus we have a somewhat paradoxical situation where we have simultaneously constitutional rights while there continues to be subordination of Israelis to religious courts. As argued above this is the essence of the Jewish State and Aharon Barak himself seems to recognize this based on his statement that: "A Jewish State is a state in which the Hebrew Law forms an essential role and in which the wedlock are decided by the laws of the Torah" (Margolin, 1997, p. 11).

Similar things could be said about the "Basic Law: Freedom of Occupation." In this case, despite a basic law that guarantees the right to work, Israelis of Arab origin are prevented from substantial parts of the labor market on the pretext that the work is in the security industry or is tied to the security of the state. Further, Israelis of Arab origin cannot buy lands or apartments and live in cities and villages which are considered "Jewish." In this situation the rights, mobility and freedom of occupation of the Israeli Arabs are violated, and today this violation is given a constitutional legitimization by these two Basic Laws.

The fusion of nationality and religion not only makes it impossible to have a constitution, but also undermines the rule of the law, and forces the state to be run by arrangements that contradict the law.

The need for arrangements that often contravene the laws is caused by the commitment of the Israeli elite to democracy, on one hand, and the fact that the Israel's political system draws much of its legitimacy also in the international arena, from the perception that it is a democracy, on the other hand. This makes it impossible to legislate laws that openly discriminate based on religion or ethnicity and obliges the state to turn to arrangements, which are beyond the laws. One way of doing it is to give certain organizations a status, of which the law has no complete control. One can point out at least two such bodies: The official Chief Rabbinate and all sort of 'Zionist' or 'Jewish' institutions such as the Jewish national Fund (*hakeren hakayemet leYisrael*) and the Jewish Agency. The distribution of powers between the rabbinic courts and the civic ones mean that the Israeli law has at least two independent sources. The distribution could not be defined by the (civic) law, since, at least formally, the rabbinic courts are autonomous to judge according to the *Halacha* (Weiler, 1976; Kimmerling, 1994, p. 127). The result is that the relation between the civil courts and the rabbinic courts is a matter of an arrangement rather than that of the law.

The operation of the Jewish National Fund is also more a matter of an arrangement than a matter of the law. The Israel Land Administration (ILA) is the governmental agency responsible for managing the public lands of Israel. Yet, as far as ownership is concerned, the public or state lands in Israel consist of lands that belong to the state, and the lands of the Jewish National Fund. Though the lands of the Jewish National Fund are effectively under the administration of the ILA, formally these lands do not belong to the state but rather to "the Jewish People". Consequently their administration is more a matter of arrangement than that of the law. One of the justifications for the unusual status of the JNF (and similar institutions of the Zionist Movement and the Jewish Agency) was the need to direct funds only to the Jewish population, and that the lands of the JNF, which belong to the "Jewish People" could be used only for the settlement of Jews. In other words, since the Israeli law forbids discrimination, and this principle is supposed to direct the operations of the ILA, this would not hold for the JNF. This arrangement is used to prevent Israelis of Arab origin from buying land or from living on land which belongs to the JNF. To make things worse, the ILA occasionally transfers lands to the JNF, thereby increasing its lands, or the lands that formally do not belong to the Israeli state (Rubinstein, 1996, pp. 308 – 309).

It is interesting to note that though the JNF is supposedly a Jewish body, the rule that its lands are designated for Jews alone is not a written rule but rather an acquired custom (Rubinstein, *ibid.*). Thus, even the administrators of this supposedly Jewish body had preferred to leave the discrimination to an arrangement rather than to express it by a written law.

In March 2000 the Israeli Supreme Court ruled on the Kaadan matter, partially upholding the appeal of an Israeli of Arab origin family who had sought to purchase a house in the Jewish municipal community of Katzir. According to Shafir and Peled and many others this was "a path-breaking decision" in which the Supreme Court ruled that it was illegal for the state to discriminate between its Jewish and Arab citizens in the allocation of land, even when it is done indirectly, through the so called "Jewish national Institutions" (Shafir & Peled, 2002, p. 132.) Thus, Shafir and Peled conclude that "in that decision the court determined that the ethno-national interest of Zionism in 'Judaizing' the country cannot override the principle of equality" (p. 274). Yet, not all shared this assessment and Gad Barzilai actually concludes the opposite, namely that "in the Kaadan the court emphasized the Jewishness of the state as the precondition to any allocation of rights to Arabs, citizens of Israel ..." (Barzilai, 2000, p. 450).

Barzilai refers to clause 19 of the verdict where the court says that the ILA policy is dictated also by "special purposes", among which are to prevent the transfer of the land to "undesirable elements", and to conduct a "security policy" and enable national projects, such as the absorption of *Aliyah* (Jewish immigration), the dispersing of the population (*pizur uchlusin*) and agricultural settlement. The expressions used by the court to describe those "special purposes" had been interpreted by the ILA, and usually conceived by the general public as synonyms with allocation of lands to Jews. While the court acknowledged that the ILA is guided by those "special purposes" it did not declare these rules unconstitutional. Yet, what the court did say that when these "special purposes" collide with the "general purposes" that should guide the ILA (as the principle of equality), a "balancing formula" should be constructed which would decide whether or to what extent the "special purpose" overcomes the "general purpose." Yet the court did not find it necessary to create a "balancing formula" in this case since in the present case there was no such collision so the "general purpose" could have been maintained in its entirety. Thus, the court did not rule that the "special purposes" were not constitutional, but rather that they did not apply to the present case.

Furthermore, it is not clear to what extent the Kaadan case had set precedence. Thus, Kedar and Yiftachel note:

> However, the material implications of this milestone decision are not yet clear: the court was careful to confine the decision only to Katzir, and not to other Jewish settlements, especially Kibbutzim and Moshavim, which form the vast majority of rural settlement blocked to Arabs. Further, more than five years after the decision, a range of legal and institutional means has prevented the Kaadans to actually live in Katzir. It appears that the High Court's watershed decision about the illegality of discrimination against the Arabs in the allocation of state land will not be easily expressed in a new geography of Arab-Jewish relations in Israel. (Kedar & Yiftachel, 2006, p. 143).

The fusion of faith and nationality is not compatible with the rule of the law. Thus it does not only demand a judicial definition of "a Jew", but also of "an Arab" and to distinguish between different kinds of Arabs. While compulsory conscription to the Israeli army is not normally applied to "the Arabs", it is applied in various degrees to some Arab groups like "the Bedouins" or "the Druze." Such legislation is cumbersome and perhaps impossible. Consequently the issue of the conscription to the army is regulated by arrangements rather than by the law. According to the Law of Security Service (*chok sheirut bitachon*) 1986, the duty of military service applies to all the permanent residents of Israel. Yet, according to Rubinstein "the law is not enforced upon all the residents" (Rubinstein, 1996, p. 300). The Supreme Court Ruling in the case of Hasona (Bagatz 53/56) debated the petition of an Israeli Druze who claimed that since he belonged to one of the minorities he should not be conscripted against his will.

The Supreme Court rejected the plea while asserting "it is not for us to investigate and assert what motivated the authorities not to apply the law until today to one group or another. It was their right to call the petitioner to the flag and since their action was not illegal we see no reason to intervene" (Rubinstein, 1996, p. 301). In this ruling the Supreme Court acknowledged the right of the authorities to apply the law arbitrarily, thus legitimizing the non-existence of the rule of the law. Indeed, the origin of the practice according to which the males of the Druze community are conscripted is not the law but an arrangement, that is an agreement between the state and the elders of the congregation (Rubinstein, *ibid*.) This is a clear violation of the rule of the law because it is obvious that the elders of the Druze community have no lawful stand, which enables them to commit the males of the Druze congregations to conscription to the army. Further, this arrangement invokes the question "Who is a Druze?" Thus it would be impossible for someone considered by the Israeli state as a Druze to avoid conscription by claiming that he is not "a Druze" but rather "an Arab". The Israeli state, does not only impose Jewish identity upon those it considered to be Jewish, but also "Druze" or "Arab" identity according to its will, without any regard to the way that the citizens identify themselves.

It should be emphasized that for those who are considered as 'Arabs' who are not suitable for military service Recruiting Orders are not issued in the first place, and consequently the youngsters are exempted apriori without presenting themselves in the Recruiting Station and or even applying for an exemption. The whole process demonstrates further the absence of the rule of law. For those Recruiting Orders are not issued for every youngster who reaches the age of seventeen as the rule of law demands, but according to a record which exists alongside or beyond the Citizens Record and which divides the latter into 'Jews' and 'Arabs'.

The fact that the fusion of religion and nationality and its distorted derivatives are not formulated by the law makes any reform in the law or any "constitutional revolution" useless. This is because the discrimination against the Arabs is not set by the law or in legislation or in any formal explicit rules. In other words, to an Israeli who is of Arab background it is not clear at all what he or she should do, or what are the conditions he or she should fulfill, in order to become equal to the Jews.

The fusion of religion and nationality does not enable the existence of the rule of law and forces Israel to be run by arrangements. The tendency towards a political community run by arrangements is enhanced also by the blur of the distinction between the religious community and the nation. Religious communities are run by arrangements, as had most of the historical Jewish communities. The fusion of religion and nationality increases the temptation to import the arrangements of the historical Jewish communities to Israel and thus contributes to a culture of (political) arrangements. This inability to sustain the rule of law in Israel impacts on its ability to institutionalize the state and its institutions.

The tendency of the Israeli Democracy to be run by arrangements should not be confused with the model of consociational democracy. The Dutch researcher Lijphart thinks that the existence of a stable democracy in divided societies is conditioned upon a unique model of policy-making and conflict resolution, which is based upon power sharing arrangements. According to Lijphart, a society, which is ideologically or religiously divided, could keep its unity and its ability to act in the political domain, if the leaders of the various contentious groups would agree to cooperate. One of the principal characteristics of consociational politics is the wish to avoid as much as possible the solution of controversial issues by legislation, as this might favor one side over the other. It also insures mutual readiness of the leaders of the contentious groups to negotiate and compromise in order to reach agreed arrangements, which will enable a peaceful settlement of the conflict (Lijphart 1968, Don Yehiya, 1999).

Don Yehiya argues that the consociational model is applied in Israel systematically in the religious sphere and only partially in other areas (Don Yehiya, 1999, p. 9). Yet, it should be noted that though consociational politics prefers the resolution of conflicts by arrangements rather than by legislation and courts, in the examples which Lijphart cited consociational politics complements the rule of law rather than replaces or bypasses it. All of the consociational democracies have constitutions. In Israel the 'flexibility' offered by the consociational democracy complements the one, which is offered by the absence of a constitution. Shlomo Avineri criticizes the Israeli tendency to rely on the judicial system in deciding upon controversial issues concerning Israel being a Jewish and Democratic state, as these controversies should be settled by dialogue and agreement between the parties and not by judicial decision, which is a "zero sum game" (Margolin, 1999, pp. 41-42). Consequently Avineri sees the absence of a constitution as an advantage: "Thank God, really thank God, that we don't have (a constitution)" (Avineri, 1998, p. 22). In this light Avineri's assertion that "the state of Israel is not the only state which sustains a democracy without a written constitution … as Britain has managed and is managed not bad without a constitution" is problematic (Margolin, 1999, p. 42). First, many would disagree with Avineri's assertion that Britain has no constitution, and indeed it is possible to fill a whole library with books, which were written on "The British Constitution" or "The English

Constitution" (Neuberger, 1997a, vol. 3, pp. 14-15). Hence there are several principles, which are considered as part of the British Constitution, one of them is "the rule of the law." As pointed above, it is doubtful whether the principles of the rule of the law apply to Israel.

Second, even if Britain does not have a constitution, which is debatable, this is indeed an exception, and it is not clear at all why Israel should adopt that exception as well. Third, even if Britain does not have a constitution, this is possible because of the deep consensus which exists there about the ways in which the government should be run. In other words, the fact that the ways to run the government are manifest and agreed upon makes it possible to do it without formulating them in one document. Yet, in Israel the reason for the absence of a constitution seems to be the lack of consensus about the nature of those basic rules. Consequently, as Mautner (2012, p. 572) observes "a formulation of a constitution, which would consolidate the Israelis around a common normative "I believe", is imperative".

Peace

In his book on nationalism Alfred Cobban posted the following question concerning Israel:

> ... there are the Jews of Israel. How can their presence be reconciled with awakened Arab nationalism? Will their history, in the territory they have conquered, be like that of a former Kingdom of Jerusalem, the crusading state which survived for generations in the heart of Islam but always as a beleaguered garrison, saved by repeated infusions of blood from the outer world? Or will Israel become one more in mosaic Near Eastern nation-states? The latter becomes more likely as both the Arabs and the Jews move away from the state founded of religious ideology and towards one based on nationalism. (Cobban, 1969, pp. 230-1).

Cobban's hope that the conflict in the Middle East would become a conflict between nations rather than between religions seems today more remote than ever. Both sides have not abandoned the concept of the religious state. As for the Arab countries, it seems that secular nationalism, in the sense that had been developed in the west and of which Cobban speaks in the quotation above, did not develop there. The resurgence of political Islam and the events in the aftermath of the Arab Spring, especially in Iraq and Syria, have proven the failure of Arab Nationalism. The same could be said also about Israel in which the fusion of religion and nationality prevented the emergence of a secular nationalism. Therefore the conflict in the Middle East appears more and more as a conflict between civilizations or religions rather than as a national conflict – as Israel seems to be a Jewish bastion stuck at the heart of a hostile Muslim world.

Indeed, Israelis should be reminded of the fate of the earlier crusader-state. Here the words of Azzam Pasha, the Secretary – General of the Arab League after the 1948's Arab defeat: "… It took us two hundred years to fight the crusaders; we are not in a hurry" (Bilby, 1950, p. 8). Those Israelis, who claim they have learned the lessons of the First Crusader Kingdom, do not suggest the Israeli State should give up its crusader character, this fusion of nationality and religion, but rather that it should "aspire for peace". As for the crusader nature of the state, the problems that it creates will be solved when peace comes. Yet, there is a double catch here: on one hand, it is difficult for a crusader state to aspire for peace, and on the other hand, it is doubtful whether the Muslim world will accept a crusader Jewish State in its midst, even when it is peaceful. My conclusion is that the separation between nationality and religion is a necessary condition for peace.

Yet, the last words must be qualified. There are those who claim that the regional hostility towards Israel is part of the global conflict between Islam and the west, and that the Muslims, or Arabs, will not tolerate in their midst any political entity which will not be Muslim or Arab. If this is the case, then the collision between Israel and the Arab-Muslim world seems to be unavoidable. Yet, it is possible to see how the separation between nationality and religion could decrease the religious tension and the impact of this collision. The existence of an Israeli Nation with a variety of ethnic and religious communities: western and eastern Jews, Arabs, Muslims, Christian and more might mitigate the Jewish image of Israel and will make Israel a real Middle Eastern nation. The fact that the Israeli state will not serve the Jews exclusively, on one hand, and the fact that the modern and rich Israeli nation (when compared to other middle eastern countries) contains successful sons and daughters of Arab origin, who are proud of their nation and also are ready to defend it, could change the attitude of the Arabs of the Middle East towards Israel.

The solution of the Israeli identity question is a pre-condition for any peace agreement. Many Israelis think that the question of Israeli identity and the question of the status of the Arabs will find answers when peace comes. Yet, the opposite seems to be the truth: a pre-condition for peace is the solution of the problem of Israeli identity. Peace is done with "the other", yet to determine who is 'the other' we must first determines who we are.

War

As noted above, even though the separation between nationality and religion might mitigate the Middle Eastern hostility towards Israel, there is no assurance that this hostility would disappear, and consequently it is possible that for the foreseeable future Israel will continue to be a "country under siege" and will have to relay on its deterrence and military powers. In recent decades, at least among the secular-Ashkenazi elite, there has been a decrease in the recognition of the importance of the security burden and in the readiness to carry this burden. According to Yagil Levy "the violation of the republican principle" brought about:

> (T)he weakening of the readiness of the middle secular-Ashkenazi class to continue and to maintain the army both in human and in financial resources, and the increase in the conditions it sets, also by political protest, for its readiness to sacrifice. Therefore, the ability of the state to conduct an autonomous military policy was curtailed, and the state was forced to take measures, which will mitigate the Israeli pugnacity – that is to decrease the burden and to match it to the decreased outcome – which has reached its climax in the Oslo Process. (Levy, 2007, p. 24).

While this change could have desirable consequences, such as the increase of civic supervision of the army and perhaps the increase of the desire for peace among the Israelis, it could also result in less desirable ramifications such as the curtailment of the state ability to take military initiatives. If we accept Clausewitz's famous saying that war is the continuation of diplomacy in other ways, then even a policy, which aspires for peace should have a military initiative option.

What Levy portrays is not a unique Israeli phenomenon, but one that had been observed in both ancient and modern societies. Plato already observed that "thin" states fight better than "fat" states, and the fourteenth century Arab sociologist Ibn Khaldun had pointed out how fierce desert tribal warriors lost their fighting spirit once they conquered a city and began to enjoy civilized life. In pre-industrial societies the problem was less consequential since soldiering was one of the main options to acquire wealth. This is not the case in modern capitalist society, which creates a certain dissonance in the modern republic. Yet there are various ways in which the contemporary (western) nation-state deals with this problem. One of these is the offering of social mobility for the non-middle lower classes and new immigrants through the service in the army (Danette-Light, 1998). Yet, the Jewish State's ability to use this option is limited. While it worked for the Mizrachim (Jews who immigrated to Israel from Arab Lands) and the religious Zionists who during the first decades after independence had been marginalized (though in different ways and from different reasons), the lowest classes in Israel, the Arabs and the ultra-Orthodox (*Charedim*), are excluded from the army by the ideology and the practices of the Jewish State.

As for immigration, the last wave of massive immigration from the former Soviet Union has been a prime source for the conscription of highly motivated soldiers. Nevertheless, the Jewish Diaspora's reservoirs of the Jewish State seem to have been exhausted. As for non-Jewish immigration it is generally not allowed into the Jewish State, on one hand, and to the extent that it exists, mainly in the form of foreign labor, as it could not be enfranchised by the Jewish State, it does not form a substratum for the renovation of the citizen body in general and the army in particular. The separation between religion and nationality would enable the inclusion of non-Jews (Arabs, foreign workers, or non-Jewish immigrants) and would add to the nation individuals who will alleviate the security burden which is imposed today mostly on the Jews in Israel.

Indeed, the failure of the Jewish State to create a civic army goes beyond the exclusion of the Arabs. As Mautner observes, though there is officially a universal conscription, only half of the eligible youth are enlisted every year: all the Arab woman, most of the Arab men, all the ultra-Orthodox woman, most of the ultra-Orthodox men and many of the religious Zionism's women are exempted from military service for "national or cultural reasons" (Mautner 2012, p. 573). Indeed, it seems to be an irony that the so-called Zionist revolution which set itself to free the Diaspora Jews from their helplessness, by creating a 'Jewish' army, ended with the creation of a state in which half of the population are reluctant to serve in the army. Further, if the readiness to serve in the army could be seen as mark of good citizenship and identification with the state, the fact that large sections of the population do not serve projects also on the ability of the Jewish State to command the loyalty and solidarity of its population.

Though the decrease of the civic motivation of the secular middle class could be attributed to a wide range of causes, it has also to do with the failure of the Jewish State to create a civic republican spirit. The fusion of religion and nationality has created a "civil religion" which is a "new interpretation" of religion (Liebman and Don Yehiya, 1983) and consequently does not appeal, in the long run to secular Israelis. Thus the main carriers of this civil religion at the present time remained those publics, which are more rooted in the Jewish religion or the Jewish tradition such as the so-called 'Religious Zionists' and the Mizrachim. It is in this respect that the increased presence in the army combat unit of people of this background, especially of the so called 'Religious Zionists', should be seen as complementary to the decrease in motivation of the secular 'Ashkenazi' middle class.

The increase of the presence of soldiers of religious background in the army in general and in combat units in particular had raised the question in academia and the general public as to the extent that the Israeli army has in the recent decades been going through: a process of "religionization". The debate was prompted by a number of recent events. They include orders given by rabbis calling soldiers to disobey orders to evacuate settlements in the West Bank, as well as actual threats made by soldiers to disobey such orders, and the refusal of religious soldiers to attend military events in which women soldiers chanted and sang. Finally, there was also the limitation imposed upon the presence of women in units where religious soldiers serve, and the increased involvement of the Military Rabbinate in the 'indoctrination' of the soldiers. According to Yagil Levy, religionization remolds the identity of the Jewish soldier who serves in the army, the secular and not only the religious, as the Jewish "national-religious" soldier (Levy, 2015).

There is a disagreement among the scholars as to whether the process of religionization is widespread and whether it is a new development. Kampinsky (2012) says that religionization is a an 'optical illusion' and that unlike the situation in the Israeli society where the status of religion is a source for the rift between secular and religious, the status of religion within the army has been principally accepted by the secular. Nevertheless Kampinsky agrees that in the recent decade there had been a controversial change in the scope of the duties of Military Rabbinate (p.329).

Indeed, 'religionization' has always been there: the Jewish State needed a Jewish army. Thus if the Israeli present civil religion is indeed "Jewish", or a "new interpretation" of Judaism, then it is the other way around: it is not the high presence of religious soldiers which had led to religionization, but rather it is religionization, or the fusion of religion and nationality, which had created the high presence of religious soldiers and religious values in the army. Indeed one institutional expression of the religionization was the establishment of the Military Rabbinate. Though initially its role was confined to technical religious assistance, like its 'civic' counterpart, the Chief Rabbinate, it represents the unity of religion and nationality: the rejection of the pluralist conception of Judaism and the need to administer one religious law to the (Jewish) army.

Like its civic counterpart, establishment of a military rabbinate was an expression of the nationalization of Judaism by the Israeli State, and a means by the state and the army to control religion. Yet, the Military Rabbinate was not initially entrusted with the education of the soldiers, spiritually or in any other way. That remained within the "secular" branches of the army, such as the Education Corps. To the extent that we are witnessing a change in the recent years it is probably due to the fact the 'religionization' was now entrusted to its more natural agents: the (Military) Rabbinate. The latter has been gradually abandoning its initial function; to provide technical religious services, instead it has been increasingly directing it sites at the secular rather the religious soldiers, with the notion of molding their spiritual world as soldiers and with a special emphasis on the "fighting spirit" of the soldiers (Kampinsky, 2010, 168 – 169; Levy, 2015). It is important to stress that this change was in fact initiated by the (secular) army that actually came to the conclusion that the administration of the "civil religion" could not be entrusted to the secular branches of the army.

It is here that Yagil Levy (2015) offers to distinguish between a process of religionization, on one hand, and what he calls 'theocratization', on the other. The latter is characterized by the increase of the penetration of "religious authorities" into the army and their attempt to influence the conduct of the army in areas which have been traditionally considered to be within the authority of the army's political supervisors. According to Levy what we are witnessing today is a process of theocratization. It is not the place here to elaborate upon Levy's 'theocratization', yet Levy and others portray a gruesome picture which goes far beyond the nature of the activity of the Military Rabbinate to arrangements with non-military rabbis and organizations, such as the settlers or heads of *Yeshivot* and *Mechinot*[8] acknowledging their status as negotiating side on issues such as military deployment in the West Bank, the integration of women in the army and other cultural arrangements (Drori, 2012, 138-139). All and all Levy points out the process interferes with the army chain of command, on one hand, and introduces into the army the authority of the Halacha as an independent religious law on which the army has no control, on the other. The Army Rabbinate, though officially under the authority of the Army Chief Command, still considers itself as subordinated to the *Halacha*, and in this sense subordinated also to the interpretation of the *Halacha* of rabbis and religious bodies outside the army.

The "invitation" for the rabbis to step in was in itself an admission of the secular in general, and the army in particular, that they have no set of values which would inspire the soldiers with a fighting spirit. In fact, it seems that to the extent that the army possessed any "secular" concept, it seemed to be one which has tried to curtail and mitigate the traditional myth of the fighting spirit of the Israeli army. According to Lebel and Luvish-Omer (2012), the high presence of the religious soldiers should be seen as "a vanguard" of a "conservative counter-culture" to the post-modernization of the Israeli army. According to them since the nineteen nineties the Israeli Army, like other western countries, has gone through a process of post-modernization partially as a response to the decrease in the motivation of the elites. A post-modern army is essentially an army of peace, which is more influenced by organizations of civil society, that seeks to mitigate the use of violence and prevent escalation. It is an army which in order to avoid casualties seeks to remove the soldier from the battlefield and prefers artillery and air warfare to traditional ground warfare. It prefers a "post-heroic warfare" in which the minimization of casualties is not a smaller factor, and sometimes even more important, than the completion of the mission. In so many words, this is an army, which is constructed to fight without "fighting spirit." Thus, according to Lebel and Luvish-Omer, "more than this process (that is 'religionization') is an attempt to bestow upon the army a 'Jewish' character in the religious or the Halachic sense, it is in opposition to the institutionalization of the army as a post-modern army" and the return to "traditional strategic realism" (p. 184).

While Lebel and Luvis-Omer perhaps identify correctly that some of the ideas associated with the high presence of the religious soldiers and values could be seen as the rejection of the post-modernist army, it is rather difficult to accept those ideas as "conservative", or as an attempt to return to the "traditional army". The "Army of God" or an army that eventually had to be run according to the *Halacha* is a fundamentalist army, rather than a traditional army. While the fundamentalist army may induce its soldiers with a fighting spirit (and this is also questionable, as many of its soldiers are secular), the encouragement of disobedience and the infringement of the chain of command, do not characterize the traditional army and undermine the ability of the army to pursue its goals. Furthermore, as Lebel and Luvish-Omer say, the traditional army requires to distant itself from the political organizations and the organizations of the civil society, a rule which had been grossly violated in the process of the 'theocratization' of the army (Drori, p. 144).

It is interesting to note that by turning to the Jewish religion to find a source for military resourcefulness the so-called "Zionist" ethos has completed a circle. The early Zionists cast themselves against the Jewish religion considering it one of the causes of the Jewish helplessness and passivity. And indeed, though religions are multi-vocal, traditional Diaspora Judaism could not be easily associated with violence and war. On the contrary, the 2000 years of Judaism without a polity, and the fact that Jews were almost always a persecuted minority led to quietism which had turned into a religious tenet "not to provoke the gentiles" (Aran & Hassner, 2013, p. 366). As Aran and Hassner maintain, the association of the Jewish religion with war and violence is a new phenomenon. In this sense, from a military point of view, 'religionization' could have become a two-edge sword, because the process of the creation of a "Jewish" army and the creation of a "Jewish" fighting spirit could have invoked the traditional Jewish quietism. In fact this has already happened before the rabbis stepped in. As we are going to see, one of the streams of the Zionist movement, that of "Spiritual Zionism", had adopted and politicized certain elements of traditional Jewish quietism. From the latter point of view, both (real) politics and the use of violence in order to achieve political and national goals were considered as unworthy of Judaism.

I believe strongly that the influence of "Spiritual Zionism" and its forefathers Ahad Ha'am and Martin Buber upon Zionism in general and

Israel in particular has been grossly overlooked. Thus, from its inception, two images of Judaism have been competing for dominance over the Jewish State. The first one, introduced in the 1950s, mixed state and military activism with chauvinism and ethno-centrism. The other was a "Buberian" interpretation of Judaism, which emphasized (political) quietism, non-violence and Jewish humanism (and see Chapter 6 below). Thus the decrease in the civil religion of the active type noted above among secular Israelis had been accompanied by the increase among them of the conception of Judaism as passive. In other words, the religionization of Zionism and Israel had led to a curious inversion: the once active secular had turned into quietists, while the once quietist religious turned into activists. Though the decrease in the readiness of the secular to serve in the army could be attributed to universal causes (including the post-modernization of the army,) it had been also enhanced by the reappearance of "Jewish quietism."

It seems, then, that the Israeli army is between a rock and a hard place. It has to choose between "the army of God", or "the army of Martin Buber." Both are problematic from the military point of view. What Israel wants is, not a "Jewish" army, but rather an Israeli civic army.

The mere addition of a mass of non-Jewish soldiers, especially of Arab origin, to the Israeli army will check its religionization as it will create a multi-religious army. In the recent debate concerning the evacuation of settlements a group of rabbis had published a ruling, which said that the Israeli Chief of Staff is bound by the Laws of the *Torah*. They will not be able to say this if Israel was to have a non-Jewish Chief of Stuff, especially one of Arab origin.

Israel and the Arab Minority

The fusion of religion and nationality, and the non-recognition of the existence of an Israeli Nation has made impossible the incorporation of Arabs or individuals of Arab origin into the national life. Officially the Israeli Arabs enjoy equality of rights, nevertheless, as noted above, Israel is administered by arrangements, rather than by laws, and practically the Arabs in Israel do not have the same rights and duties as the Jews. The Arabs are conceived of as members of a hostile nation and are denied essential rights; such as right to purchase land and live wherever they choose. Important sections of the job market, especially occupations that are linked or could be linked to the security industry (which means, in fact, most of the high technology market), are effectively blocked for them (Smooha, 2001, p. 295). The outcome is that Israeli Arabs are confined to what is known as the "The Arab Sector" ("*hamigzar haAravi*"), which is essentially rural, non-industrial and underdeveloped when compared to "The Jewish Sector." At the same time the Arabs do not have the same duties, which a "normal" Israeli citizen has, the most important being the duty to serve in the army. The reason usually given for non-conscription of the Israeli Arabs is that they are members of an enemy nation and consequently either they could not be trusted (as the Israeli right asserts), or it is immoral to demand from them to fight their "Arab brothers" (as the Israeli left asserts). The consensus in this matter is well expressed by Amnon Rubinstein (1996, p. 301):

> As it was explained in the Knesset, the custom of exemption from military service for the Arab citizens was introduced in order to prevent them to serve contrary to their will and their feelings. Indeed, an obligatory conscription was imposed upon the Druze and the Circassian communities only after the elders of the community came forward and asked to conscript the male-members of their communities. The non-conscription of the Israeli Arabs puts Israel in a unique position, unprecedented in other countries: Some 18% of the inhabitants of the state are not called to service and are not put to this important test of loyalty to the state. (Yet) this is rightful and just decision, and **as long as we do not have peace with all the Arab states it is impossible to divert from it.**

This citation is a good demonstration of the "The New Zionist Myth" and the Israeli consensus. The fusion of religion and nationality, which assumes that the Jews constitute a nation, assumes also that the Arabs constitute one, and overlooks the fact that the Arabs belong to different countries, which sometimes fight one another. What comes to light in the above citation is the paternalistic approach towards the Arabs, that is the argument that the exemption from military duty was done "to prevent them to serve contrary to their will and feelings" when there has been no attempt to find out whether there are Arabs who are willing to serve in the army, or under what conditions they would be willing to do so.

Moreover, the Israelis have never drawn the natural conclusion from their assumption that it is impossible or immoral to demand from the Arabs to fight for Israel, which would be the revocation of the right of the Arabs to vote for the Knesset. Instead we have a paradox (what Rubinstein calls "a right and just decision") where those who are suspected in disloyalty to the state, which refuses to entrust them with guns, are able to vote for and even to have seats in its parliament. Every democracy puts the parliament above the army and those who could not be trusted with guns certainly could not be trusted with their vote or with their political decision-making.

Since the service in the army is considered a fundamental civic duty in Israel and a test of loyalty and devotion to the state, many see the fact that the Arabs do not serve as a major obstacle for equality. According to the present consensus, the discrimination against the Arabs will end when peace comes. Yet, this assumption is questionable from the following reasons: (a) It is not certain at all that there is going to be peace. (b) Even the most optimists among the Israelis think that, also in peace times, Israel will have to rely on its deterring military powers. In other words, since we live in the Middle East, if the Israeli army will operate, or if it is used as a deterring force, it will probably be directed against Arabs or Muslims. So it seems that the present reasons for the non-conscription of the Arabs and the discrimination which it entails will remain also in the so-called "peace era." We find a hint of this in the words of Amnon Rubinstein above, that it would be possible to put the Arabs to the test of loyalty only when there will be peace "with *all* the Arab states." Thus, as long as there is even one single Arab State in a state of war with Israel, there can be no normalization of the situation of the Arabs in Israel.

Israel does not offer to the young Arabs who are growing up here very much. In as much as it would be difficult for the Israelis to admit, Israel has been developed into a discriminatory state originated in the confusion between nation and religion. Yet, this confusion encourages and educates racist elements, and the great danger is that the discriminatory policy towards the Arabs, based upon the confusion between nationality and religion, will become more and more a policy based also upon racism. The fear of what is known here as "the demographic problem" prompted the president of Ben Gurion University at the time (and a former army General) Shlomo Gazit to suggest "an undemocratic emergency regime" in which the birthrate of the Arabs will be curtailed[4]. Such gruesome language, which characterizes the racial margins of western democracies, was used in Israel by a President of a University. Indeed, the words of Gazit provoked strong reactions. Yet this points to the continuing deterioration of the political discourse in Israel, especially when prominent representatives of "liberal", or "left" circles, the advocates of all kind of "disengagement" programs, constantly declare that the borders of Israel should be set in such a manner as to include the least possible number of Arabs. Thus, the fusion of religion and nationality make it impossible for the Israelis to express their legitimate concerns about the formation of the national and cultural character of Israel otherwise than by the distorted language of racism.

The separation between nationality and religion and the recognition in Israel as the state of the Israeli nation will make possible the integration of Arabs into Israeli national life. Here a question arises, that is to what extent the Israeli Arabs are interested in such integration. As we are going to see, there are strong indications that had it been offered to the Arabs in Israel to integrate into the national life (including national conscription) substantial numbers would have joined. Nevertheless, there is no doubt that there will be some, and even many, that will refuse to join the nation. Their will must be respected, yet there remains the question of their status. I will discuss this question in more details later on (see below, pp. 200-214), yet what can be said now is that from the fusion of nationality and citizenship which characterizes the modern liberal democracy, those who openly declare that they do not wish to become members of the nation should not be the citizens of its state. Therefore, their citizenship should be revoked. The essential expression of this revocation would be the revocation of the right to vote for the national institution, that is the Knesset, without encroaching upon their rights to vote for the local government institutions, or their rights to their possessions and lands and the other protections that the modern liberal state offers to its inhabitants.

The recognition of an Israeli nation and the establishment of an Israeli republic would require establishing a complete equality of rights and duties to Israelis of Arab origin and their possible integration into the national life. This would mean opening up Israeli society for the Arabs, with all the vast range of possibilities and occupations it could offer, and consequently an immigration of a considerable number of Arabs to the larger cities. Therefore, it might cause a change in the "Hebrew" or "Jewish" character of Israel, and probably such a change is bound to happen. The prospect of such a change might cause Israelis, also those of democratic perceptions, to reject the idea of the Israeli nation, as they fear an encroachment on what they consider to be their national character. This is indeed a legitimate and understandable concern, but it cannot overcome the fact that any attempt to maintain the present fragmental non-integrative nature of the Israeli society with the help of the law or of arrangements is undemocratic and creates here an apartheid state under the protection of the Supreme Court. It is also democracy, then, which demands the separation between nationality and religion. Nevertheless, it is the democratic right of every nation to preserve its national character. The question which must be discussed here is how can we build an Israeli nation which would be both Hebrew and multicultural.

Consequently the Israeli concerns about the characteristics of the Israeli nation could be met by constitutional means. It is possible to set the domination of the Hebrew language (or of "a law of return", and see below, pp. 214-225) in a constitution. Indeed, constitutions are also bound to change, though by qualified majorities, yet, it is important to note that it is precisely under the present status quo that Israel risks loosing its national character given what is know here as "the demographic problem", that is the constant narrowing of the gap between the size of the Jewish population, on one hand, and the Arab population, on the other. Here those who fear for Israel's national character should be encouraged by the cultural strength of the Israeli society. In sixty-five years of independence the nation of Israel has been multiplied by more than a dozen – An unprecedented growth in the history of the modern world. In the nineteen nineties Israel had successfully absorbed about one million immigrants (that is about 20% of the total population) from the former Soviet Union. In as much as this growth had changed Israel's national character, Israel had remained essentially Hebrew. Of course, there are differences between the absorption of immigrants on individual basis and the incorporation into national life of native communities. Yet, Israeli Arabs speak Hebrew and, though isolated, were still exposed to processes of Israelization, which most likely will be enhanced if a national integration becomes an option.

Post-Zionism

Unfortunately, in the recent decades the idea of the normalization of Israel has been more and more identified with the post-Zionist idea of the "citizens' state." It should be emphasized that in as much as the thesis being proposed in this book is a post-Zionist one, it is different from the doctrines which are considered today as post-Zionist. In the current debate about the identity of Israel, the post-Zionist camp demands to dismantle the "Jewish State" and to define Israel as "The state of all its citizens". Yet, the post-Zionist "citizens' state" is essentially different from the model of the normal nation-state, or that of the republic, as proposed here. Because of the fusion of nationality and citizenship, the western liberal state is both a national state and the state of its citizens. Being national, it is not culturally neutral, and gives clear priority to the national culture. Yet, the post-Zionists, who accept the idea of the citizens' state, usually reject the idea of the national state and do not suggest the establishment of an Israeli republic. Their purpose is to turn Israel into a "neutral" or "universal" state, which lacks any national characteristics, either by the creation of a civic, a-historic, amorphous "nation", or by turning Israel into a bi-national state in which the Jewish and the Arab components would be equal, and in fact, by both.

Thus, the post-Zionist camp does not aim for the normalization of Israel, but rather to the creation of Israel as an unprecedented non-national "universal" state, or as "a kingdom of priests and a holy nation". Consequently, post-Zionism ignores the fact that Israel was established after the struggle of the Zionist movement, which was a movement for national self-determination of the "Jewish nation" (that is, the Hebrew or Israeli nation), that it had originated from within the historical *"Am Yisrael"*, and that a feeling of a common Jewish destiny has constituted a major cause for the Israelis' desire to establish and defend Israel. Post-Zionism also ignores the fact that nationalism is an essential need for most of the Israelis and contradicts their democratic wish that Israel should express this need. Consequently, the post-Zionist camp ignores the present national character of Israel, which is clearly Hebrew. Therefore post-Zionism in this form should be rejected since it denies the democratic right of the Israelis for national self-determination (See below, pp. 159-178).

In all the bi-national or multi-national countries which serve as a model for post-Zionists (Switzerland, Belgium, Spain and Canada), besides the ethno-national a particular identity there is also an overall civic-national one, or at least an attempt to create one; therefore it is questionable whether these are multinational states or multicultural nation-states. Thus the question of the overall national identity will arise even if Israel would become a federal or a consociational state, as some post-Zionists suggest, and this identity could not be anything but Hebrew. Alternatively, the post-Zionist's demand for a bi-national entity in which both components, the Jewish and the Arab, are equal does not fit these multinational democracies.

The multi-nationalism which characterizes these countries is asymmetrical, which means that the various nations which composed the multinational state do not have an equal impact on the state (Stepan, 2002). Thus, for instance, Spain is multinational in the sense that it contains three nations: Spanish, Catalan and Basque. Yet this multinationalism is asymmetric, in the sense that Spain is more Spanish than Catalan or Basque, and therefore Catalonia and the Land of the Basques are granted cultural autonomy to protect those cultures from the Spanish dominant culture, which also supplies the framework for the overall identity. Symmetrical multinational states are not stable because of the absence of overall identity. In other words, when asymmetrical multinational states approach a symmetrical form they risk disintegrating to their national components (Stepan, 2002). Since no post-Zionist suggests dismantling the Israeli state, then the Israeli parallel of these multinational structures will not be a symmetrical bi-national state composed of equal Jewish and Arab components. Instead it will be a state with an "Arab Province" with cultural autonomy within a federation or a nation whose overall identity would be a Hebrew-Israeli one (see below, pp. 130- 137).

While it would be possible to establish an Arab cultural autonomy within an overall Israeli nation, it is still arguable whether, or under what conditions, it is desirable. Consociational multinational states are stable only when there is a substantial socio-economic equality between the various national groups. A relatively successful bi-national, or bi-cultural state, like Canada, is based upon the fact that both its English-speaking provinces and especially French-speaking Quebec are at the same level of industrialization and modernization. Consequently, Quebec could provide its members the wide range of opportunities which modern society could offer. The same thing could be said about Catalonia and the Basque provinces in Spain.

In Switzerland the religious and linguistic cleavages have never overlapped the economic ones. In Israel the situation is different, as the socio-economic cleavages overlap the ethno-religious one and consequently there are great gaps in the socio-economic status of Jews and Arabs, which a consociational or a federal structure could only make worse. Here the "Arab sector" is rural and the "Jewish sector" is by and large urban. A certain immigration of Arabs to the cities is essential not only for their incorporation into the Israeli nation but also for the stability of the Israeli society.

The existence of an Arab cultural autonomy could operate in the opposite direction, which is the affixation of the Arabs to the poor underdeveloped countryside as the elites of both sections, the Jewish and the Arab, would have no interest in changing it. While those who head the Arab Section would have no interest in integration, as in this case they will loose their powers, and the Jewish elite will always fear the development of the Arab section and the political and secessionist powers which accompanies such development. So it seems that there is no great enthusiasm among the Arabs for institutional-cultural autonomy (Reiter, 1995, p. 55).

Moreover, the ecological implications of a bi-national structure for Israel should be considered carefully. In this structure the Arabs could not achieve socio-economic equality by integration into the Israeli economy and society, but only by the development of the Arab sector or province to the level that it could offer the same opportunities that the Jewish sector or province offers. This would mean not only a huge waste of resources to develop already existing industries, but ecologically it would mean the destruction of the Israeli countryside. In other words, since in the bi-national state the Arabs would not be able to live in Tel Aviv, Tel Aviv would have to come to them with all its ecological consequences. In today's Israel the locations of the big industrial centers have been already determined. Even now they impose a considerable ecological burden on the country. Consequently Israel cannot sustain the industrialization and urbanization, which a bi-national structure demands.

Thus when the available solutions for the establishment of democracies in multiethnic societies are discussed, the recognition of the existence of an Israeli nation turns out to be a necessary condition for every solution. If one possible solution is what David Laitin calls the 'competitive-assimilation game' where it becomes in the best interests of some working-class migrants to assimilate in order to enhance the life chances of their children, then the notion of an Israeli civic nation ought to exist politically and legally in order to enable such an assimilation (Laitin, 1996a; Pettai, 1996). The creation of multiple and complementary identities is another possible solution (Linz and Stepan, 1997, pp. 709-710), yet again, there is a need here for an Israeli national identity within which sub-identities (Jewish, Arab, Muslim, Christian and many others) could exist. Any consociational arrangements, federalism (territorial or non-territorial), a various degrees of cultural autonomy which are suggested for the Arab minority (Yiftachel 1990, pp. 133-4), would still demand the existence of an overall 'civic' identity which would enable both Jews and Arab to opt out from their communities into a civic or 'ethnically neutral' sphere. It should be emphasized that though this civic sphere should be 'ethnically neutral', it could not be 'culturally neutral', as it is clearly Hebrew and in this respect more Jewish than Arab.

As the notion of the Israeli republic, or the idea of the Hebrew republic, which is advocated here, should be distinguished from what is known nowadays as "post-Zionism"; it should be also distinguished from Canaanism (*kna'aniut*). The Canaanite movement, which had reached its peak in the nineteen forties, would be categorized today as "post-Zionist", and even as "anti-Zionist". Yet, there is an important difference between Canaanism and post-Zionism: the post-Zionists are indifferent to the national issue and even hostile to it, and the "citizens' state" which they present is devoid of any national aspect; while the Canaanite state was national as it embodied a territorial Hebrew nation, and by these it also shares the ideas presented in the present book.[5]

Yet, the criticism cited above against the post-Zionist "citizens' state" could be directed also against the Canaanist's "New Hebrew nation." The latter had been completely separated from the Zionist movement, and the historical Jewish People or Judaism. The New Hebrew nation would be consolidated mainly around the Hebrew language and the territory of *Eretz-Yisrael*. The Canaanist movement denied the central role of Zionism and its ideology in the establishment of Israel, and in this it had also denied the claim that Israel also was established in order to solve the 'Jewish question' (Shapira, 2003, pp. 19-23). The notion of the Israeli nation proposed in the present book means a Hebrew-speaking nation, in the sense that the American nation is an English-speaking nation. The Canaanite approach was different in the sense that its Hebrew nation was characterized by a deep Hebrew layer, which had been imposed upon it. Thus there was no place for multiculturalism within this nation (Shavit, 1984, pp. 126-127).

The approach in this book is different: the Israeli nation is Hebrew as it is a Hebrew-speaking nation and the Hebrew language and culture constitute the framework for national life. Within this framework there could be Israelis whose attitude towards the language is "technical"; others could provide their Hebraism through other dimensions. Thus, for instance, they could connect to the ancient Hebrew past or to the Jewish past in general. Paradoxically, the approach offered here could be characterized by the words of a former Israeli General who designated the secular Israelis as "Hebrew-speaking gentiles" (*goiim dovrei ivrit*). Though this former General wished to defame the secular Israelis, it seems that from the point of view of liberalism the Israeli State should relate to the Israelis as a nation of "Hebrew-speaking gentiles." Treating us as "gentiles" would mean that the State has no expectations or demands from us as Jews, and treating us as "Hebrew speaking" nation and not as "Hebrews" would mean that from the state point of view that while the Hebrew is used as the framework for national life, the nature and depth of the Hebrew cultural layer is more of a personal matter. It could be claimed, of course, that the language could not be just a formal framework and that when it is inculcated in a nation along with it are implanted cultural, cognitive and historical layers. Thus, notwithstanding liberal theory, such "technical" attitude towards the national culture is impossible, and, some would say, undesirable. Consequently, even if the Israeli republic would include in its formal national ethos the connection to the ancient Hebrews and to the Jewish history (which might seem inevitable), it should be seen as one possible interpretation of Israeli nationalism among other complementary interpretations.

Towards Normalization

In order to achieve a real normalization of the Israeli existence we must separate nationality from religion and recognize Israel as the state of the Israeli nation. Yet, contrary to the post-Zionist and the Canaanite notions of Israel, the Israeli nation was not something which had been created *ex nihilo* in 1948, but rather the outcome of the struggle of Zionism which was the movement for national self-determination of the Israeli Nation. In as much as Israel is a new entity created in 1948, it is still a political continuation of *Am Yisrael*, or the historical Jewish people. We should wish Israel to be Jewish or Hebrew in the same way that Britain is English. As there are in Britain various ethnic and religious groups (English, Scott, Welsh, Anglicans, Catholics, Jews and Muslims) who live together in complete equality of rights and duties, and yet it is predominantly English (and Anglican), so Israel, containing various ethnic and religious groups (Jews, Arabs, Muslims, Christians) would be predominantly Hebrew and Jewish. There is no necessary contradiction between the fact that France is a Catholic country (an outcome of the fact that most of the French are Catholic and the Catholic history of France) and the ability of Jews or Muslims to be equal members of the French nation. In the same way there is no contradiction between the fact that the Israeli nation is Jewish or Hebrew and the ability of Christians, Muslims or Arabs to be equal members of the Israeli nation.

Here, of course, arises the question whether the members of those groups which are characterized as national minorities in Israel, especially the Arab minority, will be interested in joining an Israeli nation which is expressively Hebrew. In as much as this question is important, it should not be confused with the question of the national identity of Israel and the Israelis. In other words, the question of the identity of Israel should be separated from the question: to what extent could the

Israeli Arabs, or others, share this identity. It is customary in Israel, in both "Zionists" and "post-Zionists" circles, to start the debate on the question of national identity by debating whether this status would be acceptable to the Arabs. Consequently the first aim of the post-Zionist programs is to solve what they consider to be the problem of the Arab national minority in Israel. Thus the post-Zionists believe that the Israelis must shed their nationality altogether. The starting point of the present book is different.

The question of the national identity of the Israelis is primarily a question, which should be decided by Israeli Jews or Israelis of Jewish origin. Not only because they constitute the majority, but mainly because they are those who had established Israel and have defended it for more than sixty years. Israel belongs primarily to them and should express their national identity even if non-Jewish groups do not want or cannot share this identity. Yet, it is important to note that national identities are not primordial and hence could be changed also by constitutional means. Consequently, when the Israelis come to decide about their national identity they should be persuaded to refine and enlarge this identity as it has been done in the western democracies, so that it would be possible for non-Jews to share it. The need for an inclusive national identity is an Israeli interest of the utmost importance. Though national identities could be subjected to reforms, these reforms are of limited nature. The Israeli nation, though not recognized, exists as a sociological fact. It is expressively Hebrew, and no constitutional process could change it, at least not in a foreseeable future. Moreover, such a constitutional process would be wrong because, though it seems to conciliate the Arab minority in Israel, it would be a severe encroachment upon the nationality and the national rights of the majority.

One of the common objections to the normalization of Israel is the claim that it would lead to the severance of Israel from the Jewish Diaspora, while at the same time it will speed up the processes of disintegration and assimilation in the Jewish Diaspora (Eisenstadt, 2002, p. 379). As we are going to see, there is no necessary contradiction between the existence of an Israeli republic and a conception of the "Jewish People" as the "Diaspora nation" of this republic (including the existence of a Law of Return, and see below, pp. 214-225). This is possible, as long as there is a distinction between the sovereign nation (that is the Israeli nation), and the Diaspora nation (that is the "Jewish people", or *"Am Yisrael"*). As we are going to see many nation-states consider themselves connected to Diaspora nations with no contradiction to being republics. Moreover, it is not obvious that normalization would lead to the breaking of ties between Israel and world Jewry. The fusion of religion and nationality creates points of friction between Israel and the Jewish Diaspora. The interventions of the Israeli government and Supreme Court in the question of "Who is a Jew" has constantly outraged the world Jewry, and especially American Jewry (Eisenstadt, 2002, pp. 371-372). The fusion of religion and nationality and the "Negation of the Diaspora" (*shlilat hagola*) ethos, which accompanies it, delegitimizes the right of the Diaspora Jews to be members of their nations and raise the question of "double loyalty."

The separation between nationality and religion will release the Israeli government from the need to intervene in the rulings of religious doctrines. These would ease the tension between Israel and the Jewish Diaspora. In addition, Jewish identification with Israel is not necessarily connected to the fusion of religion and nationality. Persons of Irish origin who live in the United States have had a greater tendency than members of other ethnic groups to identify with the Irish cause, while the Republic of Ireland had not necessarily seen them as members of its (sovereign) nation, or expected them to become ones. In the Israeli case, because of the special history of the Jews, it would be expected that among Jews all around the world there would be a tendency to identify with the Israeli republic. Furthermore, there is no necessary contradiction between the existence of an Israeli republic and the desire to maintain cultural ties with the Jewish Diaspora. This could be anchored in the constitution, as it has been done in the constitutions of Armenia and Greece, which also represent a type of nationalism known as "Diaspora nationalism" (See below, pp. 155-159).

Eisenstadt (2002, p. 379) speaks about the "creative tension" in the relations between the Jews of the Diaspora and Israel, which strengthen Jewish identity in the Diaspora. He thinks that a normalization of Israel "could slowly wear the Jewish Identity" of the Jews of the Diaspora. This view could be contested, given the fact that Judaism has existed without Israel for thousands years. As Seth Wolitz (1991), a professor of Jewish studies at the University of Texas maintains, the vision of Ahad Ha'am, according to which Israel will be a cultural-spiritual center for the Jews of the world, has not been materialized as far as American Jews are concerned, and the Jewish culture which they have created is radically different from the Israeli one. On the other hand, considering the fact that the question of the national identity of Israel involves questions of the highest importance, including questions of life and death, one must still ask whether the Israelis should give up their national identity in order that the Jews of America would be able to hold to their Jewish Identity, even if you agree with Eisenstadt. The demand for normalization of Israel and of Jewish existence means also a demand for equality among the Jews wherever they are. This includes the demand of the Israeli Jew to the right of national self-determination, in the same manner that it exists for the American Jew. Why is it that the American Jews have the right to define themselves as Jews who are members of the American nation while the Israeli Jew is only "a Jew" without a right for self-determination?

☙ CHAPTER 1 ❧
The Fusion of Religion and Nationality and the Nationalization of Judaism

Between Religious and Secular: Who are the Coercers?

The fusion of religion and nationality, or between faith and nationality, is the main cause for the split between the religious and the secular people. In Israel it is customary to blame religious sectors in "religious coercion" (*kefia datit*: the attempts to enforce religious laws on the general public) and in the lack of democratic values. Here, the classical statement had been made by Gershon Weiler excellent book *Jewish Theocracy* (1976). In this book Weiler claimed that there is an inherent contradiction between the state and the traditional Jewish law (*Halacha*). The *Halacha*, said Weiler, cannot accept the legitimacy of the state, on one hand, and cannot cope with the problems which modern citizenship put before the religious citizen, on the other. Weiler called the method the religious sectors have chosen to cope with the demands of modernity "exemption and coercion" (*petor u'kefia*): they sought an exemption from occupations and national duties which are not compatible with the *Halacha*, while trying to saturate the Israeli law and public life with rules of the *Halacha* as much as possible.

The big problem with Weiler's book is that it is not clear to what extent he thinks that the contradiction between the State and the *Halacha* is indeed fundamental, or is essentially an Israeli problem. Weiler overlooked the fact that the fusion of religion and nationality had been a major cause of the conflict between religion and state in Israel. In other words, Weiler ignored the fact that in western democracies

Jewish communities who adhere to the *Halacha* live in complete religious freedom and complete support of the principle of the non-intervention of the state in religious matters, and it had never occurred to them to use the state for religious coercion. It is important to note that this position, which supported the freedom of religion of the modern state, had been a traditional Jewish stand and usually characterizes religious minorities in general. As a religious minority, the Jews respected and supported the freedom of religion of the modern liberal state.

Moreover, historical Judaism, being a collection of autonomous communities, had been always pluralist. Each community was not only a minority among non-Jews, but also among the Jews. Had this historical structure of Judaism been transferred and maintained in Israel there would have been no reason for the various religious communities in Israel to abandon the principle of separation between religion and the state, which would have protected each one of them as a minority group from the religious coercion of the majority. Nevertheless, the fusion of religion and nationality abolished Jewish pluralism and forcefully united the Jews of Israel into one religious congregation. Consequently it had turned the various religious congregations from minority groups whose interest should have been to respect the freedom of religion, into a part of a Jewish majority who have an interest and even an obligation to enforce the religious laws. Thus Aviezer Ravitzky (1997, p. 22) remarks:

> Unlike the situation in the Diaspora in the modern era, along with the re-establishment of a Jewish public forum in the Land of Israel came a platform for confrontation and sometimes for the determination of issues. Outside of Israel, there are almost limitless opportunities for Jewish individualism and pluralism.

This was complemented by the establishment of the Chief Rabbinate, an institution, which was strange to traditional Judaism, and effectively abolished Jewish pluralism in Israel.

The definition of Israel as a "Jewish State" or as the state of the "Jewish People" compels Israel to appeal to the common denominator of all Jews wherever they are. Since Judaism today, at least outside Israel, and especially in the west, is essentially a religion, Israel had to adopt a (semi) official version of Judaism, what Liebman and Don Yehiya (1983) call "The New Civil Religion", which is a "reinterpretation" of traditional religion, or what Jonathan Shapiro called 'Jewishness':

> Jewishness is hard to define but there seems to be a tendency to connect it to the Jewish religious tradition and thus to make it more tangible. We are witnessing this development also in secular circles in Israel and abroad. This connection makes it easier to maintain the common identity of Israel and the Diaspora Jews, especially with the Jews of the United States where it is easier for the Jews to maintain their congregational uniqueness and ties with the rest of the world Jewry when all Jews are considered as members of one religion. (Shapiro, 1977, p. 22).

The outcome is that religion that is nationalized by the state and the political arena turns into a battlefield, in which this (semi) official version, or "reinterpretation" of Judaism, is determined. In this debate it would be unlikely that religious parties or religious publics would not try to impose their opinions. Many Israelis will be surprised to learn that in the early Zionist congresses the religious Zionists objected fiercely to the suggestion that the Zionist movement would undertake "Cultural Work" (*avodat tarbut*) like education, and demanded that the Zionist movement would deal only with the political and economic aspects of the Jewish problem (Don Yehiya, 1983).

As a minority in the Zionist movement the religious Zionists feared that the majority would impose upon them (and upon other Jews) what they considered as un-Jewish worldviews. But more than that, they feared that the "Cultural Work" meant the nationalization of Judaism by the Zionist movement. In their demand that the Zionist movement should concentrate in solving the political and economic aspects of the Jewish problem, they made it clear that they did not accept the idea of the "Jewish State" as it is understood today – a state that reflects Jewish contents and therefore has to deal with Jewish education and Jewish culture. Yet, since independence, the successors of "Hamizrahi" (that is Religious Zionism) have taken the opposite approach and their representatives have considered the Ministry of Education to be the Crown Jewel for which they should aspire to controp within the coalition governments. Religious Zionism's evolution should not be attributed only to internal developments within the movement or alternatively to the nature of the Jewish *Halacha* or Jewish religion, but also, and perhaps mainly, to the fusion of religion and nationality, or to the adoption of the idea of the "Jewish State". Only when their view that the Zionist movement should abstain from the cultural work was rejected, the religious Zionists found it necessary to organize in order to influence the contents of this cultural work (Don Yehiya, 1983, and see below, pp. 273 - 278).

A similar thing has happened to the ultra-Orthodox anti-Zionist congregations in Israel. In the first years of independence, and in fact until not so long ago, the ultra-Orthodox did not recognize Israel as a Jewish State and feared that the state would intervene in their freedom of religion. Consequently, their behavior had been characterized more by closure, which was meant to protect their interests, than by the attempt to influence the general character or the "Jewish" image of the state. The opposite seems to have happened in recent years: their political isolation seems to be over and for many they have turned out to be the extreme right indicator of the Israeli politics and an essential element of the religious coercion. In as much as such integrative trends are positive, it is important to note that the change originated also from the success of the "Zionists" to convince the ultra-Orthodox that Israel is indeed a "Jewish State". Aviezer Ravitzky (1997, pp. 5-6) sees this development as a victory of "Zionism", as the "Jewish State" has won the recognition of the ultra-Orthodox. Yet at the moment that the latter have recognized Israel as a "Jewish State" they have become also engaged in the struggle for keeping what they consider should be its Jewish character.

The meaning of the fusion of religion and nationality is, then, the nationalization of Judaism and the turning over of the Israeli political arena to a battle zone where the various parties, including those referred to as "secular", are trying to impose their version of Judaism upon the Israeli public. Thus, in a book by Shulamit Aloni (1997), one of the most conspicuous figures in the fight against religious coercion, there appeared a suggestion for the amendment of the National Law of Education published by her party (Ratz) in 20.7.1982. In article 12 of this amendment it was said that the aim of the national education was –

> …to help the youngster to build *a whole personality as a Jew* who identifies with the tradition of his (or her) people and its various manifestations, *full of his (or her) mission as a Jew,* full of the consciousness of the relation between the Jewish People (*Am Yisrael*) to the Land of Israel, a son of *Am Yisrael* in his land-state and a son of the Jewish people in the Diaspora, imbued with the sense of common destiny and responsibility for his people. (Zertal, 1997, p. 12, emphasis added).

There is no doubt that the religious parties, if asked, would have ascribed to this declaration and so would every so-called "Zionist" party. Yet, the question is whether the Israeli Ministry of Education has the mandate, authority and knowledge "to build a whole personality (sic.) of a Jew". It is obvious that from the point of view of modern liberal democracy the answer is negative. Had there been separation between nationality and religion, the Israeli Ministry of Education would have had the right to educate Israelis. It is obvious that there is no agreement between the Israeli political parties on what "a whole personality" as a Jew or what should be the so-called "Jewish mission" which should oblige every Israeli-Jew. Consequently there is no reason to complain about a Minister of Education from the religious party who tries to impose his version of "a whole personality of a Jew" and "Jewish mission", more than on a Minister of Education from Aloni's circles who tries to impose Aloni's versions. It is obvious that religious Jews could not remain indifferent when the aims of the state are defined in this manner, as any notion of Judaism that is transferred by the Ministry of Education, which contradicts their own, means the misleading of Jews concerning what Judaism means. A state-education, which suggests that Judaism is "pluralist", or "humanist" or "universal", despite the fact that it serves desirable democratic values, is a serious offence to the freedom of religion. It is the right of religious people to think that their religion is not pluralist, as it is the right of others to think that it is pluralist and humanist; the Israeli Ministry of Education and the Israeli State should not have an opinion on this matter.

Thus, the struggle over the official version of Judaism the state should adopt turns Israeli politics into a battlefield of religious wars. It also results in the constant interference of the state in religious matters, in contradiction to what is considered as a basic principle of the modern democracy – the principle of the freedom of worship, or more generally the separation between religion and state. The debate on the question of "who is a Jew?" is only one example of this. Every nation must decide what should be the procedures for joining the nation. In a normal nation-state these procedures are identified with naturalization. Yet, within the fusion of religion and nationality, these procedures are identified with conversion to Judaism (*giyur*). In other words, even according to the so called "secular parties" the only way to join the nation is by conversion, and so, as Ravitzky (1997, p. 21) rightly says, the debate between the secular and the religious parties on the question of "who is a Jew" is nothing but a debate on the question of "who is a rabbi?" or, "what is the legitimate process of conversion?" This debate is entirely in the religious sphere. The intervention of the Knesset, which includes non-Jews, and of the Israeli Supreme Court, on the question of "who is a Jew", are gross violation of the principle of freedom of religion. Thus the meaning of the fusion of religion and nationality and of the idea of the Jewish State is that it is impossible to separate religion from the state in Israel, at least not as it is done in western democracies. In other words, "a Jewish Democratic State" is an oxymoron and cannot exist.

The absence of a separation between religion and state is not expressed only by "religious coercion" initiated by religious circles which identify the Jewish State as actually or potentially a *Halachic* State, but also by the "religious coercion" which is paradoxically orchestrated by the State and by circles which consider themselves to be "secular". Consequently, one of the expressions of the fusion of religion and nationality is the demand of the secular public that the state should reform religion. This demand stems from the fact that the secular define themselves as Jews, but most of them are non-believers or do not wish to observe the *Halacha*. All this would not have been problematic if religion was limited to the private realm, as in a liberal democracy where the state does not intervene in the question of how individuals define their religiosity. Yet, the fusion of religion and nationality transfers the religious affiliation from the private realm to that of the State and the nation. In other words, the secular public wants Judaism as a means to define and characterize the nation, but not as a religion, or alternatively it is interested in a "lite" version of Judaism. Hence today a demand to reform

conversion is directed towards the State and the official rabbinate in order
to make conversion possible for immigrants from the former Soviet Union
who are not considered to be Jewish by the official rabbinate.

Another reason for the need to nationalize Judaism stems from the
universal nature of religion, which makes it problematic for national
purposes. Judaism today is a universal religion, which means that contrary to
what the Israelis usually think, it is possible to be a good Jew in the Diaspora.
The problem is that universal values and ideas are frequently unsuitable for
a national ethos which is usually particular and territorial. This is how A. B.
Yehoshua, one of Israel prominent writers, expresses his demand to reform
the Jewish religion in order to make it suitable for the Israeli national needs:

> If we want to uproot the option of the Diaspora – at least from
> the people who sit here - we should aspire to slowly change the
> definition of the Jew, in the clear direction of strengthening the
> national element and weakening the religious force. The distant,
> but clear, object, which we should aspire for is to set up the
> definition of the Jew, as a person who sees the state of Israel as
> his state or his country. This means to strengthen substantially
> the national element in the definition of the Jew in order not
> to allow religious or other spiritual contents to fill the empty
> space which exists in the accepted minimal definition … There
> is today a need for some religion reformers *… it is impossible, if I
> will put it sharply, to leave the religious matters only in the hands
> of the religious people. The secular, or those who are so called,
> must penetrate the religious matters not as romantic "repentants",
> but as bold reformers.* (Yehoshua, 1980, p. 66; emphasis added).

This amazing paragraph actually calls the secular (and the State) to reform
religion. The absurdity of this idea is obvious. Religious reforms are
conducted by religious people, whose religious beliefs are different from the
traditional accepted ones. In Iran or Saudi Arabia, which are fundamentalist

theocratic states, the reforms of religion are carried out also by the state. Yet it is important to say that in the latter, the rulers and most of the population are practicing believers. Yet, Yehoshua's Israeli fundamentalist theocracy is different, as it is the first theocracy in modern times, which has been established by and for non-believers. It is obvious that A. B. Yehoshua's call to reform religion by the national collective is nothing but a call for a cultural war with all its implications. To Yehoshua's credit it must be said that unlike many of the secular circles he fully understands that the "religious coercion" (as the "anti-religious" one) is inherent to the Israeli system and therefore legitimate:

> The Rabbi of Lubavitch who sits in New York could only ask, beg or persuade New York's Jews not to travel by car on Saturday … if he would have arrived in Israel it would be in his powers and his religious duty to coerce the Jews not to travel on Saturday, to study Jewish studies, and to eat kosher. (Ibid., p. 51).

Consequently the differences of opinions between the religious and the secular in Israel are about the meaning of Judaism rather than the meaning of citizenship. This had been demonstrated by the campaign titled "One Nation, One Conscription" (*am echad, giyus echad*) led by Ehud Barak, then the head of the opposition, on the eve of the 1999 elections to the Knesset, to promote the conscription to the army of the ultra-Orthodox Yeshiva students. In this campaign the slogan "we are all Jews – even the ultra-Orthodox" was used (*"kulanu yehudim – gam ha-Charedim"*), which actually meant that those who avoid the conscription do not fulfill their duties as Jews, and that even their being Jews is questioned. What becomes conspicuous here is the nationalization of Judaism, yet here it received a problematic crusader version: Since when has conscription to the Israeli army been a test for being a Jew? It is obvious, then, that the demand to enlist must be directed towards the ultra-Orthodox youngsters as citizens, and not as Jews. Yet, in Israel conscription is not according to citizenship (because Arab citizens normally are not conscribed), but rather according to the citizen's religious status, that is his (or her) being a Jew. Thus when a demand is made to the ultra-Orthodox, not as citizens, but as Jews, to conscribe, their answer is clear and obvious: we know better what Judaism means, and it does not mean service in the army, but the learning of the *Torah*. Thus, a discourse that should have been about the meaning of citizenship, turns out to be a discourse about the meaning of Judaism. It seems that in this debate the ultra-Orthodox have the upper hand, as for thousands of years the study of the *Torah* characterized Judaism more than serving in a (Jewish) army.

The nationalization of Judaism has received a "constitutional" legitimization in recent years, with the acceptance of two new Basic Laws: *Basic law: Human Dignity and Liberty*, and *Basic Law: Freedom of Occupation*, which some see as the beginning of "a Constitutional Revolution". In each of these laws there is a clause stating that the purpose of the law is "to establish in a Basic Law the values of the State of Israel as a Jewish and Democratic State". This, of course, raises the question as to who will decide what are the values of Israel as "a Jewish and democratic state". Former Chief Justice of the Supreme Court, Aharon Barak, himself a great supporter of the Constitutional Revolution and the idea of the Jewish and democratic state, maintains that we must aspire for "the universal values of Judaism" at the highest possible level of abstraction. Yet, Professor Ariel Rozen-Zvi rightly criticized Barak, claiming that his approach empties the values of Judaism of their contents, as the high level of abstraction leads to the identifying "Jewishness" with the national outlook and the neglect of that of the *Halacha* (Rubinstein, 1996, pp. 1983-1993).

The introduction of the term "A Jewish and Democratic State" into the Basic Laws was a move with far reaching consequences for the relations between religion and State. For if indeed these Basic Laws are the beginning of a constitution and if they are real Basic Laws (and this is questionable), then all Israeli legislation is supposed to be in accordance with the values of Israel as a Jewish and Democratic State. In a limiting paragraph for those Basic Laws it is said that: "There shall be no violation of rights under this Basic Law except by a law befitting the values of the State of Israel..." According to the present Israeli law, pork eating is not forbidden, and one could assume that if the Knesset would wish to legislate a law which forbids the eating of the pork the Supreme High Court would annul it on the ground that it contradicts the Basic Law: Human Dignity and Liberty. In other words, that the condition allowing the violation of the basic rights is not fulfilled. Hence it could be concluded that pork eating is compatible with the values of Israel as a Jewish and Democratic State. It is obvious why pork eating is compatible with Israel being democracy, but is it indeed compatible with Judaism? Here there is no agreement among the Jews; some say it is, others say it isn't. Yet, from the point of view of the separation between religion and the State, the State should not have an opinion in this matter. Yet, in our case, the State has made up its mind on this matter, or, alternatively it has set the right Jewish dogma – a somewhat absurd one, that pork eating is compatible with Judaism.

The fusion of religion and nationality forces the State to introduce its own version of Judaism, and maybe its own version of the *Halacha*. Secular Israelis would claim that their interpretation of Judaism, or of the *Halacha*, even if it violates the principle of separation between State and religion, is still minimal when compared to the other interpretations on the agenda. They will probably maintain also that this "secular" version of the Jewish Religion is the most compatible with the life in a modern Democratic State. Yet, the important question, which should to be answered by all those who speak about the need to separate the religion from the state and the need for preservation of the freedom of religion, is why not to do one additional step and to separate religion from nationality. This would be true especially for those who considered themselves secular. A.B. Yehoshua admits that even though he is secular he finds it impossible to separate the Jew in its national meaning (that is the Israeli or the Hebrew) from the Jew in its religious meaning:

> Any real secular position, which claims for the legitimacy of the secular Jew, should recognize that a Jew could be also a Christian-Jew or a Muslim-Jew … but it seems that in the radical secular public there will be only few who would allow the Jew to cross this border … I admit also, with all my adherence to the principle of the secular Jew, with all my belief that in Mount Sinai there had been only a welding rather than fusion of religion and nationality, I cannot accept the right of a Jew to convert to Christianity or Islam and remain a member of the Jewish people (Gorni, 1985, p. 291).

It seems that in recent years Yehoshua has changed his mind and he is ready to annex to what he sees as "our nationality" some who are not members of the Jewish faith (Yehoshua 2002, pp. 48-49). Yet, since Yehoshua readiness to accept non-Jews to what he calls "our nationality" is not accompanied by separation between nationality and religion it effectively requires the nationalization of religion, or of conversion. Yehoshua explains that he is guided also by the need to increase the Jewish people as "it becomes smaller all along history. We have lost six millions …" (ibid., p. 49). Consequently Yehoshua's readiness to accept "Christian Jews" carries the hope that eventually they will convert to Judaism and the "citizenship test" he offers, which includes the learning of Hebrew, service in the army and participation in the Israeli life (ibid., p. 46) is not a test for admission to the Israeli or Hebrew nation but a test of admission to the "Jewish people" (ibid. p. 48).

The demand to nationalize conversion is raised by other secular and non-secular as well. Thus Ruth Gavison says: "it is critical to the Zionist project in the State of Israel to widen the borders feeling of the Jewish collective beyond the *Halacha*…" (Gavison, 2002, p. 38). Gavison suggests a "joining mechanism" for the Jewish people which will be a "dramatic innovation" and "will not be religious at all" and in which "the government of Israel should be the political body which needs to accept responsibility for determining who could join" (ibid., p. 39). Moshe Lissak maintains that Gavison asks to separate nationality from religion (Lissak, 2002, p. 26). Yet this is questionable: Gavison wants to expropriate the religion from the rabbis and to deliver it to the State, something which is certainly not compatible with the principles of liberal democracy.

The most extensive monograph written about this subject is no doubt Asher Cohen's, *Non-Jewish Jews: A Jewish-Israeli Identity and the Challenge of the Widening of the Jewish Nation in Israel* (2006). The title of the book testifies to its content, and its aim is to solve the problem of the status of many of the immigrants from the former Soviet Union who identify themselves as Jews, yet are not recognized as such by the Chief Rabbinate, and consequently by the State. According to Cohen, those immigrants have already gone through "sociological conversion", which has turned them into non-Jewish Jews – they are not Jews according to the *Halacha* and to the State, yet they are Jews in their feeling, self-identification, and manners of behavior which are similar to those of most of the Jews who live in Israel. According to Cohen, what is needed now is the completion of the sociological conversion with a formal one under the state supervision. Cohen suggests *"to form the question of conversion as a national challenge"* and maintains that it could not be such *"unless in the highest levels of leadership it will be made into a national challenge … things must arrive from the prime minister"* (ibid., pp. 155-156). Indeed, Cohen sees conversion as a national project, which involves the army, community centers and even universities ("when the studies needed towards conversion will grant academic credit for a university degree"). Cohen suggests that in the process of conversion a "bonus" will be given or "a symbolic move which would testify to the joining of the Jewish collective", such as State *bar mitzvahs* and State marriage ceremonies (ibid., p. 158). From the rabbis Cohen demands "a change of the religious *Halacha* policy" or what he calls "Zionization of the *Halacha*" (ibid., p. 158).

The scope of Cohen's program turns the Israeli society and the Israeli State into a huge apparatus of conversion. I do not pretend to answer the question whether a State in which conversion is a "national project" is indeed "Jewish": but, rather to try to answer the question to what extent it is normal and Democratic. It seems that a modern State and society that invest so much energy in the question of conversion, which is essentially a religious matter, are nothing but an anachronism. The separation between religion and State is a cornerstone of modern liberal democracy, therefore the Jewish State which Cohen aspires to is not democratic, as his program means a ruthless interference of the State in religious doctrines. It seems that Cohen thinks that the democratic question is solved when conversion is delivered to democracy and is done by agreement, which includes the rabbis. Yet, it is obvious that such a ruthless and wide scope scheme to nationalize conversion is bound to have objections among religious and other circles, and even if those would be small minorities, it is still the essence of liberal democracy that there are spheres that should not be regulated by majorities.

Here arises another troublesome question from Cohen's suggestion, as well as from Yehoshua's and Gavison's: to nationalize conversion, in order to "expand" the Jewish people. Though it is not always said explicitly, it seems that the right to go through a process of "national conversion" is given only to those who immigrated to Israel under the Law of Return. Thus one must ask: why not apply "national conversion" to the foreign workers of Israel; moreover, why not apply it to Arabs or persons of Arab descent. There are many in these groups who have already gone through a kind of 'sociological conversion'. The fact that this is not suggested brings up more than a suspicion that this "national conversion" is a means for the further exclusion of these groups. If the purpose of this "national conversion" is to increase the "Jewish people" available to Israel, why must its starting point be individuals of Jewish origin, or those who claim to be such? Why can't any person, who wants to be an Israeli Jew be a candidate for "national conversion"? Furthermore, if the purpose of the "national conversion" is to solve the problems of the nation, why formulate it in religious terms and not in universal "rational" terms according to the needs of the nation, as it is conducted by other nations. In other words, why not make "national conversion" part of the immigration and naturalization laws of Israel where they will not be used as an instrument for the creation of Jews but rather for the creation of Israelis?

"Who is a Jew?"

The debate on the question of "who is a Jew?" has engaged Israel since the nineteen sixties. It represents a fine example for the confusion of religion and nationality, and the way the state and the courts intervene in religious matters and nationalize religion. In Israel the question of "who is a Jew?" is usually associated with the Law of Return. The phrasing of the Law of Return, which says that "Every Jew has the right to come to this country as an *oleh*", invites the question of who is a Jew for the purposes of the Law of Return. This begs the question whether the Law of Return could have been phrased in such a way that would not require an intervention of the State in determining who is a Jew. This question will be dealt with extensively later on (see below, pp. 214-225). Yet, the question of "who is a Jew?" was not a major issue when the Law of Return was approved, and even not during the debate on the Law of Citizenship. It became an issue with the introduction of the Population Registry Law 1965, which requires the registration of "religion" and "nationality". In other words, the debate on "who is a Jew?" and the changes which were followed in the Law of Return had no influence on the application of the Law of Return whenever there was mass immigration of distressed Jews. After the Supreme Court Ruling in the Shalit case (March 1970), limitations were imposed on the Law of Return and a section 4B was added which says that "For the purposes of this Law, 'Jew' means a person who was born of a Jewish mother or has become converted to Judaism and who is not a member of another religion and that this should also be applied to the Population Registry". Yet, the circle of those eligible for immigration by the Law of Return was widened by section 4A of the law to include "a child and a grandchild of a Jew, the spouse of a Jew, the spouse of a child of a Jew and the spouse of a grandchild of a Jew, except for a person who has been a Jew and has voluntarily changed his religion". It is obvious that section 4A was meant to enable the entrance of mixed families, and therefore not to obstruct future mass immigrations. Thus it seemed that even the religious parties understood that imposing limitations which would obstruct the nature of the Law of Return as a mass immigration law will undermine the very legitimacy of Israel. While the religious sectors were ready to accept the naturalization of whom they considered non-Jews, they were not ready to accept their registration as Jews. Consequently the debate on the question of who is a Jew was not a debate about the eligibility of the Law of Return and there was no attempt to reduce its scope as a mass immigration law. More than that, it is easy to see that the debate erupted in the nineteen sixties after the big waves of immigration were over.

The question of who is a Jew was connected to the Population Registry Law, which required the registration of "religion" and "nationality". According to this law, persons who were considered Jews could choose not to register themselves as belonging to the Jewish religion: and here indeed there were no problems, because it had never happened that immigrants who were not Jews or not recognized as Jews asked to be registered as Jews as their religion. The problem arose when immigrants who were not Jews according to the *Halacha* or according to the Registrar demanded to be registered as Jews in the nationality clause. Why registration of the nationality clause was needed at all? The answer is that Israel (at least formally) is a bi-national or a multi-national state in which the members of the various nationalities give and receive different services. After the government rejected the Supreme Court plea in the case of Shalit to annul the clause "nationality" in the registration, some claimed that issues of security were a factor in this decision. Amnon Rubinstein (1996, p. 88, note 17) says: "it is not clear whether security professionals, or the minister of security, were consulted in this matter. From the news items which were published by the press at this period it seems that their opinion was not requested".

Initially, registration was considered as a marginal administrative matter. In the years 1950 – 1958, the years of the great immigrations, the issue was never disputed, and registration was carried out according to the declaration of the immigrant. The first political crisis erupted in March 1958 following the instructions of the Minister of Interior Bar-Yehuda which institutionalized the (unwritten) norm which had existed until then according to which "a person who declares in good faith that he is a Jew will be registered as a Jew and no further evidence will be required … when both parents declare that their child is a Jew, their statement is considered as a statement by the child himself". It was said further that "for the registrar it is of no consequences that according to the *Halacha* (when one of the parents is not Jewish) the child goes after the mother … it is enough for him that the parents declare that their child is a Jew that he will register him as a Jew." (Neuberger, 1997, vol. 6, p. 78). Bar Yehuda's instructions caused a political crisis after which the Religious National Party (MAFDAL) left the coalition government.

After the political crisis Ben Gurion decided to appoint a committee whose members would be the Prime Minister and the Justice and Interior Ministers. The committee was to ask the opinion of fifty of the "Wise Men of Israel" (*Chachmei Yisrael*) well-known Jews in Israel and abroad, Orthodox and un-Orthodox, which were known as authorities in Judaism, and to ask for their learned opinion about "the registration of children of mix marriage, whose parents, both father and mother, want to register them as Jews" (Ben-Rafael, 2001). This has been perhaps the only time when the Israeli state considered the issue as a something, which had to be decided by the Jewish world rather then by the Israeli state. Out of the fifty, forty-five had answered; thirty-seven had supported explicitly the *Halacha* definition of a Jew. In his letter of the 27 of October 1958 Ben Gurion asked the Wise Men to take into account four considerations needed for understanding the problem, one of them is most relevant for our matter:

> The Jewish collective in Israel is not similar to any Jewish collective in the Diaspora. Here we are not a minority under pressure of a foreign culture, and there is no fear here of assimilation among non-Jews, which exists in some of the countries of freedom and welfare, on the contrary: there are here possibilities and inclinations or easy assimilation of non-Jews in the Jewish People, especially families of those immigrants who come from mixed marriages. While mixed marriages abroad are one of the main causes for the complete assimilation and the departure from Judaism – the mixed marriage families that come here – especially from the countries of Eastern Europe, come to complete submergence with the Jewish people. (Neuberger, 1997, vol. 6, p. 81).

The confusion of nationality and religion is obvious in Ben Gurion's letter. While he is certainly right when he says that the Israeli society assimilates the new immigrants, it turns them into Israelis or Hebrews rather than to Jews. In other words, the child of a mixed marriage will grow up as and would not be distinguished from any other Israeli. Ben Gurion, on the other hand, indeed considered Israel to be a converting entity. Thus in an interview which was given ten years after Major Shalit affair he says:

> There is no doubt that the majority of the Jewish community in this country is not in favor of religious coercion or in favor of the rule of the Chief Rabbinate with the aid of the religious political parties. And this majority undoubtfully is against making mixed marriage difficult – the marriage of people who wish to settle in the Land of Israel and consider their children and grandchildren as Jews, and not just Israelis, that is citizens of the Jewish State and not part of the Jewish people. (Ben Ezer, 1974, pp. 85-86).

According to Ben Gurion, immigration and naturalization (under the Law of Return, of course), did not only create Israelis, which for him was not a nationality but rather residence, but actually created Jews.

Following the answers of the Wise Men the policy of the government had changed. The Religious National Party returned to the coalition and its leader Moshe Chaim Shapira become the Minster of the Interior. This gave birth to the "Shapira Instructions" (January 1 1960, which were not brought to the knowledge of the government and the Knesset), according to which the registration of the nationality of the children of mixed marriages were supposed to be done according to the *Halacha*. It is important to note that Shapira's instructions applied only for registration, and not to the Law of Return (which remained as it had been before with broad "subjective" interpretation of who is a Jew).

From "Who is a Jew?" to "Who is an Israeli?": The Israeli Supreme Court and the Question of Identity

The rulings of the Supreme Court in the matter of "who is a Jew" demonstrate that within the fusion of faith and nationality it is impossible to solve the question of national identity by legal means. This was admitted by the Court when, in the case of Shalit, it turned to the government and asked for the abolishment of the registration in the nationality clause. This was the most significant thing done by the Supreme Court, beyond the confusions and contradictions, which had characterized its rulings.

The "Brother Daniel Affair"

The first case usually mentioned in relation to the rulings of the Supreme Court in the question of "who is a Jew" is the Brother Daniel affair. Yet, this affair was not a typical one, since it had appeared as a problem of the Law of Return, and not of the registration. Brother Daniel (formerly Oswald Rufeisen), a child of traditional Jewish parents, and Holocaust survivor who had rescued Jews during the Holocaust, had converted to Christianity, became a practicing Catholic and a priest in a monastery. He asked to immigrate to Israel and to acquire Israeli citizenship under the Law of Return. He claimed that he was Jewish by his nationality, though Catholic-Christian by his religion. Brother Daniel argument was not free from the confusions between nationality and religion. On one hand, he claimed that faith (religion), should not be confused with culture, language and origin (nationality). Yet, on the other hand, he claimed that the *Halacha* also considers him to be a Jew as he was "a son of a Jewish mother" and that for this reason he is entitled to Israeli citizenship according to the Law of Return. It is important to note that given Brother Daniel's actions during the Holocaust to save Jews he could have acquired Israeli citizenship through a rarely used option that is open to non-Jews by the Law of Citizenship. Yet his insistence upon acquiring citizenship by the Law of Return stems also from the fact that he wanted to be recognized by the State as a member of its nation.

The ruling of the Supreme Court was that though Brother Daniel was a Jew according to the *Halacha*, the *Halacha* test was not what prevailed in this case. Thus Judge Zilberg said:

> ... (the concept of) Jew mentioned in the Law of Return is not the same as (the concept of) Jew in the Law of Jurisdiction of the Rabbinical Courts. The latter has a religious meaning, as it is allocated by the *Halacha*, while the former has a secular meaning as its regular indication by the language of human-beings. And I repeatedly emphasis: as its regular meaning for the 'common Jewish folk'. (Neuberger, 1997, vol. 6, p. 86).

Alternatively Zilberg maintains that "(there is) a fundamental worldview that Jew and a Christian are adjectives which cannot be united in one subject – and this is accepted by everybody both the simple people and the learned ones." (C. Cohen, 1991, p. 496). Judge Chaim Cohen had the minority view maintaining that the *bone fide* declaration of the applicant is sufficient and that the registrar has no discretion in this matter.

Majority ruling in the Brother Daniel case is interesting, since in its ruling the court distinguished between what is considered as "a Jew in the religious meaning" and "a Jew in the secular meaning", without distinguishing between religion and nationality. In other words, a Jew in its secular sense was not interpreted as belonging to the Jewish nation, but rather as a popular definition or characterization of the Jew, expressed by the assertion that a Catholic priest cannot be a Jew, a definition, which was preferred upon that of the *Halacha*. In an interpretation which was given later Judge Chaim Cohen stated that in the case of Brother Daniel it was established that

> The question whether a person is a Jew for the purposes of
> the Law of Return could not be determined by the *Halacha*:
> it is a secular law. The concept "a Jew" which the legislator
> uses should be attributed a non-technical popular meaning
> … as the word is used and understood by an every day Jew
> or by Israelis *including non-Jews.* (C. Cohen, 1991, p. 496;
> emphasis added).

Thus, paradoxically, the ruling of the Supreme Court appropriated the definition of who is a Jew not only from the Jewish *Halacha*, but also from the Jews, and delivered it to the Israelis (who include also non-Jews).

The Law of Return (1950) maintained that every Jew has the right to immigrate and naturalize without establishing "who is a Jew". Therefore, in the Supreme Court ruling in the case of Brother Daniel, there was a clear invitation for the Israeli democracy to intervene in the settling of "who is a Jew?" It did not seem at the time that the Supreme Court was aware of the possibility that it was stepping into a forbidden land, or alternatively, that it was paving the way for the legislator (which included not only non-believers, but also non-Jews) to settle the issue which had appeared to be a religious one.

In a minority ruling in the Brother Daniel case Judge Chaim Cohen maintained that the test for Judaism is a subjective one, and consequently he supported the norm that had existed until that time, that is to accept the *bona fide* declaration of the immigrant. Yet, within the framework of the fusion of religion and nationality, the minority view was no less problematic than that of the majority. Cohen's claim that the immigration authorities had no discretion and had to accept Brother Daniel declaration that he was a Jew was problematic because it involved an avowed Catholic who wished to be registered as a Jew. In this case it seems as that there was no need for discretion to reject it, on the contrary, discretion was needed to accept it.

The question is whether Judge Cohen thought that the concept of a Jew ("secular" as it would be) could be overstretched (without discretion) in a manner as to include Muslims and Christians.

An interesting point was the reaction of the religious circles to the ruling of the Supreme Court in the case of Brother Daniel. Seemingly they should have protested about this ruling, which expropriated Judaism from the *Halacha*, but they had not shown any objection, and it seems that the rejection of the Judaism of Brother Daniel suited them. In other words, the religious circles in Israel acknowledged that the *Halacha* was not the only thing that had to be consulted when settling the question of who is a Jew. This had become obvious in the Shapira Instructions (1960) which were mentioned above and in the amendment to the Law of Return (1970) where it was said that "a Jew – every one born to a Jewish mother or converted to Judaism, and is not a member of another religion". It is obvious that the phrase "is not member of another religion" was intended to prevent the immigration of converts, but it is also obvious that it originated in secular, or popular, concept of Judaism, and not that of the *Halacha*.

The Major Shalit Affair

Another affair which had stirred the Israeli Public in the early nineteen seventies was that of Major Shalit. Shalit was an Israeli who had married a Scottish woman while he was studying in Scotland, came back to Israel and his children were born here. The mother considered herself non-religious and refused to convert. Shalit demanded that his children be registered in the religious clause as persons without religion and in the nationality clause as Jews. The registrar rejected his appeal and registered the children in the religious clause "Jewish Father, Foreign Mother" and in the nationality clause "not registered". Shalit went to the Supreme Court. Shalit's argument involved essentially two statements: (a) Membership in the nation does not necessitate religious affiliation. (b) The nationality should be defined according to ethno-cultural identification, rather than biological or racial origin.

It is obvious that Shalit separated nationality from religion, and had there been available the concept of Hebrew or Israeli nation, he would have demanded to register his children as Israelis, or Hebrews, as he actually did for his third child.

The problem here concerned the Population Registry rather than the Law of Return, as it was obvious that Shalit and his family were citizens. Yet for him it was a matter of principle. Indeed, in the middle of the debate, in an unprecedented move, the Supreme Court addressed the government and suggested the abolishment of the nationality clause in the Population Registry, thus admitting that the problem could not be solved by legal means alone, but has to be solved also through the political system. Chief Justice at the time, Shimon Agranat, said that *"the problem is not legal, but ideological ..."* (Lahav, 1998, pp. 413-415). Moreover, the Court had pointed out a direction for solution – the abolishment of the nationality clause. Seemingly only a formal step, but it might have promoted the idea of separation between nationality and religion (Shapiro, 1996, p. 66). The government rejected the appeal of the Court and by that returned the decision to the Court, which ruled in favor of Shalit.

There were several contradictions between the ruling in the Shalit case and the ruling in Brother Daniel case. The majority in Brother Daniel case had rejected the subjective test, but accepted it in the Shalit case. Here are the words of Judge Zussman, who represented the majority view:

> The registration is nothing but the registration of details as were given to the registrar ... only one condition was set, without it being mentioned in an order, that when one of

> the details was evidently false, and this is clear to all, such
> as when a grown up man appears before the registrar and
> asks to be registered as a five years old … in this case the
> registrar will refuse to register his age, as he cannot be a part
> of a false registration.

It is important to note that the test was not completely subjective and
the registrar had some discretion. However, the question that arises
here is whether registration of a child of a non-Jewish mother as a Jew
could not be considered as evidently false. In the Brother Daniel's ruling
the Court said that a Jew is "whoever is normally recognized by the
average Israeli as a Jew", and in Israel it is indeed usually maintained
by the average Israeli that a child of a non-Jewish mother is not a Jew.
Indeed, the minority Judge, Landau, maintained that the registrar had
a reasonable basis to reject the motion of the registration, and that it
is impossible to reach unequivocal conclusion by the "popular test"
(assuming the registrar was the "average Israeli").

Judge Berenzon, on the other hand, thought (as he thought in the
case of Brother Daniel) that "the popular test" could be applied here. Yet,
according to him, in this case it is decisively in favor of registration as a Jew.
Referring to a member of 'Al-Fatah' of East Jerusalem who had been born
to a Jewish mother and who had been captured and charged with terrorist
actions, Berenzon protested against those who support the application of
the *Halacha* test for registration in the nationality clause:

> According to this doctrine, the head of the terrorists from
> east Jerusalem, who was born to a Jewish woman and a Muslim
> man, who wanted to kill, annihilate and to destroy the State
> of Israel, will be considered as one of us and as a member
> of the Jewish nation, while the son and daughter of a Jewish
> Major, who fights the wars of Israel, will be considered as

lacking Jewish nationality. One's soul is terrified to think of such consequences in the State of Israel.

This had been answered by minority Judge Zilberg:

> The son of the Jewish mother, a member of "Al-Fatah", is a miserable, wicked Jew, of whom there are many in the circles of the new Jewish left. The children of the petitioners, on the other hand, are poor nice non-Jewish children, that because of the stubborn objection of their parents to religion did not win an entering ticket to the Jewish nation. "Judaism" is not a prize given to a person, like a doctorate of honor for his rights and deeds for it; Judaism is a religious and juridical title which applies, or given, only under certain conditions which the children of the petitioners failed to fulfill. (Rubinstein, 1996, p. 178).

These arguments testify to the confusion of both judges. The argument which Berenzon had put forward for registering Shalit's children as Jews (being "the son and daughter of a Jewish Major who fights the wars of Israel") are arguments for their citizenship or nationality, rather than for their Judaism. Though the words of the minority Judge Zilberg sounded convincing, they were confused as well. Because if the member of The Al Fatah is indeed a member of the Jewish nation, then he ought to be put on trial as a traitor rather than as a terrorist (something Zilberg does not suggest).

Consistent in his approach was Judge Chaim Cohen who maintained, as he did in the case of Brother Daniel, that the only test is the subjective one, where the only condition is the lack of *bone fide*. (Rubinstein, 1996, p. 176). Yet, the confusion of faith and nationality is manifested also here. In a liberal democracy religious affiliation is considered a private business, therefore it is possible to see as a Jew someone who declares himself to be one, and yet belonging to a nation is different. That is, the fact that a person declares himself *bona fide* as a Frenchman does not make him one. A membership in a nation is also an objective and formal matter.

The ruling in the case of Shalit had provoked legal and political reactions. In a motion by Ben Menashe against the Minister of the Interior he demanded to erase the registration of his children as members of the Jewish nation claiming that it had been done without his declaration and despite his objection. The Court had ruled that in the light of the Shalit precedence (the subjective test) the registrar is not allowed to write down anything that the one who delivers the declaration did not ask for and that "whoever does not want to belong to any nationality has the right not to declare a specific nationality". Again, this decision testifies to much confusion. First, it assumes that it is enough for a person to declare that he belongs (or does not belong) to a certain nationality in order to make (or to deny) this person a member of this nationality; that is, it assumes that national membership is only a matter of subjective consciousness. Furthermore, it assumes that the renunciation of nationality is not entailed by any consequences concerning the civil status. In other words, in a liberal democracy persons who renounce their nationality do it by renouncing their citizenship, while the debate and the ruling in the Ben Menashe case meant that the only thing that had changed following the ruling was the registration, and had no connection to the civil status of Ben Menashe.

The Aftermath of the Shalit Case

The ruling in the case of Shalit led to a change in the Law of the Population Registry (and the Law of Return). Under the new laws a Jew was one who was born to a Jewish mother or converted and was not affiliated to another religion. After this change Shalit's ruling (the subjective test) could no longer serve as a precedent, as the law now defined who is a Jew for the purposes of registration.

The amendment of the Law of Return (and the Law of the Population Registry) by adding the definition of a Jew marked a watershed in the relation between nationality and religion. Until then, in the absence of a definition of a Jew, there was still a possibility, theoretical and practical, of distinguishing between a Jew in the national sense, on one hand, and Jew in the religious sense, on the other. It was still possible to claim that those who were admitted to the country as Jews or those who were registered as Jews in the nationality clause were Jews by their nationality (and not necessarily Jews by religion). The amendment of the Law of Return and of the Law of Population Registry changed this. For now it had been settled that Jewish nationality is defined in religious terms and by religious affiliation (though, as noted above, not strictly according to the *Halacha*). In other words, this amendment is probably the only place in the Israeli law where the fusion of faith and nationality is defined. Indeed, this change invoked reactions, as people demanded to revoke their registered nationality, for they maintained that the nationality, now defined by religious criteria, was not their nationality. Such was the case of Shtaderman against the Minister of Interior. The Judges rejected his motion, claiming that the registration was done at the time according to his declaration and that any change requires a document that would show the change. Thus, because of the new law, which defined a Jew for the purposes of Return and Registration, the court did not see nationality as a mere subjective thing, and therefore demanded an objective proof (such as a document).

The confusion of the Court was manifested also in Shalit's second motion (1972), when he demanded to register his third child as a Hebrew (the registration as a Jew was impossible now under the new laws). The Court rejected the motion while maintaining that there was no difference between the Jewish nation and the Hebrew nation. According to Judge Berenzon these two names "are nothing but synonyms and are used without significant distinction, not in the traditional sources and not in the spoken language". This was a very strange argument, since in contemporary Hebrew language there is a clear distinction between "Hebrew" and "Jewish" and most of the Israelis would see a discrepancy between the proposition claiming that "Israel is the State of the Hebrew nation", on one hand and the proposition claiming that "Israel is the State of the Jewish people", on the other hand.

The Tamarin Case

Similar arguments were made by the Court in the Tamarin case (1970). The petitioner, an Israeli citizen, was registered in 1949 according to his declaration, as a person without religion and a Jew by nationality, since he thought that it was important to distinguish between the Jewish nationality and the Jewish religion. Yet, he claimed that the change of the law after the Shalit's ruling had changed his mind about whether he belonged to the Jewish nation and that he feels himself as belonging to the Israeli nation. It is important to note that Tamarin did not deny the existence of a Jewish nation, but claimed that he did not belong to this nation and demanded either to register him as Israeli or, if rejected, to erase his registration as a Jew in the nationality clause. Tamarin's error was obvious. He thought that there were two nations – a Jewish nation and an Israeli nation, therefore his motion appeared contradictory. The Court who rejected Tamarin's appeal, shared with him the same assumption, that if there was an Israeli nation, it should have existed alongside the Jewish one. These were the words of the District Court's Judge Shilo:

> There is no need here to try and define the concept of "the nation", since, as a Judge who is living among his people and even from my judicial knowledge, I can say with no hesitation that there is no Israeli nation which exist separately from a Jewish nation. … It is impossible to see at this moment even the beginning of the separation of the nation into two, a Jewish nation and an Israeli nation, and certainly it doesn't seem that there exist any consolidated features of two separated nationalities. This conclusion is true even if it is agreed that

numbers are not the essentiality of nation building, there could be small and even very small nations. (Rubinstein, 1996, p. 140).

Tamarin appealed to the Supreme Court and was rejected. Here are the words of Chief Justice Agranat:

> Where a certain people inhabit their land and in their midst a group of persons, who until now were part of them but wish now to be completely separated and demand for themselves the status of a new nation, then it must be said that the recent historical experience suggests, that usually in such cases the principle of national self-determination does not hold, for it was meant for nations rather then for shreds of nations. If you deny this, it might lead to the national and social disintegration of the whole nation. (Rubinstein, 1966, pp. 106 – 7).

Thus, the term "the Israeli nation" appeared for the first time at the Supreme Court in a distorted form. Not as a replacement of the false concept of "the Jewish nation", but as an addition to it. It didn't seem, from its rulings, that the concept of the Israeli nation reminded the courts of similar concepts such as "American nation" or "French nation".

The *Ani Yisraeli* Case

The notion of the Israeli nation had to wait almost forty years before it reappeared at the doorsteps of the Israeli High Court in 2008. This time it followed an appeal by a group called *Ani Yisraeli* ("I am Israeli") to direct the Population Registrar to register them as Israelis in the nationality clause. The group headed by Uzi Ornan, a former leading member of the Canaanite movement, consisted of some other known figures in the Israeli public, one of them was Professor Joseph Agassi mentioned above. Here, unlike the Tamarin case, there was no room for misunderstanding of the nature of the Israeli nation. For, unlike

Tamarin, who argued for the existence of an Israeli nation alongside with a Jewish one, *Ani Yisraeli* actually denied the existence of a "Jewish nation" (though they sought to change the registration in the nationality clause only for themselves). In other words, it was clear to the court that the group was using the term 'Israeli Nation' as parallel to that of the French Nation or American Nation, and not as a "shred nationality" asking for recognition along some 140 nationalities already recognized by the Registrar.

The High Court's ruling was delivered in October 2013 and the motion was rejected. Two main reasons were given by the court for the rejection. The first one, which had captured the headlines, was a repetition of the court's position in the Tamarin case: the plaintiffs had not introduced any new evidence, or had not proven the existence of the Israeli nation. The second argument, less noticed, but perhaps more important, was what the court called "the constitutional Jewishness of the state": Recognition of an Israeli nation would mean the denial of the Jewishness of the state, which has attained a constitutional status since the Tamarin case. The court maintained that this constitutional status was created by the acceptance of the notion of the "Jewish and Democratic State" as something that forms and directs "the Israeli constitutional law", and was expressed by the insertion of the clause "Jewish and Democratic State" in the two basic laws which had started the so called "Constitutional Revolution" and in many other laws (see above, pp. 80-81). One of the laws mentioned by the court was the Party Law of 1992. Paragraph 5.1 of this law stated: A party, which denies that Israel is a Jewish and Democratic State could not run for elections. Since, as the court rightly observed, the *Ani Yisraeli*'s motion challenged the very notion of the Jewish and Democratic State, thus we have here an interesting paradox. Had the group tried to form a party and run for the Knesset in order to acquire a majority for the recognition of the Israeli nation, it would have been declared as unconstitutional and denied access. In other words, constitutionally it had become impossible to recognize the existence of the Israeli nation. One could only wonder why the motion was not rejected immediately as unconstitutional and why the court needed to enter the first argument about whether or not the Israeli nation exists.

As for the court's demand to "prove" the existence of the Israeli nation, the problem is that the Israeli State had never set "objective" criteria for the establishment of nationality for the purposes of registration in the nationality clause. In fact the Israeli State had been very generous in its recognition of such nationalities. As the plaintiffs observed in their motion, Israel recognizes for the purposes of registration in the nationality clause some 140 nationalities. Some of the nationalities are recognized "proven" nation-state's nationalities (Italian, Polish, British etc.) [Which could create another problem: how can an Israeli citizen be registered as "Italian"?] Yet, the list also contains ethnic groups such as the Kurds, and communities such as the Samaritans and even a peculiar Assyrian nationality. Since many would doubt the existence of Samaritan or Assyrian nations, and since the State of Israel had not set the criteria for establishing these as nationalities, the question that arises is why make an exception in the case of the Israeli nationality? It would not be difficult to guess the answer.

The generosity of the Israeli State in its recognition of the non-Israeli nationalities stemmed from the fact that the State's main interest was to distinguish non-Jews from Jews. Thus, the State was not really interested in the question whether the nationality, which was declared was "real" or not, but rather that it was non-Jewish, or that it did not include those who were considered by the state as Jews. The State could be generous in its recognition of those nationalities also because nothing "real" followed this recognition. In other words, those nationalities were not necessarily entitled for any kind of self-determination or autonomy within the Israeli system. The case of the Israeli nation, as the court perfectly understood and wrote, was different:

for the recognition of the existence of the Israeli nation challenged that of the Jewish nation because it also included the Israeli Jews, and from this recognition would follow fundamental changes in the Israeli reality.

Yet, the question of "proven" nationality should be laid also at the doorstep of the court. What are the "proofs" for the existence of a Jewish nation? In an article published in *Ha'aretz* as a reprise to the rejection of the motion Joseph Agassi wrote that the court has adopted an 'ethnic' concept of nationalism which enabled it to reject the notion of the Israeli nation, on one hand, and reaffirmed that of the Jewish nation, on the other. Indeed, from the civic nationalism's point of view, as the court admits, the notion of the Jewish nation, lacking common citizenship, territory and government, had almost nothing to commend itself. Yet, as we are going to see, the notion of the Jewish nation does not fit easily even within the concept of ethnic nationalism, especially because it lacks common culture and common language (see below, pp. 140-143). The Israeli nation, on the other hand, is not devoid of ethno-cultural elements such as language and culture. Paradoxically the only 'objective' advantage which the notion of the Jewish nation has on that of the Israeli nation lies within the sphere of civic nationalism, that is in realm of consciousness: most of the Israelis of Jewish origin identify themselves as belonging to the Jewish rather than to the Israeli nation.

Though the plaintiffs expressed a great disappointment at the rejection of their motion, the case did signify an "historical" moment: for the first time the traditional question which had preoccupied the court until then – "who is a Jew?" – was replaced by the question "who is an Israeli?" As Agassi noted, the court offered a discussion of the question what is a nation, which related to contemporary readings and which also included modernists like Gellner and Anderson. This meant that the court, though it reaffirmed the existence of the Jewish nation (and the non-existence of the Israeli one), no longer felt that it could be taken for granted and that it had to be established within the framework of the modern study of nationalism. Though the court also referred to both Agassi's book mentioned above and the Hebrew version of the present book, it seems that it had preferred to take a very narrow concept of the Israeli nation, not necessarily compatible with what was offered in both studies. Yet, had the court's assertions concerning the nature of the Israeli nation turned into question marks, they would form the very basic questions concerning Israeli nationhood which are discussed in the present book: Is there an Israeli nation? To what extent and how is it related to Judaism and Jewish history? What would be its relation the Jewish Diaspora? What would be its relations with the Israeli Jewish and non-Jewish ethnic minorities or 'nationalities'?

The Fusion of Religion and Nationality and the Reform of Religion

The fusion of religion and nationality has prevented the liberalization of the Israeli State until now. It has also prevented the various religious communities which live in Israel to make the necessary reforms in their religion in order to make it suitable for the Israeli life. The main problem had been considered by Weiler to be the question of authority:

> Is there, according to the *Halacha*, any authority to the government of Israel? Opinions differ on this matter. But it seems that the general agreement according to *Halacha* conception could be summarized as follows: the government has the authority to legislate laws needed for the welfare of the society and for the maintenance of law and order. Thus the government could issues laws, which are not in the *Torah*, but it has no authority to issue a law, which contradicts the *Torah*. (Weiler, 1976, p. 206).

According to Weiler in the case of a collision between the *Halacha* and the State an a priori preference should be given to the law of the State.

Yet, from a democratic point of view, this demand is problematic, because there is no inherent difference between "conscientious disobedience" and "religious disobedience". In both cases the issue is the collision of the law of the State with the conscience of the individual, and from a democratic perspective, it is impossible, to demand an unconditional obedience. On the other hand, it is obvious, that a nation could not function, and a State could not exist, without the rule of the law, and that the collision with religion carries with it the potential break of the rule of the law. Yet, the solution which was accepted in western liberal democracy, the separation between religion and the State, does not mean the subordination of the religion to the State, as such subordination means exactly the opposite, which is the absence of a separation. According to the idea of separation, both the religion and the State operate in different spheres and consequently they do not usually collide. Of course, when they do sometimes collide it cannot be established *apriori* that religion should yield to the State.

Thus, to make the separation between religion and the State possible, the traditional State and the traditional religions had to change. In other words, the liberalization or the State and the reforms of religions were necessary conditions for the effective separation between the religion and the State. The reforms of the state were meant to abolish the religious confessional state and to recognize religious pluralism and the freedom of worship as basic elements of the State. Yet all these reforms could not have been sustained without parallel reforms of the religions, as in democracy it is impossible for the State to be tolerant in a society that is intolerant. Thus religious publics had to acknowledge that the state should not be used for imposing religious doctrines. Reform of religion was needed also to prepare the religious person of the Middle-Ages for modern civil life. Judaism did not escape those demands, and since the 18th century various Jewish publics, especially in the west, had recognized the need to reform religion in order to integrate into the local nations (Ben-Rafael & Ben-Chaim, 2006, pp. 89-117). On the other hand, the Jewish ultra-Orthodoxy was born as a reaction to modernity and resistance to religious reform. Hatam Sofer (1769–1832), which is considered by many as its founder, had set the uncompromising rule that "the *Torah* forbids on anything new (*chadash asur min ha'Torah*)" (Eisenstadt, 2002, 19-20).

Yet, reforms did not skip Judaism, not even Orthodox Judaism, as Orthodox Jews could not have lived in America as they had lived in Eastern Europe: there is a great difference between the Jewish communities of Eastern Europe which had neither the desire, nor the ability to integrate into the local national life, and the Jewish communities of the United States, whose sons and daughters see themselves (and are perceived by their compatriots) as Americans. The rabbis in America were demanded to answer the question how can a Jew be a good Jew, on one hand, and a good American, on the other. Consequently, "ultra-Orthodox" in the sense of the traditional Orthodoxy are a small minority within the Jews of America and America has created its own version of "modern Orthodoxy" which looks for "a way to express its attachment to the Judaism of the *Halacha* with the unequivocal desire to be part of the modern world, the American society and the Jewish world …" (Ben-Rafael & Ben Haim, 2006, pp. 246 -249). Charles Liebman and Stefan Cohen (1996, pp. 96-122) think that in the Orthodox communities in the United States there is a more positive attitude towards democracy and liberalism than in the Orthodox communities in Israel.

Religious Zionism was also not exceptional. Yeshayahu Leibowitz maintained that Religious Zionism was founded on the promise to reform Judaism, a promise which was not fulfilled (Salmon, 1996, pp. 132-133). Evidence that the promise was not fulfilled is demonstrated by the fact that the so called "Religious Zionist Camp" identifies itself today as "Orthodox", though its founders had rebelled against the traditional religion by joining of the Zionist movement, and its sons and daughters are different from the "real" Orthodox (that is the ultra-Orthodox, or *"Charedim"*) in their modern life-style. Thus, Don Yehiya remarks that the gap between the modern life style of the religious Zionists and their Orthodox commitment to the *Halacha* had given birth for tensions among the youth of the second generation which had led to fundamentalism that is to a political and religious radicalism (Don Yehiya, 2003, pp. 190-191).

Why is it that, in Israel, the religious sectors, in general and religious Zionists in particular, have avoided religious reforms? What is it that distinguishes the rabbis in Israel from those rabbis (Orthodox and un-Orthodox) who live in America or other liberal democracies? According to Leibowitz one of the reasons for the absence of reforms is the absence of separation between religion and state, which makes it possible for the various religious groups to find convenient arrangements which enable them to live according to the medieval *Halacha* in a modern country. Yet to the major obstacle for reforming the *Halacha* – the fusion of religion and nationality – Leibowitz did not relate, as he accepted it. This identity has made the question of reforms different from the one faced by the rabbis abroad in two essential elements: (a) unlike the pluralist conception of Judaism in the west, the Israeli conception of Judaism had been monist; (b) In Israel, the question of the reform of the Halacha was identified with the question of "the *Halachic* State", or "the *Torah* state", that is a state which is run according to the *Halacha* (A. Cohen, 1998).

As for the important distinction between pluralism and monism, it is important to see that the reforms of Judaism in the west had been conducted within the framework of a pluralist conception of Judaism. In as much as the existence of the historical *"Am Yisrael"* was assumed, it has been perceived as a collection of voluntary communities, and consequently the reforms were conducted within the communal framework rather than a Jewish collective one. This meant that the reformers were not guided by the desire for the consent of "the Jewish people", but mainly by the aspirations and needs of their communities. The pluralist framework and the principle "acquire your own rabbi" (*ase lecha rav*) were important elements in these reforms as the option of moving from one religious community to another not only increased individual freedom of religion, but also had made the rabbis more attentive to the needs and aspirations of the members of their communities, if only from the fear they might lose them. All this is different in Israel, since because of the fusion of religion and nationality the Jews in Israel (and in fact all over the world) are recognized also as a single religious community. This means that the Israeli rabbis, or the reformers, have to respond not to the needs and aspirations of their religious congregations, but to the needs and aspirations of a nation (which includes also secular people).

Indeed, Leibowitz had suggested to reform the *Halacha* in order to achieve "a *Torah* state", and thought that this reform would be such that the secular Israelis would be able and would want to accept, even if it involved a change in their life styles. Indeed, it is possible to reform the *Halacha* in order to make it acceptable for the secular or close to secular Israelis. Yet, within a monist approach, this would mean making this version the only one for the entire Israeli community. From a religious point of view this would mean the complete annihilation of the *Halacha* as it is known today. It would mean that the rabbis would have to legitimize forms of living, which would lead to the disintegration of (their own) religious communities. If the Jews of Israel would have perceived themselves as a collection of religious communities, then it would have been possible to speak about *reforms* of the *Halacha* or *reforms* of religion (according to the desires and needs of the various religious communities) rather then *a reform* in the *Halacha* or the religion.

Another important element which is related to the fusion of religion and nationality and which makes the reform of Judaism in Israel different from the reforms carried in western democracies, is that in Israel the question of reformed religion has turned out to be identified with the question of *"Halacha*'s state", or *"Torah*'s state," that is a state which is run according to the *Halacha*. This identity is prominent, at least from the nineteen fifties, in the writings of Leibowitz. Thus when Leibowitz (1976, p. 195) suggested that "according to the conception which has been consolidated in the *Halacha* the Jewish people (*Am Yisrael*) is a public entity which has no state-political functions, and a person of *Yisrael* is a person that has no civic duties and civic roles in the state", he seems to bind both questions and to seek an answer for both.

However, these are indeed two different questions, and therefore even if *Am Yisrael* will remain without state-political functions, the problem of the *Halacha* conception that "a man of *Yisrael* is a man that has no civic duties and no civic roles in the State" remains, both for "a man of *Yisrael*" in Israel and "a man of *Yisrael*" in democracy in general. The situation in Israel, as Leibowitz maintains, is indeed unique, as it has a Jewish majority and consequently when religious persons shrink from their civic duties or from essential occupations and roles in order to observe their religion, they might cause other Jews to sin. Yet, this does not mean that the State ought to be run according to the *Halacha* but only that the reformers have to take it into account. Indeed, Leibowitz in fact admitted that the desire for the *"Torah*'s State" does not follow from the need to reform the *Halacha* in order to make it suitable for modern State and society but that it is rather "a religious apriorism". This is because the *Halacha* covers all aspects of Jewish life:

> Therefore, from this perception, the national revival and political independence are in a known sense a religious a priori, a precondition for the attempt to implement the *Halacha*, and what we have done is not just legitimate, but also the performance of the first order which falls upon a public who

wishes to maintain the *Torah* – to acquire independence, the government, by itself, in order to try to implement what it wants to implement. (Ibid. p. 197)

Thus the need for a (Jewish) State comes from the need to fully implement the *Halacha*; consequently it is a religious apriorism. Indeed, Leibowitz had set here a radical *Halacha* ruling when he said: "the *Torah* was not meant to be observed by religious Jews but by the collectivity of *Am Yisrael*". By this he rejected the traditional conception, according to which salvation will come by the return of individuals to the *Torah*, in favor of collective action. Here Leibowitz entangled himself in a contradiction; A well known fact about his teachings is that he identified Judaism with the observation of the *Halacha* (*Torah u-mitzvot*), and that he based this identity on what he called "an historical empirical evidence", (that is, the fact that for thousands of years Judaism had been such.) Yet, his assertion that that the existence of a (Jewish) State is an *a priori* condition for the *Halacha* is a bold innovation, which does not appear in traditional Judaism. Here also appears, though not explicitly, the "Zionist" claim that non-Israeli Jews are *a priori* "deficient" Jews, because they don't live in a Jewish State. Because if, according to Leibowitz, a 'Jewish State' is a religious *apriorism*, what would be the Jewish status of those Jews who live abroad?

Further, according to Leibowitz, reform in the *Halacha* in order to achieve a *Halachic* State should be carried out by the religious Zionist public, as this public had already made the first move when it rebelled against the rabbis by joining the Zionist movement. By this Leibowitz was a part of the general inclination, which characterizes the so-called "Zionists" in Israel, which is to nationalize religion or to appropriate it by the State or by democracy.

Leibowitz had been considered by the Israeli public, especially those of liberal circles, as a religious man who endorsed somewhat liberal ideas concerning the relations between religion and State. Yet, Leibowitz's demand to separate religion and State did not spring from a liberal worldview, but from his understanding that this separation was a necessary stage towards the establishment of a *Halachic* state. His approach towards religion was fundamentalist: The assertion that the State is "a religious *a priori*" and that its aim is the realization and implementation of the *Halacha* is the similar to the views of fundamentalist Islam concerning the relations between the State and the *Sharia*.

From historical point of view, Leibowitz's assertion that religious Zionism was established because of the desire to establish a *Halachic* State is false, at least in as much as the first generation of its founding fathers is concerned. The latter insisted on the separation between religion and the Zionist movement and adhered to Herzl's famous slogan "Zionism has nothing to do with religion." (and see below, pp. 273 - 278).

Israel and the World Jewry

Indeed, the adoption of "The New Zionist Myth" in the nineteen fifties had put Israel on a route of collision with the American Jews, when Ben Gurion and spokesmen of the political establishment of Israel began to use ideas of "the negation of the Diaspora", against American Jewry in general and American Zionists in particular. Ben Gurion declared that he had no part in what was called in those days "Zionism" by the members of the World Zionist Organization, because they did not consider themselves as living in the Diaspora, and did not intend to immigrate to Israel. Ben Gurion said that the Diaspora is "a miserable, poor, doubtful experience of which nobody could be proud of – on the contrary it must be completely rejected." (Shimoni, 2000, 56). From the point of view of the American Zionists it was a change of direction, because before independence, and since the establishment of Zionism, they had not considered themselves as potential immigrants, but interpreted their Zionism as being supportive of the Zionist aims. Further, they did not consider themselves as living in the Diaspora, but as free sons and daughters of their own country. Thus, in the 23rd Zionist Congress in 1951 (the first one after independence) Rose Halperin, the President of "Haddassah" (The Womens' Zionist Organization in America), set herself against Ben Gurion and the political establishment of Israel when she said that the Diaspora meant a status of deprivation of rights and coercion, and consequently does not apply to the Jews of the United State (Ibid.).

The disagreement between the American Zionists and the government of Israel in the nineteen fifties demonstrated how the fusion of religion and nationality could become a source of strains between Israel and the world Jewry. Traditional Judaism, or historical Judaism, the one which had developed in the Diaspora, was "non-Israeli". To the extent that it had considered the Land of Israel as sacred for all the Jews, and all the lands outside *Eretz Yisrael* as "the Diaspora", it anticipated the end of the Diaspora in the End of Days with coming of the messiah. Consequently, for the present and for any foreseeable future, it was possible to be a good Jew everywhere and in this sense traditional Judaism has been a "universal religion" (Ben-Rafael & Ben-Chaim, 2006, p. 54). This universalism was challenged by the appearance of the Zionist movement, which has given Judaism also a national – territorial dimension. However, under normal conditions, which mean the separation between nationality and religion, the establishment of Israel should have abolished this national-political dimension of Judaism by transferring it to the Israeli state, letting Judaism become once again "a universal religion". This would be especially true, considering the fact that the Jews have become members of their local nations. In other words, the historical Diaspora was not only a religious concept, but also a way of life: it meant poverty, deprivation, alienation and even death. Yet for contemporary Jews, especially those who live in liberal democracies, "the Diaspora" has retained only its religious dimension.

Thus, the establishment of Israel and the integration of Jews into their local nations could be seen as additional stages in the universalization of Judaism. Consequently, the claim that Israel is the State of the Jewish people might be interpreted as the delegitimization of the right of the Jews to be members of various nations, because it invokes the question of "dual loyalty". A well known anti-Semitist argument was that the Jews could not be equal members of the nations in which they are living because their loyalty is given to their congregation rather than to their country. The unprecedented creation of a sovereign Jewish State, which sees itself as the state of all Jews wherever they are, could indeed invoke and strengthen this anti-Semitist argument.

Thus, since the nineteen fifties, a so-called "Zionist" ethos has been created, which aimed at the deligitimization of Jewish existence outside of Israel. According to it, a person could not be a Jew in the real sense unless he lived in Israel. Thus, as A.B. Yehoshua explains, one of the meanings of the "bold reform" in Judaism, which he offers and which was discussed above (pp. 78-85) is a deligitimization of Jewish existence in the Diaspora. The following rather long quotation is from an article published by *Haaretz* in 1988:

> If a young man had come to me and said that he wanted to emigrate to France or America, I would have answered him like that: I am sorry that you abandon us after all the toil that your fathers and the fathers of your fathers invested in the establishment of a Jewish State in which the Jews will realize their independence and the totality of their identity. But it is your moral right (based, by the way, on the Human Right Proclamation) to change your identity as millions have done during the history (otherwise, there would have been no America, no Australia, no Argentine). Yet, there is one condition: That you will become a Frenchmen and not Jewish-Frenchmen; that you will become American and not Jewish-American. France is no longer a hotel

but the homeland for many millions who had invested in it their blood and their marrow, who had nurtured its language and food, fought for its values of freedom and equality. Go and become a Frenchman, deepen yourself in what that is French, fully identified with the interests of France, and be ready to die for her. The same goes for the United States, New York is not just a transfer station for making money in the stock exchange (if you do not lose it in one collapse or another) and then to leave. But it is a home for millions who struggle, among other things, against the monstrosity of urbanization. Go also to Harlem and feel the pain of the black members of your new nation. Yet for this the new emigrant is not ready. He just want to get into the Jewish "bubble", to belong and not to belong, covered by the famous cliché of "alienation", thinking of Jerusalem while sitting in Chicago or London and what is most important – actually to be committed to nothing. Not there and not here. And this is immoral! Not from Jewish point of view, but form a human general one.

One who reads Yehoshua would find it difficult to decide whether he wants to rob the Jews who live outside of Israel of their nationality or of their religion or both. These Jews live in "a Jewish bubble" and treat their countries as "hotels". Must the American Jews expose their scars and medals to Yehoshua to satisfy him that an "American Jew" is indeed "American"? Haven't the Jews fought the wars of the United States? Haven't they created with other millions immigrants its culture? Haven't they marched in its protest parades? The accusation of the western Jews of "retrieving from important and central spheres of life" is not only baseless, but also carries with it an old familiar anti-Semitic flavor.

Yet, the nationalization of Judaism is not just about the delegitimization of the Jewish existence in the western nations by robbing them of their national identity, but also it is about robbing them of their religion. This is how the second article by Yehoshua published in *Haaretz* a week later (6.1. 1989) ends:

"… and we should erect clearer borders between the total Jewish existence, that is the Israeli, and the partial one, that is the Jewish existence." Thus, by identifying the total Jew with the Israeli, Yehoshua turns the Israeli *Epicurus*, who would never set a foot in the synagogue (not even a reformed one) to a better Jew than the Rabbi of Lubavitch. In a similar manner Ben Gurion maintained that:

> The Jew in the Diaspora, whether he recognizes the fact or not, has a *split personality*. In part he is a Jew … and in part he belongs to the non-Jewish environment in which he dwells. … *In Israel, on the other hand, the Jew is one hundred percent Jewish and one hundred percent human, that is a member of the human race*, because he is a son of an independent people, which is member of the family of people with equal rights. (Ben Ezer, 1974, p. 72)

Alternatively Ben Gurion said that the Jews in the Diaspora were "human dust, who try to stick to one another maybe more than other groups in the same conditions." (Gorni, 1990, p. 87). Gorni maintains (ibid., 88) that Ben Gurion had not accidently incorporated in his words in the 25th Zionist Congress (1961) the Talmudic phrase "Anyone who lives abroad is like one who has no God", words which had invoked sharp reaction form the leadership of the American Jewry. According to Shulamit Aloni, one of the pillars of Israeli secularism, the Rabbi of Lubavich is not an Israeli, but rather "a defective Israeli" as 'Essentially, he prays to be the 'next year in Jerusalem', but does not arrive. For every Israeli, Jerusalem is his real 'capital' (Aloni, 1987, pp. 11-13). Yet it seems that "a defective Israeli" is also "a defective Jew" and thus Aloni maintains:

> Here, Jewish existence is not just words and ties among people possessing a common origin, but a fact of life, a worldview, and language, culture and all the rest. Here we have a system of Hebrew education and Israeli culture that enable people to live

with a feeling of integrity and belongingness. A Jew in Israel is at home. He can walk around in bedroom slippers. Everyplace else he is obliged to be on his best behavior and wear a necktie" (Ben Ezer, 1974, p. 43).

This how the secular Jews in Israel, who were characterized by an army general of religious origin as "Hebrew speaking gentiles", have turned out to be better Jews than the Lubavicher Rabbi. Yet, Aloni, when she speaks how the Jews in Israel can "walk in slippers" certainly doesn't refer to the ultra-Orthodox, and I doubt if she refers to the religious Zionists, or the "settlers". I am not sure to what extent those could "walk around in bedroom slippers" in Aloni's circles.

As noted above, the fusion of religion and nationality forces the Israeli government to intervene in religious doctrines and especially to monopolize the definition of "who is a Jew". The intervention of the Israeli government in the question of who is a Jew, which meant, among other things, a religious delegitimization of Jewish communities abroad, had occasionally enraged American Jews (Eisenstadt, 2002, pp. 371-2). As a reaction to the Israeli pretention to monopolize Judaism and to its authentic representation, Seth Wolitz (1991), a professor of Jewish studies at the University of Texas, published an article in the *Jerusalem Post* at the time of the First Gulf War, titled *"The American Jew is American First"*. The article was published as a response to an article by Uri Gordon who was the President of the Zionist Council in Israel and the head of the Department of Immigration (*alia u-klita*) of the Jewish Agency at the time. In this article Gordon complained about the low number of *"olim"* (Jewish immigrants) from America and demanded a radical change of thinking from the Jewish leadership in America as far as *"aliya"* is concerned. Wolitz's answer was that Israelis should acknowledge that the American Jews are American first. Yet, they do not feel themselves to be less Jewish than the Israeli

Jews, but rather that they or their fathers had chosen a different course than Zionism. The differences between the Israelis and the American Jews are both cultural and political. Indeed, anyone who reads Wolitz's article comes to the conclusion the author thinks that Israeli Jews and American Jews are members of different nations, both politically and culturally. Notwithstanding Wolitz, it seems that the fusion of faith and nationality answers also to the needs of substantial parts of American Jewry and there is no certainty that when the question of separation between nationality and religion and the establishment an Israeli republic, will become a realistic option, the leadership of American Jewry will support it.

As Wolitz points out, American Jew's "identification to Israel is tinged with idealism and expectations of unrealistic performance." Indeed, one of the outcomes of the fusion of religion and nationality is the over involvement of the Jews of the world in Israel's internal affairs. The mobilization of American Jewry for Israeli internal struggles has become accepted norm in Israeli politics. This involvement of non-citizens in national questions of the utmost importance, which might decide the fate of many Israelis, is very problematic. World Jewry is naturally sensitive to what is going on in Israel. This sensitivity makes them Israel's greatest friends and defenders. It also sometimes makes them Israel's harshest critics, when they perceive that actions taken by Israel are immoral (including actions which are similar to those occasionally taken by their own governments). These are things that shame them as Jews (Eisenstadt, 2002, pp. 369 – 370). This is not fully an Israeli problem, as it testifies to the fact that the Jews of the world have not freed themselves yet of Diaspora's conceptions. Yet, it is important to see that the fusion of religion and nationality plays here an important role, for they accept the idea that Israel belongs to them, and thus they are responsible, one way or another, for its actions. Further, accepting the fusion of religion and nationality, those Jews see Israel as a religious-moral community rather than a political-national one; as a community which should stand to "Jewish standards" (moral or religious), which also means that the rules which apply to Israel are different from those which apply to other nations, hence what Wolitz refers above as a 'unrealistic expectations'. As already said, to a great extent this is their problem and not ours. Yet there is no doubt that the separation between nationality and religion will make it easier for the Jews of the west to solve their identity conflicts.

ℭℛ CHAPTER 2 ℬ⟨
Nation States and the Uniqueness of Israel

Not until very long ago the notion of Israel as abnormal entity was taken for granted by the Israelis, and was part of the official "Zionist" ethos (though this abnormality contradicted the aims of classical Zionism). This opinion was also shared to a large extent, by political scientists. Yet, in recent years, maybe as a reaction to the post-Zionist criticism, the question whether or to what extent Israel is indeed normal, or, alternatively, what are the conditions for the normalization of Israel, has come forward. Surprisingly, though the model of the nation-state is the accepted norm today, the question of the separation between nationality and religion and the recognition of an Israeli nation has rarely been discussed in this debate. On one side of the debate stand the supporters of the Jewish State who consider it to be indeed "a nation like all nations". To the extent that they could be called "Zionists", the innovation in the current debate is that while in the past the supporters of the Jewish State emphasized its abnormality and uniqueness, today they are inclined to see Israel as normal. They support their position mainly by the argument that even if the notion of the Jewish State does not fit the classical model of the nation-state, this model is no longer accepted today in its classical from, or alternatively, it has never been the only possible model for the national state. On the other side of the debate stand the critics of the Jewish State, usually identified as 'post-Zionists'. The latter indeed perceive the Jewish State as abnormal, but set the "citizens' State" as a normative model for Israel, a model which differs also from that of the nation-state. Here also the deviation from the nation-state is explained by the argument that the nation state is no longer accepted or desirable, mainly because the age of nationalism is over. Thus those who are called "Zionists" and those who are called "post-Zionists" share the rejection of the model of the nation-state. Consequently within the debate on the identity of Israel the option of the separation between nationality and religion and the recognition Israel as the State of the Israeli nation is ignored.

Here, we must ask the following questions: To what extent does the model of the classical nation state serve as a normative model for contemporary liberal democracy? To what extent the deviations from this model or the changes that it has gone through can indeed "normalize" the Israeli case? To what extent the model of the citizens' state could serve as a normative model for modern liberal democracy in general and for Israel in particular? These questions will be dealt in this chapter.

Nationalism vs. Multiculturalism

The multi-ethnic or multi-national reality in the new non-western democracies, the deviations of some western democracies from the classical nation-state and the changes of the ethnic composition of western democracies following immigration from third world countries, all these have brought political scientists to question the model of the nation-state, at least in its classical interpretation, as a normative model for contemporary democracy. This model demanded cultural homogeneity and consequently all western democracies have conducted open or covet policy of assimilation. A conspicuous example for this is the French republican approach that in its name France has conducted in the nineteenth century an aggressive policy of assimilation towards cultural and lingual minorities which lived on its soil and which was directed at new immigrants as well (Linz, Stepan, Yadav, 2004). In the United States the assimilation policy was expressed by the notion of the "melting pot", which meant that the new immigrants should give up the cultures of their original countries and become Americans (Glazer and Moynihan, 1970). In Israel this approach was expressed by the idea of "The negation of the Diaspora", yet contrary to the American and French cases, the demand for cultural homogeneity was not directed towards all the citizens, but rather to those who were considered Jews. Taylor (1998) says that the melting pot or the "republican approach" had an advantage as it had succeeded in reducing to a minimum the exclusion of the immigrants. Frenchmen of today are surprised to learn that one of four Frenchmen has a grandfather who was born out of France. In other words, in the twentieth century, France has become a country of immigrants – without the French perceiving themselves as such. The assimilation policy enabled the immigrants to become members of the nation.

Various reasons have made the melting pot or republican approach unacceptable today. Some claim that in the multiethnic reality of the new democracies in Eastern Europe and the Third World this approach could not be implemented by democratic means, and could even lead to ethnic cleansing (Linz, Stepan Yadav, 2004). Yet, consolidated western nation-states did not escape the question of the relation between democracy and culture: globalization seems to erode the status of the nation-state, and one of the results of this erosion was the appearance of separatist movements whose struggle reaffirmed and emphasized the existence of a dominant national culture in the traditional nation-state (Ake, 1997). Another important cause was the waves of immigration to western democracies. Those immigrations were different from the past as the new immigrants were sometimes religiously and racially different from the inhabitants of the host country, which tended to emphasis the cultural-ethnic aspect of the absorbing nation and made assimilation more difficult. Furthermore, unlike former waves of immigration, the new immigrants sometimes refused to assimilate and wanted to keep their original culture. The ability of the new immigrants to keep their original culture has been made possible also by technological advancements in the means of communication and transportation, which enable new immigrants to be in touch with their countries of origin. All these factors made the assimilation policy that had characterized democracies in the past more difficult to implement; if not unattainable (Taylor, 1998; Huntington, 1993). Already in 1963, before the change in the American immigration laws (1965) and the waves of "New Immigration" that followed it, Nathan Glazer and Daniel Patrick Moynihan claimed in the introduction of their celebrated book *Beyond the Melting Pot* that the "most important point in the 'melting pot' is that it has never happened." Glazer and Moynihan claimed that the American reality was pluralistic. And indeed, one of the main criticisms against the melting pot was that it had failed.

While western liberal democracy has become multicultural in fact the theory of liberal democracy had also changed, or alternatively, there had been a change of the conception of liberal democracy by the elites in the west. Until the nineteen fifties there had been a tendency to ignore the cultural aspect of liberal democracy, or to ignore the fact that, being a nation-state, liberal democracy had a dominant culture, which it imposed by various means on its citizens. According to the liberal ethos (expressed by the "social contact" theory) the State is created as a contract between equal individuals who seek to secure their "natural rights", especially the rights for security and welfare. "The right for culture" had not been considered as a natural right in classical liberalism. In as much as the individuals who had associated in the State had a culture, its place according to the liberal theory was in the private realm and it should not have a political or institutional expression. The State itself had been considered culturally neutral, that is as evenly remote from the various private cultures of its citizens. The fact that the State or the nation had a culture was not denied, of course, but this culture was "universal", as it was identified with "progress", "democracy" or "the republic", while the cultures of the various groups (religious, ethnic and others) had been considered as particular sub-cultures. Thus classical liberal democracy did not recognize the existence of cultural (or other) collectives within the citizen body, only the existence of individuals.

This conception of liberal democracy had change also because of the processes described above and instead the cultural-national aspect of liberal democracy was emphasized. The national culture was conceived as a regular culture, though dominant alongside other minority cultures. From this point of view liberal democracy was no longer culturally neutral. This awareness of the national-cultural aspect of liberal democracy entailed awareness of the problems this cultural aspects raises from liberal point of view. It was argued against the model of the nation-state that the liberal state should be culturally neutral and therefore cannot prefer the national culture (which is biased in favor of the majority group) over the cultures of the various ethnic groups. It was further claimed that the right for culture is a natural right, and therefore minority cultures should be protected (Margalit and Halbertal, 1998, p. 100). Others claimed that the oppression of ethnic cultures hinders the autonomy and development of members of these groups (Kymlicka, 1989; Brunner and Peled, 1998, pp. 108-112). Thus, it was claimed, that the liberal state should recognize collective rights, and from the nineteen sixties it has become possible to discern the abandonment of the melting pot approach in favor of multiculturalism. The change did not concentrate only on the issue of immigration and was of a more general nature. It has found an expression in movements that aspired to conserve and strengthen local languages and cultures in Europe, in the demand for recognition and autonomy for native minorities in the United States, Canada, Australia, Russia and other places, and in the appearance of movements, which objected to the assimilation of Afro-Americans (Brubaker, 2001, pp. 531-533).

The multicultural approach in its extreme version negated the nation-state, as it claimed that the state should be culturally neutral or should recognize and give equal status to all the cultures under its rule. Yet, in more moderate versions it meant a conception of a multicultural nation. Further, while sometimes negating the nation-state, the multicultural approach had been effectively implemented within the framework of the nation-state. The outcome was the legitimization of political organization and struggle of ethnic and cultural groups within the framework of the nation-state. Legitimization for immigrant groups to operate in "exile", that is to be supportive of the interests of the old country without being accused of "dual loyalty", and legitimization of multiple and complementary identities is allowed (Smooha, 2002a, p. 425).

The critics of multiculturalism emphasized that liberal democracy needs a substantial amount of consensus, which could only be supplied by the existence of shared national culture (Taylor, 1998; Resnick, 1997). According to Resnick democracy needs a sense of community that the classical liberal market theory could not supply:

> Citizens do not constitute a passing group that comes together at one moment to do certain things and break up at the next. Its members share deeper affinities with one another, cultural and historical attachments, moral bonds, and the need for basic security. I'm not certain whether such models as a social contract help us in this regard. Suffice it to say that without common values that are at the basis of the life of a citizen, it is unlikely that democracy can endure. (Resnick, 1997, pp. 116-17).

John Stuart Mill expressed similar ideas, previously in the nineteenth century:

> Free institutions are next to impossible in a country made up of different nationalities. Among a people without fellow-feeling, especially if they read and speak different

language, the united public opinion, necessary to working of representative government, cannot exist. (Mill, 2010, p. 235).

The supporters of multiculturalism maintain that the source for solidarity in the multicultural society could be "constitutional patriotism", or "political patriotism." (Habermas, 1998), which means a commitment to liberal democracy and its institutions. As Charles Taylor says, because of what seems to be the failure of the melting pot there is a great temptation in the present multicultural society to abandon republicanism and to adopt individualist approach, or what Sandel (1996) calls "Procedural Republic". The advantage of "Procedural Republic" is that it emphasizes the principles of individual rights, freedom and equality, which are assumed to be shared by members of all cultures and avoids discussing "the general good", or the national character of the State, which in multicultural society might become a source of dispute. Yet, Taylor thinks that a Procedural Republic could not supply the sense of solidarity which is needed for democracy; Linz and Stepan also emphasize that though "constitutional patriotism" is an important element for legitimization of what they call "State-Nation"; it is not enough and other elements are needed, not necessarily 'rational' or 'universal', but rather symbolic or emotional – the same kind which characterizes the classical nation-state (see also Canovan, 2000). In other words, it would be difficult to find solidarity and willingness to sacrifice for the public good, elements which are considered as required of good citizenship, among coincidental publics. Alternatively, in as much as human beings are altruists, it seems that their willingness to sacrifice or to contribute to the public is greater when they identify the public with their own nation, and that this desire declines sharply when foreign publics are concerned (Ake, 1997).

This could also be seen from a different point of view. The supporters of "constitutional patriotism" assume that any collection of individuals is democratic and consequently that democracy has no cultural or national context. Yet, it is not certain that any association would accept majority rule, or the need to protect human rights. It seems that the theory of "constitutional patriotism", like the social contract theory, assumes that this is the "natural" or the "rational" thing to do. Yet, this assumption is indeed contextual – it is clearly "modernist" or "western" and not necessarily shared by traditional cultures. Thus, if we do not consider modernity as "natural" or "universal", then we must see democracy as depended upon a cultural context, and that it is not always possible to distinguish between the political aspects of this culture, on one hand, and its historical, religious or ethnical aspects, on the other. As such, Taylor says that the apprehensions which exists in western democracies relating to last waves of immigrations are not motivated only by the desire to preserve the national-ethnic identity, but also from the desire to prevent the entrance of individuals who do not share the local culture where the latter is seen also in its larger context as including the elements which support the democratic regime. It is also a very well known criticism against multiculturalism that in its demand to preserve and protect particular cultures, which are usually traditional and suppressive of various groups in their midst, especially women, multiculturalism could undermine the human rights of the members of these particular minorities (Muller-Okin, 1998).

The events of 9/11 and their aftermath have raised the question of solidarity in liberal democracy and perhaps marked a change in the attitude towards multiculturalism, at least in its extreme version. An example was the shock Britain experienced after the terror events in London on 7.7.2005, when it had been revealed that those acts of terrorism were carried out by British of Muslim origin. A conspicuous expression for the change in the attitude towards multiculturalism, at least in its extreme version, was the "Multiculturalism Speech" of the British Prime Minister Tony Blair delivered on 12.8. 2006, in which he had called upon the Muslim Radicals to "conform" to British "essential values" or else "don't come here". Among these essential values he mentioned those directly connected to democracy such as "belief in democracy, the rule of law, tolerance, equal treatment for all", yet also those related to the nation – "respect for this country and its shared heritage - then that is where we come together, it is what we hold in common; it is what gives us the right to call ourselves British".

Another criticism against multiculturalism is the argument that in as much as multiculturalism is tolerant towards the existence of different cultures, it does not encourage contact between the cultures, and could sometimes encourage and serve alienation and hostility between cultures and thus may be used as an instrument for exclusion. An example of this argument is the fact that in France Le Pen and the racial right adopted multiculturalism and in its name demanded to protect the French culture from extinction by the prevention of the integration of foreigners (Brubaker, 2001, p. 536). Similarly Brubaker has pointed out that a differentialist policy in Germany was used as an instrument for the exclusion of new immigrants. Therefore, while denied citizenship, foreigners had received in many cases education in segregated, homeland- oriented classes. What was unique in the German case, says Brubaker, was that because of the domination of the differentialist (or multicultural) approach, even in "liberal" of "left" circles, the solution to the problem was not seen in terms of incorporating immigrants and their descendants as full citizens, but rather in extending political rights (such as the right to vote in the local elections) along with social, civil and economic rights, to resident foreigners. This differentialist policy led to the creation of what Brubaker calls "benevolent, paternalistic, and egalitarian (or pseudo-egalitarian) *apartheid*", as it institutionalized separateness (Brubaker, 2001, pp. 537-538). As such, multiculturalism could have severe socio-economic implications because when it isolates the cultural minorities and prevents their integration in the dominant culture, it also denies them the economic advantages of such integration. As Brunner and Peled suggest, sometime the multicultural approach towards a certain minority is adopted as 'compensation' for denied individual rights (Bruner and Peled, 1998, pp. 124-128).

The argument that multiculturalism could be a means for discrimination and exclusion is especially important for the Israeli case. Here Shlomo Avineri, one of Israel's leading political scientists, has argued that Israel enables cultural pluralism more than many western democracies (Margolin, 1999, p. 41). This pluralism is expressed by granting the Arabs a certain amount of cultural autonomy: "The right of the Arab public to receive education in the Arab language" and that the existence of such an education is "one of our most serious achievements" (Avineri, 1998, p. 23). Avineri says that while many suggest cultural autonomy as a solution for the problem of the Arab minority in Israel and even see this as a revolutionary solution, such autonomy already exists, and the important question is how to improve it. Yakobson and Rubinstein expressed a similar position (2009, pp. 118-123).

If we put aside Avineri's somewhat strange claim that "almost no national-ethnic-lingual minority in any western democracy possesses such right", considering multi-national democracies, such as Switzerland, Canada, Belgium and Spain, which had even institutionalized the cultural autonomy of national or linguistic minorities within the framework of a federal state, there is a certain amount of truth in his claim that Israel is much more multicultural than many western democracies. However, this fact points to the problematic nature of multiculturalism, since, given the discussion above, the question which should be answered is to what extent this multicultural approach to the Arabs is intended to answer the needs and rights of the Arab minority, or to exclude them from the majority, or to what extent the multicultural approach towards the Arabs had been adopted as a "compensation" for the absence of rights as individuals.

Indeed, Israeli multiculturalism locks the Arabs in a ghetto (which is called in Israel *"hamigzar"*, that is the "Arab Sector") and makes their integration into the dominant culture impossible. Consequently Avineri could be right when he criticizes the French liberals about their position in the debate concerning the Muslim head cover, the *chimar*, saying "their liberalism stops at the doorstep of the French school" (Ibid., p. 19). But the French system, as opposed to the Israeli system, is still ready to accept, under its own conditions, the Muslim girl as a Frenchwoman. Yet, the system in Israel is not ready to accept the Muslim girl under any condition, or at least, until today, it has not declared what are the conditions that the Muslim girl must fulfill in order to be accepted. Thus, Israeli multiculturalism is exclusive. It is not only that it makes integration impossible, but it aims to prevent integration and to preserve the distinctions between Jews and Arabs. Thus, while France wants the Muslim girl to take off the head cover, Israel wants her to keep wearing it.

In the last decades there seems to be a retreat from the multicultural approach, at least in its extreme version, which delegitimized the nation-state, towards what Brubaker calls a "moderate assimilation". Taylor emphasizes that contemporary immigrant communities in western democracies are interested in integration, yet they want to do it in their own way, and certainly not in the same way as it had been accepted by previous generations of immigrants. The insistence of the Hispanic Immigrants on Hispanic studies does not mean that they do not wish to become English-speaking Americans, but rather that they want their integration to be as painless as possible while keeping their original culture as much as they can, and, what is especially important, while contributing to the American culture. It is obvious that by this they are changing the meaning of being American, as previous generations of immigrants have done, yet they seems to be doing it consciously; while in previous generations this sense of their role in codetermining the national culture arose only retrospectively. Thus, the notion of the "melting pot" made way for that of a cultural evolution, which is codetermined also by the new immigrants (Taylor, 1998, pp. 149 - 150). It is obvious that such approach is irrelevant for Israel, as Israel lacks, at least formally, an overall Israeli identity, that is it lacks a national assimilative entity.

Multinational States, or Multicultural Nations?

There are also western democracies, which are characterized sometimes as bi-national or multinational, and as such, seem to deviate from the model of the nation-state. The common examples are Switzerland, Canada, Belgium and Spain. What characterizes these four liberal democracies are consociational arrangements, which means that as opposed to the classical nation-state where there are rights only to individuals, in these democracies, alongside a complete equality of rights and duties for all the citizens, there are also collective rights to national, lingual or ethnic minorities, and the system operates according to the principle of equality, consent and cooperation between these groups. Constitutional arrangements are designed to meet those purposes, that is to facilitate the participation of the various groups in the government: proportional representation, autonomy (cultural, institutional or territorial), right of veto to prevent decisions which would encroach upon minorities, and politics by negotiation in order to reach a consensus (Lijphart, 1997, Smooha, 2000, p. 569). One of the common ways to do it is by the Federal State and consequently all the democracies mentioned above are Federal States where autonomy is given to the various groups through the sub-units and by participation in the central government (Stepan 2002).

Then, to what extent do these four democracies deviate from the model of the nation-state? This question is important to the present book also because these four countries were used by post-Zionists as an example for their desired bi-national citizens' State.

It is important to mention that there is no agreement among political scientists as to whether these democracies are multinational States or multicultural or multilingual nations. Nevertheless, in these democracies, it is possible to discern at least formally, alongside the bi-national or multinational structure, a nation-state structure, or at least an aspiration for one. Alfred Stepan (2002) offers a criterion for distinguishing between multinational countries and multilingual or multicultural nations: multinational States are those that possess: (a) More than one lingual-territorial minority (which could be characterized sometimes also by religion or culture); (b) Significant political groups, which aspire to establish political sovereignties, or independent states, based upon these cultural-territorial identities. Stepan claims that the case of Switzerland is the least problematic, and it is common to see it as a multi-lingual nation. The Swiss cantons are indeed lingual, yet the four parties which participate in the "Magic Formula" of power sharing which forms the base of the government since 1958 are overall Swiss parties, and there is no party of any important element which suggests secession (ibid.) It is important also to emphasis that Switzerland is a republic and that the Swiss constitution explicitly recognized the existence of "a Swiss people".[6]

Yet in these western democracies identified by Stepan as multinational, (i.e. Belgium, Spain and Canada), it is possible to discern the recognition in the existence of an overall national identity or a desire to create one. The Belgian constitution, in as much as it defines Belgium as a federal State on lingual bases, acknowledges the existence of the Belgian nation: In a chapter titled "The Belgians and their rights" it defines "a Belgian" as a citizen with equal duties and rights. The Spanish constitution gives a wide cultural autonomy to Catalonia and the Basque Land alongside the recognition of a Spanish nation. Thus the second paragraph of the constitution declares "The Constitution is based on the indissoluble unity of the Spanish Nation, the common and indivisible homeland of all Spaniards; it recognizes and guarantees the right to self-government of the nationalities and regions of which it is composed and the solidarity among them all".

The situation is different in Canada. As opposed to Spain, in which the "Spanish Nation" has been traditionally conceived as an historical entity (as Spain had been one of the first to consolidate into a nation-state (Gellner, 1994a, p. 29), even if a Canadian nation does not exist, it is in the process of consolidation. The Canadian scholar, Charles Taylor, says that discussions of the relation between nation and state often assume that it is always the nation that seeks to provide itself with a state. However, the process sometimes moves in the opposite direction. In order to remain viable, States sometimes seek to create a feeling of common belonging. According to Taylor, Canada is a State, which is looking for a nation (Taylor, 1998, p. 145). Thus, it seems that these multinational democracies have developed "complementary national identities" – as it has become possible for individuals to identify without a contradiction, and even in a complementary manner with both the ethno-national unit and the general civic-national unit. Linz, Stepan and Yadav argue that most Catalans (or Basques) identify as Catalans (or as Basques), and also as members of the Spanish nation (though sometimes as Catalans/Basques more than as Spaniards, and sometimes more as Spaniards than as Catalans/Basques). Similarly, most of the Flemish and the Walloons identify both as Flemish and Walloons, on one hand, and as Belgians, on the other (though some as Flemish/Walloons more than as Belgians, and others Belgians more than as Flemish/Walloons) (Linz, Stepan, & Yadav, 2004, pp. 25-31).

The divergence of these western and other democracies from the traditional model of the nation-state prompted Linz and Stepan (1996, pp. 25-27) to offer the model of the state-nation, as an alternative substitute for that of the nation-state for those multinational democracies. The state-nation is different from the nation–state in being multi-national and characterized by institutional and political approach, which respects and protects national and cultural minorities. Yet, it is still able, (like the nation-state), to create solidarity and loyalty among its citizens. The institutional expression of multinational character of the nation-state is federalism – while the "we feeling" is created because, in as much as the political system encourages multiple identities, it still molds them as complementary.

Though the model of the state-nation is offered as a deviation from that of the nation-state, Linz and Stepan emphasize that it is difficult to define the differences between the two models, and that it is plausible to maintain that every stable multi-national state is also a nation-state, as it demands a certain degree of identification and loyalty and rejects the demand to disintegrate the state into its national or particular components. Linz and Stepan emphasize that it is impossible to establish the loyalty that exists in state-nations only upon "constitutional patriotism" (Habermas, 1998), that is upon the commitment to liberal-democracy and its institutions. Though the latter constitutes an important component of the legitimization of the state-nation, it is not enough, and additional elements are needed, not necessarily "rational", but rather symbolic or emotional, that is the same as those, which characterize the classical nation-state.

Consequently, the existence of an overall national identity in the state-nation is expressed by the nature of the federal regime in Spain, Belgium and Canada. Stepan emphasizes that multinational States are characterized by "asymmetrical federalism", which means that within the federal system certain provinces are given excessive rights (mostly cultural) to prevent their secession (Stepan 2002). Before they had turned into multinational States, those were, at least constitutionally, regular nation-states which had preferred to cop with secessionism of national minorities by the asymmetrical federalism. In the case of Spain, this federalism emphasizes the fact that there is an overall dominant Spanish identity and that the asymmetrical federalism is supposed to protect the national minority culture from the dominant Spanish culture. Alternatively, the meaning of the asymmetry is that the existence of complementary identities characterizes only the inhabitants of Catalonia and the Basque Land, while the inhabitants of the rest of the provinces of Spain identify themselves directly as Spaniards, which means that for them Spain is a regular nation-state.

In addition to the distinction from the classical nation-state, Linz, Stepan and Yadav (2004, p. 9) distinguish the "state-nation" from yet a third model which they call "pure" or "extreme" multi-nationalism. In this case all resemblance to the classical nation-state is lost and the state is conceived as a confederation of nations where each nation is a nation-state in potential. The constitutional expression of such confederation could be a symmetrical federalism in which the state is conceived as culturally neutral and evenly remote from all the sub-units from which it is composed. In this case the state is being emptied of all symbols and meanings that usually evoke the "we feeling" while turning into a mere administrative system. Linz Stepan and Yadav think that symmetric multinational systems fail to create the "we feeling", which is needed for the existence of liberal democracy and consequently they are not stable as they threaten to disintegrate in any moment into their national components. Thus, Linz Stepan and Yadav do not think that the western democracies that are sometimes conceived as multinational (Spain, Belgium and Canada) are of the third type of "pure" multinationalism. Alternatively, it could be said, that if they are such, or aspire to become such, it means that they risk disintegration into their particular national components.

To what extent is this discussion relevant for Israel? First, it is important to note that Israel does not necessarily pass Stepan's test for a multinational state. While the Arabs are indeed a lingual and ethnic minority and demands to create an Arab national autonomy were raised by Arab politicians and intellectuals, there has never been an Israeli Arab separatist movement, or a demand to build a sovereignty or a State based upon the ethnic or the lingual cleavage. Furthermore, even in the case of a future Palestinian State, the Israeli-Arabs not only never expressed a desire to be a part of this State. On the contrary, they explicitly rejected suggestions coming from various elements within the Jewish society to "swap" territories with the future Palestinian State which would have resulted in putting their cities and villages under Palestinian authority.

Yet, even if we consider Israel to be a multinational country, the difference between the multinational democracies mentioned above and Israel is clear. If it is possible to consider Israel as a multinational country, there is no overall Israeli national identity that could serve as a framework for the creation of complementary identities (Israeli-Jew, Israeli-Arab, Israeli-Muslim and so on). On the contrary, the situation in Israel is that the national identities are not complementary, but in fact, antithetical. Any suggestion to cast Israel according to the model of these multinational countries would have to assume the existence of an overall Israeli national identity alongside the particular ethno-national Jewish, Arab and others. This last point should be emphasized because the post-Zionists – when they suggest casting Israel as one of these consociational democracies – suggest also casting it as a symmetrical bi-national state which lacks an overall national identity (Yakobson & Rubinstein, 2009, pp. 148-156, and see below, pp. 159-178). Alternatively, there seems to be a contradiction in the post-Zionists' approach: In as much as they seek the abolishment of the Jewish State, they do not seek its disintegration as a State or as an administrative system. Yet, a symmetrical bi-national structure leads to disintegration. It is clear, then, that the establishment of Israel as a multinational republic requires the existence of an overall Israeli identity. It is also clear that as the Spanish identity, which exists alongside the Catalan and Basque identities is indeed "Spanish", in the sense that it is not culturally neutral, so the Israeli overall identity would be Hebrew.

It is possible to see the asymmetrical multinational state from a slightly different angle. David Laitin (2007) maintains that the classical nation-state, the one that aspires for cultural homogeneity, is not suitable for the 21th century, and models of multinational states should be examined. Laitin identifies a national minority as a lingual minority (Ibid. 58-9). Consequently, the multinational state would be also multilingual, but it would not be a symmetrical multilingual state. According to Laitin, post-colonial states have developed a lingual model, which he calls 3 +/-1 (three plus minus one) (ibid., pp. 88-92). This means that every citizen needs two to four languages in order to be able to enjoy the services and the occupational options that those countries can offer. Laitin brings as an example India where the English (which was the language of the colonial rule) and the Hindi are languages which every Indian must know – if he or she wants to make use of the various options which the country could offer. Yet, in those states which belong to the Indian Federation where the official language is not Hindi, and it is the language of the educational system, the roads signs and all other official documentations, there is a need for a third language, which is the local sub-state language. As for the plus minus one, those who live in states in which the official language is Hindi need only two languages (which accounts for 3-1); while within the states of the Indian Federation there are national minorities which the Indian constitution protects, (for instance in the matters of elementary education.) Members of these minorities need 3 + 1 languages (if they live in a state whose official language is not Hindi).

In as much as the model that Laitin suggests is multilingual, it is clear that it is not symmetrical. There is not a similar status to all the languages, and those whose mother tongue is Hindi are not required to learn additional languages (besides the English). From this it is also clear that the overall Indian identity is not neutral towards the variety of the national minorities in India, as it is more Hindu. Though Laitin thinks that the model of the nation-state is inadequate, it is still possible to consider multinational or multilingual India as a nation-state.

What are the implications of Laitin's model for Israel? Israel had not inherited a post-colonial language, yet it is possible today to consider English as a national language, at least in the sense that every Israeli who wishes to succeed economically or professionally should have an elementary familiarity with the English language. The Hebrew language is necessary in Israel. Consequently, the model that seems to be suitable for Israel is two minus one, or maybe three minus one. Thus, Israelis whose mother tongue is not Hebrew, especially Arabs, would have to learn an additional language. As such, it is obvious that the overall Israeli identity according to this model would be Hebrew.

Laitin's model (as well as Linz and Stepan's) is that of a federal State, yet, it is still questionable whether the Israeli multiculturalism should be casted in this form. As noted above (pp. 63-64), there are good reasons not to do so. Further, unlike the post colonials societies in Asia and Africa set as examples by Laitin, which are characterized by a linguistic variety, in Israel, at least from a linguistic point of view, the situation is very simple: most of the Israelis, if not all of them, speak Hebrew, and the dominance of the Hebrew is clear and unquestioned. Indeed, in as much as Laitin considers the model of the nation-state inadequate, he still points to an exception as, according to him, the former Soviet countries are developing according to the model of the classical nation-state. Yet, this could be truer for Israel, as the dominance of the Hebrew language here is much higher than that of the national languages in those countries.

Ethnic Democracy

In post-communist Eastern Europe we encounter what might look like a deviation from the classical model of the nation-state. Countries such as Latvia, Estonia, and Slovakia were defined in their constitutions as the States of the dominant ethnic nationality and not of a nation that is identified with the citizen-body. The Israeli sociologist Sammy Smooha emphasized the resemblance between these countries and Israel and suggested that Israel is an archetype of a special type of democracy –"ethnic democracy" which he distinguished from liberal democracy, or a "civic democracy". "Ethnic democracy" combines the dominance of one ethnic group with the existence of limited individual and collective rights to those who do not belong to the dominant core nation (Smooha, 1990, p. 391; Smooha, 1997, pp. 199-200).

Smooha's notion of Israel as an 'ethnic democracy' did not flatter Israel as a (liberal) democracy, yet it was an attempt to 'normalize' Israel and Israeli national identity by classifying it alongside other democracies that are 'ethnic' (Smooha, 1990, p. 391; Smooha, 2000, pp. 565-6; Smooha, 2002, p. 477). Indeed, Smooha's model was heavily influenced by the classical typology, which divided European nationalisms into western/ civic/liberal on one hand, and eastern/ethnic/illiberal, on the other hand. Within this typology, Zionism, as an Eastern European phenomenon has been traditionally classified as 'ethnic' (Shimoni, 1995, pp. 46-51). Here, the reawakening of Eastern European 'ethnic' nationalisms had also contributed to the idea that maybe Israel is not unique in its national identity, (as it was assumed before). Indeed some of Smooha's examples of ethnic democracy discussed below are from contemporary Eastern Europe, namely Estonia, Latvia and Slovakia.

Smooha's model came under attack from both 'left' and 'right'. The debate tended to focus on the question whether the 'ethnic' political community that the model describes in general, and Israel in particular, could be properly termed a 'democracy' (Dowty 1999; Smooha, 2002, p. 495). The criticism from the left considered the concept 'ethnic democracy' as a contradiction in terms and consequently the countries, which are 'ethnic' as non-democratic, or, as 'ethnocracies' (Ghanem, Rouhana and Yiftachel 1998; Yiftachel 1999). It also questioned the stability of this model, especially in the case of Israel (Yiftachel, 1992). The main thrust of Smooha's critics from the right was the well-known criticism against the civic/ethnic typology of nationalism, that is the idea that there is no pure civic nationalism, or that there is no 'neutral' nation-state and that consequently, as Alan Dowty (1999, p.9) observes 'Israel's link to ethnicity is not unique'. From this point of view Israel was a western liberal democracy, though maybe stained (Neuberger, 2000). One of the bold attempts to see Israel in this light has been Alexander Yakobson and Amnon Rubinstein's *Israel and the Family of Nations* (2009).

Yet, there was something in common to Smooha and his critics from both left and right. While they disagreed about the question to what extent the ethnicity of Israel would render it a democracy, or about what, if anything, is to be done in order to improve the democracy in Israel, they all shared the notion that Israel's national identity is not unique. Some classify Israel according to the traditional typology alongside with other countries that are 'ethnic'; others would classify it with other countries that are 'civic'. Still others see the dichotomy civic/ethnic as invalid. Yet, all seem to agree with Dowty (1999, p. 8) that Israel 'is not a category by itself'. There are many other States in which ethnicity is likewise closely intertwined with the definition of the State'. To the extent that the Israel was singled out as unique, its uniqueness was attributed either to external conditions or to the absence of certain policies rather than to its link to ethnicity.

To what extent, then, is Israel's national identity unique when compared to those "ethnic democracies"? Here it seems that, notwithstanding Smooha, the fusion of religion and nationality and the absence of a recognition of a territorial civic nation, which characterizes the present national ethos in Israel is indeed unique, and that to the extent that it could be labeled as 'ethnic', as Smooha claims, it would be so unique as to create a category by its own. As we are going to see, unlike the case of Israel, all eastern-European countries cited by Smooha as 'ethnic' still retain the basic identity of citizenship and nationality. In other words, to the extent that these countries consider themselves as belonging to a particular ethnic nation, they still recognize the existence of a territorial 'civic nation' which is identified with the citizen body, and which is multiethnic. While this 'civic' nation is indeed culturally biased in favor of the dominant ethnicity, it still enables members of non-core minorities to integrate into the dominant culture and to be equal members of the (territorial) nation.

Israel national identity and the ethnic/civic nationalism dichotomy

The traditional typology had divided European nationalism into two categories: western civic nationalism, and eastern ethnic nationalism. According to this typology, west-European nationalism was civic, that is it had a territorial, or civic or political definition of the nation, while East-European nationalism defined the nation ethnically or culturally (Plamenatz, 1973). Indeed, this classical dichotomy lies at the base of Smooha's model of 'ethnic democracy'. To what extent, then, can the fusion of religion and nationality be classified as 'ethnic'? Indeed, as predominantly East-European national movement, Zionism has been traditionally classified as 'ethnic'. Yet, I distinguish here between pre-independence Zionism, which was a movement for national self-determination and 'Zionism' as a post-independence formal national ethos of Israel. It is the link to ethnicity of the current post-independence 'Zionist' ethos that I wish to examine now.

As Rogers Brubaker notes, the notion of 'ethnic nationalism' is somewhat misleading, because it immediately invokes the notion of a national identity which is based primarily upon blood ties, race, common (biological) origin, and so on. Yet, while ethnic nationalists certainly invoke all those elements when they speak about the nation, their prime goal seems to lie elsewhere. What they are really interested in is the success or predominance of a certain culture, which they identify with their ethnicity (Brubaker, 1999, pp. 59-60). This means that all nationalisms considered as 'ethnic' are also, to a certain extent 'civic', because they are ethno-cultural (Brubaker, 1998, p. 299). The 'civic' potential lies in the fact that culture, as opposed to descent, is something that could be acquired, which makes it possible for members of other ethnic groups to join the dominant culture (which 'belongs' to the dominant ethnic group) in the nation building process, thus creating a territorial multiethnic (civic) nation. It was in this respect that Will Kymlicka (1995, p. 24) remarks that '[w]hat distinguishes 'civic' nations from 'ethnic' nations is not the absence of any cultural component to national identity, but rather the fact that anyone can integrate into the common culture, regardless of race or color'. As most 'ethnic' nationalisms are indeed ethno-cultural, 'ethnic' countries could at least potentially integrate or could allow integration into the dominant culture. Here pre-independence Jewish-Zionist nationalism was not different as it was ethno-cultural and identified the national Jew as "Hebrew". Yet, the post-independence Israeli case is different for its national identity does not have a cultural element and is based solely upon descent. Consequently it does not allow, even potentially, the integration of members of non-Jewish minorities into the dominant culture.

Indeed, as it has been pointed above, the fusion of religion and nationality certainly cannot be classified as civic nationalism. Yet, in as much as we accept Brubaker's notion of ethnic nationalism, it could not be classified also as "ethnic nationalism", as it is not ethno-cultural.

Israel does not have a constitution, which should define the Jewishness of the Jewish State. Here it might be helpful to use Israeli Supreme Court Rulings, as the later is considered by many Israelis, as a sort of substitution for the constitution, or as an institution which contains in its rulings the constitutional foundations of Israel. Alan Dowty, asks 'of what, minimally, does the "Jewishness" of the Jewish State consist?' He points out that the Israeli Supreme Court, in dealing with the eligibility of parties to participate in elections, had tried to answer this question. Acceptance of Israel as a "Jewish State", the court ruled, means at least: (a) maintenance of a Jewish majority, (b) the right of Jews to immigrate, and (c) tie with the Jewish communities outside Israel (Dowty, 1999, p. 10).

What would strike one immediately in the ruling of the Supreme Court is that this minimal definition of the Jewishness of Israel lacks any cultural elements. Thus, for instance, it does not say that the (minimal) Jewishness of Israel means the predominance of the Hebrew language or any "Jewish" culture.[7] All it says deals with demography and descent rather than with culture: A Jewish State is one that has a Jewish majority and gives predominance to Jewish immigration.

There are several reasons for the fact that the fusion of faith and nationality creates a national identity, based on descent and not on culture. First, but not necessarily the most important, is that the fusion of religion and nationality resulted in the adoption of the (Orthodox) religious criterion for belonging to the nation: a Jew is someone that either was born to a Jewish mother or has converted to Judaism (Smooha, 2001b, p. 50).

Putting aside the question of conversion, this definition has no cultural dimension and is based upon descent only. As for conversion, this has a cultural element, yet the non-missionary character of (traditional) Judaism makes it negligible. Any attempt to reform conversion has to tackle the problem that there is no agreement among Israelis or among the Jewish communities on any (reformed) version of conversion. This brings us to the second reason for the absence of a cultural dimension in the "official" definition of the Jewishness of Israel: not only is there no agreement among Jews to one accepted version of Judaism, but also, today Judaism is a universal religion in the sense that Jews are members of various nations and various cultures. Thus, defining the "Jewish People" culturally or ethnically is almost impossible. This leads us to the third and most important reason for the absence of any cultural definition of Jewishness of Israel: the absence of agreement among Israelis about what Judaism means. All in all, we come to a somewhat odd definition of the Jewish State: A Jewish State is a State in which most of the citizens have a Jewish mother.

Thus, Smooha's ethnic democracy Eastern European examples have chosen to express their links with ethnicity in clear cultural terms (the most important being the predominance of the national language). In those countries members of the dominant ethnic group are privileged because they share the culture which the State has declared as privileged; while in Israel it is the other way around – A certain culture (that is the Hebrew culture) is privileged, because it is shared by an ethnic group which has been declared by the State as privileged.

Ethnic democracy, post-Communist Eastern Europe, and Israel

When they regained independence after the collapse of the Soviet Union, both Latvia and Estonia legislated citizenship laws which automatically conferred citizenship upon those who were citizens of these countries on the eve of their annexation to the Soviet Union and to their descendants, while the other (mainly Russian speakers who had settled in both countries at the time of the Soviet occupation), were made eligible to apply for citizenship in as much as certain conditions were fulfilled: Residency requirements, speaking the local national (titular) language and a declaration that the candidate had never been connected to the Soviet occupation. From all those conditions, the most demanding one was the language barrier, (as most of the Russian speaking minorities in both countries did not speak the local language.) The outcome of these laws of citizenship was a drastic change in the social and political status of some third of the total population of these two countries. The Russian speaking minorities had turned from 'citizens' (in as much as this concept could be applied to the dictatorships of the Soviet era) to 'strangers'. The fact that the mastering of the national (titular) language in both countries had been made precondition for working in the public sector led to a wide dismissal of Russian speakers who were replaced by members of the local 'ethnic' nationality. All in all, the non-inclusive policy in both countries carried with it obvious social and economic advantages for those who were considered as members of the core 'ethnic' nation (Linz & Stepan, 1996, pp. 402-3; Smith G. et al., 1998, p. 94).

Indeed, there seems to be much resemblance between Israel, on one hand, and Latvia and Estonia, on the other, in the predominance of one ethnic group, (i.e. the Jews), which are considered as the group which 'owns' the State, and in the social and economic advantages which come from this ethnic dominance. Yet, some important differences should be observed as well. First, both Estonia and Latvia still retain, beside the notion of an 'ethnic' nation, also a notion of a civic nation which is created by the fusion of nationality and citizenship. Moreover, the laws of citizenship (which meant the denationalization of the Russian speakers) were justified also by the vision of the nation-state in which the nation and the state overlap, that is in which the citizen-body constitutes a nation (Smith G. et al., 1998, p. 97; Linz & Stepan 1996, pp. 432-3). In other words, both Latvia and Estonia are republics, which means that in their constitutions they entrust sovereignty to 'the people', which is identified with the citizen-body that is multiethnic.

It should be emphasized that citizenship in both countries was defined on the basis of the pre 1940 citizenship (which was 'civic' and included also individuals who were not ethnic Estonians or ethnic Latvians, among them individuals of Russian origin.) Furthermore, the citizenship laws in Latvia and Estonia still had made it possible for Russian speakers to join the (civic) nation. The criteria, which would have made them eligible for citizenship, were indeed civic: residence, knowing the national (titular) language and so on. Svetlana Diatchkova (2005, p. 113) remarks about Latvia that 'regarding the "full membership" of minorities in the core nation and in the state, their exclusion is not systematically based on ethnicity, for proficiency in the State language and loyalty to the Latvian nation-state are much more important conditions for inclusion than ethnicity'. Thus, in both Latvia and Estonia, exists in addition to the concept of a core ethnic nation also a notion of a civic territorial nation. The symbiosis between the two concepts is visible in the preamble of the Estonian Constitution. Priit Järve notes that the preamble, which, according to him, constitutes 'the legal foundation of the ethnic democracy in Estonia', uses two different concepts: [*eesti rahvus*] which means Estonian (ethnic) nation and [*Eesti rahvas*] which means 'the people (citizens) of Estonia regardless of their ethnic origin. According to Järve, the former refers to 'ethnic nation' and the latter to the 'civic nation' (Järve, 2000, p.1, p. 7). Järve quotes from the preamble:

> Unwavering in their faith and with a steadfast will to secure and develop a state which is established on the inextinguishable right of the Estonian people [in Estonian: *Eesti rahvas*] to national self-determination […] which shall guarantee the preservation of the Estonian nation [*eesti rahvus*] and its culture throughout the ages, the Estonian people [*Eesti rahvas*] adopted […] the following Constitution. … (Järve, 2000, p. 1).

Järve's interpretation of the preamble is very similar to Smooha's (2001b, p.73):

> The logic of the Preamble, not very explicit though, is simple: the citizens (all ethnic groups together) establish a state and adopt a constitution to preserve one ethnic group— the Estonians— and its culture. Thus, one ethnic group has manifested its specific claims to the State in which it establishes itself constitutionally as a single core ethnic nation. (Järve, 2000, p. 7).

In a more recent paper Järve (2005) seems to abandon this interpretation and sees ethnic democracy in Estonia an intermediate stage towards liberal democracy (see below).

Yet, it seems that both, Järve and Smooha, ignore and fail to quote the civic elements of the preamble. First, it should be noted that self-determination is proclaimed as a right of the Estonian civic nation, rather than the right of the ethnic nation. Furthermore, before the preservation of the ethnic Estonian and its culture is mentioned, the preamble states that the purpose of self-determination is 'to protect internal and external peace and provide security for the social progress and general benefit of present and future generations'. These could be interpreted as republican statements that refer to the future of the Estonian people that is the 'civic nation'. Therefore, it seems that as far as the constitution is concerned, 'ethnic democracy' is expressed more in terms of cultural domination and privileges, than in purely ethnic ones: it establishes the domination of the Estonian culture and not that of the Estonian ethnic core nation. While cultural domination entails a 'favored status in general and on the job market in particular when compared to individuals who are not fluent in the Estonian language' (Järve, 2000, p.13), it is still important that this bias in favor of the core nation is expressed in cultural terms and that as far as citizens' rights and welfare are concerned the state is indeed 'ethnically neutral'.

Indeed, Estonia is a republic: Chapter 1 article 1 of the constitution states: "Estonia is an independent and sovereign democratic republic wherein the supreme power of the state is held by the people". Here, the people are identified with the citizens and not with the core ethnic nation. The same is true for the Republic of Latvia: Article 1 of the constitution of Latvia states that 'Latvia is an independent democratic republic' while Article 2 of their constitution states: "The sovereign power of the State of Latvia is vested in the people of Latvia".[8] Thus, at least from a formal point of view, the constitutions of both Latvia and Estonia have made the provisions for the creation of a multi-ethic (civic) nation. An analysis of Slovakia's constitution, also singled out by Smooha as 'ethnic democracy', yields similar results. Like in the Estonian case, it seems that the Preamble of the Constitution of Slovakia expresses "[T]he ethno-national ideological foundation of the Slovak Republic" (Van Duin, 2001, p. 123):

> *We, the Slovak nation,* mindful of the political and cultural heritage of our forebears, and of the centuries of experience from the struggle for national existence and our own statehood, in the sense of the spiritual heritage of Cyril and Methodius and the historical legacy of the Great Moravian Empire, proceeding from the natural right of nations to self-determination, *together with members of national minorities and ethnic groups living on the territory of the Slovak Republic,* in the interest of lasting peaceful cooperation with other democratic states, seeking the application of the democratic form of government and the guarantees of a free life and the development of spiritual culture and economic prosperity, that is*, we, citizens of the Slovak Republic,* adopt through our representatives the following Constitution. …(Emphasis added).

Again, the symbiosis between the notion of the ethnic nation and that of the civic nation could be easily discerned. The ethnic bias of the preamble is obvious: it singles out the Slovak heritage or Slovak 'ethnic nation'. Nevertheless, it also contains important civic elements: it is still a declaration of all the citizens, including the minorities, and is ratified equally by all of them. In other words, as the preamble and Article 1 of the constitution declares, Slovakia is a republic in which, as Article 2 declares, "State power is derived from citizens". This seems to refute Smooha's claim that 'in its constitution Slovakia declares itself as the State of the Slovak nation rather as the State of its citizens' (Smooha, 2002, p. 476). In addition, the preamble contains also a republican declaration which says that the purpose of Slovakia is also "lasting peaceful cooperation with other democratic states", "the application of the democratic form of government", "the guarantees of a free life" and "the development of spiritual culture and economic prosperity"; all are clearly republican statements which relate to the welfare of the citizens or the civic nation rather that that of the core ethnic nation.

The constitution, then, distinguishes between the Slovak 'ethnic nation', on one hand, and the citizen body, which constitutes a 'civic' nation, on the other. It is interesting to note how the meaning of the word 'we' changes throughout the preamble. It starts with the Slovak 'ethnic nation' ('We the Slovak Nation') yet at the end of the preamble it refers to the 'civic' nation ('we, citizens of the Slovak Republic'). According to the preamble, the Slovak civic nation is made of the Slovak ethnic nation plus 'members of national minorities and ethnic groups' who joined it. The careful wording of the preamble should be noted here: it does not say "We the Slovak nation, ..., together with other national minorities and ethnic groups", but rather "... together with *members* of other nationalities and ethnic groups". Thus, members of other nationalities have joined us, the Slovak (ethnic) Nation, as individuals, not as collectives, to create the 'We', which is the citizen body (or the Slovak 'civic nation') of the end of the preamble. Thus, according to its constitution, though Slovakia is a multiethnic State it is not a multinational State, but rather a nation-state and its citizen body constitutes a civic (Slovak) nation.

Though Smooha draws some of his evidence for the existence of ethnic democracy in Eastern European countries from their constitutions he ignores the fact that, unlike Israel, all his East-European examples are republics. Indeed, it could be claimed that Estonia, Latvia, Slovakia and many other post-Soviet East-European countries are republics only in name. Therefore, Brubaker (1996, p. 105) dismisses all republican or constitutional declarations of these countries as something which is directed mainly towards international audience and does not affect the 'ethnic' political and social reality. Indeed, as Smooha rightly observes, within the formal framework of republicanism it is still possible to conduct 'ethnic' policies, as the core ethnic nation numerical majority enables it to 'rule democratically on its own account without the necessary political support and legitimacy of the none-core groups' (Smooha, 2001b, p. 37). Though the Slovakian constitution was ratified by the citizen body, the Hungarian parties in Slovakia did not vote in favor of the constitution, while in Estonia and Latvia the Russian speakers could not possibly ratify the constitution because they were not citizens. On the other hand, Brubaker's position is sharply repudiated by Kuzio (2001, p. 148) who claims that "the majority of the former European communist states can no-longer be defined as 'ethnic' or 'nationalizers'. The majority of them are territorial, civic and inclusive democracies … as defined by their willingness to allow integration for all into the societal culture."

Nevertheless, without entering the debate between Kuzio and Brubaker we can establish how Israel is different. At least on the formal or constitutional level Latvia, Estonia and Slovakia recognize the existence of a 'civic' nation and make provisions for the integration of non-core minorities into the dominant culture. Whether integration would happen, its scope and shape are dependent upon State policies (or the wish of the members of the dominant core nation), and the wish of the members of the non-core minorities. Indeed, one of the features of an ethnic democracy, according to Smooha, is that it has a 'no assimilation policy' (Smooha, 2001b, p. 27). Yet, in the case of Israel it is not that Israel has a 'no assimilation policy', but rather that it is impossible for it to have an assimilation policy. In order to have such a policy, there must be a concept of a national entity that assimilates. The Estonian, Latvian and Slovakian cases are different. Since there is a notion of civic nation, integration is still an option. When Linz and Stepan discuss 'ethnic democracy' in both Estonia and Latvia they say that in both countries there are in fact two competing models: the dominant model is of 'ethnic democracy' which indeed has a no assimilation policy. Yet the other model 'makes a major effort to assimilate minorities into national culture and give no special recognition to minority political or cultural rights' (Linz and Stepan, 1996, p. 429).

In as much as Linz and Stepan consider the first model as dominant, it seems that in recent years an integrative approach has developed. Whether or not the original meaning of the laws of citizenship was to dispossess the Russophones or even to drive them out of the country, the present policies of both Latvia and Estonia seem to be of an integrative nature. This was no doubt also a result of international and especially of European pressures and supervision, as both countries had applied and were eventually accepted to the European Union (Kuzio, 2001, p. 145, Järve, 2005, pp. 76-7, Diatchkova, 2005, p. 112; Yiftachel and Ghanem, 2004, p. 776). Furthermore, there are also indications that the Russophone minority in these countries – while having no interest and ability to assimilate into the 'ethnic' or core nation, acknowledges that the local languages should be mastered by the Russophones. Consequently they 'well might be loyal citizens of Estonia and identify with the 'state-nation' of Estonia (Stepan, 1998, p. 234 and see also Laitin, 1996b, pp.11-12). Indeed, it seems that in the short run the minorities in Smooha's

Eastern European examples accepted relatively quietly their new condition and the 'ethnicization' of the state because many of their members considered the possibility of joining the (civic) nation in the long run to enjoy the social and economic benefits from which they were deprived in their present status.

All this analysis is completely irrelevant for Israel. As there is no Israeli civic nation, it is impossible to include in the nation any non-Jewish minorities. Thus, unlike the case of Latvia or Estonia, the Arab minority of Israel has no similar incentive to support the ethnicization of the state, not in the short run and not in the long run. Indeed, according to Smooha, the best that Israel could hope for is 'improved ethnic democracy'. The latter is conditioned, so it seems, by peace and by the establishment of a Palestinian state, which will make members of the Arab minority in Israel more receptive towards the so-called 'Jewish-Zionist' character of the State.

Yet, even in this improved ethnic democracy the Arab minority will not integrate into the social and economic Israeli infrastructures, but will only benefit from the new opportunities which will be created by the peace, that is cultural and trade relations with the Arab world and serving as mediators between Israel and the Arab world (Smooha, 2000, p. 613). Even in the 'improved ethnic democracy' the Arabs are not expected to enjoy the same benefits, which Israel confers upon its Jewish members. In this respect, Oren Yiftachel (1992, p. 115) has pointed out that Smooha's model of 'ethnic democracy' is not stable and Smooha's claim that 'the Arabs do not intend to hurt the State or dissociate themselves from it … must be contingent upon the Arabs making some gains within the Israeli economy or political system. … Such gains have not been achieved, casting doubt over the accuracy of Smooha's observations.' Yiftachel's observations could be contested, and it could be claimed that the Arab minority, though the poorest sector in the Israeli society, has gained substantial benefits within the Israeli "ethnic democracy" (when their situation is compared to the situation of Arabs in Arab countries), and that until now, there are no indications of secessionism among the Arab minority in Israel. Nevertheless, it is obvious that the model of ethnic democracy carries an inherent contradiction. In as much as the commitment of the Israeli elite to democracy is genuine – as Smooha himself claims – and in as much as this commitment is transferred to the Israeli public as a basic characteristic of Israel (alongside with its being "Jewish"), it is obvious that Yiftachel's observation is well founded, and not only for Israel, but for the model of ethnic democracy in general. Furthermore, it is possible to question Smooha's claims about the stability of ethnic democracy in Israel, given the events of October 2000, or the recent publication of what has been known as "The Future Vision Documents" by four important bodies of Israel's Arab sector, suggesting Israel be transformed into a non-national State ('a state of all its citizens') or a bi-national state (see discussion below, pp. 204-214).

It is questionable, then, whether Israel could be seen as an archetype for the model of ethnic democracy, as Smooha claims, or only as its variant, or indeed 'a category by its own'. Smooha questions whether his Eastern European examples will follow Israel and produce a 'viable ethnic democracy'. Yet, the viability of the ethnic democracy in Israel seems to be its 'stability', that is the fact that it is a political dead end. Setting Israel as an archetype of ethnic democracy prevents Smooha from giving enough credit to the possibility that ethnic democracy in East-Europe, though not 'viable', could be interpreted as a means for nation-building or as a transitional phase towards a liberal democracy, a conclusion reached by two of his fellow researchers, Järve (2005, pp. 78-9) and Diatchkova (2005, p. 114).

Ernest Gellner's division of the spread of nationalism in Europe into time zones could be helpful here. According to Gellner (1994b, pp. 113-18) the industrialized world is bound to conform to the 'nationalist imperative', which demands the existence 'high cultures' linked to strong States. The

Eastern European type of nationalism rose in what Gellner calls Time Zone III, which was characterized by the existence of several competing weak or 'low' cultures, on one hand, and a weak political systems, or States, on the other. According to Gellner, the difference between the so called 'civic' or western nationalism, on one hand, and 'ethnic' or eastern nationalism, on the other, should not be attributed to the narrow-mindedness or the brutality of the (ethnic) nationalists, but rather to the fact that, unlike the case in the west, in the east there was no ready high culture and consequently "in order to make them conform to the nationalist imperative …was bound to take a great deal of forceful cultural engineering." (Gellner, 1983, pp. 100-1). Gellner's observation means that once this 'national imperative' is satisfied by the creation of a high culture that is married to a strong State the distinction between East and West disappears. From this point of view, the whole concept of 'ethnic democracy' could become problematic, as Smooha's Eastern European examples could be seen not as a different type of democracies, but rather, as countries which take different kind of democratic measures needed to carry out this 'cultural engineering'. Thus, David Laitin sums up the outcomes of his and other's research concerning the possibility of the assimilation of minorities in the post-Soviet states:

> The results of the research are directly in the opposite to those scholars of the post-Soviet world who claims that there are "primordial" eternal identities. Yet, if Bavarians could have been developed to "Germans", surely Ukrainians could develop to Russians. And If Italians in New York could become Americans, surely Russians in Talin could become Estonians. (Laitin, 1996b, p. 4).

Similarly, Vello Pettai (1996, p. 49) argues that the Latvians are not moving towards consociational or ethno-political structure but rather to the establishment within one or two generations of 'cultural hegemony within the borders of their state, similar to the achievements of the French culture in France'. Alternatively, if we wish to retain the concept of 'ethnic democracy', then it becomes transitional. Yet, Smooha's model precludes such a possibility: ethnic democracy could either move towards an 'improved ethnic democracy' or fall back to non-democratic regime: it could not cease to be 'ethnic' and become a 'civic' western-type nation-state. By this Smooha seems to project from his Israeli archetype onto his Eastern European examples: it is impossible indeed to interpret ethnic democracy in Israel as a means for nation building or as transitional.

In addition, Israel could not serve as an archetype for ethnic democracy, because the prevailing cultural conditions in Israel are very different from those in Smooha's East-European examples, (or in Gellner's Zone 3 countries.) The predominance of the Hebrew culture in Israel resembles more the countries of Gellner's Time Zone I, where both a strong State and a strong culture exist. This predominance is unquestionable, it is not just political,s but social: it could not be attributed only to the 'ethnicity' of the State or to its nationalizing policies. In Gellner's (1983, pp. 50-8) terminology, the Hebrew culture is a 'high culture', which creates a homogeneous medium in which a modern industrialized society could function. If 'ethnic democracy' was needed during the first years of independence to create an hegemonic Hebrew 'high culture', to day it is used as an instrument for the marginalization of the Arabs. Thus, today in Israel ethnic democracy is not necessary for nation building, at least it is not necessary to achieve a cultural hegemony. Unlike the Estonian case, in which the Russophones do not speak the Estonian language, most Israelis – if not all – speak Hebrew. Neither is it the Latvian case, in which the Russophones are the majorities in the cities (Linz and Stepan,

1996, p. 432). The situation in Israel is somewhat unforeseen in Gellnerian terms: it is the case where the Israeli or Hebrew nation already exists, yet it is not recognized by the state to which it is supposed to be 'married', nor it is recognized by its own members. What the Hebrew high culture needs now is a formal civic definition, which would establish the formal conditions for membership in the Nation.

Israel as a Diaspora Nationalism

The most comprehensive attempt in recent years to normalize the Israeli case is Yakobson and Rubinstein's important book *Israel and the Family of Nations* (2003, 2009). This book was written explicitly to defend Israel mainly, so it seems, from post-Zionist's criticism. Though the book was written from a so-called "Zionist" point of view, the authors' approach is certainly different from what has been accepted in the past. As noted above, not very long ago, the notion of the uniqueness of the Israeli case had been the accepted wisdom both among academic scholars and among the so called "Zionists". The new and bold aspect of Yakobson and Rubinstein's book is their claim, based upon a vast comparative material, that Israel is a western liberal democracy, or that it is indeed "a nation like all nations".

Thus, the authors set themselves against the idea that the Israeli 'Law of Return' and Israel's relation with the Diaspora demonstrate Israel's unique relation to ethnicity or religion. Yakobson and Rubinstein say that there are other countries, which have a special relationship with a Diaspora, and consequently, many countries have "laws of return" which make it easier for members of the Diaspora to naturalize. One of the examples which Yakobson and Rubinstein introduce is that of the German law of return, (paragraph 116 in the German constitution), which grants automatic citizenship to refugees and uprooted people of German descent. Yet, Yakobson and

Rubinstein claim, "the Federal Republic of Germany is indisputably a liberal democracy" (ibid., p. 128). From this, they conclude also that Israel is "a clear liberal democracy".

Yet, there is an important difference between Israel and Germany – Germany is a republic, while Israel is not. In its constitution Germany is defined as a republic or as the State of "the German people" (preamble). When Article 8 of the constitution declares that "all Germans have the right to assemble peacefully", it identifies "a German" with a German citizen. Thus, according to Article 116 "a German" is "a person who possesses German citizenship or who has been admitted to the territory of the German Reich within the boundaries of December 31, 1937 as a refugee or expellee of German ethnic origin or as the spouse or descendant of such person." Two things should be noted here: a) According to the German constitution every German citizen is "a German", which includes, of course, persons who are not from ethnic-German origin. b) The language of the constitution concerning the persons for whom the law of return applies should be noted: they are not defined as "Germans", but as persons of "German origin". They become Germans the minute they have been admitted to a German territory. In other words, though Germany has a law of return, which gives automatic citizenship to persons of German origin, Germany is not the state of the "ethnic Germans", but rather, the state of the German civic territorial people. This is, of course, extremely different from the Israeli case.

Yakobson and Rubinstein fail in a similar manner when they draw a comparison between Israel, on one hand, and Greece and Armenia, on the other. Yakobson and Rubinstein maintain that Israel's type of nationalism should be classified as a special type known as "Diaspora nationalism". The two other nationalisms, which usually have been associated with this type of nationalism, are Armenia and Greece. Here Yakobson and Rubinstein follow Anthony Smith who, in a paper which was dedicated to the question how unique Jewish nationalism has been, rejects the notion of uniqueness and emphasizes the similarity between the Armenians, the Greeks and the Jews, especially that all three groups are ethno-religious groups which had turned out to be completely identified with a certain religion or church – the Armenians with the Gregorian Church and the Greeks with the Greek Orthodox Church (Smith, 1995a, p. 1).

Yakobson and Rubinstein (2009, p. 86) claim that the relation between Israel and the Jewish Diaspora is not unique and that Armenia and Greece, like Israel, retain a unique relations with their Diasporas and that each of them have "law of return" whish makes it easier for members of the Diasporas to naturalize. Yet, from Smith's claim about the similarity between Jewish nationalism, on one hand, and Armenian and Greek nationalism, on the other, it is impossible to deduce what Yakobson and Rubinstein are suggesting; that the formal national identity and the regime of Israel are equal to those of Armenia and Greece. Smith is dealing with nationalism and national movements for self-determination. However, here we are dealing with definitions of formal identities and with the structure of the regime (that is after independence). Therefore, even if there is a resemblance between Israel, Greece and Armenia, especially in regard to the relations they maintain with their Diasporas, unlike Israel, both Armenia and Greece are republics. In other words, the latter distinguish, at least constitutionally, between the Diaspora nation and the republican civic territorial nation, and entrust sovereignty to the latter.

As Greece recognizes the existence of an ethno-religious Greek nation and sees Greece as its homeland. Greece is not the State of this ethno-religious nation, but rather of the Greek territorial nation (which includes persons who are not ethnic-Greeks and do not belong to the Greek Orthodox Church). The Greek constitution proclaims that the Greek government is based upon the principle of popular sovereignty. Article 4 of the constitution states that,

"All Greeks are equal before the law" and that "Greek men and woman have equal rights and equal obligations".[9] It is obvious that the Greek constitution identifies "a Greek" as a Greek citizen and not as an ethnic-Greek. According to the Greek constitution, the Greeks constitute a people in the republican sense. The Greek "law of return" uses the term "ethnic-Greek" to designate those who are entitled for simplified naturalization procedures, and distinguishes it from "the Greek" which is used in the constitution.[10] Thus, from the Greek constitution's point of view, ethnic Greeks (that is members of the Greek Diaspora) have to go through naturalization processes (though simplified) in order to turn into citizens-Greeks, that is members of the Greek republican people. It is possible, of course, that all these republican statements have no influence on reality and, as Yakobson and Rubinstein maintain, the existence of a Turkish and Macedonian minorities in Greece created difficult problems and it is not certain that the Greeks were able to cope with these problems better than Israel has succeeded in coping with the problem of the Arab minority. Yet, one must ask why, (at least in the formal constitutional level), Israel was not declared as a republic; and why it does not distinguish between the civic territorial people, on one hand, and the Jewish Diaspora nation, on the other. This distinction clearly exists in the Greek law.

Like Greece, Armenia is a republic. The preamble of the Armenian constitution declares that the source of the constitution is in "The Armenian People". The constitution declares the commitment: "to ensure the freedom, general well-being and civic harmony of future generations" – all are clearly republican statements which identify the people with the citizen body. Paragraph 15 of the Armenian constitution declares that "Citizens, *regardless of national origin*, race, sex, language, creed, political or other persuasion, social origin, wealth or other status, are entitled to all the rights and freedoms, and subject to the duties determined by the Constitution and the laws". It is important to note that the constitution does not say "citizens *regardless of nationality*", but rather "*regardless of national origin*". This means that, unlike Israel, officially Armenia is not a multinational state, but rather a nation-state; it is comprised of people of various ethnicities, or of various national origin, but not of various nationalities. This means also that the Armenian constitution identifies "ethnic Armenian", not as an Armenian but rather, as someone of "Armenian origin". Thus article 14 of the constitution, which simplifies the naturalization procedures of ethnic-Armenians states: "The procedures for acquiring and terminating citizenship of the Republic of Armenia are determined by law. *Individuals of Armenian origin shall acquire citizenship of the Republic of Armenia through a simplified procedure.*" In other words, persons of Armenian origin, or of the Armenian Diaspora, in order to become "Armenians", that is members of the Armenian republican people, still have to go through naturalization procedures, though simplified.

Thus, Greece and Armenia are different from Israel, as those countries distinguish between the sovereign republican people and the Diaspora nation and demand from members of the Diaspora nation to go through naturalization procedures if they want to become members of the sovereign republican people. In Israel, on the other hand, there is no distinction between the sovereign nation and the Diaspora one, and the automatic citizenship conferred upon each immigrant who is considered Jewish only demonstrates it. The examples of Greece and Armenia show that a republican regime does not necessarily preclude special relations with a Diaspora nation.

The Post-Zionist Myth

The question of the uniqueness of Israel has also been brought up (perhaps mainly) by those referred to here as "post-Zionists". Yet, in as much as the latter share the notion of the abnormality of Israel, the model, which they introduce as a solution was abnormal as well. Unfortunately, normalization in Israel has been increasingly identified with the post-Zionist notion of the "citizens' State", according to which the Israeli State should be culturally neutral, or a symmetrical bi-national State, which equally reflects Jewish and Arab cultures. Consequently, it is different from the model of the nation-state offered here according to which the state gives priority to the national culture, which is clearly Hebrew.

The critics of post-Zionism are often accused of over-generalization. Tom Segev (2001, p. 112) claims that "there is no consolidated post-Zionist ideology", and Yehuda Shenhav, editor of the academic journal *Theory and Criticism* devoted to the promotion of "post-national, post-Zionist, Marxist and feminist thinking", testifies that post-Zionism is an "empty label". Similarly, Raz-Krakotzkin says that "post-Zionism is a sort of a general concept invented in order to push it into the same basket and defame those who do not completely identify with the establishment ... (Livne, 2001). Indeed, this may be so, yet the same could be said about what is known in Israel as "Zionism", yet it has never prevented post-Zionists from criticizing "the great damages" that "Zionism" has inflicted upon "the Palestinians and the Mizrachim (those who immigrate to Israel from Middle Eastern countries)" (ibid.). In other words, it is arguable whether the so-called "post-Zionism" is more ambiguous and less discerning than the so-called "Zionism". The post-Zionist myths have been to a great extent a reaction to "the New Zionist Myth" and as such they carry many of its basic ambiguities, especially the notion of the fusion of religion and nationality.

It seems that the best starting point for a discussion on post-Zionism, would be its characterization by one of its first and most outspoken protagonist, Uri Ram (1996). Unlike some his fellow post-Zionists, Ram thinks that post-Zionism could be defined and thus he recognizes in it six central orientations which contradicts the present "Zionist" ethos:

(a) Civic Israeli orientation (as opposed to Jewish ethnocentrism);

(b) An individual orientation (as opposed to collectivist one);

(c) An orientation to identify with "The State of Israel" (as opposed to the tendency to identify with *"Eretz Yisrael"* (*The Land of Israel*);

(d). An orientation to relate to the present and the near future (as opposed to the remote past and future);

(e) An orientation for cultural universalism and normalcy (as opposed to cultural particularism);

(f). Political tendency towards the left, especially to the *"Yesh Gvul"* movement[11] (as opposed to the tendency to the right and to *"Gush Emunim"*).

Ram opposes "post-Zionism" to what he calls "Neo-Zionism", and by this he divides the history of Zionism into three stages: (a) Traditional Zionism which, according to him, existed until the Six Days War; (b) Neo-Zionism, which had become dominant after the Six Days War and which is identified roughly with the Israeli right; (c) post-Zionism. In the present book I prefer a different categorization: (a) classical Zionism (until 1948); (b) "The New Zionist Myth"; (c) "post-Zionism". Thus I think that Ram, like most if not all of the Israelis, does not distinguish between Zionism as a movement for national self-determination (until independence) and the post-Independence State-Zionism called here "The New Zionist Myth".

As for Ram's first orientation, the civic Israeli orientation, indeed, the idea to turn Israel from a "Jewish State" into a "citizens' State" has turned out to be the central post- Zionist doctrine. Yet, it is important to note that the notion of the "citizens' State" which the post-Zionist are trying to promote, is different from that of the nation-state or the republic which is advocated by the present book. The latter identifies citizenship with nationality and consequently the liberal nation-state is both a national State and a State that belongs to its citizens. Yet, the post-Zionists, though they accept the notion of Israel as a State, which belongs to its citizens, reject, or at least remain vague, concerning Israel as a national State or as a republic. Thus, in his fifth orientation Ram conjectures that post-Zionism aspires for "cultural universalism" as opposed to cultural particularism or Jewish ethnocentrism. Yet if, as Gellner says, the modern State "has a monopoly on culture in as much as it has a monopoly on legitimate violence and even more than that", then post-Zionism rejects the notion of Hebraic Israel and sees Israel as cultureless or as culturally neutral. Ram maintains:

> Post-Zionism … is a political and cultural project … (which involves) an ideological and political struggle for the change of the Israeli collective identity … (which means among other things) an aspiration to the separation between nationality and state in Israel, that is an aspiration for the creation of universal legal framework in which there is no special stand for national tradition or to any ethnic group. (Michman, 1997, p. 81).

Thus, post-Zionists do not aspire for the normalization of Israel, that is for Israel to be a normal nation-state, but rather, to strip Israel from any national aspect, or as Ram phrases it (2006, p.153): "to untie the Gordian knot between the State and nationalism in Israel and by this to amend the democracy". Therefore, they aspire toward the creation, maybe for the first time in modern history, of a "universal" or a "neutral" State – "a kingdom of priests and a holy nation". In other words, post-Zionists are also post-nationalists (ibid., pp. 153 – 6), and in most cases even anti-nationalists: there is no post-Zionist nation or something close to it. The negation of any national aspect from the post-Zionist entity is expressed also by the fourth post-Zionist's orientation mentioned by Ram, that this entity is oriented towards the present and the near future. The post-Zionists occasionally criticizes the Zionists for inventing the national history; yet the post-Zionist "nation" does not have a history at all, not even an invented one, and we will come back to this subject.

It should be noted that Ram, like many other post-Zionists, does not demand the separation of religion from nationality – though they sometimes seem to express this demand (and see Kimmerling below) – but he demands the separation of nationality from the State, which is the creation of a non-national State. By this, he accepts, like many post-Zionists, the fusion of religion and nationality, or that the Jews are indeed a nation, but he actually deprives it from any political expression, that is, he rejects the idea that this identity or any other national identity, would be expressed by the State. In other words, while one of the traditional objections to Zionism has been that the Jews are not a nation (since Judaism is a religion), Ram does not deny the existence of "a Jewish nation", but rather, its right for self-determination. Thus, many post-Zionists are inverse "Zionists", or to that extent "cultural nationalists" or "Spiritual Zionists": they acknowledge the Jews as a nation while denying its right for self-determination. Similarly we can find in Kimmerling, another outspoken figure of post-Zionism, the following surprising declaration:

> Israel was established as a State of inhabitant-immigrants and as a Jewish national state on part of the ruins of the Palestinian society. Yet there is no doubt that the Jews in Israel constitute a nation and consequently entitle from a political and moral point of view to a self-determination and a sovereign state. (Kimmerling, 2001, p. 124).

The fusion of religion and nationality is noted, yet it seems to be limited to the Israeli Jews who constitute the nation. It could be assumed that the Arabs, unless they convert, could not join this "Jewish nation", even though it is a "post-Zionist" one. Nevertheless, after this unexpected recognition in the "Jewish nation" and its right for "self-determination and a sovereign State", it seems that this is not what Kimmerling is willing to grant it. Thus, he recommends "remolding of the State as consociational democracy" in which "there are more than one cultural, lingual, ethno-national, ethno-religious or national unit … in this situation the State, including it symbols and identity, must be neutral towards its subunits …" (ibid., p. 95). As such, the right of the "Jewish nation" for a "sovereign State" turns out to be nothing, but the division of the sovereignty between two "nationalities": "Jewish" and "Arab" within a "neutral" State. One can easily discern here the influence of classical liberalism's notion of the culturally neutral State.

The influence of classical liberalism is marked also on another post-Zionist orientation, the second in Ram's list: Individualism, as opposed to the collectivism, which characterizes the Zionist approach (see also Shapiro, 1977, pp. 25-34). It is indeed not difficult to understand Israeli's escape to "individualism" after so many years of the dominance of "The New Zionist Myth". The latter was essentially collectivist: it did not recognize the right of Jews in general and Israelis in particular to chose their own nationality and their own religion by enforcing upon them membership in the so called "Jewish People". Furthermore, it did not recognize the existence of an Israeli nation and subordinated the Israelis to the endless journey of the "Ingathering of the Exiles". All of this was also cloaked by a so-called "socialist" veil, which elevated collectivism along side with asceticism and contempt towards the "materialist" enjoyments of life. Nevertheless, the retreat to individualism is not an Israeli only phenomenon, and we have mentioned, within the current notion of a multiculturalism, there is a tendency to concentrate on human rights, or on what Sandel calls "procedural republic" (Taylor, 1998, Sandel, 1996). They do this in order to avoid the republican discussion and the decisions about the general character of the community, as such decisions could prefer a certain culture. Such an approach, so it was claimed above (pp. 125-133), raises the question of social solidarity. As we have seen, one answer which was given by multiculturalists to the question of solidarity among the citizens is Habermas' civic approach, or "constitutional patriotism", which finds its expression in another post-Zionism orientation which is mentioned by Ram, "orientation in space" which aims towards the State ("the State of Israel"). According to this approach:

> The collective is an aggregate of citizens who live in a common territory, under a common constitutional government, and conduct a common life. The democratic collective does not need a myth of origin or historical continuation or essential belonging. Identical communities could exist "below" the level of the State, or also "above" it, yet not necessarily with direct relation to the State which is supposed to be a republican democracy of all its citizens (and only of them). (Ram, 2006, pp. 178-9).

Indeed, the notion of the post-Zionist "citizens' State" testifies to a basic misunderstanding of the political unit. Aristotle, when he discussed the identity of the *polis*, said that if a wall had been built around the Peloponnese Peninsula it would not have created a *polis*. He meant that it was impossible to mark a certain territory and declare it as a *polis* and its inhabitants as citizens, as the political unit demands a bond between its citizens, which goes beyond the fact that they are living in proximity. The idea that all the inhabitants of a certain territory that is marked by the borders of Israel could be declared as "citizens" or as a "republican "people", thereby creating liberal democracy, has nothing to commend it. Why would "an aggregate of people who live in a common territory" accept the principle of majority rule? Why would it accept the principle that the State should support individual's rights? Why would it support equality for women? Why would "an aggregate of individuals" agree to become "a democratic republic"? There is something paradoxical in the fact that the post-Zionists, some of them post-modernists, adopt the idea

A NATION LIKE ALL NATIONS

that the consent to live in one state is "rational" or "self evident". This idea, originated in the Enlightenment's social-contract theory is a "modernist" idea *per se*. Alternatively, as mentioned above, "democratic culture" could not be separated from the national one. Consequently democracy could not be an occasional aggregate of persons. It needs a consensus, which is supplied by the nation.

The revival of classical liberalism, or post-Zionists' retreat to "procedural republicanism" is not coincidental, as the establishment of the political community on individual's rights enable the post-Zionists to overlook the question of duties which is connected to the question of social solidarity and hence to the national question. One of the conspicuous expressions of solidarity had been the readiness to serve in the national army.

The question for the post-Zionists is what would motivate the citizens in the "citizens' State" to fight for it and defend it? It is very difficult to find a post-Zionist thinker or anyone who supports the notion of the "citizens' State" who would openly support a mandatory conscription of the Arabs. In this spirit, Azmi Bishara, an enthusiastic supporter of the bi-national citizens' State, rejects the idea of mandatory conscription for the Arabs, claiming that an "individual's rights are firmer than his duties". As such, Bishara's democratic Arab nation (probably the only one in the Middle East) would have been established under the protection of Jewish bayonets. The absence of solidarity and readiness to contribute leaves the market as the only element upon which the post-Zionist could count. Kimmerling recommends the establishment of "a professional voluntary army" as, according to him, "the time for universal conscription has passed". Here we encounter the paradox of post-Zionist, some of whom came from Marxist and post Marxist circles, do not hesitate to regulate through the market, issues of great public importance.

Notwithstanding Kimmerling, in as much as the time for general conscription had passed, the national State still has a reserve army, which potentially includes the whole nation. Nations rely on professional armies in times of peace. However, in times of war, sometimes a general conscription is needed. Therefore, even if general conscription passes away, as Kimmering himself says elsewhere (1994, p. 137), the concept of citizenship includes the principle of readiness to serve. Indeed, it seems that the post-Zionists tacitly and even openly assume a situation when peace prevails, and it is not a coincidence that post-Zionism had reached its peak during what that was called here "the peace process" of the Oslo Agreement. There are those who claim that after the collapse of this process, there has been a retreat to what is known as "Zionism" (Segev, 2001, p. 133; Livne, 2001).

Kimmerling and other post-Zionists' attempt to bypass the question of the conscription of the Arabs by the demand to establish professional voluntary army, raises the question, why the post-Zionists think that the Arabs could not identify with the "bi-national" "universal" and "culturally neutral" post-Zionist Israeli State? There are two possible answers to this question: (a) the Post-Zionists conjecture (what seems rather obvious) that post-Zionist Israel will remain predominantly Hebrew and consequently more "Jewish" than "Arab", consequently the Arabs would not be able to identify with it: (b) Even if the post-Zionist State would be indeed neutral or symmetrically bi-national still the Arabs could not identify with a state which is half Jewish or not completely Arab. Both answers point to the fallibility of the idea of the citizens' State.

Indeed, the question of social solidarity and the ability to achieve it within "the citizens' State" troubles post-Zionists as well. Here comes their demand for an Israeli "civil religion" which will replace "the national religion". Civil religion is a system of myths, rites and symbols common to the citizen body, which provides the solidarity needed for the stability of the political community. Indeed, part of the post-Zionist civil religion is reflected by Ram's orientations: universal values concentrate around the universal State and the ideas of democracy and humanism. Yet, as Kimmerling maintains, a civil religion could not be established only upon universal elements:

> Indeed, there is no society in the world that is wholly built upon universal elements, on pure rationality, on the absolute autonomy of the individual from the public. A society without a certain amount of particularism, tribalism, ethnocentrism, irrationalism, collective myths and "sacreds", which are encored in the past ("tradition", "historical consciousness", "founding fathers" and so on) could not exist. (Michman 1997, p. 314).

Yet, here Kimmerling, Ram and the other post-Zionists are in disadvantage when compared to the "Zionists". For, in as much as the Zionists, according to the criticism directed towards them by the post-Zionists, are relying on an invented national order and national history, "The New Zionist Myth" still provides a national order, and "the Zionist history", even if invented or imagined, could still be a source of "heritage", "national consciousness" and "founding fathers". All this is blocked for the post-Zionists, for together with Israeli nationality they reject also its history. If Benedict Anderson is right when he says that "the idea of a sociological organism moving calendrically through homogeneous, empty time is a precise analogue of the idea of the nation, which also is conceived as a solid community moving steadily down (or up) history" (Anderson, 1983, p. 26), then there is no post-Zionist nation. Thus, one of the post-Zionist orientations mentioned by Ram is the orientation towards the present and near future as opposed to the primordial past (ancient Israel) and remote future (salvation in the End of Days), which characterized what he called "neo Zionism", or what we call here "The New Zionist Myth". Tom Segev (2001, p. 92) describes post-Zionist Tel Aviv as a city "of light-spirited inhabitants: they do not live for the past, nor for the future, but for life itself".

Consequently, as the post-Zionist myth of Israel denationalized Israel, it also had to de-historicize it by the rejection of any historical aspect of the post-Zionist entity. Post-Zionist "neutral" Israel could not be the political continuation of the historical Jewish people, or the product of Zionism, the national movement for self-determination, which originated in Judaism with the aim to solve the Jewish problem. As noted above, the negation of the historical aspect of the State is also characteristic of the classical liberalism. The individuals, who are united by the social contract, in as much as they lack common culture, they also lack common history, or at least they do not consider themselves as having common history. Therefore, the liberal state, at least from classical liberalism theory, does not consider history or collective memories as a source for solidarity and social mobilization, on one hand, and for political action, on the other.

The real liberal democracy, as it has a national dimension, so it has an historical one, which also influences the shaping of the national interests, not because history is binding (as the romanticist nationalism suggests), but because it also shapes the democratic will of the members of the nation. In other words, it is impossible to see the liberal State as "service State" in the narrow materialistic sense. Furthermore, the common historical consciousness is one of the sources of the feeling of common destiny and hence also a source for solidarity and civil mobilization. The post-Zionist stand is characterized by the negation of the historical dimension in being relevant in shaping national interests. This is demonstrated by one of the so-called "New Historian", Ilan Pape. According to Pape the Israeli War of Independence was, or at least should have been, "A boy scouts' tour" of strong Jewish colonialists against a Third World weak and disunited Arab world. Yet, there is a small problem in this thesis, which is the large number of fatalities among the Jews. This is how Pape introduces and solves the problem:

The new picture casted doubt on the claim that the Jewish community in Palestine had faced annihilation on the eve of 1948. The documents revealed a disunited Arab world and an Arab Palestinian community without a military capability to threaten the Yishuv … Why did the Jewish community suffer so many casualties? The policy of Ben Gurion, who was trying to defend isolated settlements, led to some desperate battles. … research points out that many casualties were cause by the battles over the city of Jerusalem. These battles could have been avoided as the involved sides – the Israeli and the Jordanians have reached an agreement about non belligerency in all other fronts. (Pape, 1995, p. 42).

I do not wish to enter a discussion here on this highly contested (to say the least) historical thesis, especially about the so-called agreement between the Israelis and the Jordanians. Yet, Pape adopts here the model of the liberal "service" State in its most vulgar form. The Israelis were to blame for the large number of fatalities because they have introduced into the war irrelevant considerations. If the purpose of the State, to use Hobbes's words, is "a particular security", and if there should be no place for considerations which originate in historical consciousness, then the Israelis should not have fought over Jerusalem or remote places, and then the number of casualties would have been dropped drastically (and justifies the "Boy Scouts' journeys theory"). Yet, nations are also historical entities, or at least conceive themselves as such, and they fight for what their members think worth fighting, and not what the (new) historian conjectures for them.

Jerusalem, then, cannot be a part of the post-Zionist civil religion. As we have seen, Kimmerling, unlike Ram, thinks that civil religion should have particular characteristics: "tradition", "historical consciousness", and "founding fathers". What of these does he allow for post-Zionist Israel? Kimmerling sets the example of the civil religion in America as it was described and characterized by the American sociologist Robert Bellah (1970). The latter had characterized "civil religion" as holidays, rites and beliefs, which are considered "sacred" among Americans and thus used as a source of civic solidarity and mobilization. Kimmerling maintains that the Americans have succeeded in creating a civil religion, which could be shared by Americans of all religions[12]. Yet, Kimmerling's interpretation of Bellah is problematic. First, Kimberling's assertion that the sacreds, which Bellah identifies in "American civil religion" are "entirely secular", and that the civil religion in America is "secular", does not follow at all from Bella's findings. On the contrary, Bellah emphasizes that in as much as the American civil religion is not Christian, it had taken many of its symbols from Christianity in particular, and from Judeo-Christian tradition in general. Thus, it emphasizes the role of God and the idea of the Americans as the elected people and God's messengers on earth. Bellah emphasizes that this is not "a secular" religion, and that it makes use of concepts that only a believer could use, moreover, it demands from the American citizen to be believers, that is to belong to a certain religion, and that in the present situation it would be very difficult for a political candidate who runs for office and does not exhibit any religious affiliation to succeed.

The question that arises here is whether Kimmerling would be ready to accept a post-Zionist Israeli civil religion, which draws from Judaism – but is not Jewish – (therefore it could be shared also by non-Jews), as the American civil religion draws from Christianity, but is not Christian? I doubt it, as he would have certainly considered it as an affront to the "native element" – i.e. unfairness to the Israeli Arabs. Therefore, within his post-Zionist "neutral" State Kimmerling demands to change the symbols, "to consider the replacement of the flag, especially because its origin is religious – the 'tallit' – and it reflects the current theocratic tendency." The religious origin of the Israeli flag constitute a hindrance for an Israeli democracy. This is not the way that many democracies in Europe, who mark the cross in their flags see it. Among these democracies, Britain, Denmark, Norway, Sweden and Swiss (a consociational democracy which Kimmerling occasionally set as an example for post-Zionist Israel), not to mention the crescent in the flags of Muslim countries where there are also non-Muslim minorities. This demonstrates the falsehood of the notion of the post-Zionist's "neutral State", as the cross marked in those flags testifies to the Christian origin of those nations and thus gives a cultural priority to Christianity, yet without preventing non-Christians to be equal members of those nations.

Moreover, post-Zionists are usually proud of their sense of (universal?) justice. Here the question arises, from this point of view, since the other two principal religions of the west, Christianity and Islam, gave birth to many nations who give expression to their origin in their civil religion and their symbols. Wouldn't it be fair that there will be at least one nation, Israeli, which originated in Judaism, and which gives an expression of this origin in its symbols and civil religion?

As noted, Kimberling's answer to this question is negative, for he fears hurting "the native element". Yet, in as much as the American native element is concerned, that is the Indians, Kimmerling is not so sensitive. This is how he describes, following Bellah's examples, the meaning of Thanksgiving Day, which is a part of the American civil religion, a civil religion which Kimmerling considers to be reasonable:

> (It is) a family collective holiday for all the American citizens, in which the American once a year thanks his God and history for giving him the promised land, a land of milk and honey, and have made an American out of him. The first Turkey, which the members of the Indian tribes offered those who had come off the Mayflower had made the Indians, at least theoretically, partners in America which was established over the ruins of their cultures. Then comes **the sacred American**

> **Independence day,** the Labor day … and more sacred days, people and places … (Michman, 1997, p. 314 emphasis added).

I wonder if Kimmerling would have agreed to a post-Zionist "Israeli Thanksgiving Day", in which "the Israeli thanks his God and history (sic) for giving him the Promised Land, a land of milk and honey and made an Israeli out of him"? Would he settle for an "Israeli Thanksgiving Day" in which the Israeli thanks the local Arab natives for the Humus and the Falafel they gave to the members of the First and Second *Aliyot* to make them "at least theoretically partners in Israel which was established over the ruins of their cultures." Also, what about Independence Day? Would Kimmerling be ready to accept *hei be'Iyar tashach* (14.5.1948) as the "sacred" Independence Day of the Israeli nation?

The answer is, of course, negative. In fact, Kimmerling suggests abolishing Israeli Independence Day altogether, or in his words, "to cast and redefine 'Independence Day' as the day of the declaration of the State" (Kimmerling, 2001, pp. 98-9). The difference is obvious: Independence Day marks a day in which a nation had won independence, while "the declaration of the State" is nothing but an administrative move. This suggested change stems from the fact that Kimmerling, like other post-Zionists, does not consider Israel to be a nation, but rather "a State", that is an administrative apparatus, which is meant to regulate the relations between the various ethnicities within it. Thus, while America is entitled to a day of Independence (yes, the 4th of July is American Independence Day, not "the day of the declaration of the American State"), Israel is not so entitled. Yet Kimmerling does not stop here. He further suggests that "Israeli Memorial Day should be designated also for all the victims of the Israeli-Arab conflict" (ibid.). By this he deprives the Israelis one of the pillars of any civil religion – Memorial Day for those who had died for their country.

In his classical paper on the civil religion in America, the same which Kimmering considers as reasonable, Bellah emphasizes the importance of Memorial Day, which is "an important event for the whole community which means a recommitment for the martyred dead, to the spirit of sacrifice and to the vision of America" (Bellah, 1970, p. 179). Benedict Anderson says that "No more arresting emblems of the modern culture of nationalism exist than a cenotaph and tombs of Unknown Soldiers" (Anderson, 1983, p. 9). This is denied for the Israelis by Kimmerling – they are not entitled for a Memorial Day for their dead, but to "all of the victims of the conflict between the Israeli and the Arabs". This astonishing suggestion comes immediately after Kimmerling notes that the remolding of the holidays in the post-Zionist State should be such "that it will speak to the hearts of most of the citizens, or a least will not hurt their feelings". One might wonder how Kimmerling's suggestion to remold Independence Day satisfies these conditions. It is important to note that Kimmerling's suggestion for such a Memorial Day does not come only from consideration for "the native element", or because he thinks that the Israeli Arab could not identify with the dead of the War of Independence, but also from his hostility to nationalism, and his complete misunderstanding of the nature of the nation-state and because his post-Zionist State is not a nation-state. For if Kimmerling would have wanted only to show consideration to the Israeli Arabs he should have said that the Memorial Day of the post-Zionist State should be for the victims of the Israeli Arab conflict until the establishment of the post-Zionist State, and from that day on, only the dead of the post-Zionist State would be added. Yet, according to Kimmerling even his post-Zionist State is not allowed to mourn its dead without mourning also all the victims of the conflict, which might include also its enemies.

Furthermore, when Kimmerling, following Bellah, describes the main characteristics of the American civil religion he chooses, not unintentionally, its more "universal" characteristics and omits those which could be problematic from a post-Zionist's point of view. Thus, Bellah emphasizes (and Kimmerling does not tell us) that the Americans had considered themselves descendants of the ancient Hebrews; as "chosen people"; that they saw their emigration from Europe as "Exodus", and America as the promised land, as "New Canaan", to which God had led them to establish a nation of law and order which would be a light onto the nations. America has turned out to be "the New Jerusalem". Here one might ask whether Kimmerling, who praises the American civil religion and seems ready to accept it, would have accepted an Israeli civil religion, which would have considered modern Israel as a successor of ancient Israel (which seems almost inevitable). Of course, this ethos is rejected by Kimmerling and by his post-Zionists colleagues. This is Kimmerling's view, as seen in a critical review of Yehezkel Dror's book: *"The Renovation of Zionism"*, on the relation between post-Zionist Israel and ancient Israel:

> Yet, Dror's main wrath is directed towards the aspiration for "normalcy" … Dror acknowledges that it is possible to have here a State which is increasingly integrated in the Middle East, a State which flourishes economically, technologically, scientifically and culturally, a State in which there is ***a Hebrew Speaking Jewish majority, which historically relates to the periods of the First and the Second Temples and even designates once a year a memorial day for the Holocaust.*** But, if the main identity of this State would be Israeli, and it would serve as an overall mutual identity for all the inhabitants of the country, this would be a morally invalid State (from Dror's point of view – M. B.) though it might be legitimate … Thus, what that bothers Dror above all, and probably most of the Jewish inhabitants of this country, Zionists or not, is the accelerated acceptance of the "citizens' State" formula as a possible identity for this collective. (Kimmerling 1997, pp. 87-8; emphasis added).

It should be noted that according to Kimmerling, it is not post-Zionist Israel which is related to the First and the Second Temple, but within post-Zionist Israel there is a majority which relates to the First and the Second Temple. In other words, the relation to the First and Second Temple is not a characteristic of the civil religion (that is of the collective), but of a group within it. Consequently, America could envisage itself as a successor of the ancient Hebrews and modern Israel cannot. More astonishing is Kimmerling inability to include the Holocaust in the Israeli civil religion: it is not post-Zionist Israel, which designates a Holocaust Memorial Day, but the Jewish majority does. Here it should be noted that the Holocaust and its remembrance have become part of the American civil religion, and the Holocaust Museum in Washington is recognized as an official museum of the government of the United States. In another place Kimmerling shows more generosity when he is ready to accept the Holocaust Memorial Day "in its present form, yet with an emphasis on its universal lessons." (Kimmerling, 2003, p. 99).

So it seems that the post-Zionists have replaced "The New Zionist Myth" with a myth of their own – the myth of the universal or neutral State. Their purpose is not to replace the ethnocentric nationalism of "The New Zionist Myth" with inclusive liberal nationalism, but rather to denationalize Israel, that is to turn it into a "universal" or "neutral" State, probably the first in the history of the modern world. This myth is well anchored in the western tradition (yet not in western practice, for such a State does not exist). It draws from classical liberalism, which tended to ignore the national character of liberal democracy. It draws also from the Marxist and post-Marxist traditions, as it does from the post-Modernist rejection of (the western) nation-state. Nevertheless, it seems that what has made the myth of the non-national universal State so accepted among Israeli intellectuals, "Zionists" and "post-Zionists" alike, is their acceptance of the main tenet of "The New Zionist Myth", that is the fusion of religion and nationality.

In other words, to the extent that Israeli intellectuals, Zionists and post-Zionists, are nationalists, they identify their nationality as Jewish. Yet, Judaism today, as Christianity, is a universal religion. Thus, contrary to what "The New Zionist Myth" declares, it is possible to be a good Jew and not to be Israeli. In other words, religions, unlike nations, do not have political aspects and consequently they do not need States of their own. Paradoxically, the ethnocentrism of "The New Zionist Myth" could easily become non-political nationalism or what that is called today "cultural nationalism" or both. It is of no surprise that Chaim Gans, who examines the right of the Jews for self-determination reaches the conclusion that this right must not necessarily be implemented by a State and could also be implemented by a community or a sub-state autonomy (Gans, 2006). Similarly, Yael Tamir, who opens her book *Liberal Nationalism* with a dedication to her parents who educated her as "a Zionist" ends the book with the rejection of the nation-state and the adoption of "cultural nationalism" as the only one which is compatible with liberal democracy (Tamir, 1993, pp. 163-7).

A different post-Zionist stand is that of Shlomo Sand. Unfortunately, in the fierce debate that surrounded his *Invention of the Jewish People* (2009) Sand's post-Zionist stand went relatively unnoticed. Thus, unlike other post-Zionists, Sand calls for the establishment of an Israeli Republic (p. 21). Further, Sand does not preach for a culturally neutral State or symmetrical bi-national State. He sees no problem with the existence of hegemonic culture; or in the fact that "the symbols of the State derive from Jewish tradition" (p. 305); or for that matter, in having a repealed Law of Return only for persecuted Jews (p.312):

> Democracy need not be culturally neutral, but if there is a State
> supra-identity that directs the national culture, it must be open
> to all or at least seek to be so, even if the minority insists on
> staying out of the hegemonic national bear-hug … if the word

"Jewish" were replace by the word "Israeli" and if the State thus
becomes open and accessible to all the citizens, who would be
able to navigate its identity landscape at will then Israel could be
seen as a democracy. (p. 306).

There is no doubt much in common between these ideas and the ideas
expressed in the present book. Yet, there are also some important
differences. In as much as Sand does speak about Israeliness, he does not
speak, (at least not directly), about an Israeli nation. In fact it seems that
Sand's learned introduction of both the history of nationalism, and the
research study of nationalism is used more for the deconstruction of the
Jewish nation rather than for the advocation of an Israeli nation-state. True,
Sand speaks about Israeliness and he also speaks of an Israeli hegemonic
culture and he even says that it could be "Jewish". Yet, for instance, the
feature, which is considered as the most important character of a nation is,
as Sand himself acknowledges, a "cultural linguistic continuum" (p.38). Yet,
if Sand considers Israeliness as a nationality, then there is no doubt that this
linguistic continuum is supplied by the Hebrew language. In other words,
unless Sand wants to reconstruct the Israeliness from a scrap, Israeliness
could not be even conceived without the Hebrew. Yet, the Hebrew language
is hardly mentioned by Sand, not as a feature of Israeliness, on one hand,
and not in his historical analysis, on the other.

Similarly, to the extent that Sand discusses Israeliness, he seems to focus
on its cultural aspects and does not say much on its political or legal aspects.
While he calls for the establishment of a republic, the concept does not seem
to receive the appropriate treatment in the book. In this case, Republic, or
the nation-state, does not mean only a cultural hegemony, but also a political
and a legal one. While Sand seems ready to accept cultural hegemony which
would be "Jewish", it is not clear whether he would be similarly ready to
accept a "Jewish" sovereignty with all its political and legal implications.

❧ CHAPTER 3 ☙
The Israeli Nation

From Zionism to Zionist Myth

The fusion of religion and nationality in Israel, or the notion of Judaism as both a nationality and religion, and the notion of Israel as the State of the entire Jewish people whose aim is the promotion of Jewish interests, above all *"The Gathering of the Exiles"* and salvation, was rightly named by Agassi as *"The New Zionist Myth"* (Agassi, 1993, pp. 253-7). Contrary to the accepted dogma this was not the dominant conception in the Zionist movement and it had achieved its dominance after independence.

Zionism was the movement for national self-determination of the Jewish nation and its goal was also to give a solution to the "Jewish problem" through the realization of the right of self-determination of the Jewish nation. The fusion of religion and nationality assumes that this "Jewish nation" is identical with the historical Jewish people, and as such, has existed from time immemorial or about three thousand years. Here arises a question: To what extent had there been "a Jewish nation" before the appearance of the Zionist movement? The romanticist concept of nationalism sees the nation as a primordial entity, such that has existed from time immemorial. However, this notion of "the nation" is not accepted by most researchers in the field of nationalism today. It is agreed that nations and nationalism are a modern phenomena – though there is controversy concerning the question to what extent, if at all, the nations are related to ethnic or religious groups of the pre-industrial world (see below, pp. 232- 252). The famous sociologist Ernest Gellner says that we should not let the romanticist rhetoric, which characterizes movements for national self-determination to confuse us. The latter treated the nations as "sleeping beauties" which existed from time immemorial, and waited for the movement for national self-determination to wake them up towards independence. Yet, in most of the cases, it is nationalism, which creates nations and not vice versa. In other words, movements for national self-determination (or elites) occasionally speak on behalf of nations which do not exist and which they create.

As we are going to see, the Zionist movement was not an exception, and "The Jewish nation", which it had talked about in the nineteenth century, did not exist: The historical Jewish people – *"Am Yisrael"* - had been an aggregation of communities (part of them had been going through accelerated processes of disintegration because of the influence of the industrial era and the emancipation) and it lacked any national characteristics, such a common language or territory, on one hand, and common consciousness: a desire to live in a common state and under a common government, on the other. Parts of the historical *Am Yisrael* had aspired through the emancipation to become members of the nations among which they had lived, and for others the aspiration for a national independent government had been conceived as blasphemy and *"dechikat haketz"* (forcing the end). Alternatively, to the extent that there had been "proto-national" phenomena among the Jews, those were limited to Eastern European Jewry (Chlenov, 2003). But also here Zionism had been just one expression alongside other national expressions such as territorialism, autonomism or Bundism.

Indeed, the Zionist movement, influenced by romanticist nationalism, had considered the Jewish nation as an accomplished fact and sometimes addressed the entire "Jewish People" (Agassi, 1993, p. 83). Though Zionism had comprehensively addressed the Jews it was clear to the Zionists from the start that the Jewish nation would not be identical to the entire Jewish people, and that a considerable number of Jews, especially in the west, where the emancipation had been at an advanced stage, would choose to stay in their places. Herzl had thought that these Jews of the emancipation would support his scheme because it would have relieved them from the Eastern European Jewish masses, who were constantly emigrating to the west, thereby threatening the western Jews' integration into their local nations. In a communication circulated on the behalf of the Preparatory Committee of the First Zionist Congress it was said that the purpose of the Congress was to establish an executive committee which would aspire "to establish a safe and endurable national home *for those Jews who can not or would not assimilate in their local countries"* (Elon, 1975, p. 251; emphasis added).

Despite the fact that Zionism addressed also the western Jews and Jews from Western Europe were among its founding fathers, Zionism was largely an Eastern European movement. As Ben Gurion noted, in America, Zionism "was from the outset only a movement of aid to European Jewry and the Jews of the rest of the countries outside the United States" (Ben Ezer, 1974, p. 71; Shimoni, 2000, pp. 51-3). Moreover, even as an Eastern European movement the Zionists had to accept the fact that since it was unable to offer an immediate solution for the Jewish problem, many Eastern European Jews preferred the American individual solution to the Jewish problem rather than the collective one offered by Zionism.

To the extent that the Zionist movement considered the "Jewish people" as the natural reservoir for the members of the nation, it had also made efforts to distinguish the emerging nation from the historical Jewish people. In as much as it had been a continuation of the historical Jewish people, it had been also a rebellion against it. Even though the fathers of "Political Zionism" refrained from accepting any decision concerning the culture of the emerging nation it was still culturally different from the historical Jewish people. First, the nation was modern, with all the cultural consequences which followed its being modern. It was obvious to the founding fathers of Zionism that the existence of national life was conditioned by a modernization and transformation of the historical Jewish people. Also, although there had not been any formal decision in this matter, Hebrew had become the language of the nation. In other words, a spoken Jewish language was not chosen as a national language, but Hebrew, which had been revived from a language of prayer. Thus, from the start, the "Jewish nation" was identified as a "Hebrew nation". It was in these two cultural features – modernity and Hebraism, that the emerging nation was distinguished from the historical *"Am Yisrael"*.

The gap between the Hebrew nation and Judaism had increased even further and acquired a different form by the influence of "Practical Zionism" in which the Labor Movement was dominant. "Practical Zionism" rejected the idea of the immediate establishment of a State and that of a mass immigration (which were the pillar stones of "Political Zionism") and replaced it with notion of the piecemeal evolution of an elite community of pioneers (*halutzim*). Consequently the "myth of the *halutz*" was central in Practical Zionism. The Labor movement's ideology had been clearly anti-religious and the *"myth of the halutz"*, which was central in Practical Zionism, had identified the national Jew, or the Hebrew, with the *halutz* while sharply contrasting it with the Diaspora Jew and emphasizing the Hebrew cultural aspect of the nation. For some Practical Zionists the notion of the utopian society was conceived as a target of its own, for others as a means for the creation of the necessary conditions for mass immigration. Yet, in the absence of a definite future moment for the establishment of the state, or for the mass Jewish immigration, "what might have conceived as tactics (i.e. the elite utopian society) had practically turned out to be a target of its own" (Vital, 1984, p. 10).

All these tended to further widen the gap between the 'Jewish nation' or the 'Hebrew nation' and the historical Jewish people. While every Jew potentially could have become a Hebrew, in fact the members of the nation were a small minority within *'Am Yisrael'*, which included the members of the Jewish community in Palestine, the *Yishuv*, along with Jews who were about to immigrate or to make an immediate *aliya* to Palestine.

Even though tendencies to identify nationality with religion had existed in Zionism from the start, those were not necessarily dominant. One could point at two essential elements of the distinction between nationality and religion in classical Zionism: "will"and "culture". The element of will had distinguished between those Jews who were willing to become members of the nation, on one hand, and those who were willing to be members of other nations (i.e. not to immigrate to the Jewish homeland), on the other. This element was identified also with another element – that of the Jewish plight. The assumption was that a nation would develop among the distressed Jews. The other element was the cultural one, which marks the modernity and the Hebrew nature of the nation, where those are presented not only as different from the traditional *Am Yisrael*, but occasionally as antithetical to them. Roughly it could be said that the element of the *will* was dominant in Herzl's Political Zionism, and the element of *culture* was dominant in Practical Zionism and in the Labor Movement. Yet, we could usually find the two elements - of will and of culture - among Zionist thinkers of both traditions.

It is important to note that in as much as pre-independence Zionism endorsed the fusion of the "Jewish nation" which Zionism represented and the historical *Am Yisrael*, it was more because it identified nationality with (Jewish) ethnicity rather than with (Jewish) religion. While the two identities had much in common, they were not the same. Conceiving Judaism as an ethnicity rather than as a religion enabled the Zionists to "free" themselves from religion and to conduct the cultural "Hebrew Revolution" (See discussion below, pp. 283-293).

Even though the Zionist ideology did not necessarily identify nationality and religion, there had been several elements in the development of the Jewish community in Palestine (*Yishuv*), which enhanced the tendency to identify nationality and religion. Such was the nature of the definition of the *Yishuv* by the Ottoman and British rule, which identified the Jewish community in

Palestine as a religious community rather than as a national one. Unlike the case of Eastern Europe, where there was a tendency to identify minorities mainly as ethnic or national minorities, under the rule of Islam the tendency was to identify minorities as religious minorities. The main reason was the religious nature of the Ottoman Empire. This meant that the minorities within this Empire had chosen to express their differences from the Muslim Sunni majority by religion, and the Ottoman Empire recognized these minorities as religious groups, which were entitled for religious autonomy according to the system of the *millet* (Esman, 1988, pp. 271-2). Even though the British Rule abolished the special status of Islam, it kept the definition of the minorities in Palestine as religious minorities. In this sense the existing fusion of nationality and religion is a continuity of the conception of the Jewish community set by these regimes. On this matter, Israel Kolatt contends:

> The establishment of constitutional framework to the Jewish religious life did not come from the development of the Zionist ideology or from the structure of the Yishuv in 1921. It was the British Mandatory regime, which imposed the pattern that organized the Jewish life of the Jewish religion. This constitutional framework set to a large extent until today the religion's life in Israel. The questions: what would have been the fate of the religion in the *Yishuv* without this decision of the Mandate government; Would it have been possible to develop religious institutions on voluntary basis according to the principle of separation between religion and State?; or would the social system, because of its own necessity, link the religious institutions to the civil regime one way or another – these are all matters of historical speculations. (Kolatt, 1994, pp. 333-4).

The fact that the Practical Zionists had preferred a slow development of the *Yishuv* under British sovereignty and postponed the establishment of the State to indefinite future (Agassi, 1993, pp. 102-9) enhanced the tendency to identify nationality and either Jewish religion or Jewish ethnicity. Anthony Smith says that ethnic groups, whenever they wish to become nations, have to adopt territorial and civic elements of national identity. Probably the crossroad in which the ethnic group adopts these elements is when it establishes a State. Then, because of the fusion of nationality and citizenship that characterizes the nation-state, territorial and civic elements will enter the national identity. In the pre-State stage, the tendency would be to identify the nation more by ethnic or religious elements. Alternatively, "cultural nationalism", which does not necessarily aspire for a State, would tend also to define the nation by ethnic or religious traits. Consequently the tendency to identify religion and nationality was even bigger in non-Zionist Jewish nationalisms (Bundism and Autonomism), which sought to establish cultural personal autonomies (Kolatt, 1996, pp. 239 – 240). The absence of a territorial or civic element and also the fact that such personal autonomies were a continuation of Jewish traditional practices, had increased the tendency to rely on the traditional basis of "who is a Jew" (Ibid.).

Here an important factor in enhancing the fusion of nationality and ethnicity was the Eastern European ethnic, nationalism's worldview, shared by the Zionist leadership, which identified nationality and ethnicity. The fusion of nationality and ethnicity is not the same as that between nationality and religion, yet under certain circumstances they reinforce one another. Furthermore, the Eastern European worldview at the beginning of the 20th century, especially the one which was popular in socialists circles, was that the best way for self determination of national minorities was by cultural personal autonomy. The Austrian Socialist party considered it as a solution to the problem of national minorities within the Austro-Hungarian Empire and the Bund had adopted it as a solution for the national question in Russia. There is no doubt that this idea had its influence on the leadership of the *Yishuv*, whose background was both Eastern European and Socialist.

The fact that these kind of autonomies were in a sense a continuation of traditional Jewish practices (such as the Ottoman *"millet"* or the Eastern European "Kahal"), the fact that the *Yishuv* had been formally defined by the British Mandate as such an autonomy and the postponement of the establishment of the State to an indefinite future, enhanced the tendency of the *Yishuv* to view itself as a personal national autonomy. When Ben Gurion phrased the aims of Zionism in the nineteen thirties, he spoke on the establishment of a "national autonomy". And even though he tried to distinguish it from the "personal cultural autonomy", that the Jews had in certain cases in eastern Europe and from the Ottoman *"millet"*, it seemed different in the rights that the Jewish community had which went beyond culture, but it was not different in the manner that the community was defined. Though Ben Gurion denied it this was a personal and not a territorial autonomy, it did not include those who were not Jewish who lived among or near Jews (for instance in mixed cities), or alternatively it included only the Jews who live in the midst of Arab population (Ben Gurion, 1931, pp. 110-130). It is important to stress also that when Ben Gurion had later adopted a federal solution for Palestine, he adopted a "federative-autonomy" model, which meant that the Jewish unit in the federal State was still an autonomy of the kind described above.

Gorni suggests that the basic "socio-cultural" assumption of Gen-Gurion was that "the autonomous structure is the one which fits the society in *Eretz Yisrael* ... consequently the way in which the Jews will organize is not dependent on the character of the regime, whether it would be the Mandate Government or when the time comes a government of the inhabitants of Palestine." (Gorni, 1993, pp. 34-7). This conception had increased the tendency to identify nationality and religion (or ethnicity) in the *Yishuv*, and more than that, had relieved the *Yishuv* from any discussion on the status of non-Jews in the future State, which could explain why we do not encounter much discussion on constitutional and civic questions in the pre-independence *Yishuv*.

It would be beneficial to demonstrate how the absence of a State and Jewish sovereignty had increased the tendency to identify religion or ethnicity with nationality in the days of the *Yishuv*. One of the problems Ben Gurion was trying to cope with was the contradiction between the interest of the Jewish worker and that of the Arab worker, as the demand of the labor movement for "Hebrew labor" meant the rejection of the Arab worker. According to Ben Gurion there was no contradiction between the interests in the long run: the low wage of the Arab worker and the possible endless flux of Arab workers from neighboring countries had made the increase of the value of the work impossible; This, in turn, had made impossible the modernization and development of the country which were necessary for increasing the wage and level of life of the Arab worker (Ben Gurion 1931, p. 101). Yet, the "Hebrew labor" meant, in fact, separation between Jews and Arabs, which was based upon the fusion of religion and nationality (or ethnicity and nationality), as it was not clear how the Arab worker could take part in the "Hebrew labor". It is obvious that if a Jewish sovereignty existed the problem could have been easily resolved: (a) the immigration of workers from neighboring countries could be blocked and thus preventing the entrance of cheap labor into the country. (b) It would have been possible by legislation to set minimum wages and decent labor conditions. (c) It would have been possible to protect by legislation the Israeli industries. All these could have been done without the necessity to distinguish between the Jewish and the Arab workers.

The New Zionist Myth

Though the tendencies to identify nationality with religion existed in the Zionist movement from the beginning, this fusion had not been necessarily dominant in the Zionist ideology prior to independence. The dominance of the fusion of religion and nationality, or "The New Zionist Myth" is a post-independence phenomenon. Here the testimony of Ben Gurion is important as he, perhaps more than anybody else, had been responsible for the creation of the New Zionist Myth. Ben Gurion thought that the ideology of classical Zionism did not fit the post-independence reality, as classical Zionism had been essentially an Eastern European movement. The establishment of Israel and the abolishment of Eastern European Jewry, if by extermination, or by emigration to America and Israel, had turned Israel and the United States into the central Jewish centers and had made the Zionist ideology irrelevant. For the Israelis, the myth of national liberation had become a reality; while in the United States, according to Ben Gurion, Zionism has been from the beginning only a movement for helping the Jewry of countries outside the United States, and America's Jewry had never intended to immigrate to Israel (Ben Ezer, 1971, p. 71).

Politically (though not necessarily religiously) the term "Diaspora" had become anachronistic, at least in as much as the western Jews were concerned. The latter, especially the Jews of America, were not Jews who lived in the "Diaspora", but rather equal members of their nations. Further, according to Ben Gurion the danger of this ideological vacuum tended to increase under the influence of post-independence immigrations. Those who come from the refugees camps in Europe ('she'erit hapleta') were motivated by plight rather than by "Zionist" ideology, that is, they did not come to be "pioneers" (halutsim) who wished to build the country, but simply to save themselves. Neither was the immigration from the Arab countries "Zionist" as it was motivated by the traditional Jewish salvation ideas. Ben Gurion claimed that "for the Jews of Muslim countries the verse 'vetechezena einenu be'shuvcha le'tsion be'rachamim' ('May our eyes behold Thy return to Zion in mercy') means more than any Zionist literature, that most of them, have never heard of."(Adler and Kahana, 1975,

p. 14). Ben Gurion feared this ideological vacuum as *"be'ain chazon ipara am"* ("without a vision the people would parish").

The irrelevance of classical Zionism that troubled Ben Gurion so much, was nothing but an expression of a normal process, in which the ideology of a movement for national self-determination becomes irrelevant after the movement had achieved its goal – national independence. The next step should have been the disestablishment of the Zionist movement and the transference of its rights and duties to the Israeli Republic, while adopting and cultivating an Israeli republican ethos based, among other things, upon the ideas of national liberation and constitutional government. Yet, the founding fathers rejected the establishment of the republic and the republican ethos and adopted instead a "New Zionist Myth", which was nothing but a political dress of the religious messianic idea of the "End of Days". This identified the nation of Israel with the religious mythical *"Am Yisrael"*, and not with the Hebrew nation, and national liberation with the ingathering of the exiles and the establishment of a "perfect society" (*chevrat mofet*) according to the biblical prophesies, and not with independence. Israel, and in fact the entire "Jewish people" continued also after 1948 to be in the stage of the struggle for national liberation, which had justified the continued existence of the Zionist movement and its institutions, as well as the non-recognition of the existence of an Israeli nation. Sacher remarks on this rejection of the republican ethos in *A History of Israel* (1976, p. 471):

> Israel's leaders might have interpreted Jewish Statehood as the expression of a national liberation movement, something every former colonial people would have understood. The term was scarcely mentioned, however, in the addresses and writing of Ben Gurion, Sharett, or Eban. Rather, the Israeli statesmen chose to discern a profounder explanation for the 'miracle' of rebirth in the historical and theological roots of the Jewish people.

Ben Gurion was clearly aware of the difference between the "New Zionist Myth" that he was introducing and classical Zionism. Thus, in an interview by Ehud Ben Ezer, Ben Gurion says:

> I distinguish between the Zionist ideology – the offspring of 19th century Europe – and the messianic longings of the Jewish people for national redemption in the land of their fathers, which are the fruits of the Prophets of Israel and had existed in the Jewish people throughout all the years. (Ben Ezer, 1974, pp. 69-70; Adler & Kahana, 1975, pp. 11-14).

Anita Shapira (1997, p. 228) suggests that Ben Gurion's new approach as it was expressed in the nineteen fifties could be metaphorically called "post-Zionist", and Menachem Brinker calls Ben Gurion "the first Post-Zionist" (Brinker, 1997). Similarly Yehuda Reinharz distinguishes between "Old Zionism" and "New Zionism":

> In previous times, before the Land of Israel had become open for every Jew who wants to enter it, all had considered the concentration of the Jews in their homeland as the essence of Zionism. This was agreed also by those who did not consider joining the immigration process by themselves. It had been the agreed solution for the problem of the Jews of Eastern Europe, and all the Jews have understood it as a paradigm of the essential Jewish situation. … Yet, there was another special problem that is the required healing needed for the hurt identities of the Jews of the West. Today, as the Diaspora is continuing even though the State of Israel is accessible, the situation of the Jews in the west had turned out to become essential, and the problems of the identity of the western Jews had turned out to be the burning issue of the New Zionism. The attempts to deal with this problem – which sometimes are being carried out halfheartedly – are

the main task for the New Zionism, which is supposed to
be more implementable for our time that the Old Zionism.
(Reinharz, 2000, p. 44).

With "The New Zionism", or the "New Zionist Myth", the irrelevance
of classical Zionism was rectified as the existence of Jewish communities
in the West had turned out to be a "Jewish Problem" and consequently
a "Zionist" and Israeli "problem". Thus, unlike "Old Zionism", which
considered itself mainly as a solution to distressed Jews, the "New
Zionism" mainly approached a well off Jewish public with recognized
American nationality.

The meaning of the introduction of "the New Zionist Myth" was
that from the ruling elite's point of view the Jewish religion and the
Jewish tradition had become an essential source of national values.
Being a Jewish State in this sense meant it belonged to all Jews wherever
they were. The fact that Judaism is a religion, at least as it is considered
by both Jews and non-Jews in the west, meant that the State should have
adopted "Jewish values" originated in the Jewish tradition. The nature
of the mass Jewish immigration from the Arab countries, which was
essentially traditional, had also influenced the adoption of "The New
Zionism". Thus, Liebman and Don Yehiya (1983) point out the radical
change in what they call "the civil religion" in the nineteen fifties. At the
base of this radical revolution was the change from a civic approach that
was confrontational towards religion ("the confrontational approach"
or "Berdichevskian approach"), to a "New Civil Religion" ("the new
interpretation approach").[13] Liebman and Don Yehiya locate the
ideological turning point in the nineteen fifties with the adoption of
what was known as the "Jewish Consciousness Program" by the Israeli
education system. The goal of the "New Civil Religion" was "to unite
and integrate the society around the conception of the Jewish tradition

and the Jewish people; it no longer sought the creation of a new Jew and a new Jewish society (Labor-Zionism) or the unification and integration of the society around the symbols of statehood (statism, or *mamlachtiut*)" (Liebman & Don Yehiya, 1983, p. 62). Yonatan Shapiro (1996, p. 58) remarked on the change in the nineteen fifties:

> We have returned, by this tradition, to the pre-national period when the Jews had been a religious community. National ideas were added to the religion commandments ... and by the recitation of religious habits and traditions, symbols and myths, the religious tradition was presented as an expression of the 'Jewish-Israeli' nationalism".

There were other reasons for the dramatic change in the nineteen fifties in the worldview of the ruling elite and the adoption of the New Civil Religion. According to Anita Shapira (1997, p. 230) the fifties were years of the political radicalization of the left-wing Mapam, the days of Hazan's "second fatherland" (that is the Soviet Union) and that the need to introduce an overall ideological alternative to the labor's left-wing radicalism "seemed to Ben Gurion of no less importance than the acquisition of weapons for the IDF." "The New Zionist Myth" fitted here as it was a general utopist ideology (very close also to the elite's socialist utopians ideas), and also because it introduced the idea of *"am levadad yishkon,"* ("a people that shall dwell alone"[14]), which offered a resistance to "foreign" ideas and wished to establish the utopian ideas only upon Judaism. Baruch Kimmerling also thinks that the choice of a "western orientation" as opposed to the "eastern Communist orientation" was an important motive for the adoption of the fusion of religion and nationality (Kimmerling, 1994, p. 130). The "New Zionist Myth" suited this western orientation as it basically interpreted "Zionism" and Judaism in religious terms, which suited the concept of Judaism in the West and particularly in the United States. Another ideology, which the New Zionist Myth was supposed to counter-balance was the Canaanite ideology which had become more popular after independence among the young generation.

Yonatan Shapiro gave a different explanation (1977, pp. 22-23). According to Shapiro, fusion of religion and nationality had "an internal ideological logic" and that in its adoption after independence it is possible to identify a return to well entrenched traditional Jewish conceptions. A somewhat similar explanation relates the adoption of the New Civil Religion to the character of the immigration from the Arab countries in the fifties and sixties (Liebman & Don Yehiya, 1983). Indeed, as we have seen above, one of the reasons which Ben Gurion gives to adoption of "The New Zionist Myth" was the fact that the immigrants from the Arab countries were not "Zionists", that is they were not motivated by the "pioneering will" to build a Hebrew nation, but, as members of traditional societies, were motivated by the messianic biblical ideas. Consequently they needed a mobilizing ideology which was different from the one offered by classical Zionism (Ben Gurion, 1957, p. 11).

Some reasons for the adoption the fusion of religion and nationality were related to the Holocaust. There was here, undoubtedly, also a sincere wish "to embrace" the Jews wherever they were and offer them protection, a wish which originated also by the guilt feeling created by the inaction of the *Yishuv* and the Zionist leadership during the Holocaust. Yoram Kaniuk points at what he calls "the abolition of the Hebrew rebellion in its midst" by the establishment of the Jewish State:

> At the moment when the Palestinian Jew (*'Eretz-Yisraeli'*) the son
> of the Hebrew and Zionist rebellion, has started to feel guilty
> towards the refugees of the Holocaust, then, in this dreadful
> junction, the new Israeli has been melted, the one who is not
> Jewish any more, yet neither he is Hebrew. This is why Israel is

today the State of the Jewish people, and the revival movement
had been for nothing, as Israel is not the State of its citizens, and
without emancipation and a complete change of values there
would be no Hebrew sovereignty. (Kaniuk, 1987, p. 2).

Already before Israel's independence Uri Avnery had blamed the "old
leadership" that it had turned to save the Jewish culture now out of
guilty consciousness because of its failure and lack of will to save the
Jews during the Holocaust (Shapira, 2003, p. 29). Indeed, the Holocaust
raised questions not only related to the actions of the Zionist leadership to
save the Jews of Europe, but also about the policies of Labor dominated
Practical Zionism between the two World Wars: The rejection of the idea
of mass immigration, on one hand, and the adoption of the notion of slow
evolution towards statehood, on the other.

Beyond this, the annihilation of the Eastern European Jewry had
grave consequences for the vitality, survival and legitimacy of the
new Israeli State. This Jewry was the principal reservoir from which
the new nation was supposed to draw its members, yet this Jewry
was exterminated almost completely. The Zionist movement had
turned out to be a rare case, if not an only case, of a national self-
determination movement, which had lost its own people on its course
for self-determination. It is said that the principle of national self-
determination pushes nations to seek statehood. Yet, sometimes it is
the other way around and States are looking for nations. The newly
created state was in a desperate need of a nation, and the myth of the
"Jewish people" seemed a way to answer this need. The notion of the
Jewish State as a solution for the Jewish plight had always been the basis
for the international legitimacy of Zionism. Though the Holocaust
might have "proved" that Zionism was right, its consequences might
have been interpreted as if it was no longer needed. Hence, the need to

emphasis not only the relation to Diaspora Jews, but also the constant hostility and dangers that the Jews were facing in the Diaspora.

An important motivation for the adoption of "the new civil religion", and the rejection of republicanism, originated in the wish to exclude rather than to include. The wish was to exclude the Arabs of Israel. As Sammy Smooha claims, the Israeli 'ethnic democracy' is used in Israel as an apparatus for the exclusion and domination of the Arab minority. In as much as the Arab exclusion had been a continuation of pre-independence attitudes, and the newly accepted fusion of nationality and religion, this exclusion was also shaped by the fact that as Israel came into existence it found itself at war with the Arab world.

Here I would like to stress a point which had been relatively unnoticed – the implication of the ferocity of the resistance of the local Arab Palestinian population in the War of Independence, which surprised the *Yishuv*. It is important to recognize that the most difficult days of the War of Independence were in January and February 1948 (before the invasion of the Arab States). During this time the *Yishuv* almost collapsed under the attacks of the local Palestinian Arab population. Until the invasion the numbers of fatalities among the Jews was about two thousand five hundred. These also projected on the will and the hope to incorporate the local Arab population in the future State.

It is important to stress that all these reasons, causes and motivations for the adoption of a fusion of religion and nationality as the basis for the legitimacy of the Israeli State could not explain why liberal democracy and republicanism were rejected. In other words, they could not explain why the founding fathers did not think that what they had identified as an ideological vacuum could be filled with a republican-democratic ethos. Consequently, adopting the fusion of religion and nationality should be seen also as a testimony for the lack of democratic and republican spirit of the founding fathers and the fact that they have not completely been able to free themselves of traditional Jewish conceptions.

The Hebrew Nation – The Conceptual Framework

"The New Zionist Myth" was clearly anti-republican. Yet, to what extent were the principles of classical Zionism suitable for a republican government? Had Israel been declared republic in 1948, who were supposed to be the sons and daughters of the Hebrew or Israeli nation? Here it would be important to note that the U.N. Partition Resolution had imposed a republican form of government on the new State. In as much as it was identified by the resolution as "a Jewish State", it was also required to be a constitutional regime, which gives equality to all. Generally speaking, the international legitimization that the Zionist movement had been working to obtain had assumed the separation between nationality and religion. The preamble of the Mandate which repeated the words of the Balfour declaration declares:

> Whereas the Principal Allied Powers have also agreed that the Mandatory should be responsible for putting into effect the declaration originally made on November 2nd, 1917, by the Government of His Britannic Majesty, and adopted by the said Powers, in favor of the establishment in Palestine of a national home for the Jewish people, it being clearly understood that nothing should be done which might prejudice the civil and religious rights of existing non-Jewish communities in Palestine, or the rights and political status enjoyed by Jews in any other country.

The distinction between the "Diaspora nation" and "the sovereign nation" is being made here twice. First, in Palestine there would be established a national home for the Jewish people, but not for all the Jews. In other words, alongside the Jewish national home in Palestine, Jews will also live in complete equality in other countries (that is as members of other nations). Second, there should be no contradiction between the existence of a Jewish national home and the civil (and religious) rights of non-Jews – within the Jewish national home will live in complete equality non-Jews.

To what extent, then, did the principles of classical Zionism fit the establishment of an Israeli republic? Had Israel been declared as a republic in 1948, who were supposed to be the sons and daughters of the Israeli or the Hebrew nation? The first membership layer would have consisted of 625,000 members of the pre-independence *Yishuv* who fought for its independence. Yet, the *Yishuv* was also a part of the Zionist movement, which was a movement for national self-determination whose aim, in the words of the First Zionist Congress, was "to establish a secure and lasting national home *for those Jews who cannot or will not assimilate into their present homes*" (Elon, 1975, p. 225). Thus, in 1948 there were still concentrations of non-Hebrew Jews who lacked national self-determination (that is they would not or could not assimilate in their local nations) from which the Hebrew nation was about to draw more members. The first immediate group was that of the remains of the European Jewry (*she'e'rit haplayta*). After the Second World War it had become obvious that this group (which was at that time in refugee camps in Europe) could not and would not remain in Eastern Europe. Most of them wanted to immigrate to Israel, as their 'Zionism' was more an outcome of the Holocaust rather than of pre-war Zionist ideology. Moreover, with the gates of other countries blocked, immigration to Palestine was also the only option. Here is the testimony of Richard Crossman, member of the Anglo-American Committee, which was appointed after the Second World War to examine possible solutions in Palestine and the situation of the remaining Jews in Europe:

> In the first place, I had reached the conclusion that Zionism, whether we like it or not, was a bare necessity for the existence of Eastern European Jewry. History, reaching its climax in the Nazi persecutions, had made these few survivors of the

Polish, Hungarian and Rumanian Jewish communities into members of a Jewish nation. Some of them, no doubt, might rebuild their lives in Europe, either in their old occupations or as communists. But the vast majority must either emigrate or perish; and if they emigrate, they would desire to join their kinsmen in the national home. It was not the product of Zionist organization, but the expression of the most primitive urge, the urge for survival. (Crossman, 1947, p. 166)

A second circle of potential immigrants into the Hebrew nation were the Jews from Muslim countries. These Jews had lived as 'tolerated' under the Islam and the Ottoman Empire. Yet, the dissolution of the Empire, the rise of Arab nationalism and the establishment of Israel had changed all this and the Jews the in the Arab world were now part of the "Jewish Problem". As Jewish and Arab nationalism had appeared simultaneously in the Middle East, it had become accustomed to consider the hatred to the Jews and their deportation from the Arab countries as a reaction to the establishment of Israel. Yet, it could be assumed that even if Israel had not been established, there would have been still a Jewish problem in the Arab countries with the abandonment of the Ottoman tradition – which had been relatively patient towards the Jews, and the adoption of European nationalism. As the latter was imported from Europe, so were some of its romanticist and anti-Semitist elements. Under the influence of this nationalism the situation of minorities (not only Jews) has been worsening in the Arab countries (Lasker, 2006, pp. 7-8).

It is clear, then, that as the appearance of nationalism in Europe had raised the question of the national identity of the Jews, so the appearance of Arab nationalism would raise the question of the Jewish national identity in the Arab countries. In this context the important questions are: To what extent the Jews had wanted to be part of Arab nationalism, on one hand, and to what extent Arab nationalism had wished to include them (Crossman, 1947, pp. 137-8). Another question is whether there are nations in the Arab world (either a pan-Arab nation or Arab nation-states), that is: Whether there are in Arab countries the cultural and political homogeneity that characterize the western nation-states. The existence of a nation presupposes a certain degree of modernization, industrialization and the existence of a wide middle class, which the Arab world seems to lack. The existence of nationalism in the absence of real nations means that in the Arab world, notwithstanding the nationalist rhetoric, it had been impossible for minorities to assimilate in the national culture. Alternatively, if Arab nations do exist, it is very difficult to see how they could have integrated the Arab Jews as equal member citizens, given the fact that those countries are defined as Muslim countries and the civic and democratic element in their identity is weak. The recent reawakening of fundamentalism or political Islam only strengthens this point further.

An additonal circle of potential immigrants to the Israeli nation had been the Soviet and Eastern European Jews sitting behind the "Iron Curtain". The Soviet Union was a multinational dictatorship which did not recognize the right of self-determination of the various nations within its territory, nor did it recognize the individual's right of national self determination – that is the right of persons to choose their nationality including the right of emigration. Thus, the realization of the right of the Jews for national self-determination, if by integrating into their local nations, or by immigrating to any other nations, (including Israel), had to await the downfall of the communist regime. Indeed, ever since the fall of the communist dictatorship, a substantial part of the Jews of the former Soviet Union has chosen to immigrate to Israel.

So far we have discussed the 1948's potential membership in the Hebrew nation among distressed Jews or Jews without national identity. Yet, in countries where Jews enjoyed security and equality, and were considered members of their local nations, lived Jews who considered themselves as national Jews and as a part of the Zionist movement. The establishment of Israel had created a new situation whereas those Jews could realize their right for national self-determination. Consequently, another circle of sons and daughters of the Israeli nation were those Jews of the west who wanted to fulfill their right for self-determination in the Israeli republic.

The 'Seventy-First Nation'

In addition to all these Jewish publics, in 1948, there was also another non-Jewish public whose members were then potential candidates for the Israeli nation: The local Arab population. Their joining the Israeli nation was required from the principle of territorial citizenship, according to which the nation-state aspires for civil equality of all its inhabitants. Israeli children used to be taught that Israel was created of people who came from "seventy languages". While Israel has absorbed into its nation those 'seventy nations' and thus fulfilled its obligation to them, Israel had not fulfilled its obligation towards the seventy-first 'native nation' - the Arab population - partly because of the confusion between nationality and religion and partly because of the fact that Israel was established through war against the Arab world. The Israeli solution in 1948 was to create a fictitious citizenship for the Arabs without considering them as members of the nation. Thus, an Israeli citizenship was enforced upon the Arabs, which had lived within the Israeli borders after the War of Independence. In as much as this step was required by the U.N. Resolution of 29 November 1947, it was still problematic, as citizenship means, among other thinks, the identification of the citizens with the State – the last thing that could have been expected from the Arabs living within the Israeli borders who were in 1948 an enemy defeated in war. The fact that until 1966 the Israeli Arabs had been under a military regime showed that the State did not consider them citizens, but rather potential enemies. Furthermore, it is impossible to conjecture that the enforcement of citizenship upon the Israeli Arabs had been made as a first step in a nation building process and towards their incorporation into the national life. This had become impossible because of the adoption of the fusion of religion and nationality.

The fusion of religion and nationality, or the notion of the "Jewish State", is not the only obstacle for the incorporation of Arabs or of people of Arab origin in the Israeli national life: Pan Arabism, Palestinian nationalism or Islamism – in as much as these world views exist among Israeli Arabs they will constitute an hindrance for the integration of the Arabs when Israel is declared as a republic. Nevertheless, there are also indications for the existence of tendencies towards integration among the Israeli Arabs. Benziman and Mansour point out that in 1954 the Israeli authorities had issued a registration order for service in the security forces which included also the Arab population and that this order was received with "a certain enthusiasm," by many Arab youth who presented themselves in the conscription offices. Yet, after the registration nothing happened and the Arab youth were not conscripted. Benziman and Mansour say it is not clear whether the registration order was issued to encourage Arab integration or to cause a massive exodus from the country of Arab youth who would have refused to conscript (Benziman & Mansour, 1992, pp. 117-8).

A somewhat surprising testimony for the existence of such integrative tendencies among the Israeli Arab population had come from someone who could be considered their greatest opponent – the former MK Dr. Azmy Bishara. Being a pan-Arabist, he wrote with obvious dismay that the Arab population in Israel was in a crisis which –

… Would lead eventually to its division into two main movements: One movement would stress integration, which is

Israeli identity, including service in the army, and I think that in some sections of the Arab population, towards the end of the century, there would be the demand to serve in the army, something to which I object. The second movement would turn into the direction of national autonomy. (Bishara, 1995, p. 47).

Those words were written in 1995 and it is possible that things have been changed since then. Indeed, the recent publication of the so called "Visionary Documents" point to another source for the objection to idea of the Israeli nation – post-Zionist ideas of the 'citizens' State and the bi-national State which had become common in certain segments of the Arab intellectual elite (see discussion below, pp. 204-214). Anyway, it should be taken into consideration that when the Israeli republic will be established a part of the Israeli Arab population would refuse to join it. This wish should be respected. There will remain a question of the civic status of those who refuse to join. In his proposal, as it appeared in Agassi's book, Kook maintained that what was not done in 1948 should be done now. This means, recognition of an Israeli nation and a call for the Israeli Arabs to join it as individuals while those who would refuse could not be citizens but only residents.

The execution of Kook's plan today is more problematic than it was in 1948, as it might look as a large-scale disenfranchisement of the Israeli Arab who would refuse to join the nation. In 1948 things were different, as the Arabs who found themselves under Israeli rule were defeated enemy and did not expect the Israeli citizenship to be conferred upon them. To the claim that the disenfranchisement of the Arabs is undemocratic it could be answered that to a large extent the current Israeli citizenship of the Arab is fictitious and that within the proposed plan it would become possible for those Arab who would desire it to gain real citizenship, that is full equality. Furthermore, the main political meaning of the disenfranchisement would be the denial of the right to vote to the Knesset, not the denial of rights of residency, and it does not necessarily have to include the right to vote to the local authority. Yet, in every country the rights of a resident are less than those of a citizen and it is obvious that those who will live in Israel as residents could not attain certain positions in the job market for which citizenship is usually considered as a necessary pre condition (such as positions in the state public service).

Another disadvantage of Kook's plan is the fact that it contravenes some U.N resolutions which aimed at the reduction of stateless persons, culminated in *The United Nation Convention on the Reduction of Statelessness*, which came into effect in 1975 and which demanded from all the states which are members of the United Nation to reduce as much as possible the stateless persons within their jurisdiction by conferring upon them citizenship.[15] Yet, it could be claimed that the abolition of the right to vote for the national institutions is not similar to the denial of the rights of residency nor does it mean the denial of the protection of the State or making those persons stateless.

A resemblance to Kook's plan could be found in the citizenship laws of the Baltic republics of Estonian and Latvia. Notwithstanding the fact that this legislation seemed to contradict the international law, the international community accepted this move with understanding and even accepted these countries as members of the EU (see above, pp. 143-155).

Nevertheless, if Kook's plan is adopted, it could not be denied that if many of the Israeli Arabs would refuse to join the Israeli nation there could be a problem both from a democratic and national point of view. A country which many of its inhabitants have a status of residents and do not enjoy full political equality could hardly be called democracy. From a national point of view the existence of a large national minority that cannot or would not participate in the national life would be a continuation of the current problematic situation. Thus, in the long run, the existence of a stable democratic Israeli nation depends on the joining of most of the Israeli Arab population. Furthermore, a real separation between the Jewish religion, or the Jewish ethnicity, on one hand, and the Israeli nationality, on the other, could exist only if the nation would consist of a considerable number of Arab persons, that it of persons who are clearly of a non Jewish origin.

The Future Vision Documents

The 'Future Vision of the Palestinians Arabs in Israel' (2006), known also as 'The Future Vision Document', was published by The National Committee for the Heads of the Arab Local Authorities in Israel (NCHALA) and followed by three similar documents published by three different Arab organizations[16]. The documents suggest dismantling the Jewish State and reestablishing Israel as a citizens' State or as a consociational bi-national democracy, and in fact as both. By this approach, they could be seen as a variant of current post-Zionism. Thus, as we are going to see, the criticism directed against post-Zionism is valid also in the case of these documents (see above, pp. 159-178).

Indeed, though the drafters of the *Future Vision Documents* do not mention it, it seems that they are influenced by the examples of the western multinational countries discussed above (pp. 130-137) when they demand to organize Israel as consociational democracy (Kaufman, 2008). Yet, the 'Future Vision State' portrayed by the documents is still very different from the multi-national democracies in the west and carries with it many of the abnormalities and deficiencies of the present Jewish State, as it also lacks an overall civic-national identity.

As noted above, stable multinational States are characterized by the existence of complementary national identities. The case before us is different, as the national identity of the Arabs in Israel, which is portrayed by the drafters of the documents, is confrontational to and alienated from both, the other (Jewish) nationality and the (future vision) state. This alienation appears already in the introduction of the document of the NCHALA in what the drafters call "the historical narrative". The spirit of the narrative is well described by Ghanem and Mustafa: according to them "The future vision related specifically to the question of the historic rights and to the being of the Palestinians 'the native inhabitants of the homeland', which means, that most of the Jews are immigrants to the homeland of the Palestinians." (Ghanem & Mustafa, 2008, p. 89). This means that from the point of view of "historic rights", Palestine, or *Eretz Yisrael*, is the homeland of the Palestinians not only in the simple meaning that they are the 'natives', but rather that the were supposed to be the sovereigns, or that Palestine or *Eretz Yisrael* was supposed to be an Palestinian-Arab nation-State. Thus, the establishment of Israel does not mean only the human suffering, the refuge and the discrimination suffered by "the natives", but in its essence it is an embezzlement of national rights. I do not want to get into the debate about what is known as the "Palestinian narrative". Yet, this narrative means a total delegitimization of Israel, which no reform could fix – unless Israel would turn into an Arab or Palestinian State. Charvit (2008, p. 60) described the situation very well:

> It is not yet clear, whether with the fulfillment of the Future Vision in full; the binary conception which divides the conquerors from the conquered will disappear. At the most it would become a confrontation between an ex conqueror and a retired conquered, between the old time oppressor to the old time oppressed. The demand for full partnership and to change the State comes from suspicion and separatism, which is wholly preoccupied with power sharing. (See also Reiter, 2008, pp. 151-152).

Thus, the Future Vision documents were not drafted by patriots who are trying to change the nature of their government, nor by an alienated minority trying to create a State that would also be "its own", but rather by an alienated group attempting to improve its conditions, at the same time maintaining their alienation. The Vision Documents are paradoxical: While they speak about reform of the Israeli State which amounts to the abolition of the "Jewish State", it does not seem that the drafters identify with the new Vision State, more than they identify with the present Jewish State. The Future Vision is confrontational towards the Future Vision State and preoccupied with what the Arabs could get from the new state, and says nothing about what might be expected of them as duties in the new consociational democracy. The Documents indeed raise the demand for equality of rights, but say nothing about the equality of duties of the Israeli Arabs (Reiter, 2008, p. 151). Thus, for instance, the Documents say nothing about whether the Arabs would be ready to go to the army and defend the Future Vision State.

The question that arises here is, why the drafters of the Vision Documents did not think it would be possible for the Arabs to identify with the new Vision State? There are several possible answers to this question. One theory is that although the Documents aspire to abolish the Jewish State, it seems as if the Future Vision State would remain Jewish, (at least in the sense of the sociological dominance of the Hebrew culture.) Moreover, the national character of the Documents raises the suspicion that even if the new State would be a symmetrical bi-national State, the Israeli Arabs could not identify with it because they could not identify with anything that is not a purely Arab national entity. To this mix, one must add the problem of national security, and especially the conscription to the army. Future Vision Israel would need an army. The drafters rightly assert that the needed reforms should not be conditioned by peace in the Middle East. Yet, the meaning of this is that it is possible that the new State would still be in conflict with the Palestinians or other Arab States. Thus, from the perception of an Arab nationalist point of view it seems that the circumstances, which are usually considered as preventing the identification of the Arabs with the "Jewish State", would prevail also in the "Visionary State".

Complementary to the nationalists, the antagonist attitude of the documents to the Future Vision State of their own design is the fact that the main interest of the documents is placed more in the political-cultural-symbolic realm, and less in the improvement of the socio-economic situation of the Israeli Arabs. The reasons for this are obvious: there is a clear contradiction between the national-cultural revival, which the documents demand, on one hand, and the improvement of the socio-economic situation of the Arabs, on the other. One necessary condition for socio-economic equality is the complete opening of the Israeli job market for the Israeli Arabs. Another condition would be to enable them to live wherever they choose. These two basic demands (which are not met by the present Jewish State), do not appear in the visionary documents – at least not in the same open clear and bold manner in which the demands for collective rights appear.

The reasons for this are obvious. The cultural revival, or the recognition of the Arabs as a "national native minority", presupposes the existence of an "Arab sector", as exists today in the Jewish State. Thus, a radical national world view which characterizes the Visionary Documents would object to emigration to the cities, because it would mean a partial integration into the Israeli society, and lead to a partial eradication of the "Arab sector", that is of the "Israeli-Palestinian-Arab nation". In addition, the way to socio-economic equality passes through integration into the present Israeli economy, that is, also into institutions and industries, which, from the point of view of the Documents, represent the so-called "colonialist State" which disinherited the Arab-Palestinians. In other words, the Future Vision State would still have an "Aircraft Industry" and other technological industries that will be part of the military-industrial complex. It is obvious why the Documents would hesitate to demand the opening of those institutes for the employment of the Israeli Arabs.

From the Documents' point of view the way to socio-economic equality lies essentially in the collective equality and development. Charvit remarks that the Documents show clear preference "to demand for the State's non-intervention in their business (of the Arabs) at the expense of the promotion of integration and partnership" (Charvit, 2008, p. 57), and that "the attitude towards Israelization could not be mistaken, the preferred option is withdrawal" (ibid. p. 59). The document of the NCHALA declares "the targets which are supposed to be in the central demands of the Arab Palestinians in the next two decades", out of seven demands only one is concerned with socio-economic equality (and even this is phrased in a very general and vague manner). There is no clear demand for freedom of occupation or living, and the discourse slides immediately to the collective level. The example for "affirmative action" is taken from the realm of "Lands" or budgets allocated to the Arab sector (and not an affirmative action, for instance, in the universities).

Another precondition for the integration of the Arabs in the Israeli economy has to do with the education they are going to receive. One of the obstacles which prevents the integration of the Arabs in the job market is the fact that though most if not all of the Israeli Arabs speak Hebrew, the Hebrew of many of them is not up to par. The Israeli economy is Hebraic and consequently a higher standard Hebrew instruction as well as occupational training in Hebrew are needed. So far, the Israeli State has prevented such an education from the Arabs, also as a means for their exclusion from the Israeli society. One would expect of the Visionaries that alongside their desire to protect the Arab culture against the dominant Hebrew, there would also be recognition that in Israel the Hebrew language is essential for the Arabs, and that Arabs should demand an increase of level of Hebrew teaching. Yet, the attitude which the documents exhibits towards the Hebrew is, again, essentially confrontational.

In addition, there seems to be a contradiction between the aspirations the documents express for the modernization of the Israeli-Arabs and their demand to teach in Arabic. The fact that the Arabic language is an obstacle for modernization is admitted by the drafters of the NCHALA's document themselves, and this is because of the "the linguistic duality between the society (the spoken popular language) and the education institutions (the classical literary Arabic), something which overloads the educational process and the development of high thinking capabilities."

The problem stems from the fact that the classical literary Arabic, or the Modern Standard Arabic – MSA (which is usually perceived as the language of education) is not suitable for modernization. It is not the mother tongue of the Arabs and its acquisition amounts to that of a new language. Furthermore, it is the language of the Koran, and there is an (religious) objection to reform it, in order to make it suitable for modern life (Marbry, 2013). Of course it is possible to develop the Arabic into what Gellner calls "High Modern Culture" in which industrial society could function. Yet several questions arise here. Why Israel, which is not an Arab country, would be successful where all the Arab countries seem to have failed? (Haeri, 2000). The second question is why to invest national resources in this when there is an available Hebrew language, in which the Israeli society is already functioning as a modern industrial society, and when the Israeli-Arabs already speak Hebrew. Here also arises the demand made by the documents for an Arab University. It is not clear at all what good this would do for the young Israeli-Arabs. It seems obvious that under normal conditions, if and when the Israeli job market is open for them, the young Israeli-Arabs would prefer to study in the Israeli Hebrew universities. And alternatively, encouraging them to go to an Arab university could severely damage their future and the chances of their integration in the Israeli society and economy.

Here, the Israeli Druze poet and academic Salman Masalha voiced a completely different opinion. In an article titled "Arabs, Speak Hebrew!" published in the Daily *Ha'aretz* on September 27 2010, Masalha called on Israel's

Ministry of Education to do away with the country public schools system's Arabic curricula and demanded to replace it with Hebrew and English course modules. According to Masalha the reason for the low performance of the Israeli Arab students is mainly that there are being taught in Arabic. The gap between the performances of those who study in Arabic, on one hand, and other foreign languages like English (and Hebrew), on the other "exists in the entire Arab world" and "has nothing to do with Zionism or Israel". According to Massalha, "everybody knows that the Arabic taught in schools is compared with Hebrew or any other foreign language, but it is not the language Arab children speak at home." The fact that "The mother tongue they speak at home is totally different from the literary Arabic taught at school", eventually creates a situation which perpetuates "linguistic superficiality that leads to intellectual superficiality." (see also Salameh, 2011).

The political and socio-economic exclusion of the Arabs in Israel is direct outcome of the "Jewish State" and cannot find its solution within the Jewish State. Yet, this problem would not find its solution in the Future Vision State, which carries with it many of the presupposition of the "Jewish State". On the contrary, what seems to be a problem in the Jewish State, receives a legitimization in the Vision State: The informal exclusion of the Arabs in the Jewish State accepts a constitutional legitimization in the structure which is supposedly bi-national and which perpetuate the civic and socio-economic inequality. Thus, it is not surprising, that among the Israeli Arabs there is not much enthusiasm for the idea of the bi-national State (Reiter, 1995, p. 55; Smooha, 2008, p. 132).

To what extent, then, are the documents conducive to the creation of an Israeli Nation-State? Here Agbaria and Mustafa (2011) argue that the documents do not only challenge the notion of the Jewish State, but also "the political continuity of collective identity of the Palestinian people" by proposing a new formula: Instead of 'two states for two peoples', they propose 'two States for three peoples'. The latter would mean that the Palestinians would exercise the right of self-determination as two different peoples: the first within a Palestinian Nation-State and the second within the Israeli State as an indigenous minority (p.726). Consequently, according to Agbaria and Mustafa, the documents represent an "embryotic" Palestinian-Israeli identity (p.731). Nevertheless, these might be possible implications from the publication of the documents, rather than their spirit: to the extent that they represent different national "Palestinian-Israeli" identity, this is not a hyphenated complementary identity, but rather a new national identity. Thus, and here I agree with Agbaria and Mustafa, "the challenge remains how to create the integrative identity of Palestinian-Israeli whose Israeliness is not a coerced Israelization?" and that "the question is how to remain a Palestinian and become Israeli?" (p. 732).

In sum, the confrontational tone of the Documents does not seem to be conducive to the creation of an Israeli nation-state. This pessimistic conclusion should be qualified given the fact that they were formulated within the world view associated with the ideology and the practice of the Jewish State and in which the notion of an Israeli nation-state is not on the agenda. Furthermore, it is not clear to what extent the documents represent the opinions of the Arab public or an elitist discourse (Ozacky-Lazar & Kabha, 2008). It might be true, as some have suggested, that they constitute an improvement of the present situation and that the documents manifest an attempt to stabilize the relations between the Jewish majority and the Palestinian minority, and that this is, in fact, a recognition of the State of Israel and a desire for a dialogue (Jamal, 2008). This is indeed a possible interpretation of the Documents. Yet, it is important to emphasize that if the Documents carry with them recognition of Israel, it is rooted in pragmatism, rather than sympathy (Jamal, 2008, p. 28). Anyway, even if the Documents indeed mean the stabilization and the improvement of the relations between the Jewish majority and the Arab minority, which is desirable, it still means that the "Vision State" would not become also the State of the Israeli Arabs, but, at the most, an "an improved Jewish State".

More is needed for equality. That is what is needed the evolution of an Israeli national consciousness among Israelis in general and Israeli Arabs in particular. It is true that the change in the character or the Israeli State from a Jewish State to an Israeli nation-state is above all the business of the (Jewish) majority. Yet, the questions posed above by Agbaria and Mustafa should be laid down before the (Arab) minority as well. There have been not few cases in which important carriers of national ideas were members of minorities also because they considered nationalism as an instrument for equality and integration. In as much as the Irish nation is Catholic, within its originators were members of the Irish protestant elite (Avineri, 1998, p. 2); and in as much as Pan Arabism was linked to Islam, many of its key ideologists were Christians. Similarly, the Indian Muslim Ulama objected to the division of the subcontinent and the establishment of Muslim Pakistan and supported the Indian Congress Party (Friedman, 1971).

In addition, Arabs or people of Arab descent have emigrated to western liberal democracies and become members of the local nations. If someone of an Arab descent could become an American or British, why not Israeli? It is possible that the conflict between Israel and parts of the Arab world constitutes a hindrance for a part of Israeli Arabs, but not necessarily for all of them. National identities are not primordial; thus what is required is to mold both "Arab Identity" and "Jewish Identity" from confrontational to complementary identities within the framework of an Israeli nation. Thus, the "victim discourse" of the Documents should be replaced by the questions: Under what conditions the Israeli Arabs could and would be willing to participate as equal members of an Israeli nation-state? What kind of cultural autonomy do the Israeli Arabs seek?

The model of the nation-state is not uniform and enables various degrees and forms of participation – if by integration as in the French or American republican version; or if by a cultural national autonomy as some of the consociational States discussed above. Other questions that need to be raised are: To what extent the national symbols needed to be changed or revised in order to make it possible for the Arabs to identify with the State? And how could the history of the Israeli Arabs be incorporated into the Israeli national history?

Here, some would say that the history of the Middle East makes it impossible to have anything but a confrontational Palestinian narrative. Yet, I think, that the idea that the history of the conflict in the Middle East constitutes an insurmountable obstacle for the creation of an Israeli nation-state is arguable. Without entering the question whether the Palestinian narrative is true, it is certainly contested. Further, it is usually said about national narratives that they are invented. Thus it is certainly possible to invent another non-confrontational one. Ernest Gellner once said that Romanticist thought had emphasized the need for a vivid national memory, yet in the process of nation-building too vivid a memory could become an obstacle, and there is also a need to forget.

Thus, in the process of the Israeli nation building, the Israeli Arabs no doubt will have to forget. Yet, it is important to stress they are not the only ones who will have to forget. This does not mean that one has to lie or to reinvent history. If the horrible history of the Afro-Americans in the United States had become part of the American national ethos (and an Afro-American has become the President of the United States) it is not necessarily impossible for the 'nakba' to become part of the future Israeli national ethos (and for an Israeli of an Arab descent to become an Israeli Chief of Stuff, or Prime Minister). In America this was made possible because the discourse was non-confrontational at least in the sense that it did not question the legitimacy of the American State and the American nation. On the contrary, Martin Luther King demanded his rights as American and in the name of the

American dream. Thus, it is possible that the time has come, or would come, where the Israeli Arabs should demand their rights as Israelis.

I think that if there is an element in the Vision Documents upon which Israeli national identity could be built, it is not to be found in what is written in it, but rather in what they do not say. In as much as those documents are confrontational, they do not demand to dismantle the Israeli State, if by the establishment of an Arab or Palestinian State in its stand, if by dismembering it to a Jewish and an Arab component. Alternatively, there is no demand to join a future Palestinian State and there is a strong objection to any territorial exchange within a future Israeli-Palestinian arrangement. It is possible that that the reason for the absence of those demands is sheer pragmatism. However, it is also possible it means that eventually Israeli Arabs may want to be Israelis.

The Relation with the Diaspora Nation

The recognition of an Israeli nation does not mean that Israel could not see itself as uniquely related to what it identifies as its "Diaspora nation", that is the historical Jewish people. There are many States that consider themselves as connected to Diasporas, yet define themselves as republics. One of the ways to express the connection with the Diaspora nation is the existence of a "Law of Return", which usually means expedited naturalization procedure for members of the Diaspora.

Israelis concieve of Israel's "Law of Return" defining the relation between Israel and the historical Jewish people. Consequently this law has acquired a transcendental status, as it is the ultimate expression of the fusion of religion and nationality, hence it is a nation-constituting law. Yet, within the framework of an Israeli republic, or an Israeli nation-state, the law loses its transcendental status. We should ask to what extent Israel needs a law of return, or under what conditions the existence of a law of return would be compatible with the separation between nationality and religion and the existence of an Israeli democratic republic.

One of the criticisms of the law of return is that it gives preference to the immigration of a specific ethnic or religious group, i.e. the Jews, and that is not democratic. Yet, a law of return as such does not contradict democracy because it deals with the relation of the State with individuals who are not members of the (territorial) nation, that is who are not citizens of the State. In other words, it does not discriminate between the citizens as individuals. Furthermore, the right of every nation to preserve its national character is recognized by the international law. The international treaty for the abolishment of any form of racist discrimination accepted by the United Nations on 21st of December 1965 establishes in paragraph 1(3) of the first part that "nothing which is said in this treaty cannot be interpreted against the lawful instructions of States which are members of the treaty concerning residency, citizenship and naturalization, as long as these instruction do not discriminate against a certain nationality" (Rubinstein, 1996, p. 297; Gans, 2006, pp. 201-2).

In other words, while a State is not allowed to discriminate against a certain nationality, it is allowed to discriminate for a certain nationality. As such, there is no hindrance for Israel, if it wishes to preserve its national character, to allow immigration according to a certain ethnic key. However, it should not discriminate against any members of religion or nationality that wants to enter the country. Thus, in addition to the law of return, Israel also needs regular laws of immigration, which will regulate immigration according to the rules which are customary among the nations: family relations, the potential contribution to the nation, occupations needed by the market and so on and so forth.

As noted, many States have laws of return through which the State encourages the immigration of a certain ethnic group (or sometimes groups), which it prefers. This encouragement usually acquires the form of simplified naturalization procedures for those ethnic groups. The list of countries that have laws of return in one form or another is long. Alongside Germany, Armenia and Greece, which were mentioned above, Spain allows simplified naturalization processes for Andorrans, Portuguese, and citizens of Latin America, the Philippines, Equatorial Guinea, and Jews of Spanish origin. Similarly, Turkey allows simplified naturalization processes for persons of Turkish origin. The same is true for Bulgaria, Croatia, Finland, India (up to four generations), Hungary and Japan. China's immigration laws give preference to "ethnic Chinese", including those who have lived outside of China for many generations. Consequently immigration to China has been predominantly "ethnic Chinese". All these countries consider themselves as having diaspora nations. It is important to point out that a nationality-based immigration policy had been conducted by the United States when the immigration quotas for various nationalities had been set according to the ratio of the matching ethnicity within the American people. This policy stemmed from the desire to prevent a change of the national character of the United States by immigration. There is no doubt that the American Laws of Immigration were aimed to give priority to immigrants of north-west Europe over those of eastern Europe, not to speak over immigrants from the eastern hemisphere. Even though the immigration laws had been amended several times, the quota based upon "national origin" had remained an essential element of the American immigration laws until the nineteen sixties (Johnson, 1998). This did not prevent the United States from being an immigration country open to immigrants from all over the world.

Unlike in Israel and Germany, in all of the countries mentioned above, the naturalization of members of the preferred group is not automatic. Hence, the immigrant, even though he or she immigrates by the right of return, still has to go through (simplified) naturalization processes. In other words, a member of the Diaspora nation who wants to become a member of the territorial nation must go through naturalization processes. Consequently those countries distinguish between the ethnic Diaspora nation, on one hand, and the multi-ethnic territorial nation on the other. The subordination of the member of the Diaspora nation to naturalization procedures (though simplified) also means that unlike the Israeli case, all other countries are not obliged to naturalize the member of the Diaspora nation and retain the right to reject his or her motion (Gans, 2005, pp. 211-215). As for Germany which, like Israel, confers immediate citizenship to those who use their right of return, it is important to emphasize, as Gans does, that this law applies only to refugees or uprooted person of German origin and not to persons of German origin in general. In other words, it applies to the German ethnic minorities of east and central Europe that were either deported, or did not want or could not integrate in their resident countries. This does not apply, for instance, to American or British of German origin, which are subordinated to regular immigration laws.

The automatic citizenship, conferred upon those considered as Jews could be problematic from a republican point of view from two reasons. First, automatic citizenship means that there are no procedures for joining the nation or the citizen body. This tends to blur the distinction between the citizen body and the Diaspora nation. Here it is important to note that the Law of Citizenship of 1952 had actually imposed citizenship. In other words, the automatic citizenship was not given to a Jewish immigrant who had applied for citizenship, but every one who had immigrated under the auspices of the law of return had turned automatically into a citizen. Thus, an application for citizenship (which could be interpreted as a request to join the nation) was not required. More than that, conferring immediate citizenship on those who had just descended from a plane or a ship entails the degradation of citizenship, as the naturalized person should have some amount of identification with the State and the nation, a reasonable understanding of the political system which is a precondition for democratic participation, a desire to integrate and more. Since the liberal State could not look into the hearts of the people, it is generally accepted that in order to become a citizen a new immigrant or resident should fulfill some conditions which are essentially technical, like residency of several years, knowledge of the language, or the basics of the constitution, and so on.

Notwithstanding the problematic character of conferring an automatic citizenship, it would have been still possible to see the act of immigration by itself as expressing a will to join the territorial nation. Indeed, it seems that the German Law of Return presupposes this principle when it accords automatic citizenship to refugees or uprooted persons of German origin upon their arrival on German soil. Yet, paragraph 2 of the Israeli Law of Citizenship (1952) made it impossible, as it had established that every Jew born in Israel would accept his or her citizenship under the auspices of the Law of Return. The reason given for this odd paragraph was the desire to create equality between the immigrants Jews and those who were born in the country. Though, as Amnon Rubinstein remarks, it had been possible to create such equality if the law said that every Jew who immigrates to Israel is entitled to citizenship, as if he was born here (Rubinstein, 1996, p. 878). While in such a case there would be different naturalization procedures for Jews and non-Jews, it would have been possible to see immigration as a sort of naturalization process, which turns the Jewish immigrant into a member of the territorial nation.

Paragraph 2 of the Law of Citizenship in its strange wording united all the Israeli Jews when it established that they are granted citizenship by virtue of the right of return, yet it distinguished between the right of citizenship of Israeli born Jews, on one hand, and Israeli born non-Jews, especially Arabs, on the other. While the former right for citizenship was entailed from their right of return, the latter right of citizenship was entailed from birth.

Paragraph 2 of the Law of Citizenship (1952) abolished, in fact, the existence of an Israeli territorial nation.[17]

An important difference between the current Israeli Law of Return and Laws of Return in other countries is in the degree of importance and centrality. In other countries, the Law of Return usually appears as paragraphs of immigration laws; while in Israel the Law of Return is central, as it is considered as a nation-constituting law. There is another important unique aspect of the Israeli Law of Return, in that it defines the Diaspora nation according to religion; while in other countries, the Diaspora nation is defined according to origin or ethnicity. The definition of a Diaspora nation according to religion is more problematic than defining it by ethnicity or origin – in that religions are most often multi-vocal. As such, a religious definition of the Diaspora is likely to create controversies. At the same time, a definition of the Diaspora by religion forces the State to intervene in religious matters, which contradicts the tenets of liberal democracy. In other words, when the Greek Law of Return grants "ethnic Greeks" expedited naturalization rights and demands from them proof for their Greek origin, the outcome of the verdict of the State in this matter is likely to be less controversial than that which establishes whether or not a certain person is "a Jew". There is no question that the Israeli legislature was aware of this difficulty when it added the religious definition of a Jew as a factor for the purpose of return (a child of a Jewish mother and member of no other religion and those who convert to Judaism) also an 'ethnic' one, which extend the Law of Return until the fourth generation of Jews, which means that origin also counts. Here it seems that an Israeli Law of Return, which gives special naturalization rights to every person of "Jewish Origin", would be less controversial. Such an 'ethnic' Law of Return would not grant converts the right of return, as they are not persons of "Jewish" origin, and this is another advantage of an ethnic formulation. This not only makes it unnecessary for the State to intervene in the controversy of "who is Jew" (which is an intervention of the State in religious matters), but also prevents a situation in which persons wish to convert because they want to immigrate to Israel. For persons of non-Jewish origin (whether or not they are converts) the road will be open to immigrate and become Israelis by the regular laws of immigration that the Israeli republic is bound to have.

The uniqueness of the Israeli Law of Return in its present formulation turns it into a bad immigration law, leaving Israel with practically breached borders. Originally and justifiably, this law was intended to enable mass unconditioned immigrations of distressed Jews; hence the definition of the right of return had to be as wide as possible (see above, pp. 85-86). Yet, what was the advantage of the Law of Return – enabling mass immigrations – turned out to be a disadvantage of the law as an immigration law, as the inclusive policy, or the wide range of "Jews" recognized by the law, means that Israel is loosing control over immigration. In the past, the fact that Israel has been a country in a tate of war, on one hand, and relatively poor, on the other, still regulated immigration. It had been reasonable to assume that those who immigrated to Israel had done so because they dentified with Israel or because they were distressed Jews. All this has changed during the last decades. Israel has become a relatively wealthy country and a preferred destination for immigration, and consequently it needs, like any normal country, regular laws of immigration. The Law of Return, as an immigration law, does not allow Israel to control immigration unless it controls the definition of "who is a Jew?", which is very problematic.

So it seems that within the present Law of Return there is a hidden alliance between Israelis who consider themselves secular and liberals, on one hand, and the Orthodox rabbinate, on the other. From a liberal point of view the approach to the question of "who is a Jew?" should be "liberal", and probably the answer to the question should be that a Jew is someone who declares him or herself to be a Jew. Yet, when such a widening approach would be implemented within the present Law of Return, combined with the fact that Israel today is an attractive country for immigration, it would encourage mass conversions made for the purpose of immigration to Israel. It would be possible for the foreign workers inside Israel to convert to Judaism in order to become Israeli citizens, or to anyone living abroad simply to convert in order to be eligible for immigration to Israel. In the current case those who actually regulate the immigration are the Orthodox rabbis and their hard-line approach towards conversion make it difficult to become a Jew. This approach has the tacit approval of the "secular". This is inappropriate and this is one of the reasons that the Law of Return, as a mass immigration law, should eventually be abolished.

Within the fusion of religion and nationality, or the "New Civil Religion", the Law of Return and the Law of Citizenship as formulated in the nineteen fifties were not just immigration laws but nation-constituting laws. In other words, the Law of Return has received a transcendental status as a constitutional manifestation of the fact that Judaism is a nationality. In fact it is more than constitutional, as constitutions could be changed, it is transcendental; it is "above" the Israeli democracy and not subjugated to the Israeli democratic will. It is also eternal, because this law is necessary as long as there is even one Jew who lives outside the borders of Israel. Yet, within the framework of an Israeli republic, or that of the separation between nationality and religion and recognition of an Israeli nation the law loses its transcendental status and eternal necessity. The questions that we have to address are: What were the needs that the law of return was supposed to meet in the first place? To what extent are those needs relevant today? And to what extent could regular immigration laws meet those needs?

A NATION LIKE ALL NATIONS

The aim of the Zionist movement was to solve the "Jewish Problem" – the physical and the socio-economic distress of the Jews. In this sense, it is important to see that today only remnants remained of the historical Jewish problem. Those exist in the former Soviet Union where the national status is unstable, and it is still not clear to what extent civic nations into which Jews could integrate were created there, and to what extent the Jews are willing to integrate into these nations. Thus, it seems that the era of Jewish mass immigrations, in as much as the Jewish problem is concerned, is over. Yet, the Zionist movement had spoken on behalf of the right of national self-determination of the Jews in general and not necessarily of distressed Jews. This meant that all Jews, wherever they are, had the right to become members of the new nation. Thus, within the framework of the adaptation of the Jewish world to the new situation created by the establishment of Israel, it should have been necessary to enable the Jews who wanted to take advantage of the new option to become Israelis. However, this could have been a temporary situation only. In other words, when persons emigrate from their country, they or their descendants lose the citizenship or their right for the citizenship of their country of origin. Consequently, if it had been possible in 1948 to see the Jews all over the world as those who had exiled from their country and thus entitled to Israeli citizenship, it seems reasonable that after more than sixty years of independence, in which those who have wanted to realize their right for an unconditioned Israeli citizenship could have done so, the Jewish world would adapt to the new situation. In other words, the automatic right for self-determination as Israelis could not be kept for the Jews forever. In this sense it would be wise to declare that the Law of Return in its present formulation would be valid for few more years before its abolishment. Of course, after the abolishment of the Law of Return the option for immigration would be open (for Jews and non-Jews) through regular immigration laws. Alternatively, Israel could still maintain immigration laws, which would grant simplified naturalization processes for persons of Jewish origin.

There will be probably those who would object to the assumption that the "historical Jewish Problem" has come to a solution, suggesting that western liberal democracies are not immune from anti-Semitism and that the persecution of the Jews could repeat itself again. Yet, in order to give an answer to this possibility there is no need for the present all embracing Law of Return. A "Proposal for National Debate", published by Hillel Kook and Shmuel Merlin in the daily z on 18.4.75 included the following suggestion:

> The new basic laws, which will be discussed by the next Knesset, should include legislation that will establish that also members of all religions and nationalities will be able to immigrate to Israel. Their number will be set by the needs of the country and naturally the majority of the immigrants will be Jews. … Consequently, such legislation overlaps, to a large extent, the practical need of a Law of Return. Nevertheless, it has to include also a clause, which says that every person who is a Jew or because he is considered a Jew he is persecuted in his country, and wants to find shelter in Israel, the gates of the country will be open for him beyond the immigration quotas set by the law.

We can see here how the Law of Return loses its central and transcendental status and turns out to be a clause in the immigration laws, as it is done by other nations.

Yet, there are few things that need to be said about Kook and Merlin's proposal. First, the proposal was written in 1975, before the collapse of the Soviet Union, and before Israel had become an attractive destination for immigration. After the great waves of Jewish immigration from the former Soviet Union, the assumption presented in the above suggestion,

224 | A NATION LIKE ALL NATIONS

(namely that naturally the majority of immigrants to Israel would be Jews) is arguable. While this is not necessarily a problem, if we wish to meet "the practical need of the Law of Return" it is still possible to include also in the immigration law a clause that will give preference to people of Jewish origin as discussed above.

In the above suggestion Kook and Merlin distinguish between those who are persecuted as Jews – who are entitled to immigration beyond immigration quotas of the future – and all the others whose immigration would be regulated by ordinary laws of immigration. Their suggestion seems to fit both the aims of Zionism and the separation between nationality and religion. The careful wording should be noticed here: "every person who is a Jew or because he is considered a Jew he is persecuted in his country", which makes it unnecessary to establish whether or not this person is a Jew: it is enough that the person is persecuted as a Jew. Yet, it seems that Kook and Merlin's phrasing in this manifest is two narrow and the category of "stateless Jews" should be added to those who are persecuted as Jews (it should be remembered that the manifesto was published before the collapse of the Soviet Union). The Jews of the former Soviet Union might not necessarily fall within the category of "persecuted Jews", but rather that of "stateless Jews" (a concept which Kook had used elsewhere).[18] They were stateless, because under the totalitarian Soviet regime they were denied their right for self-determination, meaning, the right to choose their nationality.

Nevertheless, the obligation of Israel to open the gates of the country beyond the immigration quotas to those who are persecuted as Jews and for stateless Jews raises some other tough questions. As noted above, one of the reasons that the Law of Return in its present formulation could be abolished is the fact that the historical Jewish problem has been almost completely disappeared. However, it is still possible that a Jewish Problem will appear in the future and the question is under what conditions will Israel be obliged to solve it, and whether or not this solution will necessarily by a Law of Return. In other words, if new Jewish publics which will be either persecuted or distressed will be discovered, would Israel be obliged to rescue them as in the case of the historical Jewish problem? It seems that the separation between nationality and religion means, among other things, the recognition that Judaism is a universal religion or universal Church, and that the special relations of Israel with its Diaspora should not necessarily acquire the form of immigration, but rather of culture and, wherever there is a discrimination and persecution of Jews, also by supporting the struggle of the Jews for equality, in diplomatic appeal, to the responsible governments, as other nation-states show towards their Diasporas while still acknowledging their legitimacy.

Is There an Israeli Nation?

Until now I have discussed the Israeli nation as if it existed, though unrecognized. Yet, is there an Israeli nation? This raises another question, "what is a nation?" I don't want to enter here into this elaborate question which has vexed many scholars in the last two hundreds years or so, but for the present discussion we need a definition, temporary as it may be. The famous sociologist Ernest Gellner suggests two provisional definitions for a nation:

> 1. Two men are of the same nation if and only if they share the same culture, where culture in turn means a system of ideas and signs and associations and ways of behaving and communicating.

> 2. Two men are of the same nation if and only if they recognize each other as belonging to the same nation. … If and when the members of the category firmly recognize certain mutual rights and duties to each other in virtue of their shared membership of it. (Gellner, 1983, p. 7).

These two definitions represent two aspects of the nation: the common culture, on one hand, and the common will or consciousness, on the other. It is possible to combine the two definitions into one provisional definition, which will demand that both, the cultural and the voluntary components would exist. According to this definition, in its social, economic and cultural elements, Israel resembles a mature nation, on one hand, while the voluntary component is wanting, on the other hand – a group whose members do not consider themselves a nation do not meet a basic condition for nationhood.

On the eve of Israel's independence it was already clear that the Hebrew entity that had been created in Palestine was clearly distinguished from the historical Jewish people. Richard Crossman, a member of the Anglo-American Committee established after the Second World War to examine various solutions in Palestine and also the conditions of the Jews in the refugees' camps in Europe testified regarding this matter:

> When I reflect on my impressions of Palestine, I see that the Jews of the national home have become a nation. The issue is not whether or not the Jewish people shall return to Zion, but whether political recognition shall be given to an accomplished fact. There are excellent books describing of Arab nationalism but there is no book … which gives even an inkling of the nationhood of the six hundred thousand Jews of Palestine. (Crossman 1947, p. 202)

In another place Crossman says:

> Just as the Englishman who immigrated to the States ceased to be an Englishman and became an American, so the Jews of the national home had lost the separate characteristics of their countries of origin, and become fused in a single nation. The national home was not a synthetic colony, composed of Jews of

fifteen different nationalities, but a new Palestinian community, aggressively nationalist, self consciously Hebrew, the nucleus of a brand-new Western State planked down on the seaboard of the Arab world (ibid., p. 167).

On the eve of independence the Israelis were distinct not only from non-Hebrew and non-modern Jews who had lived in the Diaspora, but also from modern American or British Jews. If we take Gellner's characterization of the nation as community, which possesses a homogeneous high culture, and which could support the division of labor needed in industrial society, then Israel and the Hebrew culture meet these conditions. According to Gellner, nationalism appears because of the demands of industrial society, which depends on the existence of large homogeneous unit characterized by high culture. The homogeneous cultural medium enables the communication and high mobility, as a precondition for the division of labor of the industrial society. The only system that could ensure the creation of such medium is the modern state, especially through its educational system. As Gellner notes "The nation-state holds the monopoly of legitimate culture in as much as it holds the monopoly of legitimate violence and even more so". Thus, "modern man is not loyal to a monarch or a land or a faith, whatever he may say, but to a culture (1983, p. 36)". The acquisition of this culture is what enables the modern person to acquire also the professional mobility, which is a precondition for respectful life in modern society. This mobility, though, exists only within the national medium.

Gellner's theory confirms the existence of an Israeli nation. There is no doubt that Israel has developed a Hebrew homogeneous cultural medium, which enables the high mobility of individuals and the development of a modern industrial society. For most of the Israelis, if not for all of them, the ability to make a respectful living is related to their sharing of the Hebrew culture. It is this high Hebrew culture through which the Israelis operate a modern industrial society and it is the Hebrew generic training they receive by the national education system, which enables them the mobility in this industrial society. This mobility is limited, of course, to the national culture medium or to the geographical borders of Israel. Many Israelis today seem to possess the illusion of universal mobility (no doubt an inheritance of their "universal" Jewish past), yet for most of them emigration, if possible, will entail a decrease in the standard of living. Indeed emigration no longer tempts the descendants of the "wandering Jew". They are no longer east-European universal (non-national) poor Jews who consider emigration as a way to improve their standard of living, but rather Israelis, sons and daughters of a relatively rich nation and as such connected by their navels to their Hebrew culture, granting them this wealth.

Yet, this should be qualified because in the present situation the social and occupational mobility characterize only the Jews of Israel and do not apply to the Israeli Arabs who are prevented from many jobs, especially those related to the modern industrial society. A clear expression to the immobility of the Arabs is the separation between the Jewish and the Arab populations and the confinement of the Arabs to the non-industrial countryside. Hence, it is obvious that the creation of an Israeli nation means not only the granting of civic rights to the Israeli Arabs, but also the opening of the Israeli society and the vast spectrum of its occupational options for the Arabs. A creation of an Israeli nation also means the emigration of a part of the Israeli Arab population from the countryside to the big industrial cities.

In order to enhance the mobility of the Israeli Arab a formal opening of the Israeli society is not enough. They should be equipped with the means that enable such mobility, above all, proper Hebrew. It seems as if the Israeli education system has never taken care that the Israeli Arab should receive a proper Hebrew education, which would enable them to move freely in the

Israeli society, if because of the confusion between nationality and religion, if because of the desire to perpetuate their immobility.

The existence of an Israeli nation is demonstrated also by its proven absorption capabilities. In less than seventy years of independence the nation has been multiplied by more than a dozen. This seems to be unprecedented national population growth. While the various waves of immigration changed the character of the nation (though, some would claim not enough) the nation remained Hebrew. Even though most of the immigrants had come from unindustrialized countries in Eastern Europe and the Middle East, Israel has developed into a modern industrialized nation. In the past, this success had been usually attributed to Zionist "ideologies", such as that of the "negation of the Diaspora", which had been to a certain extent the Israeli version of the American "melting pot", in which state apparatuses were used in order to detach the new immigrants from their original country which was considered "exilic" or "backwards" for the creation of "new" or "modern" Jew. Yet, ascribing the successful absorption of immigrants mainly to Zionist ideology would probably mean yielding too much to ideology, especially in the recent decades when the official Zionist ethos has been somewhat on the decline. In those years Israel had successfully absorbed a million immigrants from the former Soviet Union. The absorption capabilities of the Israeli society stems from its being a "melting pot" like any other modern dynamic nation, and not necessarily because of "melting pot" policies of the government (to the extent that they exist today). The latter were more needed in the first decades after independence when the country had been less developed and less industrialized. At the present time, new immigrants who want to take advantage of all that Israel has to offer have to master the Hebrew language and other basic skills needed for functioning in an industrial society. In a sense, a real Israeli national education system does not exist or is still wanting, as it is divided between "Jewish" and "Arab" education systems and there are quasi-autonomous education systems for various Jewish ultra-Orthodox sections. Yet, the Israeli education system has managed to give those basic skills needed for the functioning in modern society to the majority of the nation.

The strength of the Israeli society is expressed also by the processes of Israelization, not only of the new immigrants, but also of the Israeli Arabs. There is an interesting phenomenon here, where a public, which formally had not been included in the political nation, is increasingly identified and identifies itself with the sociological nation. Presented here are relevant aspects from Sammy Smooha's research. Smooha criticized what he called "the radicalization thesis" which was accepted by Israeli Orientalists, which suggested that since 1967 the Israeli Arabs have gone through a process of radicalization and segregation. According to Smooha, the Israeli Arabs are more close to the Israeli Jews than to the Palestinians who live in the occupied territories – both culturally and politically. Smooha sees the Israeli society as a society that has a basic solidarity, not only among the Jews, but also between Jews and Arabs (Smooha, 2001b, pp. 274-6). Smooha's conclusions can be contested (ibid., pp. 245 – 249). However, I do not intend to argue that it follows from Smooha's conclusions that the Israeli Arabs would accept the idea of an Israeli Nation. Smooha himself repeatedly declared that a bi-national Israel is the option preferred by Israeli Arabs.

The survival test is often one of the important indications for the existence of a nation. In his book *A Nation Reborn*, Richard Crossman (mentioned above) had this to say regarding the policies of Ernest Bevin, the British Foreign Secretary on the eve of Israel's independence:

> … The fact that the Jews of Palestine were compelled to fight and to win a war of independence proved to the Western world that they were indeed a nation. … As far as I know there is only one test on whether an ethnic community is indeed a nation. That test is war. … It was Ernest Bevin, the man who believed that

it was only a religious community, who compelled the *Yishuv* to pass this test triumphantly. Moreover, the War of Independence brought a second and equally important advantage to the new nation. It was demonstrated that Israel was not, as her Arab neighbors believed, a British satellite, the advance guard of British imperialism ... There is nothing like a clash with western imperialism to establish the credentials of a new member of the United Nations (Crossman, 1960, pp. 85-6).

Indeed, according to the international law, the survival and viability of any State – not necessarily a nation-state – constitutes a basis for its legitimization (Dinstein, 1971, p. 91). Yet, it is important to see that Israel is not a regime, but a nation, and its ability to survive is linked to its nationhood. Thus, the existence of a popular army, extensive mobilization of reserve army in war times, and also the high motivation of the Israeli soldier, testify to the existence of an Israeli nation. Not long ago, the so-called "New Historian" Ilan Pape, criticized the myth of "few against many", on which generations of Israelis had grown up. According to this myth in Israel's War of Independence, the Israeli few prevailed upon the Arab many. According to Pape, in many of the battles in the war the numbers of combatants was even on both sides – which he considers to be a refutation of that myth (Pape, 1995, p. 42).

Assuming that Pape's thesis is correct, the fact that the *Yishuv* which numbered 625,000 persons on the eve of independence, could mobilize from its midst numbers which would match those of five so-called Arab "nations", in addition to the local Palestinian Arab population, testifies to high organization and motivation capabilities which only characterize nations.[19] It was Clausewitz who suggested that the victories of republican France over the European coalition after the revolution were not the product of the skills of the French generals only, but mainly, because for the first time in European history a national army based upon general conscription of highly motivated citizens was used in battles. The same was the case in Israel's War of Independence: The Hebrew national army was not confronted by mobilized nations, but only regimes, or alternatively, by a local population that was not organized.

Was There a "Jewish Nation" Before the Appearance of the Zionist Movement?

The uniqueness of the fusion of religion and nationality is expressed not only by the abnormality of Israel, but also in its being very problematic from point of view of the research study of nationalism. The notion of Judaism as both nationality and religion is problematic from the point of view of the current study of nationalism because it assumes a "primordial" nation, which has existed from time immemorial (or, at least, three thousands years). There is an ongoing debate in the study of nationalism on the question to what extent, if at all, there is a continuation between the modern nations and the ethnic forms that these nations consider as their origin. On one side of the debate stand the modernists, whose conspicuous representative is Ernest Gellner, who see the so called ethnic origin of the nation as contingent, sometimes a fiction, and in any case unnecessary and even obstructive for nation-building. On the other side stand the primordialists or the ethnicists, whose conspicuous representative is Anthony Smith, who agree that nations are product of the modern age, yet they suggest that the nation is shaped to a large extent by former ethnic sentiments and structures (Hutchison, 1994, pp. 1-38).

While both modernists and primordialists agree that nations and nationalism are modern phenomenon, they disagree also on the reason for the appearance of modern nations and nationalism. Modernists consider the nation as an outcome of the industrial age, and the nation as instrumental in the desire of the members of the nation to integrate into modernity. Primordialists, on the other hand, would not dispute the claim that the nation is also a product of the hardships of the industrial age, but they see also an important cause, if not the most important one, for the appearance of nationalism, in the attempt of various ethno-cultural groups to protect their culture. The modernist sees "national culture" as an instrument for nation building and for achieving the "good life", while the primordialists considers the revival and protection of the national culture as the prime goal of nationalism.

The division between "modernists", and "primordialists" or "ethnicists" is a coarse one, and certainly does not represent correctly the current study of nationalism. There will be many who would disagree the labeling of Smith as "primordialist" and also among modernists there are important differences (Ben Israel, 2004, pp. 451-491). Yet it seems to me that this binary division is the best starting point; I will try to qualify it in what follows.

Paradoxically, Israel seems to fit the paradigms or even to be the archetype for both modernists and primordialists. In the introduction to the Hebrew edition of his *Nations and Nationalism* Gellner said that the case of Zionism does not present a problem for his theory of nationalism (Gellner, 1993). According to Gellner, modern Israel is furnished with all the cultural equipment needed in the modern world: a literate population, a mass public education system, a common modernized language, a modern system of communications and legal system, in short, a 'high culture' of the kind required by the mobile, anonymous society which industrialism creates (Smith, 1996b, p. 377). While Modern Israel is indeed a Nation it could be claimed that before the rise of Zionism, the Jews had nothing which would commend them as such: they did not live in the same territory, nor did they speak the same language, and did not even aspire to live under a common government. Therefore, it could be claimed that Israel was constructed *'ex nihilo'* and could serve as an exemplary model or archetype for modernism.

On the other hand, Israel and Zionism have served as an exemplary model for Smith's ethno-symbolism and some would say that Israel serves as an archetype for Smith theory of nationalism, or even that the Smith's theory of nationalism is actually based on Zionism (Ben Israel, 2004, pp. 113-114). As Smith puts it "(to) assert ... that there is simply no connection between the age-old Jewish yearnings and pilgrimages to Zion and the modern ingathering of Jewish exiles into Palestine, is to miss, not only the element of ethnic ascription, but also the whole aspect of popular motivation and collective self-understanding which is essential to the success of any nationalism". From this point of view, in as much as Israel is modern, it is still a product of Jewish collective memory, or of the "ancient conceptions of the holy land and the chosen people, which "had retained their popular resonance through encoded collective memories, symbolism and ritual, and the generational repetition of collective aspirations" (Smith, 1995a, p.16).

As the reader has probably noticed, my approach towards nationalism, in general, and Zionism in particular is modernist, viewing the "Jewish nation" (that is the "Israeli Nation"), as a creation of the Zionist movement. Yet, in as much as my stand is modernist, it is important not to confuse the question of to what extent was there a "Jewish nation" before the appearance of Zionism?, with the question of the legitimacy of Zionism as a movement for national self-determination. Here, the modernist claim that nations are not "natural" has been used as a basis for the de-legitimization of nationalism, in general, and Zionism in particular (Hobsbawm, 2006; Ben Israel, 2004, pp. 471-2). In fact, this is what happened to Sand's *Invention of the Jewish People* (2009). Contrary to Sand's original views and intentions, his inquiry into the origin of the Jews or to the question of the invention of the Jewish nation, had turned into a fierce debate about the legitimization of Zionism and Israel. Furthermore, whatever their attitude towards nationalism was, modernists like Gellner, Hobsbawm and Anderson saw the nation as a "real" being, ontologically and epistemologically. Hence, the nation could be distinguished by its national culture and by the common consciousness of its members. Yet, post-modernists use the modernist claim that the nation is "an invention" to see it as a fiction and to deny the existence of the nation altogether (Ben Israel, 2004, pp. 476-80). As Uri Ram maintains "nationalism is perceived here as a discourse of the 'imaginative' type (Ram, 2006, pp. 20-22; pp. 177-178). In other words, the nation is nothing but a dominant "narrative" which suppresses, like all other products of modernity, particular identities; there are no American or British nations, but a society which is an assemblage of ethno-cultural groups. The nation is a suppressive fiction, while the particular culture has a real end even liberating existence.

As for the question of legitimization of Zionism and Israel, the tendency to identify this question with the question to what extent there was indeed a "Jewish nation" before the appearance of Zionism stems mainly from the romanticist notion of the nation which sees nations as primordial entities and rejects the idea of "nation building" and consequently grants independence only to existing nations. As mentioned above, many of the members of the United Nations are not in fact "nations", and certainly were not nations when they had become independent. Accepting the romanticist notion of nationalism means the delegitimization of those countries and in fact of the entire international order. In other words, even if the Palestinians do not constitute a nation today, it does not mean that a Palestinian leadership or elite is not entitled to demand independence to solve "the Palestinian Problem" by the building of a Palestinian nation-state, as the fact that the Jews who did not constitute a nation in the nineteen century did not forfeit the right of the Zionist movement to demand to solve the Jewish Problem by the establishment of a Jewish nation-state. Moreover, Israel seems to have an advantage on many other members of the United Nations, because even if there had been no "Jewish nation" at the end of the nineteenth century, this nation (the Israeli Nation) exists today. Thus, the Zionist movement had succeeded in creating a nation, while many members of the United Nations who demanded independence by the right of national self-determination failed.

Within the debate between primordialists and modernists, the Israeli academic research on nationalism in general and Zionism in particular has always tended to be 'primordialist'. As noted above, the latters, though they might agree that nations are modern, still consider the nation to be built on a pre-modern ethnic core, which suited the notion of the fusion of faith and nationality. A good example is proposed by one of Israel's leading historians Jacob Katz. According to Katz (1983) nations had existed before the appearance of nationalism, or, alternatively, nations are direct continuation of ethnic groups, which preceded them. Nationalism appears mainly as an attempt to check disintegration and assimilation processes of pre-modern ethnicities in the modern world and it appears as an ideology that stresses the ethno-cultural uniqueness and demands its preservation by political independence. Judaism had been once an ethnicity or nationality characterized by religion, and when it couldn't retain its integrity in modern times due to the eclipse of religion, Jewish nationalism, or Zionism, emerged as its successor.

The opinion that the purpose of Zionism had been the preservation of Jewish culture, originated in Ahad Ha'am's approach (see below, pp. 270-273), has turned up to be the accepted paradigm in the study of Zionism. Thus, Chaim Gans says that "Zionism is an ideology of cultural nationalism, a nationalism which focuses on the interests of members of cultural or ethno-cultural groups to adhere to their culture, to preserve it for generations, and to be supported by a state to achieve this purpose" (Gans, 2006, p. 260). S.N. Eisenstadt maintains that the purpose of Zionism has been "the fulfillment of the Jewish civilizational vision" (Eisenstadt, 2002,

p. 163). This approach represents a primordialist conception of the nation, because even if national consciousness is something new, which appears with the threat to culture, the national culture, which nationalism wants to protect, predated nationalism. Here we are entangled in what Gellner calls "the thesis of the sleeping beauty", that is the dormant nation which waits to be woken up by the movement for national self-determination. Hence Katz (1983, p. 3):

> Judaism was called a nation by Jews and others also in the period that predated nationalism. … We are not exaggerating when we are saying that as far as national consciousness, the attachment to the homeland, language and so on, the Jewish nation was ready for nationalism in the second half of the nineteenth century, no less, and probably more, than any other nation in Europe (See also: Don Yehiya & Susser, 1999, p. 20).

Katz and others could be right when they conclude that one could find in the Jewish tradition national motives. Yet, as a counterbalance to these motives there were other motives which opposed nationalism, such as the a-political and even anti-political nature of traditional Judaism, the passivity and the waiting for the messiah and so on (Weiler, 1976). Yet, the big difficulty with the Katz's thesis, or with the "Sleeping Beauty" thesis, in as much as Judaism is concerned is that if, as Katz maintains, in the nineteenth century the Jewish nation had been ready for nationalism more than any other nation, why, as Katz himself acknowledges, when Jewish nationalism had emerged (and in fact until the present day) it had not affected the vast majority of the Jews but only a small fraction within them? (Katz, 1983, pp. 31-5).

The fact that the vast majority of the Jews had not become national Jews, and many of them even objected to Jewish nationalism, receives the following formulation by Hedva Ben Israel, a leading Israeli expert on nationalism:

It seems to me that this is an unprecedented phenomenon, that
there has been within a nation for the last two hundred years a
dispute as to whether or not the Jews constitute one nation, or
just one religion whose believers belong to various nations. …
Only among the Jews, since the emancipation, the question has
penetrated to the depths of the Jewish existence and has never
been resolved. The territorial dispersion and the variety of
adopted cultures were, of course, the material background for
the dispute. But there was also a spiritual basis for the dispute,
rooted in the different interpretation of the religion and the
national vocation. (Ben Israel, 2000, p. 20; 2002, p. 16).

What Ben Israel describes not only contradicts Katz's "readiness" theory, but
also raises the question of whether or not the Jews indeed were a nation, as
one of the pre-conditions for nationhood is the awareness of the members
of the nation as being members of one nation. Yet, according to Ben Israel
the absence of national consciousness (and a national culture) among the
Jews does not question the nationhood of the Jews, but rather paradoxically
turns out to be a characteristic of the Jewish nation.

Even if we accept Katz's thesis that Jewish nationalism is an attempt
to preserve Jewish culture and identity as a response to the disintegration
processes of Middle Ages Judaism in the modern age, not all the members
of the ethnic group (what Anthony Smith calls *ethnie*) responded in a
similar manner. In other words, Katz's idea that nationalism is the only
response from the so-called "peoples" or *ethnies*, is also objectionable. In the
Muslim world, and especially in the Arab world, it seems that the response
to modernity is religious fundamentalism rather than nationalism. Within
Judaism there were other responses to modernity, aside from Zionism,
such as ultra-Orthodoxy (i.e. fundamentalism) that tried to preserve Jewish
identity by seclusion, alternatively another reaction was the assimilation into
the local nations accompanied by the emphasis on the religious aspects of

Judaism (Chlenov, 2003). Furthermore, there were other forms of Jewish nationalism, like Bundism or autonomism, and there is no way to establish whether Zionist Jewish nationalism is a more authentic continuation of the Jewish Middle Ages *ethnie* than, for instance, Jewish ultra-Orthodoxy, Jewish communal life in America, or a Yiddish autonomy in Eastern Europe. In fact, as noted above, from a cultural point of view, the Hebrew culture created by Zionism, could be interpreted as antithetical rather than a continuation of tradition (Middle Ages) Judaism.

Another question which arises form Katz's thesis is that of the ethnic distinctiveness and the political unity of the "Jewish people". Katz maintains that:

> Nobody at the end of the eighteenth century doubted that the Jews were an ethnic group, distinct from the local population wherever they had established a community. The same goes for the unity of the Jewish communities around the world, which also was not questioned.

The emphasis which Katz puts on the ethnic distinctiveness of the Jews, from their point of view, as well as from that of their surroundings, points out that the Jews were a nation or a "proto-nation" even before the age of nationalism. Yet, Katz's decisive assertion that the Jews indeed were an ethnic group (or nationality) on the eve of the age of nationalism could be disputed. According to the ethnographer Mikhail Chlenov (2003, p. 256) the various models of Jewish identity which had existed in the Middle Ages and in the modern age were more dependent upon the character of the society in which the Jews were living rather than on internal Jewish traits. The Middle Ages model of Judaism was corporative and "included organically both religious and ethnic characteristics" (and in this sense indeed resembled Katz's notion of Judaism in general). Yet, when the corporative organization of the Middle

Ages society disintegrated, the Jewish corporation disintegrated and vanished along with it. The new Jewish identities which had emerged were dependent upon the societies in which the Jews were living (Ben Raphael & Ben-Chaim, pp. 57 – 87). Contrary to Katz's assertion, the famous saying by Clermont-Tonner after the French Revolution: "We must refuse everything to the Jews as a nation and accord everything to Jews as individuals", testifies that the model that was developed in western Europe after the French revolution and according to the ideas of the Enlightenment, had been one which identified Judaism as a religion rather than as ethnicity. After a while this model had become, especially in the United States, what Chlenov (2003, p. 187) calls "Ethnic inclusiveness, which means being included in the national or ethnic forms of the countries of their residence, while maintaining religious distinctiveness". However, the model of Jewish identity that had emerged in Eastern Europe was indeed different:

> Among the east-European Ashkenazi Jews, as opposed to their brethren of west Europe, was created a complex of cultural recognition traits, which had separated them from the various cultures that surrounded them and which had defined them as a national group. They spoke Yiddish, which was very different from the Slavish or Latin surrounding languages. They had lived in a relatively dense area, in the Pale of the Settlement in the Russian Empire, in Galicia (which belonged to Austro-Hungary) and in Rumania. They had also represented the specific form of culture and the behavior characteristics, which is clearly recognized as a distinctly ethno-cultural model. (Chlenov, 2003, p. 263 see also: Evron 2002).

Yet, as Chlenov remarks, it was not only the demographic differences between Eastern and Western Europe Jews, which had dictated the dominance of the ethnic or nationalist component in the Jewish identity as it was complemented also by "the very nature of the political philosophy of Russia and eastern Europe ... in this part of the world the dominant view even today has been that the whole humanity is divided to ethnic, or national groups (which for them are the same), and that all these groups have the right for self-determination" (And see also Ben-Rafael & Ben-Chaim, 2006, pp. 71-76). Furthermore, the differences between East and West could be explained also by the differences in industrialization and nation-building processes that were much more advanced in Western Europe (Gellner, 1983). Advanced industrialization meant the dissolution of the Middle Ages ethnies, and the emergence of the nation state creating the cultural medium, which could potentially assimilate the Jews. In other words, the division of Eastern Europe countries to national-ethnicities complemented the absence of the nation-state. In addition, the "Jewish plight" which meant poverty and persecutions and which could be seen (from a modernist point of view) as a prime cause for the emergence of nationalism characterized Eastern rather than Western Europe.

These differences between Eastern and Western Europe could explain why the various forms of Jewish nationalism originated in Eastern Europe. Indeed there were also nationalist conceptions different from Zionism: the Yiddish nation of the autonomists and the Bundists was different from the Hebrew nation of the Zionists. As a result, it is not possible to point to the Hebrew culture as a more authentic continuation of Middle Ages Judaism than the Yiddish culture. Moreover, even if these different nationalisms competed for the same public (which was not always the case), they were not necessarily contradictory. It is a fusion of religion and nationality, which makes us consider autonomism and Zionism as contradictory. The existence of a Hebrew nation in Palestine does not necessarily contradict the existence of a Yiddish speaking autonomy, or autonomies, in Eastern Europe.

The notion of a Jewish Yiddishist nation raises the question whether the Jews were one or perhaps several ethnic groups. While what they had in common was indeed religion, it was still possible to distinguish between Eastern European Ashkenazi and Western European Ashkenazi Jewry and those were distinguished further from the Sephardic Jews. Also among the latter it was possible to distinguish between the North African communities, those of the Balkan, and those of the Middle East (Smith, 1995a, p. 8). Even if ethnicity is indeed a "proto-nationalism", (which is controversial), then it seems that on the eve of the age of nationalism there was in the historical "Jewish People", or within the "Jewish civilization", a potential for the appearance of several nationalities.

If we accept Katz's assertion about the ethnic distinctiveness of the Jews and their being ethnically conscious, and even if we assume that ethnic distinctiveness and consciousness are "proto-nationality" which has the potential to develop a national movement, it is impossible to establish apriori whether or not a certain ethnic group will develop a national consciousness or from what degree of ethnic distinctiveness such a consciousness will emerge (Akzin, 1980, p. 31). Ernest Gellner points at what he considers as "the weakness of nationalism", which means that for every actual nationalism there are ten potential ones, groups that are identified by common culture they inherited from the agrarian world, and they do not even bother to fight for the realization of this potential. In fact, these groups have no interest in preserving their culture and they reconcile with its extinction and with their absorption into the more successful cultures (Gellner, 1983, pp. 43-50). According to Gellner there is nothing inherent in the 'ethnie' that obliges it to struggle for the preservation of its culture and there is nothing in the national ideology or the ethnic or national culture, as such, which will cause the ethnic group to unite around it and to fight for its preservation. Only a small fraction of a nation – i.e. the elite or the leadership of the national movement – are motivated by the national ideology as such.

According to Gellner, for nationalism (and the national ideology) to grasp the masses it needs to provide for their material concerns. In other words, the struggle for national self determination is not motivated directly by the threat to the culture, but by the fact that the members of the cultural or ethnic group identify their material distress with their being a members of a different culture, and see the mutual struggle for national self-determination and for cultural revival as a means to overcoming their distress. Only then a national ideology that stresses the importance of national culture and the need to preserve it could turn into powerful engine among the masses. Gellner gives a clear priority for the need to better the material status over what the romanticist ideology usually considered as the prime motif of nationalism – the desire to preserve the culture and uniqueness.

Katz also distinguishes between the influence of the national ideas of those who had been known as the "Forerunners of Zionism" (Kalisher, Elkalai, Hess) who operated in the first half of the nineteenth century when the emancipation process had been at its heights and bestowed optimism concerning the fate of the Jews, when compared to the influence of the national ideas after what had been considered as the failure of the emancipation. According to Katz, the limited influence of the Forerunners of Zionism testifies "the extent to which the force of an idea is limited when it is not tied up to a social need" (Katz, 1983, p. 31). Katz also contends that Jewish-Zionist nationalism needed the Jewish plight and the recognition of the Jewish masses and that Zionism offers a way out from this distress, in order to turn from a mere idea, into a real force. In other words, without Jewish distress, there would have been no Jewish nationalism in general, and Zionism in particular. Moreover, if distress is indeed an important and even necessary condition for the emergence of nationalism, then the question to what extent nationalism would evolve among a certain ethnic group depends also on the extent to which its members share the distress. Therefore, even if we consider Judaism as an ethnicity, not all among this ethnic group had shared the Jewish distress (for instance, American Jews).

Does Israel Have a Navel? Anthony Smith & Zionism

In a debate which was held at Warwick University, on 24.10.95, only few days before his sudden death, Ernest Gellner described the quarrel between himself and Anthony Smith as between modernists and primordialists: between those who think that nations have always existed or that their past is important, on one hand, and those who think that the whole story of nations and nationalism started in the modern era, sometime in the eighteenth century, and what that had happened before that is irrelevant, on the other. In short, according to Gellner, the debate boils down to the question – Do nations have navels? According to the modernist approach, which he shares, some nations have navels, other do not – and in any case it is not important. Smith's answer is that nations *do* have a navel, or a cluster of navels, and that possessing navels is a necessary condition for nations. Navels are necessary for nations because nations are 'born' out of their ethnic past. They are also necessary, in the sense that the navel (or navels) constitutes or delivers a certain 'ethnic core', without which the nation could not have been constructed.

As noted above, the division of the field of study of nationalism between modernists and primordialists is a very coarse one. Many would probably object to the label 'primordialist,' which Gellner attaches to Smith's theory of nationalism. Smith himself distinguishes between the perennial approach (that is 'primordialism') and his own 'ethno-symbolism' (Smith, 2009). Yet, Smith did not object to Gellner's summation of the debate between them as a debate about the question 'do nations have navels?' (Smith, 1996a).

What would be Israel's navel of navels according to Smith? Smith deems necessary for national revival of the ethnic group 'a collective belief of common origin and descent … associated with a specific territory which they regard as their 'homeland' (Smith, 1995a, p. 5). In the Jewish case "religion has been both the source and the vehicle of shared memories" (ibid., p. 6). As Smith puts it: "It was ultimately religious and political vision, rather then the needs of modernity, that inspired and mobilized many Diaspora Jews to become Zionists and take the arduous road to Palestine" (Smith, 1996a, p. 337).

Israel's, or Zionism's navels seem to be the 'ancient conceptions of the holy land and the chosen people', which "had retained their popular resonance through encoded collective memories, symbolism and ritual, and the generational repetition of collective aspirations" (Smith, 1995a, p. 16). This is, of course, the accepted "Zionist" formula. Thus, when Katz speaks about the readiness of the "Jewish nation" for nationalism, he means, of course, the common historical memories of dispersion, on one hand, and the hopes for revival and redemption in the Land of Israel, on the other hand.

That Zionism, as many other movements for national self-determination, had employed the concept of the 'chosen people' is perhaps undeniable. Yet, as Breuilly has rightly argued:

> To refute modernist objections to ethno-symbolic and perennialist ways of telling a long-run story of continuity, it is not enough to demonstrate a long and continued history of certain names. Rather, one must show that these names are used for the same purposes and in the same ways from generation to generation. (Breuilly, 2005, pp. 18-19).

In other words, while it could be true that, as Smith says, that the myth of 'ethnic election' characterizes nationalism and that it had originated in traditional religion (Smith, 2000, p. 272), the question involved here is whether the 'ethnie' selected by traditional Judaism and the one which selected by Zionism were indeed the same.

Indeed, to the extent that Jewish tradition employed the concept of "the nation", it was identified with faith, or, as Smith points out those 'encoded collective memories' were concerned with 'the people as a whole, *the community of practicing believers*' (Smith, 1995, p. 7). Yet, as we are going to see in the next chapter, classical Zionism had rarely approached the Jewish nation as a community of practicing believers and mostly distinguished between the "Jewish nation" and the historical *"Am Yisrael"* and sometimes even set the former as antithesis to the latter. Furthermore, Smith and Katz's assertion about the centrality of the messianic ideas in Zionism is also questionable. Herzlian Political Zionism certainly was not directed by such ideas, and as for practical Zionism, as Katz himself admits, "the historical role that the pioneers had seen before their eyes was not the fulfillment of the messianic promise, not even in its national incarnation" (Katz, 1983, pp. 32 – 3), meaning that they were aspiring for the establishment of a elite socialist utopian society rather than for the "gathering of the exiles" of the biblical prophesies.

Smith's assertion that it was 'ultimately religious and political vision, rather than the needs of modernity, that inspired and mobilized many Diaspora Jews to become Zionists and take the arduous road to Palestine' could be also questioned. The historiography of Zionism counts five waves of immigration (*Aliyot*) prior to the establishment of Israel. Only the first two, which were by no means mass immigrations, were motivated by 'political vision', which was certainly not the 'religious vision', which Smith refers to. The mass waves of immigrations (part of the Third *Aliya*, the Fourth *Aliya* and the Fifth *Aliya*) which were relatively mass immigrations were motivated by the 'plight of the Jews' and it is not coincidental that those waves of mass immigration started when America had imposed restrictions on immigration in the nineteen twenties. In other words, had America remained open for Jewish immigration, it is rather doubtful whether, as Smith says, many Jews would 'become Zionists and take the arduous road to Palestine'. After the establishment of Israel one could discern three waves of mass immigration: the remains of European Jewry immediately after independence, which was clearly motivated by plight. The mass immigration from Arab countries: here the situation is more complex: those were certainly motivated by plight, caused by the creation of Israel and also by the emergence of Arab nationalism. Nevertheless, coming from predominately traditional agrarian countries, the Jews were motivated also by the traditional religious vision of the 'Ingathering of the Exiles'. Yet, it is still doubtful whether they would have chosen the Israeli option if they had other more materialistically attractive options (Lasker, 2006, pp. 7-8). The third wave of mass immigration came after the collapse of the Soviet Union. This immigration, as many have noted, was predominantly motivated by the desire to improve the standard of living rather then so called 'Zionist' ideology

Examining the history of mass immigrations to Israel seems to disprove Smith's notion of its being motivated by a religious-political vision, rather than driven by the demands of modernity. Nevertheless, it is still possible to claim that the Zionist movement use the "collective memory" while reinterpreting and secularizing it (Avineri, 1994), otherwise how could we explain the centrality of *"Eretz Yisrael"* in Zionism. Can we say, then, that Palestine, or *Eretz Yisrael*, constitutes the navel of Israel? Smith certainly seems to think so:

> That is why, even among many secular intellectuals who had embraced socialism and whose conception of restoration was a return to agrarian labor, Palestine retained its hold: only in the land of the forefathers, where Jews had once been free and their own masters …could the Jews retain their self-respect and dignity through autoemancipation. (Smith, 1995a, pp. 8-9).

Smith mentions in this respect the Uganda debate at the 1903 Zionist congress where 'some western intellectuals and professionals like Herzl' who wanted to consider the possibility of Uganda as a safe haven for the Jews were opposed

248 | A NATION LIKE ALL NATIONS

and defeated by 'many of the secular Russian Zionist intelligentsia', 'to ensure continuity within the secular domain of the old religious idea of restoration to Eretz Yisrael'. Similarly, Eisenstadt maintains that what has made Zionism different from other Jewish reactions to modernity and what had turned it to the most radical and revolutionary of all Jewish responses was the assumption and insistence that the 'rebuilding' of a Jewish collective identity was possible only in its "natural, national and territorial" surrounding, that is in Palestine (Eisenstadt, 2002, pp. 163-164).

There are, indeed, two questions involved here: a) to what extent was Palestine necessary for Zionism? b) to what extent did the Zionists think that Palestine was necessary for Zionism?

Was Palestine indeed necessary for Zionism? This is not an easy question to answer. However, a short intellectual exercise could help. Let us assume that at the end of the nineteenth century, and in the first two decades of the twentieth century, Palestine was neither a part of an empire nor a colony of an empire, but rather a sovereign nation state like England or France. In other words, let us assume that at that time Palestine had not been considered as "empty", or as country, which was legitimately open for European colonization. If that had been the case, according to Smith and those who consider Palestine as necessary for Zionism then there would have been no Zionism. For it is hard to see how Zionism would have emerged in defiance of the international order demanding to dismantle a legitimate sovereign nation-state. In fact, the famous, albeit often criticized Zionist slogan: "A land without a people for a people without a land" shows that the fact Palestine was considered "empty" was used to legitimize the Zionist claim to it. Would Smith say that under these conditions Zionism would not have emerged?

This would not be true for Herzl and Political Zionism that were motivated by the Jewish plight and demanded a political solution for the Jewish Problem. This was quite independent of the question of Palestine. To this Smith could have answered that in such a case, if a "Zionism without Zion" movement for national self-determination would have been established, it would have been doomed to a failure. Indeed, it is not easy to tell how such movement would have developed, if at all. Yet, as many have noted, 'Zionism without Zion' characterized many nations, which had considered themselves as a continuation of the ancient Hebrews. The most conspicuous example is, of course, the Americans. The founding fathers of the American Nation saw the Americans as the rightful inheritors of the ancient Hebrews, and America as New Canaan or New Jerusalem (Bellah, 1970). Therefore, if the Americans could have been 'Zionists without Zion', there is no reason to assume, a priori, that the Israelis could not have done the same. In fact, in the draft of the charter for Uganda – which had already gained the approval of the British government – Herzl suggested to call the settlement in Uganda 'New Palestine' (Rabinowicz, 1958, p.61).

Furthermore, the idea that there could be no Jewish nationalism without Palestine is refuted by the other forms of nationalism which have emerged among the Jews: there were 'Autonomism' and Bundism which favored the establishment of a Jewish autonomies in the Diaspora, and territorialism, which sought a non-Palestinian nation-state solution to the Jewish Problem. To this Smith would probably answer that Zionism was the only successful form of Jewish nationalism. Yet, the failure of the other forms of Jewish nationalisms was also due to the fact that East-European Jewry was exterminated in the Holocaust. One could imagine the fate of Zionism would not have been much different had Rommel's *Afrika Korps* conquered Palestine. Moreover, as Smith himself notes, the Zionist solution had an advantage in the sense that it sought a solution in a form of a nation-state. The modern world, says Smith, does not seem to tolerate autonomies and *millets*. It could be claimed that Zionism was successful, not because of the Palestinization of the Jewish problem, but rather because its territorialization in the form of a nation-state.

Yet, to what extent did the Zionists think that Palestine was necessary for Zionism? This would bring us to the Uganda debate. Smith seems to belittle both the intensity and the importance of this debate. Following his ethno-symbolism, Smith seems to consider the outcomes of the debate, the 'reaffirmation' of Palestine, as "natural" and obvious. Yet, this was hardly the case. First, it would be a gross mistake to view 'territorialism', the movement within Zionism that supported a non-Palestinian solution to the Jewish problem, as a weak offspring of Zionism. Zionism and Territorialism were born at the same time. The forefathers of 'Political Zionism' had not considered Palestine as obvious, and this was true even in the days of *Hovevei Zion*, prior to the establishment of the Zionist movement by Herzl. Pinsker, in his *Auto Emancipation* states that "We do not need a holy land, but a land of our own", and until his death had refused repeated requests to change both his opinion and the text of *Auto Emancipation* with regard to the necessity of Palestine (Elroi, 2011, p. 5). Similarly, in his "Jewish State", Herzl asks "Palestine or Argentine?", and answers "We shall take what is given to us, and what is selected by Jewish public opinion".

The dividing line in the Uganda debate was not between eastern and western European; nor was it between secular and religious; nor between those who received Jewish education and those who had come from assimilated homes (Benyamini 1990, pp. 27-28). In Russia, many socialist-Zionists, headed by Nachman Sirkin supported the Uganda plan. On the other side of Europe, many English Zionists had turned into ardent territorialists. Surprisingly, there had been a strong center of supporters for the Uganda Plan within the Hebrew *Yishuv* in Palestine, headed by Eliezer Ben Yehuda, forefather of modern Hebrew (Luz, 1988, p. 355). The latter had turned into an ardent supporter of the Uganda plan, and his newspaper *Hashkafa* become the mouthpiece of the territorialists in Palestine. To those who claimed the Ugandists were turning their back on the past, Ben Yehuda answered that if Zionism wishes to be consistent and honest with itself, it must announce publicly: "We have all turned our backs on the past, and this is our praise and our glory" (Luz, 1988, p.273). As Luz (1988, p. 265) points out, "there were also quite few who straddled the fence. Writers like Berdichevsky (sic) and Y.H. Brener typified the uncertainty of many Zionists".

On the other spectrum of the supporters of the Uganda solution stood the religious Zionists, who had comprised the largest party in the Sixth Zionist Congress that debated Uganda (Don Yehiya, 1983, p. 124). Later historians saw the Mizrahi's support of the Uganda Plan as "one the most bizarre episodes in the history of Zionism" (Eliav, 1987, p. 87) or alternatively maintained that it was an episode soon to be replaced by "the return of the movement to its origin" (ibid., p. 95). Others suggested that the Mizrahi's support for the Uganda Plan was given half-heartedly and stems more from their loyalty to Herzl (Luz, 1988, p.267). Notwithstanding all these considerations, it is important to note that the Mizrahi's vote on Uganda was coherent with their position on the "Culture Question" which will be discussed below, (pp. 273- 278) and well rooted in the Mizrahi view of the Zionist movement, as a political instrument for the solution of the 'Jewish Problem'.

The Uganda debate offers a unique test-case for the debate between the modernists and the primordialists. According to the latter, the national homeland is not chosen, but rather dictated by the national ethnic core. However, from a modernist point of view, it is possible for a nation to choose its homeland. Yet, in most, if not all cases, the option does not exist – as a people who undergo the processes of nation-building already live on a certain territory, and there is no reason or possibility to remove them from this territory. The Uganda debate offered a rare, if not unique, test-case: Since the Jews constituted a "Diaspora nation", without any recognized Jewish center, the choice of a homeland had become a real option and the question was raised. The very fact that the question was raised and the ferocity of the debate show that Palestine was not self-evident and constitute a further corroboration of modernism.

∝ CHAPTER 4 ∾

Classical Zionism &
the Separation between Faith and Nationality

The fusion of religion and nationality has become central to what is known today as 'Zionism', in that Yaakov Salmon (2000, p. 116) has suggested that 'in Jewish nationalism there was not an influential thinker or movement which demanded the separation between nationality and religion or that believed in such separation'. Similarly, Don Yehiya and Susser (1999, pp. 14-15) say that few national movements in the west have attached such importance to the religious component in their national identity as Zionism. According to them, the dominant trend in modern Jewish nationalism is to see the State of Israel as the political expression of a unique national entity, which is distinguished by both religion and ethnicity. Horowitz and Lissak (1990, p. 186) maintain that 'all the branches of secular Zionism have kept, at least, the negative component of the fusion of religion and nationality – there was no movement in Zionism which was ready to legitimize conversion from Judaism, without seeing it as a cessation from the nation (*Klal Yisrael*). Yonathan Shapiro says that this identity has its 'internal ideological logic' as 'there was never a separation between religion and nationality in Jewish history, and consequently it is difficult to separate them today in Israel'. According to Shapiro, this is the reason why Israelis were not able to define a social status of a Jew who is a member of the nation, without necessarily being a member of the Jewish religion (Shapiro 1977, pp. 22-23).

To what extent, then, was the notion of the fusion of religion and nationality shared by the forefathers of Zionism? And if it was shared by them, what are we to make of their demand for normalization? While answering this question, it is important not to confuse it with the question of the mutual relations and influences between the Jewish religion and the Jewish nationality: the separation between nationality and religion could exist also when the nationalism is saturated with religion. Shlomo Avineri has pointed out that the myth of secularization and the myth of separation between State and religion, which characterized modern liberal democracy has identified the rise of nationalism with secularization and with rebellion against religion. Yet, according to Avineri, to the extent that those elements exist, they have characterized the initial stages of the national movement and that national ideology is in fact not a rebellion against the religious past but an attempt to reinterpret it. Avineri claims that 'every national movement must discuss in a new and transformative way the religious aspect of its past' and the outcome is that nationalism is saturated with religion. (Avineri, 1994, pp. 9-10; Smith, 1996c, p. 98).

If by the separation between nationality and religion we mean the establishment of 'Walls of Separation' between them, then it is obvious that we could not find them in Zionism, or in any other movement of national self-determination. However, the fusion of religion and nationality, which is currently attributed to 'Zionism', is different from the examples cited by Avineri. To the extent that Catholicism is interwoven in Irish nationalism, there is still an Irish nation that is separated from the Catholic religion – in the sense that not all Catholics are Irish, and also in the sense that Protestants or Jews could be Irish. In a similar manner, the existence of a Polish or a German nation should be mentioned.

When we approach the question of the separation between nationality and religion in classical Zionism, we should not try to establish to what extent Zionist ideology was 'secular', but rather to what extent there was a recognition that a person could be Jewish by religion, yet not Jewish by his nationality and vise versa: to what extent was there recognition of the fact that a person could be Jewish by his nationality, and yet not Jewish by his religion. In other words, we are trying to examine to what extent the Zionist teachings could have formed the base for a multi-religious territorial nation.

One of the corollaries of the fusion of religion and nationality in contemporary Israel is the notion of the 'Jewish State', as a State that must reflect a 'Jewish' content. When we approach the question of the separation between nationality and religion in classical Zionism, we are also trying to establish, from cultural point of view, to what sense, if any, the culture of the emerging nation was envisaged as 'Jewish'.

In the following section, I will argue that unlike the accepted dogma, we can find in classical Zionism strong elements of separation between nationality and religion. This separation was based upon two elements: will and culture. The Jewish nation was envisaged as composed of those Jews that were willing to join it, and eventually to immigrate to the Jewish homeland; while those who chose not to do so (especially in western countries) would remain members of their local nations. The second important element which distinguished between Jewish nation and the historical Jewish People was that of culture: the emerging nation was envisaged as both Hebrew and modern, as opposed to the varieties of popular cultures which characterized the historical '*Am Yisrael*', on the one hand, and the cultures of the Jews who chose to become members of their local modern nations, on the other hand. Moreover, this national culture was not envisaged as one that must have a 'Jewish' content.

Here, I will not try to establish the extent to which those elements of separation between nationality and religion were dominant in Zionism; rather only to show there were enough of them to refute the present dogma that sees this identity as self-evident, and perhaps to point to different routes, which were available on the eve of independence. If the separation between nationality and religion is indeed a precondition for normalization or reinvigoration of Israel, then looking back to classical Zionism might prove a great help.

"Zionism has nothing to do with religion" – 'Political Zionism' and the Separation between Nationality & Religion'

The distinction between nationality and religion was a basic principle in Political Zionism. In a letter Herzl distributed on behalf of the preparatory committee of the First Zionist Congress, held in Basel in 1897, he called for the establishment of an executive committee, which would seek "to establish a permanent and secure national home for those Jews who cannot or will not assimilate into their present homes" (Elon, 1975, p. 225). Herzl used the same language when he approached the Anglo-Jewish aristocracy. The latter, while subscribing to the idea of Jewish solidarity, felt resolutely British and were concerned that Herzl's presumption to speak on behalf of the 'Jewish People' would blur the line between their religious identity (as Jews) and national allegiance (as British). Herzl called for the formation of a Society of Jews to promote the acquisition of territory for such Jews as were unable to assimilate (Pawel, 1990, p. 301). By 'assimilation' Herzl did not necessarily mean the conversion or secularization of the Jews, but rather their national assimilation, their being absorbed as Jewish members of their local nations. Moreover, Herzl thought that the establishment of a Jewish State would make it easier for those Western European Jews who wanted to assimilate, as it would divert the immigration of the Eastern European Jewish masses from Western Europe to the Jewish State. Here, the element that created the distinction between religion, and the historical '*Am Yisrael*', on the one hand, and the 'Jewish nation', on the other, was will. It was the will of the individual Jew that determined whether he belonged to the Jewish nation (or whether he wished to secede from it and become a member of his local nation). Herzl sometimes treated the 'Jewish nation' as a fact, identical to the historical Jewish people, from which Jews were allowed to opt out, as we can see from his article 'The Protest Rabbis' published in the *Die Welt*, on July 16 1897. Here, the German Rabbis who objected to Zionism were allowed to opt out from the existing Jewish nation:

> If someone wishes to secede from the Jewish nation, from which he originated, and to join another nation, he can do so. We, the Zionists, will not detain him. Nevertheless, he is considered by us as a stranger. His new-nation affairs are not our business, but also our national affairs are not his business. He has no right to voice his opinions in our matters ... But to belong to Judaism and to make Judaism their occupation, if one may say so, and to fight against it - this is something that any sense of Justice should object. (Herzl 1961 vol 7, p. 100).

The separation between nationality and religion here is clear. In as much as the Jewish nation, or "Judaism", is an accomplished fact, every Jew is entitled to secede from it and to choose another nation. Here we can see how a "primordial" conception of the nation could still go together with the separation between nationality and religion, once the right of secession is given to the individual Jews. It is obvious that Herzl did not doubt the religious affiliation of the German Rabbis and did not think that in their secession from the Jewish nation they secede also from the Jewish religion. In other words, Herzl distinguishes between the Jews as a collective, on one hand, and the Jews as individuals, on the other. The Jewish collective is identified with "the Jewish nation" or with "Judaism" and is represented only by the Zionist movement.

In other places Herzl speaks of the 'Jewish nation' as something built or to be built from 'Jewish' material (Almog 1982: 28). Here the emphasis is about Jews opting in. In both cases it is the individual will which creates the difference between the religion and the nation. In this sense Herzl was a true son of the Enlightenment, and was well within the social contract tradition. Consequently, as the will that creates the social contract originates in a social need or in the deprivation of the 'State of Nature', so the driving force of Zionism originated in the plight of the Jews. Thus, Herzl declares in the 'Jewish State' (1988, p. 92) that 'We are a People – our enemies have made us one without our consent'. In his audience with the Grand Duke Friedrich of Baden, uncle of the Kaiser, the latter has expressed his fear that the Jews in the Duchy of Baden might misinterpret his endorsement of Herzl's plan and think he wanted to get rid of them. To this Herzl answered that 'only those Jews who would want to will go … Since the Jews of Baden are content under your Royal Highness's liberal reign, they will not emigrate, and rightly so' (Elon, 1975, p. 193). The "will" that created the Jewish nation, then, was not the outcome of what Gellner calls the awakening of the 'Sleeping Beauty', that is the romanticist notion of the nation which is ready for the call of the national movement for self-determination; nor was it rooted in the need to protect the Jews from assimilation or to protect or revive a Jewish Culture. Rather, the will that created the Jewish nation was the outcome of the hard conditions of the Jews. This made Herzl's 'Jewish nation', as he himself came immediately to discover, predominantly an Eastern European nation. After his first encounter with the Russian Jews during the First Congress Herzl says: 'I have often been told in the beginning, "The only Jews you'll win will be the Russian Jews". Today I say, "They would be enough!"' (Elon, 1975, p. 246).

Indeed, the Zionists were quick to realize that their movement had been essentially an Eastern European one. This is how Nordau phrased the aims of Political Zionism:

> (Political Zionism) should bring about the release of *this part of the people of Israel, which feels oppressed,* considers itself persecuted, which aspires for rest in a peaceful life, which struggles to

achieve the right to become what it is before God and the world. Political Zionism is the Zionism of six million Jews moaning under the whip of Russia, for hundreds of thousands of Jews who are deprived of rights, of the smallest conveniences of life, who are engaged in a struggle for survival in a horrid conditions in Rumania and other countries, where the same trend prevails" (Nordau, 1937, pp. 22 – 23, emphasis added).

Herzl's "discovery" that his nation was mainly an Eastern European nation was common knowledge. In fact, it would be very difficult to find among Zionist thinkers after 1881 the current Israeli accepted dogma of "*kibbutz galuyot*" (The Ingathering of Exiles). Stemming from the fusion of nationality and religion, the latter identifies this ingathering with the relocation of the historical '*Am Yisrael*', that is of all those who are considered as Jews wherever they are and whatever they wish. Classical Zionists had seldom entertained such a notion. For classical Zionists The *Ingathering of Exiles* meant mainly from Eastern Europe. Even a pre-1881 thinker, like Moshe Hess, who had a romanticist "sleeping beauty" notion of the Jewish nation and did not consider the plight of the Jews as the main drive of Zionism, did not envisage a total ingathering of the exiles; "Jewish Statehood was to supplement, rather than totally displace continued diaspora emancipation" (Shimoni, 1995, p. 56). Shlomo Avineri remarks that according to Hess 'the Jewish commonwealth would provide an answer to the plight of the Jewish masses in Eastern Europe and the Muslim world" and that "Hess' awareness that these two large communities … would form the basis for the Jewish State is of central importance of the way Hess visualized the Jewish national society that would arise in the Land of Israel" (Avineri, 1981, p. 43). The notion of Zionism, as mainly an Eastern European movement, was shared by Zionist thinkers associated with *Hovevei Zion*. Thus, Pinsker did not think that Jewish emigration would comprise of all the Jewish communities in the world. Western Jewry will not emigrate, because they are relatively secured and free. The immigrants will come mainly from countries with a dense Jewish population. Pinsker singled out Russia (which included areas of Poland), Rumania and Morocco as the main reservoirs of mass immigration to Palestine, and, as Avineri (1981, p. 80) remarks, this was a striking forecast of the eventual structure of Israel.

In their distinction between Zionism as 'the Jewish People on the march', on one hand, and the historical *'Am Yisrael*, on the other, Herzl and Political Zionism found the religious Zionists on their side. To the extent that the Jewish tradition had the concept of "nation" it identified it with *'Am Yisrael'* and consequently it did not distinguished between nationality and religion. Yet, this nation was supposed to be redeemed by God, and the problem the Zionist movement posed for religious Zionists was – how could someone who believed in salvation by God support those who wished to promote salvation by human beings. Here the distinction between the emerging nation and the historical *'Am Yisrael'* made it possible also to distinguish between redemption by man and redemption by God. According to Rabbi Reines, the leader of the religious Zionists and the founder of the Mizrahi, Zionist Religious Party, "the leaders of Zionism came to declare simple salvation, which is not directed towards the general salvation and has nothing from the spiritual, but is just material and political":

> It is our tradition that the forecasted salvation would be general salvation for the entire of Israel (*Klal Yisrael*) ... and all the nations will unite to call His name ... but on these issues the founders of this organization (Zionism) do not hope, for even if they are going to be successful then there will be a place [in Palestine] just for a considerable part of the nation, and it will be under the custody of the state, and with the consent of all the governments, and this is very far indeed from the hoped situation of the future salvation, and how can you compare such an idea with that of the salvation. (Don-Yehiya, 1983, pp. 107-108).

In other words, for Religious Zionism at its inception the distinction between the mythical *Am Yisrael* or historical Jewish People, on the one hand, and the actual emerging nation, on the other, was a necessary condition for joining the latter. From their point of view, the fusion of religion (the historical Jewish people) and nationality meant Salvation and the Gathering of the Exiles and consequently the "forcing of the end" (*dechikat haketz*) and blasphemy. In his biography on Herzl, Amos Elon tells that in the First Zionist Congress five rabbis with grave faces came to visit Herzl in his hotel. When they left his room they were beaming with satisfaction. One of Herzl's assistants asked them with astonishment "what happened? Did Herzl promise to observe the Shabbat and to eat only kosher food?" The answer of the rabbis was illuminating: "Not at all. This would have worried us tremendously. If he suddenly had become religious and observant we could not have joined the movement because of the fear that we would have to accept him as the messiah. It is better like this." Those rabbis had no problem to join a movement looking for a solution for the Jewish existential problem, though it lacked a Jewish religious dimension. On the contrary, setting a religious dimension to the movement would have confronted the religious Jew with a dilemma as explained by those rabbis: the solution to the Jewish earthly problem would have turned into salvation and the national leader into the messiah and they would have either to consider Herzl as a false messiah, or, if they would have accepted him as the messiah they would have to watch him carefully and demand he would observe the *mitzvot*. Herzl was needed to abate the fears of the religious Zionists from the secular movement. He did it in the Third Zionist Congress in a sentence that had turned into a slogan "I can assure you that Zionism does not intend to do anything which will harm the religious conception of any stream within Judaism."

This announcement achieved its goal, and many religious Zionist considered it as a promise that the Zionist Movement will deal only with political and economic questions and not with questions that should be related to religion (Refael, 1983, p. 40). A very illuminating communiqué was sent by Rabbi Rabinowitz, one of the representatives of the Zionist Orthodox from Russia, to many rabbis asking their opinion about Zionism. He himself testifies that Zionism "is clean from any fault concerning faiths and opinions … The leaders of Zionism, also those who are secular, have not the wish or the ability to touch things which are given to the heart, and to intervene in matters of faith and religion. The differences of opinions should not become an obstacle for cooperation and eventually Zionism would bring people closer to religion and not the opposite." (Ibid., p. 47).

Indeed, Herzl's Zionism, which emphasized the political solution for the Jewish masses did not necessarily create a problem for the religious Jews: they too needed rescue. As a rule, the religious Zionists repeatedly emphasized that as long as the Zionist movement would limit itself to the solution of material problems they will not have any problem to be its members. The meaning of this was that religious-messianic ideas were given lower priority (if not discarded altogether), when compared with ideas concerned the concrete Jewish problems. This approach was also expressed by the Mizrahi's support in Herzl's position during the Uganda crisis. As Rabbi Reines stated:

> The hearts of all of us is aching when we hear the news … that we are far from our hopes in our fatherland … (Yet) we have agreed to the African offer, because we have paid attention to the needs of the people of which we are fond more than of the country – and the needs of the people who keep deteriorating both in material and spirit demand a safe haven anywhere. (Don Yehiya, 1983, p. 124).

The Mizrahi's vote on Uganda was not coincidental and stems from its position – which considered Zionism as a political tool only and from its insistence to separate the earthly redemption – the rescue of the Jews, from the messianic one – the gathering of the Jews in Palestine. As Don Yehiya notes, both Herzl and the forefathers of the Mizrahi saw "… Zionism as a reaction to problems which originated in the real existence conditions of the Jewish People, and as a movement that the source of its pushing power is anti-Semitism and the 'Jewish problem', rather than the appeal of Palestine and the Jewish salvation vision".

Herzl's distinction between nationality and religion could be found not only in the recognition that the emerging Jewish nation did not include all the Jews, but also in that it contained non-Jews who lived in its midst in complete equality. In the *Jewish State* Herzl says that:

> Every man will be as free and undisturbed in his faith or his disbelief as he is in his nationality. And if it should occur that men of other creeds and different nationalities come to live amongst us, we should accord them honourable protection and equality before the law. (1988, p. 147).

In Altneuland Herzl writes: "It is not the business of society if someone seeks his moments of elevation which connect him with God in the synagogue, church, mosque, museum of arts or philharmonic concert". In Altneuland we can also see that though the settlement in Palestine originates in the Jewish population, the means and participants come also from non-Jews: '… we were not in any way swayed by considerations of race or creed. Everyone who wanted to work the soil of Israel was welcome'. Arabs also are parts of the New Society, and one of the heroes, Rashid Bay, is an enlightened Arab who is willingly and enthusiastically participates in the New Society (Herzl, 1961, Vol. 1, pp. 133-4). Hence Gorni (1985, p. 38) says that "Herzl believed in the possibility of integrating the Arab minority into the Jewish society by its adjustment to western civilization while preserving its original culture".

Herzl's position has been sometimes interpreted, as if his State was not a nation-state, but rather a multinational state, or a citizens' state, something very close to the present 'post-Zionist' notion of Israel (Elboim-Dror 1999, pp. 246-7). Shimoni (1995, p. 96) remarks that "in Altneuland, Herzl describes 'a New Society', rather than a conventional national State. It is post-national, a polity that transcends and betters the European State". According to Shimoni Herzl's State lacks national characteristics and "culturally, it was rather inchoate: secular cosmopolitan, and pluralist rather than distinctively Jewish ... it was definitely a State *for the Jews* rather than a *Jewish State*" (Ibid., pp. 94-5). Hence, Tom Segev (1996; 2001, pp. 17-18) refers to Herzl as the "first post-Zionist". As Hazony (2003) points out, this image of Herzl as post-nationalist, or 'Post-Zionist' has become rather accepted.

If this 'post-Zionist' vision of the Herzl is true, then it means he did not distinguish between nationality and religion, as it envisages the Jews as a nationality among the other nationalities in the multinational "New Society". Furthermore, according to this vision, Herzl did not aspire to a nation-state, and consequently the equality of non-Jews in the 'New Society" is not achieved by membership in the nation, that is by non-Jews being politically and socially integrated as equals into the 'Jewish nation': equality is achieved either by the equality of the collective rights of the various nationalities or by citizenship in a culturally neutral "citizens' state", or both.

Yet, I believe this image of Herzl as post-nationalist or as post-Zionist is wrong. Indeed, it seems that Political Zionism in general, and Herzl in particular, were more sensitive than what was expected of a movement for national self determination of their time, to the necessity of tolerating different cultures within the 'New Society'. There is no doubt that liberal, cosmopolitan and pluralist concepts of society as well as a "Jewish" sensitivity to minority rights played here a very important role. Yet, all these by no means should be seen as a rejection of the notion of the nation-state but rather as the way to create one within a multicultural society. In the contemporary debate about the nature of Herzl's 'Jewish State' much emphasis has been laid on Herzl's multiculturalism as far as non-Jewish minorities or individuals were concerned. Yet, Herzl's multicultural notion of the 'New Society' was also and perhaps mainly dictated by the multicultural nature of the emerging "Jewish nation".

When in his diaries Herzl writes that 'the absence of a common language will not stop us. Switzerland is also a unified State of members of different nationalities' (Herzl 1961 vol. 2, p. 49), he refers to the Jews as being comprised of various nationalities. In a similar passage in the *Jewish State* (1988, p. 146) when Herzl describes Switzerland as a 'Federation of Tongues' and set it as an example for his Jewish State he sees it as a reflection of the multilingual or multinational origin of the Jews, rather than a reflection of the existence of non-Jewish minorities in the future Jewish State. Yet, Herzl's distinction between nationality and religion is not found only in his attitude to the Jews as multinational, but also in the fact that his "New Society" is not culturally neutral. It is a nation, or, in fact, it is a "Jewish nation."

Thus, it is wrong to suggest, what Ahad Ha'am used to say, that Political Zionism in general, and Herzl in particular, ignored the necessity of national cultural infrastructure, or envisaged a state without particular national and cultural character. Rather, that it had left the choice of the culture to the inhabitants of the future Jewish State (Ben-Zion, 2003, pp. 9-10). Furthermore, as Kaufmann put it, Political Zionism, though it admitted a distinct national character, never tried to link it to special cultural contents called "national tradition" (1961 vol. 2, p. 375). In other words, the 'Jewish State', though it was culturally distinct, was not envisaged as necessarily materializing or incarnating Jewish content or Jewish values. On the contrary, as the debate about the cultural question clearly shows, Herzl objected to ascribing in advance any cultural 'Jewish' content to the Zionist movement also, because he knew that it would lead to kulturekampf, which would eventually destroy the Zionist movement. In this respect Shimoni, (or to that matter Ahad Ha'am) is certainly right when he says that Herzl's 'Jewish State' is not Jewish. Here, again, Political Zionism's position was shared by the first religious Zionists, headed by Rabbi Reines. The latter demanded that the Zionist movement would limit itself to the political and economic aspects of the Jewish existence and would refrain from the adoption of any cultural policy. In other words, the founders of *Hamizrahi* objected to the notion of the Jewish State, as envisaged by Ahad Ha'am (see below), a notion which sees that State as the incarnation or the embodiment of Jewish values (Don Yehiya 1983).

Hence, it would be more appropriate to describe Herzl's nationalism as "formal nationalism" (Ben Israel, 2003, pp. 97-98) or "civic nationalism", which emphasizes the formal and the legal structure of the nation-state. As for the national consolidation, the Political Zionists assumed that the political, territorial (and later on also the Hebrew) framework would consolidate the nation. As Yaacov Klachkin maintained in his criticism of Ahad Ha'am and his spiritual nationalism, "we do not aspire for the country (Palestine) in order to maintain in it the ideas of Judaism. The earthly redemption is for us an aim of its own: a life of national freedom. The content of our life would be national when their form would be national" (Kaufmann, 1995, p. 68).

Yet, while Political Zionism's 'Jewish State' was not Jewish in Ahad Ha'am's sense, or in our contemporary sense, this does not mean that it was not a nation-state, or that is that it was not culturally distinct. First, it was modern and its modernity distinguished it from both popular Jewish cultures, on one hand, and the local Middle-Eastern cultures, on the other. Indeed, in the Jewish State, Herzl makes it very clear that popular Jewish cultures will have to give way to modernity:

> We shall give up using those miserable stunted jargons, those Ghetto languages, which we still employ, for these were the stealthy tongues of prisoners. Our national teachers will give a

due attention to this matter; and the language, which proves itself to be of greatest utility for general intercourse will be adopted without compulsion as our national tongue (1988, p. 146).

The "nation building" in the above passage is clear as it mentions a transformation from a multi-jargoned society to one which has, at least in the public domain, unified language in which a modern society could function. Yet, the modernity of the culture of the New Society distinguished it not only from the Jewish popular cultures but also from the Middle Eastern traditional cultures. Replying to a criticism by Ahad Ha'am that the 'New Society' in Altneuland lacks a Jewish character Max Nordau says:

It is true that Altneuland is a European sector within Asia. Here Herzl showed with great accuracy what we want and to what end we are aspiring. We want the Jewish people, after being liberated and after restoring its unity, to remain a cultured people to the extent that it had already attained this, and to become cultured to the extent that it is not yet so (Gorni 1987, pp. 33-3).

In another passage Nordau maintains:

We will never agree that the return of the Jews to the land of their forefathers should constitute a retreat into barbarism, as our enemies and slanderers claim. The Jewish people will evolve their unique essence within the framework of general western culture, like any other cultured people, but not outside it. Not within savage, cultured – hating Asianism, as Ahad Ha'am would apparently wish (ibid.).

Yet, it would be a mistake to ascribe to this modernity of the Jewish nation a 'universal' or non-particular national character. Herzl considered this particular character to be, in fact, "Jewish". In his diaries Herzl refers to the absence of a common language among the Jews, which could have hinted to the fact that they did not constitute a nation:

> Language would not be an obstacle. Switzerland is also a federal State of several nationalities. We are a nation by the religion. (Herzl, 1997, p. 95).

In other words, though we currently lack common language as national characteristic (something which should be corrected), we still have the Jewish religion as a national characteristic: The "Jewish nation" is indeed "Jewish". The distinction which Herzl had made between religion and nationality, or between the Zionist movement and religion, which was expressed by the famous slogan "Zionism has nothing to do with religion", was not motivated by hostility towards religion or from objection to its centrality in Jewish national life. On the contrary, Herzl acknowledged the religiosity of the Jewish masses, and assigned important role for the rabbis both in the Zionist Movement and in the future Jewish State: "I do not intend to harm religion in anything, on the contrary, I want to go with the rabbis, with all the rabbis" [Herzl, 1997, Vol. 1, p. 135; Hazony 2003, p. 349].

On the formal-constitutional level, it seems that Herzl, while separating nationality from religion, did not separate the State from religion, or to be more accurate, did not separate between the Church and the State. In famous passages in *The Jewish State*, Herzl likens the status of the religion to that of the military. Herzl writes regarding the rabbis that "(w)e shall keep our priests within the confines of their temples in the same way as we shall keep our professional army within the confines of their barracks", and that rabbis and generals "must not interfere in the administration of the State which confers distinction upon them". It seems that in the Jewish State religion is institutionalized, at least in the sense that the rabbis are being paid by the State. Salmon (1999, pp. 296-7) notes that the likening of the status of religion to the military suggests that religion was to be mobilized in the service of the nation, and by guaranteeing that the State would pay their salaries, Herzl sought to secure the religious functionaries' total obedience to state institutions.

As Hazony notes, the model which Herzl saw as fitting for the relation between Church and State was not the American "walls of separation", but he imagined a government such as Britain, Germany and Austria of his own day with which he was familiar, whereby religion, like the military, was politically subordinated to the government of the State, but was nevertheless an integral part of it (Hazony 2000). In other words, though in the Jewish State total freedom of religion is guaranteed, Jewish religious communities would not be given a status superior to that of the non-Jewish ones, despite the fact that Jewish religion will have a special status compared to other religions – and in this sense, the Jewish State is indeed "Jewish".

Yet, Herzl's State was not only formally or constitutionally Jewish, but rather, since most of its inhabitants were Jews, it was culturally Jewish. It was Jewish not as a result of its adherence to pre-political Jewish religion or Jewish values, but as a result of the fact that most of its inhabitants came from a Jewish stock. A good example for this notion could be found in Herzl's answer to Max Nordau who asked him what would be the status of Nordau's non-Jewish wife in the "Jewish State":

> If we have accomplished our project today, it would be impossible to deny to a Jewish citizen, that is a citizen of the existing Jewish State, the right to marry a foreigner. By this she would become Jewish no matter what her religion is. If they will have children those children will necessarily be Jewish. (Zur 2001, p. 198).

Here, we can see Herzl's notion of Jewish nationality, in a nutshell. In maintaining that Nordau's wife will be Jewish – notwithstanding her religion – Herzl, of course, means she would be Jewish by her nationality.

Herein, Herzl distinguishes between belonging to the Jewish nation, on one hand, and belonging to the Jewish religion, on the other hand. Furthermore, by maintaining that Nordau's wife and her children would be Jewish, despite not being Jewish according to Jewish law, Herzl's presupposes the assimilative Jewish character of the 'New Society'. They will become Jewish, because they live in a Jewish nation.

Ahad Ha'am's Reaction and the Birth of the Jewish State

The seeds of the fusion of religion and nationality, and the objection to normalization, was introduced to Zionism by Ahad Ha'am (Asher Ginzberg). As these turned out to be the accepted dogma of what is known today as "Zionism", Ahad Ha'am might be considered as one of the most influential thinkers, if not the most influential thinker, in the history of Zionism. This might seem a bit odd, given that he is considered as the founder of a somewhat marginal stream in Zionism – 'Spiritual Zionism' or 'Spiritual Nationalism' (which is what we call 'cultural nationalism' today.) Yet, the ideas of Ahad Ha'am became influential after the Uganda crisis and the decline of Political Zionism. Between the two world wars he had greatly influenced the leadership of the Zionist movement, and Chaim Weizmann considered himself as his disciple.

Unlike Herzl's Political Zionism, which identified the 'Jewish Problem' as the problem of the survival of the Jews, Ahad Ha'am identified the 'Jewish Problem' as the problem of the survival of Judaism, as a cultural and historical unit in the modern world (Vital 1984, p. 18). According to Ahad Ha'am, the 'Jewish People' were a primordial nation united in the past by its religion. Modernity and the fall of the walls of the ghetto had made religion inadequate for the preservation of the unity of the Jewish People, and consequently the Jewish nation had gone through stages of disintegration and assimilation. The role of Zionism was to supply through a cultural revival a new (cultural) base for the unity of the Jewish people. This is why a Jewish Center was needed in *Eretz Yisrael*, where such a culture could evolve, and all the parts of the 'Jewish People' would be attached to this center, and acknowledge it as a spiritual Jewish guide for them. As Rotenstreich (1962, p. 376) remarked: 'the geographic concentration in *Eretz Yisrael* will fulfill from pragmatic point of view the role the Jewish religion and the Jewish historical continuity.'

Clearly influenced by Hegelian ideas, Ahad Ha'am spoke about the Jewish "National Self" evolving and advancing through history putting on and taking off different forms. For thousands years the expression, or form of the "National Self" was the Jewish religion, and now this form must be taken off, while the 'National Self" ought to be expressed in the new (cultural) form of Zionism (Kaufmann 1961, vol. 2, p. 361). The evolution of the "National Self", on one hand, and the idea that Zionism is the successor of religion, on the other hand, meant that Zionism was a reformed secular version of Judaism. Zionism had become a new Jewish religion, or a new Jewish culture (Kurzweil, 1955).

To a certain extent, Ahad Ha'am distinguished between nationality and religion. He was an ethnicist or primordialist, which means he did not consider Judaism to be both nationality and religion, but rather a nationality which had a religion, and that could have "taken it off", "put Zionism on" and still remained a Jewish nation. Yet, Ahad Ha'am's "Theory of Continuity" and his claim that Zionism is a continuation of and substitution for religion, created the fusion of nationality and religion. The 'New Wall" which nationalism or Zionism was supposed to build instead of the religious "Old Wall" should be built 'in the same completeness and circumference that our forefathers had succeeded in giving to their wall" (Ahad Ha'am 1947, p. 402). Similarly, Ahad Ha'am's fusion of nationality and religion was expressed by the notion that the 'Spiritual Center', as a successor of religion, ought to have a Jewish content in order to provide the common ground for the unification of the

Jewish people. The Theory of Continuity, or the evolutionary nature of the "National Self", meant that that the "New Wall" still contained some remains of the "Old Wall", that is of Jewish religion, and consequently the present generation ought to observe part of the tenets of Judaism for the sake of the preservation of the "national Self". In other words, according to Ahad Ha'am 'The National Self' cast religious duties (though 'reformed' or 'reinterpreted') upon the national Jew, even if he was an atheist (Luz, 1988, pp. 216-17). Here appears the idea, with which Israelis are so familiar, that a "Jewish State" means that for national reasons, a certain degree of religiosity should be observed, in both the public and in the private spheres. Ahad Ha'am also demanded that the cultural content of the spiritual center be limited to what was considered Jewish, and thus in his journal *"Hashelach"*, he refused to publish Hebrew material that was not characterized as Jewish (even the poems of Hebrew poet Tchernichovsky).

Contrary to Political Zionism, where the Jewish State or the territorial concentration of the Jews created the distinction between nationality and religion, or between the Jewish nation and the historical Jewish People, Ahad Ha'am's Jewish nation was a Diaspora nation, identified with the historical *Am Yisrael*. While Political Zionism negated the Diaspora, and considered the creation of a normal territorial nation as the aim of Zionism, Ahad Ha'am saw the aim of Zionism as the prevention of the assimilation of a "Diaspora nation". In this respect, Ahad Ha'am objected to the idea of normalization. His notion of the Jews as a Diaspora nation meant the continuation of the abnormal status quo of the Jews, especially in Eastern Europe. Ahad Ha'am objected to the idea of mass Jewish immigration to the homeland, which was central to Political Zionism. The spiritual center, meant to be established by a small elite that would be specially trained for the mission. As David Vital remarked, "the answer which Ahad Ha'am gave to the question – 'What would be the fate of the Jews who will not be included in the 'center' in the

Land of Israel' was in fact a shrug: to his opinion, Palestine could not have been their salvation from the start" (Vital, 1984, p. 18).

The Debate on the 'Culture Question'

The meaning of the evolution of the "National Self" was the reformation of Judaism, or the creation of a new secular Judaism. Baruch Kurzweil (1955) says, "The problematic nature of the new Theory of Continuity of Judaism is obvious. Ahad Ha'am's Judaism is Judaism without the binding authority of the *Torah*; it is also Judaism without God." From this stemmed the great apprehensions that existed among religious Zionists concerning Ahad Ha'am and his followers. Apparently, Ahad Ha'am had appeared as someone who respected the Jewish religion and the Jewish tradition as the "National Self" contained also traditional elements. Nevertheless, Ahad Ha'am talked about the evolution of the national spirit, and considered religion as the primitive revelation of this spirit, which was supposed to be expressed now by the work for the spiritual center. The apprehensions of the religious Zionists found their expression in the struggle, which took place in the first Zionist Congresses concerning the question of culture. This debate is important to our case, as it was a prologue to the struggles on religion and State, which characterize Israel today and which were described in the first chapter of this book.

As noted above, Political Zionism abstained from any position concerning the culture of the future "Jewish State". The choice of the cultural character of the Jewish State was left to its inhabitants (Goldstein, 1991, p. 111). From Herzl's point of view, any discussion on the question of culture was irrelevant to that of national solidarity, because, as we have already seen, what, according to him, had turned the Jews into a nation at that stage was not the common culture, but rather the distress, the common enemy and the common destiny. On the contrary, such discussion could harm and lead to a war of culture, which would divide the movement. The meaning of a resolution concerning culture could be a violation of the principle that "Zionism has nothing to do with religion".

Herzl was a pluralist and his pluralism stemmed not only from a liberal worldview, but also from his conception of Zionism as "the Jewish people on the march", of which substantial parts were traditional and religious publics, all candidates for emigration. However, Ahad Ha'am was an elitist. For him, the Zionist movement was not "the Jewish People on the march", but rather, elite that would inhabit and build the spiritual center. Consequently the question of secession and that of maintaining Zionism as a mass movement did not bother Ahad Ha'am, as it had been central in Political Zionism.

The "Culture Question" had been on the agenda of the Zionist movement from its inception, yet at the beginning Herzl had it in his power to postpone the debate and the decision in this matter. Things had changed after Herzl's failures to achieve the Charter from the Sultan. When a political solution had seemed to fade away and there had been a fear that the Zionist movement would lose its momentum, the question of what should the Zionist movement do in the meantime came up. One of the answers was "Work of Culture", or "the Work of the Present", which meant the formulation and application of a program of education that would have prepared the Jews for the national task that lay ahead. This meant starting the nation-building process in the Diaspora. The pressures for the application of the "Work of the Present" came mainly from a group called "The Democratic Faction", whose members were, among others, Chaim Weizmann and Martin Buber, and which was supported by Ahad Ha'am, though from the outside as he was never a formal member of the Zionist movement. On the opposite side of the debate, stood the religious Zionists who demanded without reservations that the Zionist movement should abstain from any preoccupation in questions of values and education. Rabbi Rabinowitz, mentioned above, maintained that there is unbridgeable gap between the Orthodox and "the enlightened": "We need Rooms and Yeshivas, and they need general schools and gymnasia". He had several conclusions: a) Nothing should be taken from the Treasury of the Zionist Movement for both camps. b) The central institutions of the Zionist movement should not be engaged in the "Work of Culture", which should be left to the local Zionist organizations or the various parties, which should also finance it. c) The question of culture must not be discussed in the congress, as it might lead to agitation and breach of faith. This position was repeated by Rabbi Reines in the Third Congress and had become the official stand of the Orthodox in the future Congresses (Refael, 1983, pp. 45-46). As Don Yehiya says, the purpose of the Mizrahi was defensive: the preservation of the "purity" of Political Zionism from the attempts by the Democratic Faction, which was inspired by Ahad Ha'am, to control and enforce the "Work of Culture" (Don Yehiya, 1983, p. 138).

Why did Reines and the Religious Zionists object to the "Work of Culture"? First it should be noted that their position could sometimes characterize the behavior of minorities, which apprehend being coerced by the majorities. It seems as if the position of the Religious Zionists matched the principles of liberal democracy, as it separated between the religion and the Zionist movement. Most of the members of the Democratic faction belonged to the secular radical flank of the Zionist movement whose members sometimes expressed openly a hostile stand towards religion. To a religious Jew it seemed obvious that public funds should not be allocated for anti-religious education.

Yet, the objection of Reines and his friends to the "Work of Culture" did not stem only from the fear of anti-religious education. The spiritual father of the Democratic Faction was Ahad Ha'am, who had a positive attitude towards religion and its national role. Yet, the religious Zionists objected – for obvious reasons – to Ahad Ha'am and his Spiritual Zionism that identified

Zionism with Judaism, and sought to enforce its version of Judaism through the Work of Culture. Though Ahad Ha'am's nationalism incorporated religious elements, it was, after all, secular, and in fact, spiritual Zionism considered the Work of Culture as a substitution for religion. Therefore, in the Fourth Congress, Rabbi Rabinowitz explained why the Orthodox were apprehensive about the "Work of Culture":

> Yesterday, for instance, one of the speakers maintained that Zionism should become for us what the religion had been before. And by the way he said that that until now we had only religion, and from now Zionism will prevail. But this opinion is baseless. The religion has not passed away and will not pass away … the religion unifies the Jews and so does Zionism. It is nonsense to maintain the Zionism unites us today as religion had united us before. The religion has never stopped to unite us even today. We see Zionism as a means for the strengthening of our religion, and vise versa, if the root will dry the people will perish. (Don Yehiya, 1983, pp. 164-167).

Furthermore, the fusion of Judaism and nationality meant the nationalization of Judaism. Thus, Reines asserted that there was something rude and impolite when persons who are strange to Judaism and its spirit presumed to teach the people what Judaism is.

David Vital describes the members of the Democratic faction as "democrats", "modernists", persons of "science and method" who fiercely objected "clericalism" and "Byzantines and religious hypocrites" (Vital, 1982, pp. 190-1). Indeed, Vital's description seems to match the currently accepted vision among secular "enlightened" Israelis about the struggle between the secular and religious. Yet, according to Goldstein, the struggle was between the religious who supported Herzl's pluralist Political Zionism, and Monist secular radical Democrats (Goldstein, 1991, p. 124): "the Factionists' ambition was to create a monolithic national movement, which would match their worldview" (ibid. p. 129). Indeed, in this light we can see the decision that had been accepted by the Fifth Congress under the pressure of the Democratic Faction: "The Congress makes clear, it identifies the concept of culture with the national education of *Am Yisrael*, and considers this work as an important clause of the Zionist program and lays it as a duty upon every Zionist" (Maor, 1986, p. 191).

Maor points out that the decision, which mentioned national education that was not related to religion was resisted by the religious Zionists and led to the establishment of the Mizrahi – the Zionist Religious Party. The establishment of the Mizrahi party had been closely related to the victory of the Democratic faction in the debate about culture. An interesting point here is the direct contribution of Ahad Ha'am to two other important decisions; recognition of the existence of two separate streams within the Zionist Movement and the establishment of separate and equally funded committees for culture (one "religious" and one "secular"). These decisions were accepted in 1902, by the second convention of the Russian Zionists in Minsk. While Ahad Ha'am supported and pressed for these decisions, Rabbi Reines and the Mizrahi party objected to them. It was obvious that they had only accepted them as a lesser of two evils (Don Yehiya, 1983, p. 127). These decisions, which were accepted by the second convention of the Russian Zionists had far reaching implications concerning education and culture in Zionism and in the future Jewish State, as here, for the first time, it had been clearly decided that the Zionist movement would not be pluralist and that it would contain two principal streams: "secular" and "religious" (ibid., p. 139), where it was obvious that the division was artificial and that both camps were composed of various groups. Therefore, it is important to stress that the Mizrahi party was eventually founded not as an initiative of the religious Zionists, and as instrument for exerting political pressures concerning funding or religious coercion. On the contrary, it was founded as an attempt by the religious Zionists to defend themselves against what they considered an unnecessary intrusion by the Zionist Movement.

Ahad Ha'am and the Roots of Zionist Messianism

Yehuda Reinharz maintains that Ahad Ha'am's objection to the notion of Zionism as a solution for the plight of the Jews, stemmed from practical reasons. The doubts which Ahad Ha'am had were "pragmatic", yet his disciples in the west tended to turn his doubts into absolute principles. Indeed, Ahad Ha'am was convinced that the Diaspora would be long and even eternal, but "this was a pessimistic conclusion which he accepted with sorrow in the light of the practical limitations which faced the option of concentrating the Jews in their homeland" (Reinharz, 2000, p. 43). Yet Reinharz's assertion could be disputed. Indeed, Ahad Ha'am maintained that from various practical reasons, such as the absorption capabilities of Palestine, and the readiness and capabilities of the Jewish masses, the mission set by Political Zionism was unattainable. Beyond and aside from those practical protests, Ahad Ha'am objected to Political Zionism's notion of normalization – to be a nation, like all nations. According to Ahad Ha'am being a nation like all nations, or the establishment of a regular nation-state was not worthy of the Jewish nation. He believed "it is impossible for an old nation that has been a light unto the nations, as a reward for its plight, to be satisfied by so little; with that which many other peoples, with no name and culture, achieved in a short time, without suffering even a fraction of what it had suffered". The true reward worthy of the "Jewish nation" would be the fulfillment of the Jewish vocation, which, according to him, aims at the spread and realization of the biblical prophesies of the End of Days through the work of the spiritual center (Ahad Ha'am, 1947, p. 275).

Indeed, Ahad Ha'am's messianism was complementary to his "pragmatism" mentioned by Reinharz. According to Ahad Ha'am, the prophets understood that the small Jewish State could not prevail in a world ruled by conflicting interests of superpowers, and therefore they arrived at the idea of world peace on the End of Days, as a precondition for the peaceful development of their own people. In other words, physical redemption of the Jews is impossible in this world, and would have to be postponed until an everlasting peace prevails in the End of Days. At the same time, spiritual redemption, the one which would be realized through the spiritual center, will also advance the future physical salvation, as it dispenses the general salvation by spreading the biblical prophesies. Not much different from traditional Judaism, Ahad Ha'am's "pragmatism", or his notion of the helplessness of the Jews, was complementary to his messianism, and what he had practically suggested to the Jews in as far as their physical salvation was concerned, was not much different than what had been offered by the Jewish tradition – that is, to wait to the End of Days. Ahad Ha'am's messianism and his objection to normalization were expressed also by his contempt for the average person who was motivated by the desire to better his material situation and his rejection of the idea that materialistic deprivation catalyzes historical processes. He rejected the main tenet of Political Zionism, which considered the plight of the Jews to be the prime engine of Zionism. According to Ahad Ha'am, those who were motivated by material interests could not be trusted in the building of the spiritual center, not only because the hardships in Palestine required self-sacrifice, but because the center in *Eretz Yisrael* was supposed to become an example for Judaism at large. Only a small elite group of "priests" should be concentrated in *Eretz Yisrael*, while the Jewish masses should find the solution to their plight elsewhere (Brieman, 1950).

It is important to see how these messianic elements introduced into Zionism were connected to the fusion of nationality and religion. For once, Ahad Ha'am's utopianism was based upon the End of Days vision, making it complementary to traditional Judaism. Yet, he had replaced the traditional Jewish tenet – that in order to speed up the coming of the Messiah, every Jew must follow the Laws of the *Torah* – with the notion that in order to speed up the coming of the End of Days the Jews, as a collective or a Diaspora nation, should work the spiritual center. Also the idea of "vocation", used by Ahad Ha'am, (influenced by the romanticist nationalism of the nineteenth century), suggests that every nation had a vocation, was also a continuation of the traditional debate about reasons and purpose of the Diaspora in the new era. Indeed, one of the traditional explanations of the Diaspora was the need to spread monotheism, or the word of God among the gentiles. This idea was also used by the Jewish Enlightenment when they were faced with the question – why not abandon Judaism altogether? One of the answers given was that the Jews had a vocation, which was to spread morality, especially the ideas of the prophecies. The development of reformed, non-halachic forms of Judaism, whose members aspired to integrate into their local nation presupposed reformation of traditional Judaism, after which most of the external characteristics that distinguished the Jews from their surroundings disappeared. Thus, non-halachic Judaism tended to view Judaism as morality. Furthermore, as the reformers were aiming to integration in the local nations, the notion of salvation in *Eretz-Yisrael* also had to be abandoned. Here too, the existence of the Diaspora was explained by the need to spread this morality for all humanity (Ben Rafael & Ben-Chaim, 2006, pp. 103 – 107).

The notion of the Jewish vocation was used not only by Ahad Ha'am to oppose Herzl's Political Zionism. The anti Zionist manifesto, published on the eve of the First Zionist Congress by the executive of the Union of the rabbis in Germany, (which included both Orthodox and reformed rabbis), proclaimed that "the aspirations of the so-called Zionists to establish a Jewish national State in *Eretz Yisrael*, was in opposition to the messianic vocation of Judaism". As Yaakov Zur (2001) pointed out, both Orthodox and reform rabbis could have been united behind this vague phrasing, as they both shared the messianic conception of Judaism, (though they disagreed about the nature of the Jewish vocation.)

The appearance of nationalism, especially in its romanticist version, added a collective dimension to the notion of the Jewish vocation. Here the romanticist philosophy, especially of Hegel, had a great influence. According to Hegel, nations existed as long as they fulfilled their vocation and contributed to the "World Spirit". Hegel considered the Jews to be a nation (rather than a religious community), which in the past had made an important contribution to the "World Spirit" by spreading monotheism. The historical vocation of Judaism had come to an end with the appearance of Jesus, whose teachings signified a more advanced stage in the development of monotheism and the World Spirit. As the historical role of the Jewish nation came to an end, it should have ceased to exist. The conclusion was that the continued existence of the Jewish People could not be explained, and consequently is contingent and meaningless. It was Rabbi Nachman Krochmal (RANAK) who had turned the Hegelian equation upside down: If, after the appearance of Christianity the Jewish nation continued to exist, this meant that its existence was meaningful and that it had a vocation. The uniqueness, non-territorial, and non-political nature of the Jewish nation was attributed to the fact that, unlike other nations which had both material and spiritual elements, the Jewish nation was distinctive, as, in the course of history, it had taken off its materialistic elements and become more and more spiritual. Eventually, it was not the nations of the world that had acquired their hegemony through materialistic political power, but rather the spiritual, Jewish nation that was the true carrier of the Word Spirit (Avineri, 1981, pp. 14-22).

These motives also appeared in Ahad Ha'am's teachings – the notion of vocation as collective and the emphasis on the spirituality of the collective, while lessening its materialistic elements. The annulment of the materialistic aspects of the Jewish nation did not mean only the diminution of the importance of worldly politics, but also the disregard for the notion that

Zionism should answer for the materialistic needs of the Jews, or the disregard for individuals motivated by the desire to improve their materialistic status.

It is important to emphasize again, the profound change that the notion of vocation acquired under RANAK and Ahad Ha'am. The traditional vocation, and the one which had appeared in the Enlightenment and in non-Halachic Judaism, was attributed to Jews as individuals, or as (religious) communities. According to both RANAK and Ahad Ha'am, it was transformed and attributed to "Judaism" as a collective.

Indeed, Ahad Ha'am's messianism or spirituality meant the disregard for worldly 'materialistic' politics and its conspicuous expressions: state and sovereignty. Nathan Rotenstreich maintained that "in the ideas of Ahad Ha'am, (at least of the mature Ahad Ha'am), there are no signs that the idea of the spiritual center is antithetical to that of the 'Jewish State'; those ideas deal with the special character of the state." (Rotenstreich, 1962, p. 378). Yet, it must be emphasized that the establishment of a state was not a necessary condition for the spiritual center. In other words, there are no signs that Ahad Ha'am considered the establishment of a Jewish State necessary for the successful existence of the spiritual center; on the contrary, he occasionally expressed contempt for the characteristics of sovereignty, which he considered as antithetical to the "spirituality", or the mission of Judaism and the spiritual center. Thus, political independence was not important or essential; what mattered was that the spiritual center would authentically reflect the Jewish national "self". Thus, if a state was required, it was not an end by itself (as normally movements for national self determination maintain), but as a means to fulfill the Jewish vocation. As Avineri (1981, p. 138) notes, according to Ahad Ha'am, "the role of Zionism does not end with the establishment of the state. From several aspects, the real project will start after political independence". Thus, "to Ahad Ha'am, following the Hegelian school of thought, a state is not an end in itself, but merely the necessary foundation for the spiritual expression of the national spirit, the Volksgeist (Avineri, 1981, p. 121).

Consequently, Zionism is not a regular movement for national self-determination, whose task ends after independence is reached. Here, again, we see the notion of Zionism, as understood in Israel today, is an ongoing "eternal" project, which justifies the existence of Zionist organization – even after independence.

Ethnic Nationalism, Racism and Radicalism: Practical Zionism and the Separation between Nationality and Religion

A widely accepted view suggests that the characteristics of Zionism, especially with the respect to the relation between nationality and religion, could not be deduced from 'Political Zionism', which was dominated by the unique personality of Herzl. According to this accepted view, Herzl was unique in two important respects: First, he was exceptionally liberal. Second, Herzl came from an assimilated home, something which naturally reduced the religious or traditional element of his notion of the Jewish nation (Salmon 1999, p. 294). Furthermore, Political Zionism had prevailed only for a short time to be replaced by what had been known as 'Practical Zionism', which dominated and shaped Zionism until Israel's independence. While Political Zionism was dominated by Western Jews who had a civic approach towards nationalism, (so the argument goes), Practical Zionism was dominated by Eastern European Jews, who shared nationalist romanticist or "organic" views, which tended to stress the centrality of the religious and ethnic components of the Jewish national identity. To a large extent, this accepted view had been influenced by the classical dichotomy mentioned above between Western-European civic nationalism, on one hand and Eastern-European ethnic nationalism, on the other. To what extent, then, can the separation between nationality and religion be discerned in Practical Zionism?

Practical Zionism was a synthesis of ideas, partly "political", partly "spiritual", which had been formed already in the days of *Hovevei Zion*.

Practical Zionism shared with Political Zionism the negation of the Diaspora, the centrality of the "Jewish Problem" and the notion of the establishment of a Jewish State as a safe haven for Jews. Nevertheless, like Ahad Ha'am, the Practical Zionists emphasized the "Work of the Present". While Political Zionism assumed that the nation-building process would happened under the custody of the State, the Practical Zionists considered the process of nation building in the training of few chosen pioneers (*halutzim*) in the Diaspora in preparation for immigration to *Eretz Yisrael*. Consequently in the cultural question the Practical Zionists tended to identify with Ahad Ha'am and not with Herzl: A cultural revival was a precondition for independence (though not all Practical Zionists had necessarily agreed with Ahad Ha'am on the nature of the national culture). Yet, the main disagreement between Herzl and the Practical Zionists was about the nature of immigration and settlement in the homeland. Here too Practical Zionists tended to side with Ahad Ha'am rather than with Herzl. Herzl objected to 'infiltration' into Palestine and wanted a mass immigration in the short-range once the Charter would be granted. However, Practical Zionists wanted gradual settlement of *halutzim*, not necessarily under Jewish sovereignty; hence, the important difference concerning sovereignty and statehood. The Political Zionists demanded immediate Jewish sovereignty, while the Practical Zionists preferred a slow development – even without Jewish sovereignty, while postponing the question of statehood to an indefinite date in the future.

Unlike Political Zionism, Practical Zionism -- at least in the short term -- aspired for the establishment of elite utopian community in Palestine. For some, like Ahad Ha'am and his followers, this utopian society of *halutzim* was a purpose of its own, for others it was a necessary condition to create the conditions for the following mass Jewish immigration. Yet, as the Practical Zionists had not introduced any timetable for statehood and mass immigration, what might have been seen as a tactical purpose, had practically turned out to be absolute. (Vital, 1984, 10).

Zionism as Ethnic Nationalism

If one accepts the ethnic/civic traditional typology of nationalism, as a mainly Eastern European phenomenon, Zionism had always tended towards 'ethnic', rather than civic, definition of a nation (Shimoni, 2000). Yet, there are two points to be made here. First, as noted above, the notion of the emerging nation as predominantly Eastern European (and thus not including the entire *Am Yisrael*) was shared by *Hovevei Zion* and other Zionist thinkers of Eastern European stock who might have had a more organic or romanticist or ethnic notion of the Jewish nation. Second, as Anthony Smith points out, ethnic nationalism was also politics of cultural revolt, not only against alien rulers, but also against the 'fathers' or the traditional order (Smith, 1995b; Shimoni 2000, 87). The Zionist case was no different in this sense, and as we are going to see, in as much that Zionism could be classified as "ethnic nationalism", this ethnicism was sometimes radical and was used as means to rebel against religion, or, in other words, the ethnic (or even racial) definitions of the nation were used as a means to separate nationality from religion.

Paradoxically, Ahad Ha'am was one of the first to express this radical ethnicism, as he was the one "who gave Jewish nationalism an organic, ethnic and culturally exclusive definition." (Ben Israel, 2003, p. 97). According to his notion of 'Biological Nationalism' (*leumiut biologit*), the Jewish nation was a biological, racial or ethnic entity while Judaism is religion, or the world of beliefs and opinions of the Jewish nation created in order to defend the nation from assimilation throughout the generations. The radical elements of this theory lay in the fact that it released the Jew from all commitment to Judaism as a worldview. As Kaufmann (1961 vol. 2, pp. 366-7) notes: this meant that, 'beliefs and opinions' of Judaism were 'utterances of biological national needs that fulfilled a known task in its time'. Furthermore, since belonging to the nation was natural, it had completely relieved the individual Jew from the adoption of any 'Jewish' opinions or doctrines that could serve as precondition for belonging to the nation. Thus, in a famous passage Ahad Ha'am (1947, p. 89) maintains:

> I at least know "why I remain a Jew" or, rather, I can find no meaning in such a question any more than if I were asked why I remain my father's son. I can at least speak my mind concerning the teachings and beliefs that I have inherited from my ancestors without fearing to snap the bond that unites me to my people. I can even adopt that "scientific heresy which bears the name of Darwin" without any danger to my Judaism. (see also: Shimoni 1995, pp. 288-9).

The ethnic or biological characterization of the nation had turned the Judaism of the individual Jew into a biological fact and thus releases him from any commitment to the substance of his Judaism. Later on, Ahad Ha'am reversed course on this absolute freedom which he ascribed to the 'National Self'' and, as noted above, chose to stress another aspect of his biological nationalism – 'The Theory of Continuity', where he stresses the evolutionary nature of the national spirit and the fact that it did contain traditional Jewish elements which obliged the national Jew. Yet, his disciples and his critics had always reminded him of this point. One of his critics was the writer Micha Yosef Berdichevsky, who rejected Ahad Ha'am's notion of the commitment the (national) Jew had towards any kind of "Jewish Tradition", which he considered as degenerating and as responsible for the plight of the Jews in the Diaspora. Berdichevsky demanded a total secession from the Jewish (Diaspora) tradition and a 'reunification' with the ancient Hebrew past. Sharing with Ahad Ha'am the ethnic notion of the Jewish nation (Shimoni, 1995, p. 288), he kept repeating the words of the early Ahad Ha'am: the (national) Jew could speak his mind regarding the beliefs and opinions that he had inherited from his ancestors without the fear that the bond that united him to his people would snap (Berdichevsky, 1922 Part 2, pp. 39-40). Though he shared the idea that the solution to the Jewish problem laid in cultural or spiritual revival with Ahad Ha'am, Berdichevsky's approach did not call for the revival of Judaism, but rather, revival of the individual Jew: "Jews come first, before Judaism". In fact, Berdichevsky rejected the notion of the existence of "Judaism" as one culture, or as a collective entity: "there is no Judaism, there are Jews".

I believe that Kaufmann was right when he remarked that the importance of Berdichevsky's work does not lie in his attack on religion or Judaism, but rather in his idea of the separation between Jews and Judaism. This idea is expressed in Berdichevsky's article "*Stira u'Binian,*" that is not based necessarily on the negative attitude towards Judaism, which usually characterizes his writings (Kaufmann, 1961 vol. 2, pp. 393-5). According to Berdichevsky, national revival requires a "change of values" (*shinui arachim*), which would mean the separation of the concept of *Am Yisrael* (the "Jewish People") from any constant or limited worldview. In other words, national revival could not tolerate any constraint (Berdichevsky, 1922 Part 2, pp. 18-20). Here Berdichevsky followed the important central idea of the Enlightenment, which drew from the notion of the autonomous individual to that of the autonomous community. The principle of unlimited sovereignty, (i.e. that no constraints could be put on the sovereign, or the people), had turned out to be one of the basic principles of modern political thought. In this respect, it is not only that the subordination of *"Am Yisrael"* to the *Torah* should be rejected, and that it should be proclaimed the "Israel comes first before the *Torah*" (*Yisrael kodem le'oraita*) (Ibid. p. 20), but also that "Israel comes first before Judaism". This would include any cultural norms or "national morality" or "national vocation" such as postulated by Ahad Ha'am (Ibid. pp. 39-40). This would mean "the nation of Israel is an existential fact, and not a world-outlook". According to Berdichevsky, "we are people who happened to think in certain ways, but, our being a people is not dependent on thinking in those ways – We shall not be compelled by any abstract Judaism of one kind or another. We are Hebrews and we shall follow our hearts" or, "Israel lives in all lives and in all shapes … there is no Israeli thought, only thinking Israelis; there is no essential Israeli soul, but only sons of Israel with a human soul (Ibid. pp. 39-40; (and see also Shimoni, 1995, p. 289; Kaufmann, 1961 vol 2, p. 394). As Kaufmann notes "the notion of a human-Hebrew nationality, by the separation of the Hebrew nationalism, not only from religion, but also from Judaism at-large, is the existing fruitful idea of Berdichevsky's thought". (Kaufmann, 1932, b, p. 394).

In a way, Berdichevsky's solution to the "Question of Culture" was not at odds with that of Political Zionism. As the latter had refused to set any apriori cultural constraints upon the emerging nation and suggested those limitations be decided upon by the inhabitants of the Jewish State, it seems to have shared Berdichevsky's laissez-faire attitude towards Jewish national identity. Yet, there appears to be a tension between the absolute freedoms Berdichevsky allowed the national Jew in "*Stira u'Binan*" and the hostility he professed against religion or traditional Judaism, (something absent in 'Political Zionism'). For a cultural revival one would need a revolutionary "change of values" which would cast the modern Jew, or the "New Hebrew" as a total negation of the "Old Jew". This attitude would not only distinguish between nationality and religion, but, in fact, position them as antithetical. Thus, Berdichevsky completely rejected Ahad Ha'am's theory of continuity, and his nation did not evolve out of Diaspora Judaism, but was directly related to the ancient Hebrews. It was both "universal" and "materialistic", as opposed to the "spiritual" nation of Ahad Ha'am. It was the 'nation of the sword', rather than the 'nation of the book', more connected to the earthly materialistic elements of human existence (Holtzman, 1993, pp. 194 - 196).

Writer Yosef Haim Brenner carried this freedom of thought, which Berdichevsky gave to the national Jew to its natural conclusion. Sharing with Berdichevsky the ethnic notion of Judaism, Brenner argued that it was possible for national Jew to adopt the Christian teachings, without severing his connection with the Jewish nation (Govrin, 1985). Here we see how ethnic nationalism could form a basis of a multi-religious nation. We can examine similar views expressed by Israel Zangwill, one of the founders of Political Zionism. Zangwill held a rather racial concept of the nation, and though he thought different races could integrate into one new nation, he saw it as a long process, full of racial conflicts that could be hazardous for a nation, (especially when it is at the beginning of its independence). Consequently, Zangwill had suggested the relocation of the non-Jewish minorities in Palestine (especially the Arabs, but not exclusively, as there was a German minority he also wished to relocate). Yet, as Palestine was supposed to be cleared of non-Jewish elements, who could guard the non-Jewish holy places? Zangwill's solution to the problem is that 'The Holy Grave will be guarded by Christianized Jews, while the Mosque of Omar will be guarded by Islamized Jews' (Netanyahu, 2003, pp. 210-11). Thus, Zangwill's 'Jewish nation' which was comprised of members of the "Jewish Race" also contained Christian Jews and Muslim Jews. Another interesting example is supplied by Ber Borochov, one of the most influential socialist Zionist thinkers. Borochov maintained that Palestine was most suitable for Jewish immigration, as economically it was underdeveloped and therefore the Jews would not meet the same resistance they had encountered in capitalist countries. Furthermore, according to Borochov, the local Palestinian peasant population, (the *fellaheen)*, had a natural racial affinity with the Jews. After all, they were 'direct descendants of the Judean and Canaanite population, with a very small addition of Arab blood' (Shimoni, 1995, p. 182, Shavit, 1984, p. 120).

Thus, according to Borochov, in Palestine the native population itself could be assimilated, culturally and economically, into the incoming Jewish population. Here we can see, again, how a racial notion of the nation could be used to separate nationality from religion, and to create a multi-religious nation (Shimoni 1995, p. 184; Gorni, 1985, p. 40). Ben Gurion and Ben-Zvi had also toyed with such ideas. In a book titled: *The Land of Israel Past and Present* (1918) they suggested that the Arab *fellaheen* were the descendants of "Jewish peasants, who were forced by persecutions and hard times to separate from their religion in order to remain loyal and attached to the Jewish Land" (Bartal, 2007, pp. 129-130). This assertion was prompted by the discovery of a small Jewish *fellahin* community in the small Galilee village of Peki'in. This was seen by Ben Gurion and Ben-Zvi not only as a proof for the existence of a Jewish continuous settlement in Palestine (justifying Zionist claims), but also as a indication of a possible future bonding – as these two "ardent Zionists wanted to bond with the local 'natives', and with all their heart, they believed that it was possible, because of their mutual 'ethnic origin' (Sand, 2008, pp. 179-181). Berdichevsky, on the other hand, held a pessimistic view about the possibility of the assimilation of the local population. Therefore, in what looked as an omen for the future Israeli State, Berdichevsky says:

> The strictnesses concerning mix marriages were, as it is well known, a basis element of the existence of the Jewish race and the most important obstacle for assimilation. This obstacle, which had stop the Jews from dissolving within other nations, will be to no less extent an obstacle to the reconquering of the homeland, as the latter is conditioned by the absorption of the alien population. ... The People of Israel had behaved in this manner towards the Canaainites. It had simply swallowed them. ... any conquest which will not attempt and annex the first inhabitants to its own culture will fail. What that Israel could

have done in the past, the rabbinate-nation cannot do. And after this ability had been taken away (from the nation) and the national exclussivess had become an essential characteristic [for this nation], also in its homeland many gates will continue to be blocked for it. (Shavit, 1984, p. 120).

The distinction between nationality and religion in Berdichevsky and Brenner's writings is expressed not only by the demand to free the (national) Jew from any commitment towards the Jewish tradition or any ('Jewish') world-view, but also in the individualist nature of their doctrine (Kaufmann, 1961 vol. 2, pp. 405-17). When Berdichevsky established that "There is no Judaism, there are only Jews", he denied the existence of any Jewish collectivity, not only the traditional *"Am Yisrael"*, but also in any national sense. As such, Berdichevsky rejected not only Ahad Ha'am's notion of Jewish national collectivity, but also that of Political Zionism. From his point of view, the nation was a collection of individuals, and national revival or auto-emancipation was the sum of the individual revivals: the nation will be free when each and every member of the nation will set himself or herself free. Thus, this was not a liberal individualism, but rather, an existential individualism heavily influenced by Nietzsche's notion of the *Übermensch*; the will and ability to set oneself free could not be found in every Jew, but only in a small "elite" who would form the nation, while the rest were doomed to assimilation. Those special few will comprise the "Hebrew nation", while the many, the historical *"Am Yisrael"*, will remain in the Diaspora. Since, unlike Ahad Ha'am, Berdichevsky and Brenner did not believe that a "Diaspora Nation" could exist, it was doomed for extinction; whether physical, or by assimilation. Consequently, while he was aiming, like Ahad Ha'am, at the creation of a small elite community in Palestine, unlike Ahad Ha'am this chosen community constituted in his case a nation. Here the distinction between nationality and religion turned out to be between the 'chosen ones', the small elite who were blessed with the ability to set themselves free, and the rest (Kaufmann, 1961, pp. 417-22).

Berdichevsky had a great impact upon the members of the Second *aliya*, upon the ideology of the Labor movement, and the entire *Yishuv* prior to independence (Holtzman, 1993). In Berdichevsky we find the roots of the ethos which had become dominant in the Labor movement and in "Practical Zionism", an ethos which Liebman and Don Yehiya (1983, pp. 59-60) label as 'confrontation' approach towards traditional Judaism. The antithesis between the "New Jew" (or the Hebrew) and the "Old Jew" had not only separated the Hebrew nation from the historical *Am Yisrael* but in fact cast the former as an antithesis of the latter. It had drawn a sharp divide between the '*halutsim*', or the Jews who were members of the *Yishuv* and those who were about to make an immediate immigration (*aliya*), on one hand, and the rest of the Diaspora Jews, on the other. Thus, Anita Shapira (1997, pp. 156-7) points to the poems of Chaim Nachman Bialik which dealt with "*metei midbar*" (The dead of the desert): the myth of the Exodus, where the People of Israel were found as unworthy of entering the Promised Land. According to Shapira, this myth suited the worldview of the Zionists, as the doctrine of the revival of the individual Jew in his historical homeland tacitly presupposed the existing generation (that is the current *Am Yisrael*) was "*the generation of the desert*".

It is important to stress that in as much as an ethnic, racial or organic conception of a nation could be used as means for the separation between nationality and religion and the creation of a multi-religious nation, it could be an obstacle for the creation of a multi-ethnic nation, that is to the inclusion of those who are considered as belonging to other ethnicities. Indeed traditionally, 'ethnic nationalism' had been considered illiberal and non-inclusive when compared to 'civic nationalism'. Thus, while from Brenner's point of view regarding an individual of the Jewish race who converts to Islam still remains a member of the Jewish nation, he objected to the incorporation of Arabs in the Jewish nation (Gorni, 1985, pp. 22-61).

This objection did not stem from the fusion of religion and nationality, but rather, from the assumption that the Arabs constitute a different race or different nationality. As we have seen above, Borochov expresses a different opinion: because of the racial affinity between the Jews and the Arabs the latter could be assimilated. While Borochov and Brenner share the ethnic conception of the nation, they arrive at different conclusions, as they disagree about the racial affinity between the Jews and the Arabs.

ભ CHAPTER 5 ৯০

Republicanism in Israel on the Eve of Independence and Afterwards

On the eve of Israel's independence the fusion of religion and nationality was not self-evident, and it was possible to discern republican trends within the leadership of the *Yishuv* and the Zionist movement. In the document adopted by the Zionist leadership convened in the Biltmore Hotel in New York in May 1942, it was stated that the purpose of Zionism was the establishment of a "Jewish Commonwealth". The term "commonwealth" is the accepted translation in the United States and Britain to the term "republic". Also "The Hebrew Committee for National Liberation," established by Hillel Kook and operated in the United States during the Second World War, called for the establishment of "The Hebrew Republic of Palestine". The framework of the political and constitutional discourse on the eve of Independence was dictated, (to a great extent), by the 1947 United Nation Partition Plan for Palestine; which practically imposed a republican government on the Jewish State (even though the term 'republic' did not appear in the resolution). Consequently, on the table of the Provisional State Council (PSC) was a proposal of a constitution, proclaiming "Israel is a sovereign, independent and democratic republic". Although the Declaration of Independence did not declare Israel a republic, it contained republican elements, especially in its operative part, which laid the moves for the election of a Constituent Assembly. Also the programs of some of the parties (published on the eve of the elections for the Constituent Assembly) proclaimed Israel as a republic. This republican discourse had vanished – to a great extent – with the abolishment of the Constituent Assembly, when it was turned over into the First Knesset, without producing a constitution. Even though, in the seventh meeting of the First Knesset, in which Ben Gurion introduced his government, he still committed himself to entrench by law "the democratic and republican regime in the State of Israel".

The purpose of the following chapter is to try to address the question of the extent to which the constitutional debate, (especially on the eve of independence and in the first years afterwards), was aimed at the establishment of a republic: (a) To what extent in this discourse can we trace the attempt to solve what seemed to be the tension between the fact the State was "Jewish", on one hand, and a "democratic republic", on the other. (b) To what extent there had been a distinction between the sovereign people (the "Israeli People"), on one hand, and the Diaspora nation (the "Jewish People"), on the other. (c) To what extent did this discourse recognize that the sovereign people would also be composed of non-Jews? (d) What was supposed to be the status of minorities, especially Arabs, in the Jewish Republic? The answers to these questions reveals the fact that the concept of the "Jewish State" entertained on the eve of Independence was very different than what became accepted later.

Between a Jewish Republic & the State of the Jewish People

The Importance of a Name

The Biltmore Program, notwithstanding, the use of the term "commonwealth" (or republic) was very rare even on the eve of independence. The terms which were used to describe the new governing entity were: "Hebrew State", "Hebrew Regime" (*Shilton Ivri*). Use of the term "Jewish State" was much less common (Beeri, 1992, pp. 19 – 20). Use of the adjective "Hebrew" to describe either the future state or its organs, carried within it a republican element, as it created a territorial sovereign people (the Hebrew People) and distinguished it from the Diaspora nation (the Jewish People). Hebraism, especially under the dominance of the Labor movement, was characterized by its confrontational attitude towards Judaism, thus it was not only distinguished from Judaism, but sometimes conceived as antithetical to it. Hebraism was also territorial in the sense that it was limited to the Hebrew speaking *Yishuv* and thus distinguished it from the Jewish Diaspora. In addition, the use of the term "Jewish State" was different than the one that is currently accepted. Today, a Jewish State means a State that is supposed to reflect "Jewish" values, as it is reflected in the new Basic Laws; while in 1948, it meant a state established by Jews, or that most of its inhabitants are Jews (Aloni, 1987).

Nevertheless, the question, which still remains, is why a term that was so common in other movements for self-determination, was not in used in the Zionist case. One of the main reasons seems to be the distinction that was drawn between the "independent State" (which had full sovereignty,) and the "State" (which had limited sovereignty.) A republic meant an independent State; while Political Zionism, which had sought Jewish sovereignty within the framework of a Charter by a superpower, was aiming to a "State" more than to "independent State". Thus, even a maximalist, like Jabotinsky, was still seeking a state within the British Empire (Naor, 2004, p. 73-75). Another reason for the absence of republican discourse was Practical Zionism's approach which dominated the *Yishuv* and the Zionist movement between the two world wars, and which had preferred a slow development of the Yishuv, as a sort of National Home under British protection while postponing the question of sovereignty (whether full or limited) to indefinite future.

Another question is to what extent the forefathers of the Jewish State considered non-Jews, especially Arabs, as possible partners in the Jewish or the Hebrew state. In an interview conducted in the nineteen-sixties Ben Gurion described the doubts which characterized the debate in the Provisional Government (*minhelet ha'am*) on the eve of independence concerning the name of the new State:

In the declaration we also said that the State "will maintain complete equality of social and political rights for all its citizens, with no difference of religion race or sex", and every citizen in this state is an Israeli citizen, but not every Israeli is necessarily a Jew. An Israeli citizen can be an Arab (Moslem or Christian) or a member of another people who has settled as a citizen in this country. And for this reason several members of the Provisional Council of State had doubts as to whether it was not necessary to give the state a different name in other languages, and not Israel, since Israelite can be interpreted as synonymous with "Jew". But the council decided to leave the appellation "Israeli" for every citizen, whether Jewish of not. And it decided that the State should be called Israel in all languages. Hence it is clear that an Israeli is not obliged to be a Jew, and Israeli does not mean Jewish, for the decision was passed unanimously. (Ben Ezer, 1974, p. 87)

This rather astonishing testimony reveals a clear distinction between nationality and religion on the eve of independence. It seems, then, that for the forefathers the name "The State of Israel" meant also an identity – "Israeli", which was different from the identity "Jew". The problem which Ben Gurion was pointing at was raised in connection with the translation of the name of the state into Arabic were that the terms "Israeli" and "Jew" were identical. The problem seemed to be two-fold: On one hand, this new identity could harm the situation of "our brothers in the Arab countries", where it could raise the question of "dual-loyalty", which would be especially severe in their case. On the other hand, there was the question of the ability of the Israeli Arabs to identify with Israel. Thus, the Minister of Agriculture in the Provisional Government, Aharon Tzizling, said in the meeting of the Provisional Government: "I am against a name which would force every Arab who carries it to revolt against it". And Shertok said: "I don't want it to be called in Arabic 'Israel'. I was looking all the time for a way out, not to impose upon an Arab to identify with the Jewish People, and I can't find it" (Beeri, 1992, p. 23). We can see that the members of the Provisional Government did not consider "Israeli" as an adjective that denotes a place of residence or an administrative tool, but rather as an identity. This identity was different from the Jewish identity, and was supposed to be one with which the Arabs could identify.

Constitutions for Israel

The United Nation Partition resolution had imposed a republican government on the new State. In as much as it was called a "Jewish State", it was obliged to be a constitutional regime, which provides civic equality for all. In December 1947, as part of the procedures to carry out the U.N. Resolution, the Management of the Jewish Agency approached Yehuda Pinchas Kohn, who was the Secretary of the Political Department of the Management of the Jewish Agency, and after independence the Legal Councilor of the Foreign Office, and asked him to compose a draft of a constitution. Kohn prepared the draft and submitted it to the Constitution Committee of the Provisional State Council headed by Zerach Varhaftig on July 1 1948 (Varhaftig, 1988, p. 60). After its submission Varhaftig declared: "the Constitution Committee had decided to accept the draft as the basis for its discussions". The draft had gone through some changes and was published for the public (Y. Kohn, 1949). The publication carried the name of the Provisional State Council 1949, though it was stated at that time: "it does not have any formal authorization, and the responsibility is on the composer alone."

The draft was published in the Hebrew press. The full document appeared, among other places, in the New York Times of December 10, 1948 (Akzin, 1966a, p. 10, note 1). Thus, in an article dedicated to Kohn's constitution, an experienced reader such as Carl J. Friedrich, did not hesitate to call it: "a constitution of a republican democracy" (Friedrich, 1949,

p. 203). Indeed, the draft declared: "Israel is a democratic independent sovereign republic". Here, it is important to stress that in as much as the U.N. Partition Resolution imposed upon the two new States, Jewish and Arab, a republican regime, and in as much as Kohn's draft was initiated as a response to this demand, the term "republic" was not mentioned in the resolution, and it was originated by the author. Moreover, there were other proposals. For instance, a proposal by Yochanan Bader, a member of the Constituent Assembly and the First Knesset from the opposition *Herut* Party, repeated Kohn's words that "the State of Israel is a democratic independent sovereign republic". There was also a proposal by *MAPAI*, (the ruling party), which was prepared by a committee headed by Zvi Berenzon. The number of republican constitutional drafts that were made public since independence is probably no more than a handful. From these I would like to single out and discuss the one offered in the nineteen sixties by Professor Benjamin Akzin (Akzin, 1966b). The draft of Akzin is important to our discussion, not only because of its republican character, but also because Akzin participated in the republican debate on the eve of independence.[20]

All these republican constitutions declared that Israel is "a national home for the Jewish People *(Am Yisrael)*", or assert the connection between the new State and the "Jewish People", and the right of every Jew to immigrate and naturalize. The question is, of course, how they deal with the apparent tension between this assertion, and the demand to establish a republic. The answer to this question lies in the equality of rights and duties which those constitutions offer to all citizens without a distinction of religion, race or sex, on one hand, and that the republican definition always meant that the sovereignty was entrusted to the citizen body (which included non-Jews) and not to the "Jewish people", on the other hand. In other words, in as much as it is not clear to what extent these constitutions separated nationality and religion and recognize the existence of an Israeli nation, they still distinguished between "the people" (the sovereign) which was identified with the citizen body, and the Jewish people, while granting complete equality to all the members of the sovereign people.

Indeed, the preamble of Kohn's draft was a declaration on behalf of the Jewish people:

> We, the Jewish People … are resolved to rebuild our commonwealth in accordance with the ideals of peace and Justice of the Prophets of Israel, to open our land to every Jew who seeks entry, and to promote the security and prosperity of those who dwell within …we have maintained and accepted the words of the following constitution.[21]

In the preamble we can see the duality: a declaration on the behalf of the "Jewish people" vs. the establishment of the republic. Yet, a republican motif also appears in the preamble: "to promote the security and the prosperity of all who dwell within". Thus, the purpose of the republic is not the welfare of the Jewish people, but rather of the inhabitants of the country without distinction of religion, race, or sex. Kohn was aware of the difficulty. In the memorandum (in English) attached to the draft, Kohn states that one of the problems in the preamble is that it is not the entire Jewish people, which ratifies the constitution, but only the Jews of Palestine. Kohn suggested overcoming this difficulty by changing the first sentence of the preamble to: "We the Jewish People in Palestine". The Hebrew version, which appeared in transliteration said: "We members of the Hebrew people who reside in Zion" (Kohn, Memorandum, p. 3). It is not clear why Kohn did not use this formulation from the beginning or why he did not change the original accordingly.

This duality was also reflected in paragraphs 2 and 3 of the draft. Paragraph 2 declared that "Israel is a democratic, independent, sovereign republic", while paragraph 3 states that "Israel was chosen to become a national home for the Jewish People. It will allow to every Jew to come and settle according to the rules set by the laws of the State". In his review of the constitutional draft Karl Friedrich addressed this duality:

> The basic problems that this constitution is seeking to solve are the problems, which concern every constitutional regime. Israel is defined here as an independent, sovereign, democratic republic (clause 2) and as destined to be the national home of the Jewish People (clause 3). The latter - which is natural and understood on the background of the historical origin of the new state and the long Zionist struggle which had preceded it – is unique in the history of constitution writing in modern times. Every state is, of course, a national home for a certain people, yet I know of no constitution, which says it explicitly. This entails another provision, which is that every Jew who wishes to settle in its territory will be allowed to enter. The fate of the state is depended upon this ... and the constitution must take this vocation into account. Yet, the constitution establishes complete equality of all human beings before the law and a complete civic and political equality to all the citizens. Any kind of discrimination is forbidden, by race, religion, language or sex. (Friedrich, 1949, p. 205).

It should be mentioned here that what seemed to Karl Friedrich as unprecedented in 1948, (that the constitution would declare explicitly that the State is a home of a certain people,) is not unprecedented today, and characterizes some republics, mainly in Eastern Europe, which won independence after the collapse of the Soviet Union (See above, pp. 138-155). Anyway, because the constitution granted a complete equality to all the citizens without a distinction of religion, race or sex, Friedrich did not consider it to be a problem.

In Kohn's draft there was no direct reference to the citizen body as "people" (in the republican sense), even though it was implied. In this sense Bader's draft was more interesting. It also declared in the preamble: "We, the sons of Abraham our father, had settled our mind to rebuild the Hebrew State …". In paragraph 59 of the constitution, Bader said: "the State of Israel is a democratic independent sovereign republic based upon social justice". Paragraph 60 stated: "1. State sovereignty is granted to the people." 2. "The people exercise their sovereignty either directly or indirectly by their elected representatives in the manner and the limits set in this constitution and in accordance to the dictates of the general good". Hence, "the people" here was identified with the citizen body and not with the "Jewish People". Berenzon's suggestion mentioned above was more of a guiding line and principles for the constitution, rather than constitution draft and consequently it did not contain a preamble. Yet, the first of Berenzon's constitutional "basic presupposition" was that "The Hebrew State is a republic"; and the second was that "Sovereignty in the state belongs to the people and is maintained by the parliament which is elected by the citizens of the State and its inhabitants".

On the eve of the elections for the Constituent Assembly the various parties had published their programs. Thus, the program of MAPAI, the leading party, declared that "The State of Israel will be established as a democratic republic which is built upon the pillars of freedom, equality and justice and in which sovereignty is maintained by the people". The program emphasized complete equality in all areas "to every citizen and child" and the demand for "equality in rights and duties". Similar assertions were made in the program of the left-wing labor party *MAPAM*.

Akzin's constitution draft (1965) was not a declaration of "the people," but rather an assertion of the Knesset "by the power of its authority as the Constituent Assembly". This draft is important to the present discussion not only because of its republican character, but also because Akzin took part in the discussion about the constitution on the eve of independence. Thus, Paragraph I established that "the State of Israel is a democratic sovereign republic. Its regime derives from the will of the people as expressed in the decisions of the majority of the population and its representatives on the basis of deliberation and free exchange of ideas". Again, we see that "the people" is identified with the population, which is with the citizens. In this careful phrasing Akzin wished to distinguish between the sovereign people, on one hand, and the "Jewish People", on the other. The relations between the former and the latter were set in paragraph 3:

> The State of Israel was established in the Land of Israel in accordance with the natural rights of the peoples of the world for an independent political existence, with the desire to promise the Jewish nation the conditions for free existence and development on the soil of the nation. Without harming the principle set by paragraphs 1 and 2 above (that is the ones which declared Israel as a democratic republic – M. B.), the state sees its special aim in the cultivation of the values, the culture and the future of the Jewish nation.

The right of self-determination was attributed to the historical "Jewish nation," while the sovereignty was entrusted to the citizen body. In as much as this paragraph indicated on the special relationship between Israel and the "Jewish nation", it should be noted that Akzin emphasized this relationship should be carried out within the limits of the paragraphs which establish Israel as a democratic republic. In other words, the republic comes before the relationship with the Jewish People and the cultivation of Jewish values and culture.

It should be noted that according to Akzin, Israel derives its legitimacy from "the will of the people", which is identified with the population. The population is not just aggregation of individuals but rather "a people" who have "a will". Indeed, in an article "Notes on the Draft of the Constitution for Israel" (1949) which dealt with Kohn's draft, Akin criticized the fact that the draft gave the religious courts the authority to rule in personal matters also without the consent of the litigants. Akzin said that Kohn was influenced by the precedence of the British Mandate, as the British usually divided the inhabitants of their colonies into religious groups and imposed upon them religious courts. This was done – not out of respect for religion – but rather "because by this process they prevented the unity of the people of the colony, and assured they will remain divided". Yet, "the state of Israel has no such tendencies. On the contrary, it is interested to help all the inhabitants of the state to unite into a citizen body" (Akzin, 1966a, p. 18).

In the last decades the debate over a constitution has been dominated by two propositions for constitution: "Constitution for Israel" (*huka le'Yisrael*) which was published by a group of Law professors headed by Uriel Reichman in the nineteen eighties, and the constitution draft by the Israeli Democracy Institute "Constitution by Consensus" ("*huka behaskama*") published recently (2005).[22] In both drafts the term "republic" was not mentioned. Like the republican constitutions discussed above, both drafts declare Israel as "the State of the Jewish People" and based its legitimization on the right of the Jewish people for self-determination (Bechor, 1996, p. 208). Yet unlike the republican constitutions discussed above, they do not entrust the sovereignty to a republican "people". Thus, the draft of the Constitution for Israel "is vague in relation to the collective the affinity to which serves as a starting point for the definition of political legitimacy in Israel" (Bechor, 1996, p. 51). The introduction to the "Constitution for Israel" asserts that it receives its authorization from "the decision of the citizens of the State in a referendum". Thus, the simple republican phrasing "from the authority of the people" was avoided, as it would mean that the citizens were identified as "people". Indeed, the drafters seemed to have felt a republican urge to use the term "people", which they do by using the term "referendum", expressed in Hebrew by a two-words phrase *mish'al-am* (literally means "polling the people".) Though it contains the word "people" (*"am"*), it does not have the connotation of a republican people.

This is repeated in another place, when it is stated: "the source of the authority of the government is the will of the citizens, expressed in free elections and in referendums". For instance, the phrasing of the French Constitution: "National sovereignty shall vest in the people, who shall exercise it through their representatives and by means of referendum". The term "citizens" in "The Constitution for Israel" means an aggregate of individuals rather than "people". The same goes for the constitutional draft *"huka behaskama"* of the Israel Democracy Institute. Here, too, Israel was not declared as a republic, and the phrase used was "Israel is a Jewish and democratic state". The use of the term "people" was also avoided, when it was said: "the source of the authority of the regime is the sovereign will of the citizens, as it is expressed in the constitution and in free elections".

The avoidance in the two constitutional drafts in relating to the citizens as a "people" was not accidental, as it relied on the current status quo – which considers the citizens of Israel to be divided at least into two "peoples" – Jewish and Arabs who do not share a republican solidarity, and their attitude toward the State is not identical. Indeed, both drafts emphasized the equality of rights of all the citizens, yet they did not mention equality of duties. This was, again, not accidental and connected to the fact that the drafts do not recognize the citizens as "people" who share solidarity and consequently also duties towards the collective.

In these two drafts, the "right's discourse" intended, so it seems, to bypass the problem of solidarity among the citizens, especially the problem facing the Israeli Arabs – identifying with the Jewish State. The republican constitutions mentioned above were different. Kohn's draft emphasized that "The citizens of Israel will enjoy all rights and undertake all duties concerned the citizenship of the State" (Para. 6.1). In addition to a bill of rights, Bader's constitution contains a whole chapter titled: "The Duties of the Man and Citizen". In Akzin's draft there is a chapter titled: "Rights and Duties". In Bader's draft (paragraph 56) "every citizen must regard the principles of fraternity, tolerance and social justice, towards every other person … each person must take part in the public burdens as much as he can". In Akzin's draft (paragraph 28a) states: "It is a moral obligation for everyone to contribute to the public by useful work according to his (her) abilities."

As noted the two recent constitutional drafts, *"huka leYisrael"* and *"huka behaskama"* do not mention the duties of the citizens. This becomes more apparent in the paragraph dealing with what is considered in Israel an elementary civic duty – serving in the army. Thus, Akzin's draft declares: "every Israeli citizen and every resident in the country must participate in the defense of the State" (para 32). Bader's constitution (paragraph 57.1) states "loyalty to the homeland and its protection is the most sacred obligations of every citizen". Similarly, Berenzon's draft (para 22) states: "every citizen must participate in maintaining the security of the state and in the defense of its independence and integrity".

On the other hand, *huka leYisrael* says vaguely that "the duty to serve in the army will be as established by the law (183b)". A similar phrasing could be found in *huka behaskama*, where it is said that "The duty of serving and enlisting in the army shall be as prescribed by law (120A)". It appears that the authors of both constitution drafts wished to keep the present status quo and to bypass, at least at this stage, the question of the conscription of the Arab citizens to the army.

The Declaration of Independence

As opposed to the republican constitutional drafts mentioned above, the term "republic" does not appear in the Declaration of Independence, though a version which declares the establishment of a "Jewish republic", or a "Hebrew Republic" was offered by Uri Yadin and rejected (Shachar, 1991, p. 543, note 25). Yet, it is possible to trace republican elements in the declaration of Independence, especially in its second part, which laid down the procedures towards the elections of a constitutional assembly and the establishment of a constitutional regime (see below). First, I wish to examine to what extent there is a distinction in the Declaration of Independence between the declaring body, on one hand, and the Diaspora nation, on the other. It seems that the formula mentioned above is also maintained here: that is the establishment of Israel is justified by the right for self-determination of the historical Jewish People, which eventually becomes the right of a territorial Israeli people.

Indeed, the declaration stops short of speaking on behalf of the entire "Jewish People". After the sentence which says: "This right (of self-determination) is the natural right of the Jewish people to be masters of their own fate, like all other nations, in their own sovereign State," the first part of the declaration ends: "Accordingly we, members of the People's Council, representatives of the Jewish Community of *Eretz Yisrael* and of the Zionist Movement, hereby declare the establishment of a Jewish State in *Eretz Yisrael*, to be known as the State of Israel."

The People's Council does not represent the entire Jewish people, but only the *Yishuv* – the Jewish Community in Palestine, and the Zionist movement. Thus, the declaration made on the behalf of a collective whose boundaries were not clear, and that was defined only roughly by the public which aspires to national self-determination. It is not yet defined only by territory, as part of it is still outside this territory, and consequently represented not only by the representatives of the *Yishuv* (The Jewish community in Palestine), but also by the Zionist Movement. It is important to stress here, that the Zionist movement does not represent the entire Jewish People, that is all the Jews wherever they are, because then it should have been declared explicitly: "we the representatives of the Jewish People", rather than only a part of it; the part which aspires for national self-determination (including those Jews who were about to join Jews in Palestine, as well.) Probably what stands before the eyes of the declaring assembly was mainly the surviving remnants (*she'erit hapleita*) of European Jewry, who were sitting at that time in refugee camps in Europe (Agassi, 1993, pp. 186-7, Aloni, 1987).

Agassi criticizes this formulation and maintains, following Hillel Kook, that what was needed in the Declaration of Independence was "a declaration of the independence of the Israeli Nation as a successor of the Jewish nation" (Agassi, ibid.). In as much as this formulation does not appear, the phrasing of the declaration could still be interpreted in this light: "the natural right of the Jewish people" boils down to "our natural and historical right". The nature of the liberated body becomes clearer in the end of the declaration:

> We appeal to the United Nations to assist the Jewish people in the building-up of its State and to receive the State of Israel into the community of nations.
>
> We appeal - in the very midst of the onslaught launched against us now for months - to the Arab inhabitants of the State of Israel to preserve peace and participate in the upbuilding of the State on the basis of full and equal citizenship and due representation in all its provisional and permanent institutions.
>
> We extend our hand to all neighboring states and their peoples in an offer of peace and good neighborliness, and appeal to them to establish bonds of cooperation and mutual help with the sovereign Hebrew people settled in its own land. The State of Israel is prepared to do its share in a common effort for the advancement of the entire Middle East.
>
> We appeal to the Jewish people throughout the Diaspora to rally round the Jews of *Eretz Yisrael* in the tasks of immigration and upbuilding and to stand by them in the

great struggle for the realization of the age-old dream - the redemption of Israel.

Here, again, the duality pointed above also appears – it is the State of the "Jewish People", on one hand, and the use of "we" which defines a collective, which is different from the "Jewish People", on the other hand. The term "we", refers to a group much wider than the members of the People's Council, which appears in the first part of the declaration and is identified with the "sovereign Hebrew people", or with the "Yishuv", that is "the Jews of *Eretz Yisrael*".[23]

The last paragraph, in as much as it calls the "Jewish people throughout the Diaspora to rally round the Jews of *Eretz-Yisrael* (the *Yishuv* in the Hebrew version), in the tasks of immigration and upbuilding", it still distinguishes between the Jewish People and the *Yishuv*. There is a similarity between the call to the local Arab population to "participate in the upbuilding of the state" and the call for the "Jewish people" and in fact, individuals of both groups are being called to join the "We". It also should be noted that the appeal for the local population to join the "We" comes before the appeal to the Diaspora Jews.

Kamir, (2000, p. 499-500) observes that this paragraph:

> … is primarily a creation of a state-public, of the Israeli community. It builds the Israeli collective, and characterizes it as a voice, which calls for peace and cooperation. The new political community, more than it is defined positively, is defined negatively, by the background of the groups which it addresses: since it appeals to the Diaspora Jews and to the Palestinian Arabs, it does not include these groups.

As noted above, the apparent contradiction between republicanism and the Jewish particular character of the State is solved by the principle of equality to all citizens without the distinction of religion, race or sex. It is perhaps not coincidental that both principles, of Jewish nationalism and equality, are expressed in the same paragraph:

> The State of Israel will be open for Jewish immigration and for the Ingathering of the Exiles; it will foster the development of the country for the benefit of all its inhabitants; it will be based on freedom, justice and peace as envisaged by the prophets of Israel; it will ensure complete equality of social and political rights to all its inhabitants irrespective of religion, race or sex; it will guarantee freedom of religion, conscience, language, education and culture; it will safeguard the Holy Places of all religions; and it will be faithful to the principles of the Charter of the United Nations.

As noted above in the words of Karl Friedrich, the mere promise of the equality of rights and duties is enough to indicate a republican regime; even if the State emphasizes "Zionist" elements, like being open to Jewish immigration. Furthermore, this is a clear republican statement, whose aims are singled out relating directly to the Israeli population and not to the "Jewish People". On the whole, it should be noted that though the declaration states that Israel will be open for a Jewish immigration and called for a Jewish immigration, it did not declare what would become the main tenet of the New Zionist Myth in the coming years – that the aim of the Jewish State is to relocate all Jews into Israel.

Between the Right of Return and Citizenship

All of the republican constitutions discussed above acknowledge the right of every Jew to immigrate to Israel. As noted above, there is no necessary contradiction between the republican approach and the existence of a Law of Return, or between the existence of a special relations between the republic and what it identifies as its Diaspora nation – as long a the distinction between the Diaspora nation and the sovereign citizen body is preserved. One of the ways to preserve this distinction in these constitutions was through the separation between the Right of Return, and the Right of Citizenship, (i.e. between the right of every Jew to immigrate to Israel and his or her right to naturalize). Opposed to these republican constitutions, the Law of Citizenship (1952), which had complemented the Law of Return, established that all immigrants by the Law of Return would automatically become Israeli citizens. As noted above, from a republican point of view, the separation between Return and naturalization is preferable.

Indeed, the Right of Return had to be immediate and unconditional, as one of its rationales for the creation of the State had been to give shelter to distressed and persecuted Jews; meaning, the gates of the country should be open unconditionally for Jews sitting the refugee camps in Europe, and later on for the Jews of the Arab countries. As noted above, the Law of Return, together with the Law of Citizenship (1952) had turned into nation-constituting laws. Yet, the spirit of the Declaration of Independence did not project this attitude towards the Return, and this is also reflected by the separation between the return and naturalization in the discussed republican constitutions.

These constitutions acknowledged the right of every Jew to immigrate to Israel, yet they did not confer immediate citizenship upon these immigrants; minimally requiring an application. Kohn's constitution (paragraph 6.2) establishes that "in the future the conditions for the validity of citizenship and for its termination will be specified by the Law of Citizenship". Bader's constitution emphasizes the right of every Jew to immigrate and to enjoy the rights of a resident (Chapter 1, paragraph 2.3), and the right of every Jew, including those who reside abroad, "to purchase Israeli citizenship by giving the appropriate declaration before the Israeli authorities, as would be settled in the Law of Citizenship". Akzin's constitutional draft states: "every

A NATION LIKE ALL NATIONS

Jew, under the limits and conditions established by the law, is entitled to immigrate and to settle in it. After settlement he is entitled to acquire the citizenship of the state in the manner described by the law" (Ch. A, paragraph 4). The most specific, in this respect, is Kanzler's constitutional draft for "Presidential Republic" (1982), which specifies that a new immigrant by the Law of Return will be granted an identity card that will be valid for two years. After this period, in order to get a "Republican Citizenship Card" the immigrant will have to pass an official test and to show, among other things, proficiency in the Hebrew language and in the history of the Jewish People. Here it is important to note both contemporary non-republican constitution drafts, (*huka leYisrael* and *huka behaskama*) grant automatic citizenship to every Jewish immigrant.

The Law of Citizenship 1952 contradicted the spirit of the republican constitutions introduced here, and was not a natural continuation of the discussions that were held at the time. The Law of Return of 1950 had given the right of immigration to every Jew, yet it did not grant immigrants the right of citizenship. Amnon Rubinstein maintains that before the enactment of the Law of Citizenship (1952) in the two years after the enactment of the Law of Return (1950) "The Right of Return" was considered just that, and at least one Judge considered that when given to the immigrants, the right for citizenship would be qualified (Rubinstein, 1996, p. 878). On the agenda of the Provisional Government were 17 former drafts of the Law of Citizenship composed by the Ministry of Law. In those drafts, the Ministry of Justice refrained from entitling exclusive rights to the Jewish immigrant, and insisted upon equality between Jews and non-Jews. In the introduction to the 17th draft of the law it was said:

> The suggested law is based upon the judicial and political principle recognized in the modern law of the nations. Consequently the Israeli citizenship does not depend on

belonging to the Jewish people or the Jewish religion or the Jewish national movement, on one hand, and those affiliations are not enough to grant the status of an Israeli citizen, on the other. Residency within the borders of the state, birthplace in the same place, a declaration of loyalty to the State and so on, these are the conditions for Israeli citizenship. (Warhaftig, 1988, p. 136).

Thus, we can see that acceptance of the Law of Citizenship (1952) was not conceived as self-evident. Discussions on the topic reveal that the drafts suggested by the Ministry of Justice distinguished clearly between the right to enter Israel and the right and conditions for naturalization, which were indeed general. This is how Uri Yadin describes the meeting of the ministers committee headed by Ben Gurion on 12.5.50, during which the Citizenship Law discussed. From Yadin's description it seems it was Ben Gurion who imposed the decision in favor of the 1952 Law of Citizenship (Barak & Spanic, 1990, pp. 59 -60):

> The main question, and in fact the only substantive question, on the agenda was whether the Law of Citizenship would be a general-civic law, with no discrimination according to nationality, or would it be law that distinguishes between Jews and non-Jews. They also discussed whether Israeli citizenship would be given only after application (especially for foreign citizens) or whether it would be conferred automatically (with or without a negative option). Until the 17th draft our law was 'civic', not 'Jewish', and in most cases, gave the individual the choice of whether or not to become an Israeli citizen. … However, Rosen (the Minister of Justice) relayed some hints from Ben Gurion, on his ambiguous aspirations to make every Jew a citizen, once admitted on the fatherland soil. Yet, the minister said he did not understand the idea, and thus could not explain it. This time we understood it, and perfectly!

What could have been more simple, wider and deeper?! Very simple: every Jew as he is, half a Jew and half non-Jew, and when he comes to Israel he stops being non-Jew and becomes a complete Jew and a citizen as well! Here there is no question of naturalization, but automatic citizenship conferred upon the person without any will, or act, and without being able to avoid it by will-act; exactly like naturalization by birth … Following this conversation I have prepared the 'Law of Return – 1950'. A law of 4 brief paragraphs … and the main contained each only one line: 'Every Jew is entitle to immigrate to Israel' and 'Every Jew who immigrated to Israel become an Israeli citizen'.[24]

Between a Jewish Republic and a Citizens' State

The Zionist Narrative

When Kohn introduced his constitutional draft to the Provisional State Council (PSC) it was headed by two preamble documents. The first was called the "Constituent Act", which was based completely on UN resolution 181 of the 29 November 1947, and laid down the procedures for the constitution of the State as established by the U.N. The other document, which is more relevant here, was called "Preamble", or "Declaration to be adopted by the Jewish Members of the Constituent Assembly." The Preamble starts with the declaration "We the Jewish People" and contains what Yoram Shachar describes as the "Zionist belief narrative," which led to the establishment of the State. In a memorandum attached to his constitutional draft Kohn pointed at two problems concerning the Preamble. One problem is mentioned above; that the constitution is not to be adopted by the entire Jewish People, but only by the Jews of Palestine. As noted above, he offered to solve this problem by replacing the phrase "We the Jewish People" with "We the Jewish People in Palestine" (in Hebrew it reads: "We the Hebrew People who reside in Zion"). The other problem was that the constitution "is being enacted by a Constituent

Assembly representative, that is, at least in theory, of all the people of the State of Israel, including a substantial Arab population". The representatives of the latter will not be able to adopt a constitution with such preamble. This problem may solve itself, writes Kohn, if the Arabs boycott the Constituent Assembly. If, however, they do take part in it, it would hardly seem appropriate for such a Preamble to be adopted by a majority vote of the Jewish members. In this case, it is suggested, the preamble will be removed from the constitution and the Jewish members should, simultaneously with the enactment of the Constitution, adopt the preamble as a Declaration – of course, without the final clause ("adopt the following constitution") (Kohn, Memorandum, p.3). Yoram Shachar, who shared the story, calls it an ugly "political trick":

> By assuming that the Arab citizens of the State would not accept this document as a preamble to the constitution of the state, he says the obvious, that this historic belief-story, is the story of Zionism as told by Zionists, and not a truth accepted by all. (Shachar, 2003, pp. 552-3).

Shachar's criticism seems to be a twofold: The inappropriate anticipation that the Arabs would boycott both the elections and participation in the Constituent Assembly, on one hand, and the centrality of the "Zionist narrative" in the preamble – a narrative which is not "a truth accepted by all", on the other.

As for Shachar's criticism concerning the centrality of the "Zionist narrative" in the preamble, it seems there could not have been a preamble to the constitution (or, alternatively a Declaration of Independence), of an Israeli republic, which would not include a "Zionist narrative". Indeed, as Kohn notes in his memorandum: "It is customary for constitutions to be preceded by a preamble, setting forth the historical and political circumstances in which they were enacted. In our case, the situation is so unique that there is certainly a room for such a preamble". As noted above, Karl Friedrich also thought that a "Zionist" preamble to the Israeli constitution was unavoidable. "The Zionist narrative" might not have been a "universally accepted truth", but the fact that the emerged State was a product of the struggle of Zionism, was enough to justify a "Zionist narrative" as a preamble to its constitution. Indeed, the republic which Kohn's constitution was about to establish was not a "neutral" or "universal" State, but rather a "Jewish Republic".

As for the possible fictitious nature of the "Zionist narrative", being "the story of the Jewish people as was told by it to its convenience at the moment of the acquisition of sovereignty", it was not different from many national myths. As Orit Kamir notes, such texts should be read as "constituting texts" (Kamir, 2000, p. 477). And here we come to the Shachar's second criticism, highlighting the "ugly political plot". Indeed, there seems to be a fault in the fact that Kohn formulated a preamble, which he knew the Arab representatives could not adopt, coupled with his wishing the Arabs would boycott the Constituent Assembly. Here we may ask, was it indeed possible to formulate a preamble that would contain a "Zionist narrative" the Arab representatives could adopt? I think that Shachar believes that any "Zionist narrative" could not have been accepted by the Arabs. It is probable Kohn thought the same. Regarding the first problem, created by the clause "We the Jewish People", he had offered a solution. While for the problem created by the inability of the Arab representatives to accept the preamble, he did not offer any change they might accept.

It is obvious that for those Palestinian Arabs who objected to the establishment of the Israeli State, or alternatively considered their Arabism as an identity which made it impossible for them to live in a country which is not Arab (or Muslim), any "Zionist" narrative was unacceptable. They were not ready to accept the "Jewish Republic" on any terms. Yet, this does not mean there were no Arabs who considered their Arabism differently, and who could have accepted a "Zionist narrative" to the establishment of the "Jewish Republic", and choose to become citizens of this republic. Yet, the opening of the preamble of the constitution created an obstacle for them, as it started with the phrase "We the Jewish People…" (Similarly Bader's preamble: "We the sons of Israel our father"…). It was obvious that a non-Jew would find it difficult to consider himself as a part of this "we".

To what extent, then, was it possible to formulate another preamble that contained a "Zionist narrative", yet could also be signed by non-Jewish minorities? An interesting example for such a formulation could be found in the Slovak's constitution mentioned above (pp. 147-149). The constitution was ratified in 1992 (after the division of the former Czechoslovakia into two republics: Czech and Slovak.) The Slovak case resembles the Israeli one; as in the territory of the Slovak Republic lives alongside the "Slovak Nation", other national or ethnic minorities, especially an Hungarian minority of 570,000 (about 10% of the population of the Slovak republic). As the "Jewish nation", the "Slovak nation" also sees itself a related to a rich historical past with its heroes and ancient kingdom, that is, everything that could be titled the "Slovak narrative". In the above analysis of the preamble of the constitution I have pointed out how the notion of "We" changes through the preamble. It starts with "**We, the Slovak nation**", where "we" means the historical Slovak Nation, which is joined by individual members of other nationalities to create a new "we" that is the republican people or a civic Slovak nation, identified with the citizens which adopt and ratify the constitution. The structure of their preamble is:

> We the Slovak Nation …[Slovak Narrative] … **together with members of national minorities and ethnic groups living on the territory of the Slovak Republic** …[republican narrative] … **we, citizens of the Slovak Republic**, adopt through our representatives the following Constitution.

The Israeli republican version could have looked like this:

> We, members of the Jewish People who reside in Zion …
> [Zionist Narrative] … Together with members of other
> national and ethnic minorities who live in the territory of the
> Jewish (Israeli, Hebrew) republic [republican narrative] … We
> the citizens of the Jewish (Israeli, Hebrew) republic adopt
> through our representatives the following Constitution.

In as much as the above formulation could remove an obstacle from non-
Jews who wished to join the "Jewish republic", it was not enough to solve
the problem that bothered Kohn. For the Arab minority living within the
territory of Israel was not just a minority that lived in a territory dominated by
a different nationality, but rather a hostile minority, which presented national
demands contradicting those of the Jews (and was actually at war against the
Jewish State.) The Slovak Formulation could have suited some members of
this minority, but in the elections for the Constituent Assembly in which all
Arabs residing in Israeli territory were supposed to participate whether they
were willing to join the new state, objected, or even were hostile to it.

Who is an Israeli?

The Partition Resolution of the U.N. laid the problem that brought Kohn
to what Shachar called an "ugly trick" at the doorstep of the Constituent
Assembly. The U.N. Resolution demanded from each State, Jewish and Arab,
to automatically naturalize all those who resided in their territories, while the
Arabs who resided in the Jewish State, and the Jews who resided in the Arab
State had the option to revoke their citizenship, within one year, and choose
the citizenship of the other State. Those demands found an expression
in paragraph 1.6 of Kohn's Constitution with two changes – 1) The U.N.
resolution gave the right to revoke the citizenship explicitly to Arabs, while

Kohn's constitution gave it to non-Jews. 2) In the U.N. resolution, the revocation of the citizenship of the Jewish (or Arab) State was accompanied by a choice of the citizenship of the Arab (or Jewish) State (Gutman and Dror, 1967, p. 34), while Kohn's constitution dealt only with the revocation of the Israeli citizenship.

From a republican point of view this formulation had advantages and disadvantages. It clarified that the emerging republic was primarily a "Jewish Republic". That is that the basic citizen body, which requested independence was composed primarily of Jews; this was not a "citizen's state" nor "bi-national state", but rather a Jewish Republic which assumes a solidarity among the citizen-body. This solidarity could be found among the Jews who live in Palestine, as they were the element, which was requesting independence. Non-Jews could be a part of this republic, yet it is not clear to what extent they wanted to be included, as such, they were given the right to opt-out. In this sense, it is important to stress that this paragraph was taken from the U.N. Resolution, that indeed speaks about the establishment of a Jewish State rather than a "citizen's state".

Based on the U.N. Resolution, Israel was facing elections to a Constituent Assembly, while a substantial part of the voters, or citizens, were hostile, or part of a people who were in the midst of a war against this very State. The problem had become more acute because an Arab State was not established, so the opting-out option, which from the point of view of the U.N. Resolution was based upon the existence of an Arab State no longer existed. This is the situation that Kohn had to deal with and which brought him to the dual preambles or what Shachar called "the dirty political maneuver". It should be noted that the same problem did not exist for the Declaration of Independence, because unlike the Constituent Assembly the declaring body did not include any Arabs, but the State "was declared" by the Palestinian Jews only, who were the body that were seeking self-determination and independence. This is, perhaps, why a different approach from the one in the U.N. resolution was required.

As noted above, the uniqueness of the program of the "Hebrew Committee for National Liberation", headed by Hillel Kook, was the clear distinction that it had drawn between faith and nationality, acknowledging the existence of a "Hebrew nation" which was distinguished from the "Jewish People". Hillel Kook demanded to declare the establishment of the Hebrew republic and call the Arabs who reside in the Israeli territory to join the Hebrew nation, where all those who refuse to join the nation would have remained in the status of residents (Agassi, 1993, p. 183). In this case, the ratification of the constitution would have been carried out, as the declaration of Independence, by a Jewish citizen-body. In fact Kook's approach was expressed in the Declaration of Independence where the Palestinian Arabs are called "to participate in the upbuilding of the State". There is a resemblance between Kook and Kohn's suggestions, as both considered the Jews of Palestine as the immediate sons and daughters of the republic; while the non-Jews were allowed to opt-out (as Kohn suggested), or to opt-in (as Kook suggested). Thus, both suggestions clarified the nature of the emerging republic or of the Israeli State – though Kook's suggestion did it to a greater extent, as opting-in demanded more solidarity and identification with the State than the identification that was needed from those who chose not to opt-out.

The Jewish Republic and Minority Rights

The tension, which might have been created in the "Jewish Republic" between the republican nature of the regime, and its "Jewishness", was lowered mainly by complete equality among the citizen body without the distinction of religion, race or sex, and by entrusting the sovereignty to the citizen body rather than to the Jewish People. Thus, when the Declaration of Independence and the republican constitutions address members of non-Jewish minorities, they gave them equality as individuals, but say nothing about the collective rights of minorities. Hillel Kook said it explicitly in his testimony before the Anglo-American Committee: "If we offer complete equality of rights to non-Hebrews, we do it under the assumption that they do not constitute a nation and that they have no national rights whatsoever" (Karlibach, 1946, p. 146). In this sense the approach which characterizes these documents resembles the famous saying of the revolutionist Count Clermont - Tonnerre concerning the equality of the Jews: "To the Jews, in as much as they are human – everything; to the Jews, in as much as they are nation – nothing".

Contemporary thinkers were quick to notice this character of the Declaration of Independence. One scholar said: "though it is declared explicitly that in Israel there will be no discrimination according to religion, race or sex, it is significant that nationality is not mentioned, as it reflects the ambivalent approach of the forefathers to the problems of the national status of the Arab citizens in the Jewish State" (E. Cohen, 1997, p. 156). A similar position is expressed by Orit Kamir who said that while the Jews are recognized by the declaration as both a nation and individuals "non-Jews are recognized only as individuals" and not as "national minorities" or "ethnic groups" (Kamir, 2000, p. 498). Kamir also remarks (ibid., p. 514) that "the recognition of the Arab minority as a collective was not included in the declaration, but it is implied by the complementary instruction of the Partition Plan".

Indeed, the Declaration of Independence does not recognize non-Jewish minorities as national minorities. Yet, Kamir is wrong by seeing the status of the Israeli-Arabs today as a continuation of what had been stated in the Declaration. In post-independence Israel it is the norm to recognize the Arabs as a national minority, though with rights that are not equal to the rights of the Jewish nationality (Yakobson and Rubinstein, 2003, pp. 188-195). For many

years the word "Arab" appeared in the nationality clause of the Israeli Identity
Cards of those who were considered Arabs by the state. Furthermore, in
the present situation, the promise of the Declaration of Independence for
individual equality of rights and duties is not fulfilled: the declaration indeed
constituted a Jewish-Israeli collective, but in as much as it did so, it also called
on the Arabs to join this collective on the basis of complete equality. This
contradicts the situation today, when the Arabs are considered a nationality,
but are not equal in rights and duties as individuals.

Two questions emerge form Kamir's criticism: (a) To what extent is
she correct in maintaining that the recognition of the Arabs as a collective
is implied by the U.N. Partition Plan? (b) To what extent is she correct in
maintaining that the Declaration of Independence does not recognize *any*
collective rights for non-Jewish minorities? Both questions are related, as the
relevant paragraph in the Declaration of Independence repeats the words of
the U.N. Partition Plan.

As for the first question, the answer depends on what is meant by
"collective". If Kamir means a national collective, then the answer is firmly
negative. The U.N. Partition Plan does not recognize the Israeli Arabs
as a national minority (as it does not recognize the Jews who reside in
the Arab State as a national minority). Alternatively, if Kamir means by
"collective" a minority which has some degree of cultural autonomy, then
it seems that according to the Partition Plan this autonomy was very limited
as the Partition Plan acknowledged the existence of ethnic and religious
congregations. From this follows the answer to the second question – in
the Declaration of Independence there was no recognition of the Arabs
as members of a national minorities, yet there was in it recognition of
communities. Thus, the phrasing of the Declaration of Independence was
in accordance with both the Partition Resolution and with the Mandate of
the League of Nations. Both documents had not recognized the minorities

in the Jewish national home as national minorities, but rather as religious minorities. As noted above (p. 196), the only nation mentioned in the articles of the Mandate was the Jewish nation. The partition resolution says that the constitutions of the both States (Jewish and Arab) should contain the followings:

> Guaranteeing to all persons equal and non-discriminatory rights in civil, political, economic and religious matters and the enjoyment of human rights and fundamental freedoms, including freedom of religion, language, speech and publication, education, assembly and association.[25]

There is no mention of national rights and the wording is very similar to the one in the Declaration of Independence (see above). Paragraph 6 of chapter 2 of the resolution specifies the amount of cultural and educational autonomy that the minorities will possess:

> The State shall ensure adequate primary and secondary education for the Arab and Jewish minority, respectively, in its own language and its cultural traditions. The right of each community to maintain its own schools for the education of its own members in its own language, while conforming to such educational requirements of a general nature as the State may impose, shall not be denied or impaired. Foreign educational establishments shall continue their activity on the basis of their existing rights. No restriction shall be imposed on the free use by any citizen of the State of any language in private intercourse, in commerce, in religion, in the Press or in publications of any kind, or at public meetings.

There is no demand here for national rights, not even for "due representation" promised by the Declaration of Independence. The cultural rights which are mentioned are very limited – elementary and high schools, and this is also should be carried out within "the educational requirements of a general nature as the State may impose". It is obvious that there is nothing in the Declaration of Independence contradicting this clause. Yet, while the Declaration of Independence does not acknowledge the existence of national minorities, Kamir is wrong when she maintains that the declaration does not acknowledge the existence of "congregations" in the form of ethnic or religious groups: the promise to freedom of "culture and education" implies a recognition of a multicultural society. Furthermore, the declaration calls the Arabs to join the upbuilding of the state on the basis of "due representation" which might be interpreted as consociational arrangements, which also means recognition of congregations and minorities' collective rights. Kamir is right when she says that the phrasing of the declaration is laconic, and that the absence of specifications makes it impossible to put concrete meaning into the high language (Kamir, 2000, p. 513). Yet it is questionable whether declarations of independence are meant to be that specific; this is normally the task of the constitution. Indeed, the specifications of the collective rights of the minorities appear in Kohn's constitutional draft, which could be seen as complementary to the Declaration of Independence (Shachar, 2003, p. 553), and indeed the draft contains almost the exact wording of paragraph 6 in chapter 2 of the U.N. Partition Plan.

It should be noted that the promise for educational autonomy also includes Jewish minorities (like the ultra-Orthodox communities). Yet this educational and cultural autonomy of the minorities does not contradict the setting of the Hebrew as the language of the State. Moreover, Kohn's constitution acknowledges the existence of religious courts that deal with

Personal Code (as the U.N. resolution requires), which also necessitates the recognition of the existence of congregations.

The Archimedean Point –
The Birth & Death of the Israeli Republic

While the declarative parts of the Declaration of Independence could be controversial from a republican point of view, the second part of the declaration, "The Operative Part" which lay down the procedures for the establishment of the State was clearly republican:

> WE DECLARE that, with effect from the moment of the termination of the Mandate being tonight, the eve of Sabbath, the 6th Iyar, 5708 (15th May, 1948), until the establishment of the elected, regular authorities of the State in accordance with the Constitution which shall be adopted by the Elected Constituent Assembly not later than the 1st October 1948, the People's Council shall act as a Provisional Council of State, and its executive organ, the People's Administration, shall be the Provisional Government of the Jewish State, to be called "Israel".

This part of the declaration describes the moves towards the establishment of a republic, though it does not say so explicitly. According to this part of the declaration, elections to a Constituent Assembly should be carried out. This Constituent Assembly is tasked with drawing and ratifying a constitution within a given time and then to dissolve. After the ratification of the constitution there will be elections for the parliament, while in the interim, the "People's Council" will act as "The Provisional State Council" (PSC). This part of the Declaration was based on the U.N. Partition Resolution, yet with some necessary changes. According to the U.N. Resolution the PSC should have been established by a U.N. committee, which was supposed to receive the sovereignty from the British and then to deliver it gradually to the

PSC. Yet, as this U.N. committee was unable to function, mostly because of lack of cooperation of the British, the Jews had established in March 1948 a temporary ruling council called "The People's Council" (*Minhelet Ha'am*) which was created by a unification of the Executive of the Jewish Agency and the Executive of the "National Committee" (*Va'ad Leumi*). This body was supposed to "receive" (actually to take, as the British did not cooperate) sovereignty once the British leave. The U.N. Resolution set October 1 1948 as the last day for the establishment of the constitutional State.

The republican elements in this part of the declaration were obvious: the recognition of the necessity of constitutional government; a distinction between the constituent body (the Constituent Assembly) which ratifies the constitution, and the legislative body (the parliament) which rules according to the constitution; the notion that the source of the constitution is the people, and therefore elections for a Constituent Assembly are needed. Another important principle was the temporary nature of the government until the elections to the Parliament under the new constitution. The Provisional State Council was indeed temporal. Therefore, the powers of the PSC were set in a manifest, which the Council itself enacted on its first day (14 of May 1948) as a temporary legislative body. In other words, at this stage the PSC had set its own powers. Ben Gurion stated:

> The State of Israel was established by a revolutionary act, without elections and without a democracy, because there was no previous way, and it was important to establish the state than to be fussy about the procedures of democracy. It was necessary to establish a temporary thing- in both, the government and the legislative – something which does not draw its powers from elections, but from the revolutionary act, and in this was a great blessing. Yet, immediately with the establishment, we had not forgotten that this Temporary Council was not the supreme eternal sovereign of the State

of Israel but a temporary arrangement, and when the first opportunity arrives, the powers that the Temporary Council had assumed for itself will be delivered to the people. (Barak & Spanic, 1990, p. 79).

Ironically, this speech was delivered within the discussions in the PSC concerning the *Passage Order to the Constituent Assembly 1949,* which had a different meaning and marked a change in the work of the PSC. Paragraph 1 of the *Passage Order,* which was received on 13 of January (less than two weeks before the elections to the Constituent Assembly) established that: "The PSC will continue to preside until the convention of the Constituent Assembly. When the Constituent Assembly convened the PSC will dissolve." This order contradicted what was said in the Declaration of Independence, which set the "simultaneity" or the overlapping of the PSC and the Constituent Assembly. According to the Declaration the PSC should have ruled "until the establishment of the elected, regular authorities of the State in accordance with the Constitution which shall be adopted by the Elected Constituent Assembly". Moreover, paragraph 3 of the Passage Order, established, again unlike what was said in the Declaration of Independence, that the Constituent Assembly would inherit the powers of the PSC (Gutman and Dror, 1967). In other words, the PSC, which had been a temporal sovereign decided that its powers, or sovereignty, will be transferred to the Constituent Assembly. The cancellation of the overlapping between the Constituent Assembly and the PSC, and the transference of the powers of the PSC to the Constituent Assembly, meant that the Constituent Assembly, which was about to be elected to ratify a constitution (and not to rule) was about to become a sovereign body. No less irregular than the behavior of the PSC was that of the Constituent Assembly. The elections for the Constituent Assembly took place on January 25, 1949 and the Constituent Assembly convened on February 14, 1949. Yet, on February 16th the Constituent Assembly had enacted the Passage Law 1949 and became the First Knesset. The Passage Law stated:

> The legislative house in the State of Israel will be called 'The Knesset'. The Constituent Assembly will be called 'The First Knesset' and a delegate of the Constituent Assembly will be called "member of the Knesset" (Gutman and Dror, 1967, 91).

In other words, the Constituent Assembly, which was not elected to rule, but rather to ratify a constitution, had turned itself to a sovereign, and in the absence of a constitution, to a sovereign with unchecked powers.

This sequence of events raises the following questions: To what extent was the transfer of the powers from the PSC to the Constituent Assembly legitimate? To what extent was the turning over of the Constituent Assembly to the First Knesset legitimate? Amnon Rubinstein seems to think they were:

> The powers of the First Knesset – that is the Constituent Assembly – were set by the legislation of the Provisional State Council. …. This authority of the Council was set by the Council itself and here we reach the end of the continuity – the Declaration of Independence. … This is the beginning of creation, a creation ex nihilo, which characterizes the beginning of a new regime which does not draw its existence from a previous one. (Rubinstein, 1966, p. 49).

As for the event in which the Constituent Assembly had turned itself into the First Knesset Rubinstein does not consider it as a deviation from the Declaration of Independence as "formally it was only a change of name, which is not accompanied by a substantial change …(ibid. p. 52). Akzin, on the other hand, agrees that there was a deviation from the Declaration of Independence, yet he doesn't consider it to be a problem, as the Declaration of Independence was not a formal constitution and thus did not oblige the PSC or the Constituent Assembly (Akzin, 1966c, pp. 137-8). Also the former President of the Supreme Court, Aharon Barak, does not find any flaw in the sequence of events described above and maintains that "the instructions of the second part of the Declaration about the creation of the PSC, as the supreme power of the State of Israel, creates the basic norm of the law, an Archimedean point" (Rubinstein, 1966, p. 49). As for the Constituent Assembly he says that "the Constituent Assembly had, then, two roles ("Two Hats"): it was the body authorized to ratify a constitution and a body which had the powers of the PSC." (Barak, 1994, pp. 37-41).

Thus, Rubinstein, Akzin and Barak share the view that the PSC was acting within its powers, which were wide and unlimited, as it was created *ex nihilo*. The opinion of these senior legal experts might project on the differences between the legal point of view, and the republican or democratic point of view. While it might be true that the PSC was unlimited from a legal point of view, it is still questionable whether it was so from a republican or democratic point of view. Indeed, the view expressed by Rubinstein, Akzin and Barak leads to an unacceptable conclusion: If the Constituent Assembly would have fulfilled its task and ratified a constitution according to which a parliament (that is a sovereign) had been elected, then this parliament, being limited by the constitution, would have less power than the PSC, which according to them was unlimited. This while the parliament was elected and received its legitimacy from the elections and the constitution, the PSC was not elected at all. This conclusion is very hard to accept, and it might be the result of the separation of the legal point of view from the republican one.

According to the legal point of view, "the Archimedean point" is the self-proclaimed PSC, while according to the republican point of view the "Archimedean point" is the "people" or the principle of the sovereignty of the people. From this point of view, the state was not created *ex-nihilo*, but was preceded by "the people" who constituted it and for whom it was constituted. The powers of the PSC were not derived from itself, neither were they derived from the Declaration of Independence (as the latter had not been approved by the people), but the powers of the PSC were derived from the people. Since at this stage it had been impossible to seek the approval of the people, the PSC was established. Yet, it doesn't follow from this that the PSC was unlimited, but rather the contrary that it was severely limited. Without the possibility of receiving the approval of the people, the PSC and the provisional government should only do the minimum, such as conduct the war and do what is necessary to establish a Republican form of government. From this point of view, it does not seem that it was within the powers of the temporary ruler to create constitutional facts, and certainly not those that eventually led to the abolishment of the republic.

From a republican point of view, the question which arises is: Could a body that was a temporary sovereign (i.e. PSC) deliver sovereignty permanently to a body which had not received an authority to rule from the people (the Constituent Assembly)? In a similar manner one could point at the problematic nature of the move in which the Constituent Assembly had turn itself into the first Knesset. Here, Rubinstein's assertion that from a formal point of view that this move was only "a change of name which is not accompanied by substantial change…" (Rubinstein, 1996, p. 53) seems a bit strange. Even if we accept the legality of the move in which the PSC delivered its powers to the Constituent Assembly, then these powers were the powers of a temporary sovereign, not those of a sovereign parliament. In as much as the duties of the Constituent Assembly had changed with the Passage Order to the Constituent Assembly, and in as much as the public was aware of these changes, the elections of January 1949 were still elections for the Constituent Assembly, and not for a parliament. Consequently, the move by the Constituent Assembly contradicted its powers as defined by the PSC (as it had turned itself into a parliament), as well as the mandate it had received from the people. When a person, or a body assumes authority

without being elected, it means a revolution, or a "putsch", as shouted Hillel
Kook, who was then a member of the Constituent Assembly on behalf of
the Herut party (Agassi, 1999, p. 20).

Notwithstanding all these, it might have been possible to formulate a "Passage
Order" which would cancel the overlapping of the PSC and the Constituent
Assembly and would turn the later into a ruling apparatus, and yet would not
contradict the principle of the sovereignty of the people. In a lecture delivered
on 17 January 1949, less than a week before the elections to the Constituent
Assembly, Uri Yadin defended the "Passage Order to the Constituent Assembly"
which was enacted on the last convention of the PSC (13.1.1949). Yadin, one
of the forefathers of the Israeli Ministry of the Justice and participant in the
preparation of the judicial framework of the future state, explained that the
process of the constitution of the bodies elected under the new constitution
should have ended within four and a half months after the Declaration of
Independence (by 1.10.48 as mentioned by the Declaration). However, the war
had frustrated this timetable and the elections to the Constituent Assembly were
to take place on 25 of January 1949, thus Yadin established that:

> But now, after all the events that took place since the State was
> established, it had become obvious that the first plan could not be
> carried out. It is impossible to have the overlapping of both the
> Constituent Assembly and the PSC. Thus, the present temporal
> government should be replaced by one which would be based on
> the Constituent Assembly. (Barak & Spanic, 1990, p. 80).

The argument Yadin advanced was indeed different. The Passage Order to
the Constituent Assembly comes from the necessities of that time: the ruling
of the PSC took longer than desired (because of the war) and it is the need of
legitimate government which demanded the establishment of an elected body,
in this case the Constituent Assembly (Akzin, 1966c, p. 138). If this is what

Yadin meant, then it is rather strange that the pressure to dissolve the PSC did not come from the opposition circles (which had a clear motive), but from Ben Gurion. Nevertheless, Yadin pointed to a possible interpretation according to which a Passage Order could have been enacted. According to this interpretation the transfer of powers to the Constituent Assembly was legitimate not because the PSC was unlimited in its powers, but because it was acting under its authority to establish a republican regime. Yet, in order for this to happen the Passage Order should have explicitly said it. Indeed, Yadin notes that in the discussion on the phrasing of the Passage Order it was suggested to add to it the following instructions:

> (a) "to oblige the Constituent Assembly explicitly and in advance to give a constitution to the State"

> (b) "to set a limit of two years for the operation of the Constituent Assembly. The supporters of those suggestions maintained that 'the Constituent Assembly' should also operate within the laws of the State, and that the voters should be notified in advance, by legal orders, stating what is the principle duty of the organ they are about to elect and for how long it is going to serve" (Barak & Spanic, 1990, p. 80).

This was the stand of the majority of the Constitution Committee of the PSC and also the stand of Pinchas Rosen the Minister of Justice. This indeed shows that the majority of the members of the Constitution Committee did not consider the powers of both, the PSC and the Constituent Assembly, as unlimited. Had those suggestions been accepted, the Passage Order would have been within the limited powers of the PSC. Yet, those suggestions were rejected by the PSC and were not included in the Passage Order, and instead the position of the minority of the Constitution Committee of the council, which included also the Chair of the Committee Zerach Varhaftig, and which was also the position of the Provisional Government headed by Ben Gurion, was accepted (Varhaftig, 1988, p. 78). This position was defended by Ben Gurion:

> The people who elect are sovereign … and the Constituent Assembly could also change the name "Constituent Assembly" … a Constituent Assembly which receives a mandate from the people establishes what it establishes. (ibid.).

Indeed Yadin agreed with that interpretation:

> … Formally, then, the absolute freedom of the Constituent Assembly with regard to its duties and period was kept. If it wishes, it would go on and fulfill its original mission to give a basic constitution to the state of Israel, but if it would find it necessary, it could also avoid it … (Barak & Spanic, 1990, p. 80).

These rather astonishing words testify that the importance of the Passage Order was not only in what was written in it but also, and perhaps mainly, in what had not been included. In other words, that the members of PSC had already reconciled themselves to the fact that the Constituent Assembly would be such only by name and that it intends to turn itself into ruler without drafting a constitution. They thought that the best policy would be to hide this fact from the voters who were about to go two weeks after the publication of the Order to the elections for a Constitutional Assembly. It is important to emphasis that most of the public, including the high court judges, trusted the promise to give a constitution, and considered the elections which were held in 25 January as elections for the Constituent Assembly. Consequently what was revealed by the discussions concerning the Passage Order was an intention to mislead, which was problematic not only from a republican point of view, but also from a legal one (Negbi, 1987, pp. 26-27; Rubinstein, 1996, p. 52).

As Moshe Negbi, rightly noted, the story of the abolishment of the Constituent Assembly was a "missed opportunity" (Negbi, 1987, pp. 24-5). What had been missed was not only the fact that a constitution was not composed, but also that of an opportunity to teach the Israelis a lesson in republicanism. If the formula given by the Declaration of Independence had been followed, the result would have been not only the constitution, but also the participation of the public in a constitutional process that could unify the citizen body and give the whole system a measure of legitimacy, which it seems to lack today. Amnon Rubinstein maintains that all the laws of a present Knesset obligate us by what had been set in the Law of Passage to the Second Knesset (1951), which established that the Knesset is the legislative body. Moreover, as long as there is no other law, the powers of the Second Knesset (and every Knesset to follow) would retain the powers of the First Knesset. The powers of the First Knesset – which was the Constituent Assembly – were set by the PSC (Rubinstein, 1996, p. 48). Yet, if indeed there is a doubt in the legitimacy of the move in which the First Knesset and its powers were established, or in the legitimacy of what Aharon Barak calls "the Archimedean Point", it is questionable whether the whole system upon which the Israeli regime is based is indeed legitimate.

ભ CHAPTER 6 ৯৩
The Fusion of Religion & Nationality and the Roots of Israeli Messianism

In a letter sent in 1926 to Franz Rosenzweig, Gershom Scholem raised the following question concerning the renovation and secularization of the Hebrew language:

> People here do not realize what they are doing. They think they have made Hebrew into a secular language, that they have removed its apocalyptic sting. But that is not so… God will not remain dumb in the language in which He has been adjured so many thousands of times, to come back into our lives. (Ravitzky, 1996, p. 3).

Many would agree with Scholem on the prevalence of political messianism in Israel, which originated in politicization and modernization of a religious apocalyptic discourse. It is usually assumed that this discourse: (a) characterized the Israeli Right, especially its religious flank. (b) originated in developments within the national-religious public, especially the teachings of Rabbi Avraham Yitzhak Ha'Cohen Kook, and his son Zvi Yehuda Ha'Cohen Kook (Ravitzky, 1996; Rachlevsky, 1998). Scholem's opinion seems to contradict these assumptions, as it sees Israeli messianism as a direct product of the secularization of the Hebrew, thus unavoidable and inseparable from Zionism.

Indeed, though Zionism's apocalyptic messianism originated in the religion, (in the vision of the End of Days utopian society,) it was not introduced into Zionism by religious Zionists; and not necessarily by "right wing" Zionists. Its forefathers – Ahad Ha'am and adherents of Spiritual Zionism – were secular, and to the extent the division between left and right could be applied to those early days of Zionism, they certainly would have been classified as "left". Apart from their messianism, their Zionism was indeed 'small': it aspired towards establishing a "Spiritual Center", and not necessarily a State; which would accommodate only small elite, not the Jewish masses. Furthermore, it had looked down with contempt and apprehension on power politics, and symbols of sovereignty and statehood as unworthy of Judaism and Jews.

It was Ahad Ha'am who had introduced this apocalyptic discourse into Zionism. It was he who had objected to the normalization of the Jewish existence – to become a nation like all nations - in the name of the Jewish vocation; it was he who considered salvation, (i.e. the fulfillment of the biblical prophesies,) as the prime target of Zionism. Though Spiritual Zionism had been marginal in the history of Zionism, after independence, Ahad Ha'am's ideas became dominant, no doubt because it was shared by influential intellectuals like Martin Buber, Akiva Ernst Simon, Y.L. Magnes and Scholem himself. There is no doubt that Scholem's opinion of the unavoidability of messianism in Zionism had to do with his own messianic Zionist beliefs.

Thus, in the nineteen fifties, right after independence, a messianic apocalyptic discourse emerged within the Israeli elite. Its prime protagonists were Ben Gurion and Martin Buber. Though Ben Gurion and Buber differed on many issues, they shared a belief in the fusion of religion and nationality, the rejection of the notion of normalization, and the adoption of the Jewish apocalyptic vocation. Though this debate might sound strange to the contemporary Israeli, it contained the two poles of the Israeli messianism that exist until this present day: Ben Gurion represented one pole, referred to by Buber as – "narrow nationalism," that consisted of an etatist worldview, which emphasized the role of the State in the realization of the apocalyptic vision. It complemented the idea of the uniqueness of the Jewish People highlighting hostility of the gentiles towards it and consequently tended to become both ethnocentrist and chauvinist. The opposite pole, represented by Buber, was the moral one, which minimized the role of the State, power and earthly politics and emphasized the moral elevation of the nation – both as a collective and as individuals – in order to implement the apocalyptic vision. Here, messianism and the abnormality of the Zionist or the Israeli polity were expressed also by the idea that unlike other nations, it was not supposed to conduct its affairs by power politics and "reasons of State", but rather under the moral restraints worthy of Jews and Judaism.

The messianic discourse of the fifties was anti-democratic and anti-republican, as it rejected the notion of the sovereignty of the people: the realization of the Jewish vocation was a transcendental mission, rather than a product of the will of the Israeli people. This apocalyptic discourse of the nineteen fifties paved the way for a similar apocalyptic vision, which originated in the religious sectors around the theories of Rabbi Avraham Yitzhak Ha'Cohen Kook and his son Rabbi Zvi Yehuda Ha'Cohen Kook and which had become influential in the nineteen seventies. In this sense, Scholem's prophecy came true – God did not remain silent.

Ben Gurion as a Disciple of Ahad Ha'am

Paradoxically, the New Zionist Myth was introduced by Ben Gurion, the leader of the Labor movement and a member of the second *aliya*, whose members had been usually considered disciples of Berdichevsky, Ahad Ha'am's greatest opponent, and as those whose attitude towards religion was 'confrontational', and emphasized the distinction between the "Hebrew" and the "Jew" more than anything else (Liebman and Don Yehiya, 1983). As noted above, the main cause for the introduction of the "New Zionism", or what Liebman and Don Yehiya call 'The New Civil Religion', was what Ben Gurion considered as the ideological vacuum created after independence. Yet, what Ben Gurion was offering as "Zionism" was not only different from republicanism, but also from his opinions prior to independence – to the extent that various thinkers had described him as "post-Zionist" (see above, pp. 188-196). Somewhat surprising was the dominance of the ideas of Ahad Ha'am in Ben Gurion's "New Zionism". Anita Shapira remarked: "The language used by Ben Gurion resembled the school of Ahad Ha'am and not that of Berdichevsky, to the extent that a philosopher-researcher that had recently written a book on the teachings of Ahad Ha'am innocently introduced Ben Gurion as a disciple of Ahad Ha'am" (Shapira, 1997, p. 232).

One clear motifs of Ahad Ha'am's writings, which appears in Ben Gurion's writings, was the adoption of the notion of the abnormality of the Jewish existence and the rejection of the aim of classical Zionism to become "like all nations". According to Ben Gurion, "Judaism differs from all other religions in that it is the most national, the most Jewish, and at the same time the most universal" (Ben Ezer, 1974, p. 74). The Jewish nation was not a normal nation, as it was "the incarnation of moral will and carries an historical vision since it had appeared on the stage of history" (Ben Gurion, 1969, a, p. 1; Shapira, 1997, p. 228). Here, the idea of the Jewish vocation appears – which was so dominant in Ahad Ha'am's teachings and so strange to Berdichevsky's (and, of course, to Political Zionism). Like Ahad Ha'am, Ben Gurion identified the vocation of the Jewish nation with the realization of the vision of the End of Days and the ideas of the Prophets:

> … the spiritual cause had operated in the history of the Jewish people more than in most nations … and this spiritual cause was not only the exceptional belief which first originated in the consciousness of the Jewish people, the belief in a supreme, eternal power … but also the expectation and the belief which

> had been planted in the Jewish people by its big prophets in the
> messianic vision of salvation and redemption, the End of Days
> vision, when Israel will return to its homeland … and justice
> and grace will prevail among all nations, and they shall not wage
> war … *We should educate the new generation, those who were born here*
> *and those of the new immigration, if we want to implement them in the*
> *tradition of our great past and to train them for the aims of the future*
> *which carries redemption and salvation.* (Ben Gurion, 1957, pp. 10-
> 11; emphasis added)

The establishment of Israel was not only the first step to national salvation,
but also the first step to the general universal salvation. The relation between
the redemption of *Am Yisrael* and that of the human race is a clear motif
in the prophecies, and Ahad Ha'am gave it a sort of "natural" explanation.
His objection to political Zionism stemmed also from his assumption that
a necessary condition for the salvation of *Am Yisrael* is the salvation of the
world: only in a redeemed world there will be enough good will towards
the Jews, and only in a redeemed world the Jews could re-enter politics,
without betraying their vocation. While Ben Gurion accepted the relation
between the Jewish salvation and the general salvation, he had turned Ahad
Ha'am's equation upon its head – the reentering of the Jews to politics
had become necessary condition for the redemption of the world, and the
total return of the exiles in our generation should be seen as a stage of this
redemption. This, in fact, had turned the Israeli State into an instrument
in the realization – not only of the Jewish salvation, rather of the general
universal one.

Here Ben Gurion had also adopted Ahad Ha'am's theory of continuity.
The history of the Jewish nation is the history of a nation, which had
tried to preserve its uniqueness and to protect its culture form threatening
foreign cultures and its members from assimilation (Ben Gurion, 1969, p. 3).

Once the Jewish people had reached independence it did not give up its historical vision and did not accept the authority of foreign ideas (Anita Shapira, 1997, p. 229):

> All the people who inhabited this part of the world – now called the Middle East – have been wiped out and have disappeared from the face of the earth. And if the Jewish people … has preserved it faith, its heritage and its expectations despite everything … it is only because it has managed to maintain, as in ancient times and through the centuries of exile, its spiritual superiority. (Ben Ezer, 1974, p. 80)

This completely contradicted Berdichevsky's teachings and demonstrated the change that Ben Gurion underwent. What Ben Gurion considered as the "spiritual superiority" of the Jewish people, and the source of its power, was the source and the cause of their plight for Berdichevsky. This was also a deviation from the main tenet of Political Zionism because apocalyptic messianism, rather than the plight of the Jews, had turned out to be the main driving force, which had led to the establishment of Israel (Shimoni, 2001, p. 106).

There were several important differences between Ben Gurion's messianism and Ahad Ha'am's. First, unlike Ahad Ha'am, Ben Gurion emphasized the importance of both earthly power politics and the State (Kedar, 2013, 11-12). Second, while Ahad Ha'am postponed the "Return of the Exiles" to the End of Days, Ben Gurion's New Zionist myth demanded the immediate return of the exiles. Nevertheless, Ben Gurion's ideal, i.e. a total ingathering of the exiles, was not accompanied by any plan or a timetable for its realization, and practically had been always conceived as something which would happen in some undefined future. Consequently, the outcome was not very much different from Ahad Ha'am's notion of the Jews as a 'Diaspora nation', though, now, this "Diaspora nation" was considered illegitimate.

The third element had to do with the role of anti-Semitism and the plight of the Jews. As noted above, anti-Semitism did not play any role in Ahad Ha'am's Zionism: his Zionism intended to solve the problem of Judaism, rather than the problem of the Jews. While the plight of the Jews was no longer the driving force behind Ben Gurion's Zionism; Zionism and Israel were still a solution for it. Thus, the role of anti-semitism in the New Zionist myth was important – as it gave the latter a 'naturalist' or 'materialist' justification. Moreover, the abnormality of the Jewish State, the impossibility to become a nation like all nations, and the demand for the total ingathering of the exiles were justified also by the hostility of the other nations towards the Jews. Jews must be one nation, because they cannot be members of other nations. Thus, Israel had become the solution for both the problem of the Jews and the problem of Judaism.

There is no doubt that Ben Gurion's messianism had not stemmed only from the fusion of religion and nationality but from his socialist background as well. Indeed, Ben Gurion's pre-independence socialist utopianism predated his Jewish approach. As noted above, pre-independence labor movement envisaged the creation of an elite socialist "perfect society" in Palestine. The change from the socialist-utopian vision to the religious one was possible – not only because of the resemblance between some socialist utopias and religious ones, but also, and perhaps mainly, because both, socialism and the New Zionist myth, were, in fact "secular religions". The resemblance between socialism, (at least in its Bolshevik version) and religion, had been noted by many. As Ernest Gellner observed:

> The collapse of the Marxist societies was in effect the collapse
> of a moral order. This had been the first secular Umma or
> sacramental community, based on the doctrine of total salvation,
> articulated in naturalistic and sociological idiom rather than a

A NATION LIKE ALL NATIONS

transcendental one. But it was a moral order: the background belief accounted for everything and allocated a place to everything, it covered Morals as well as Faith, and it endorsed the state and was endorsed by it. It had its own theodicy, it explained evil, thus turning it to necessary evil, and it guaranteed that in due course evil would be overcome. (Gellner 1994a, p. 174).

Indeed, The New Zionist myth, like communism and fascism, was a product of the age of the great ideologies. It was also a myth of 'secular *Umma*', as its founding fathers were clearly secular, and it was "based on the doctrine of total salvation". Like communism, the New Zionist myth was "articulated in naturalistic and sociological idiom rather than a transcendental one". Like the role of the Dictatorship of the Proletariat in bringing about the Socialist salvation, was the role of the Israeli state in bringing about the Zionist one. Like communism the 'New Zionist Myth' demanded the sacrificing of private interests and rights of the members of the political community for the sake of the universal mission. Furthermore, like communism and like religion, it had its own theodicy (or its own devils – i.e. anti-Semitism and assimilation), which explained evil, turning it into a necessary evil, and guaranteeing in due course that evil would be overcome" (with the completion of the Gathering of the Exiles).

Martin Buber and the Origin of the Israeli Messianism

One of the prominent critics of Ben Gurion's messianic vision was Martin Buber. The latter correctly identified the dangers in connecting political ideas with messianic ones. The obvious conclusion should have been that in as much as the State, or the nation were concerned, messianism had to be either given up (or at least reduced), yet Buber, being messianic himself preferred to give up the State.

Like Ahad Ha'am, Buber's Zionism was "spiritual", which means he considered Zionism to be a movement for a cultural, rather than a political revival. Consequently, the basic messianic elements in Buber resembled those of Ahad Ha'am: the objection to normalization and the acceptance of the idea of vocation of the Jewish people, which meant the realization of the biblical prophecies and the End of Days vision, as well as the minimalization of the political and materialistic elements of Zionism and Israel. Yet, there was an important difference between Ahad Ha'am and Martin Buber to the extent that the former was secular and his messianism was godless; while Buber was a religious person and his messianism was saturated with his religiosity.

Buber's messianic vision was different from Ben-Gurion's, as it did not emphasize independence, the State, and the return of the exiles; rather the creation of a perfect society, which would be "a light unto nations" or *"mamlechet kohanim v'goy kadosh"*. Like Ahad Ha'am, Buber did not consider the establishment of the national home – as an aim for itself, but rather as a means for the realization of the Jewish cultural-spiritual renovation, which would project on the entire "Jewish Nation" (Lavski, 1990, 172). Both Ben Gurion and his critics did not see the establishment of the State as the end of Zionism (Sahvit, 1992, 71). Buber agreed with Ben-Gurion on the need for a new Zionism after independence:

> Quasi-Zionism, which strives to have a country, has attained its purpose. But the true Zionism, the love of Zion, the desire to establish something like 'the city of a great king' (Psalms 48/3) of 'the king' (Isaiah 6/5) is a living and enduring thing. (Ben Ezer, 1974, p. 117).

Like Ben Gurion, Buber acknowledged the abnormality of what he saw as "true Zionism". The latter stems from the uniqueness of Zionism, rather than the free will of the Jews:

> It was enforced upon the people. Because, unlike the national ideas of other peoples, this idea was not new; it was not the fruit of political and social revolutions, which were expressed by the French Revolution, but a continuation, a reformation, an adjustment to the form of national movements in the nineteenth century, of an ancient spiritual reality. And this reality was the holy pairing, concentrated in the name Zion, a pairing of "holy" people with "holy" land. (Buber, 1985, pp. 9-10).

This was not a normal nation, aspiring for independence, but a people upon whom a transcendental entity had cast an historic mission, from which it could not retreat. The mission was no less than the establishment of the "God's Just State" (ibid. p. 12). Here also appears the relation between the Jewish salvation and the general salvation (Ratzabi, 1999, pp. 141 – 144):

> Zion implies a memory, a demand, a mission. Zion is the foundation stone, the bedrock and basis of the Messianic edifice of humanity… (Ben Ezer, 1986, p. 58)

The disagreement between Buber and Ben Gurion, was not about the utopian End of Days society, but rather, on the way to reach it. As Buber described it, Ben Gurion's way to messianism had been through the State, or "the political element". Here, Buber disagreed, as he thought that messianism cannot be enforced, but requires essential internal change, and the creation of a new national society should be done through spontaneous processes – without the directions of the State and without "the cult of the State". Buber's messianism was not political, in the sense that the State had no role in it. Yet, it was political in the sense that it considered Judaism as a collective and a nation. It was also political, in being anti-political, i.e. by its demand to curtail, and even abolish, the political elements of the nation. In other words, in as much as Buber in particular, and spiritual Zionism in general, aspired towards the abolishment of the political dimension of Zionism, it had been political – in the sense that the 'Jewish Vocation' was supposed to be realized by a collective, i.e. by a nation: the demand from a nation to conduct its affairs by non-political means is both political and messianic. Also, messianic, was the notion of the spirituality of the nation, which meant that unlike other nations, it was not motivated by real politics or by reasons of the State, on one hand, nor by the materialistic needs of its members, on the other. In fact, as Shavit rightly says, this worldview was not less totalitarian than Ben Gurion's approach:

The criticism delivered against "the totalitarian character" of the State seemed to be delivered in the name of "liberal" values. Yet, it also stemmed from a totalitarian worldview. The intellectuals and writers which criticized "the Ben Gurionist State" on its "authoritative character" and expressed values of "voluntarism" and "creative spontaneity", as opposed to the "coercive" and "centralist" nature of "the State", had also introduced one kind of "totality" against another kind of it. (Shavit, 1992, p. 65)

Buber's apprehension regarding the national State stemmed from the fear that it might jeopardize the realization of the Jewish Vocation. Setting sovereignty as a target "could encourage the narrower sort of nationalism that sees only as far as the visible horizon" (Luz, 2003, p. 261). Thus, during the period of the debate over partition (1936- 1937), Buber was utterly opposed to the establishment of a Jewish State, claiming that it would damage the spiritual character of the Jewish people (ibid.). Other leading figures in *Brit Shalom* shared this opinion. As such, Ernst Simon said: "out of motives the gentiles will not grasp, we must be a people without a State, serving as an educational model for both the Arabs and the rest of the world" (Luz, 2003, p. 173). In his testimony before the Anglo-American Committee in 1946, Buber repeated his objection to the establishment of a Jewish national State. Buber told the committee it was obvious the prime aim of Zionist activity was not creating a State, but rather, the establishment of a perfect society (Ratzabi, 1999, p. 133). As Luz points out, Buber and *Brit Shalom* endorsed the ideal of the bi-national State in Palestine not only because they considered it to be the most practical solution to the conflict but also because it was "an ideal alternative to the national State; an alternative that could immunize the Jewish people against the virus of nationalism." (Luz, 2003, p. 173).

The idea that Zionism and Israel were not concrete political entities, but rather a tool for the realization of the highest moral values was shared by the members of *Brit Shalom*. Hans Kohn stated:

The Zionism championed by me since 1909 was at no time political. I and a group of my friends regarded Zionism as a moral-cum-spiritual movement within which we could realize our most fundamental human convictions: our pacifism, liberalism and humanism. It has been often argued that we [Jews] could not unreservedly sponsor pacifism or ethical politics among the European peoples, since it would result in our being regarded as aliens and traitors. Zion was to be the place where we would be able to realize our humanitarian aspiration. (Buber, 1988, p. 91).

This means the purpose of Zionism was not the survival of the nation, but the realization of those high values; or perhaps that the survival and the welfare of the nation were secondary to the transcendental mission, which was the preservation of Hans Kohn's universal beliefs. Indeed, Kohn was aware of the fact Political Zionism, which aspired to create a State, had been the last resort of the millions of Jews of Eastern Europe:

I assume that millions of the east [Europe] Jews will be pushed to Palestine, because they have no home in another place. They cannot live in the European countries, not only because of the hard economic conditions but also because the feeling of inferiority, contempt and enslavement of Jews, therefore they are looking for a place in which they could become masters. And then they entangle a tragedy, as in the land which they desire for life of freedom and justice sit others, who are also reluctant to give it up because of the same national aspirations. (Lavsky, 2002, p. 207).

Hagit Lavsky says that from Kohn's point of view this "was a tragic reality which would jeopardize the realization of Zionism as a Jewish mission. This leads him to abandon his original position and to consider Zionism as element which corrupts Judaism". Thus, Kohn says that *"the most difficult tragedy is that the Jews had not learned to reconcile with their fate and want to escape it, if by Zionism if by assimilation" (ibid.).* Political Zionism is a tragedy, as it requires irreconciliation with the fact "the people of Israel were chosen to suffer". Buber also made similar statements (Ben Israel, 2000, p. 27). Akiva Ernst Simon, another member of *Brit Shalom,* suggested in a memorandum to the Jewish Agency – after 1929 Palestine riots *(meoraot tarpat)* – to declare that it would settle for a "spiritual center" in Palestine and the guarantee of its safety. According to Simon, if the revival of Israel is connected with injustice, (which means a spiritual deterioration) then it is better "that the Jewish people would cease to exist while just Judaism would exist, than if the Jewish people were to continue its existence, while completely distorting and faking its image and constantly undermining the order of its historical influence" (Dotan, 1992, p. 60).

Thus, as Luz phrases it, one can find in Buber (and to that matter in *Brit Shalom*) a "martyr-like think" (Luz, 2003, p. 176). Though Buber, Simon and Khon could have not known it at that time, the meaning of their position was that Auschwitz was preferable to the "distortion of the image". Hedva Ben Israel notes that the dedication of this "group of intellectuals" to the absolute justice had been to the extent that they were willing to compromise the immigration of the refugees of Nazi persecution in Germany, before the Second World War, and of those refugees who survived the Holocaust (Ben Israel, 2002, p. 17). More than that, they were willing to compromise it even during the Second World War. Indeed, it seems that the problem of the "distortion of the image" bothered Buber and the members of *"Brit Shalom"* during the dark days of the Second World War. In August 1942 they established *"Ichud"* (a continuation of *Brit Shalom*) under the leadership of Magnes. *"Ichud"* joined the "League for Jewish-Arab Rapprochement and Cooperation" and adopted the platform of this league as a minimum platform of its own. This is how Ernst Simon, Buber's colleague, describes the establishment of *Ichud* and the meaning of its platform:

> Clause 4 contained at least the possibility of interpretation that they will not insist upon the principle of Jewish majority, but will be satisfied by numerical equality. For Buber it was a difficult concession, because for a long time he had spoken of "unlimited immigration" and thought that an understanding with the Arabs could be reached on this premise. Yet four years of Palestinian experience were enough to convince him that he was wrong. He was 64 years old and still capable to learn from reality. (Simon, 1973, p. 36).

According to Simon, the change in Buber came in the middle of the war, when Europe was occupied by the Nazis and the news of the massive extermination of the Jews were starting to arrive and a massive Jewish immigration was required. At this stage Buber and the *Ichud* were ready to establish "agreed immigration quotas", which, according to clause 3 of the platform will be subjugated to the absorption capabilities of the country "in the scope which, will promise the growth and development of the Hebrew community in Palestine towards complete and autonomous economic social and political life; while cooperating with the Arab people" (ibid. pp. 39-40). It should be noted that the limitation on Jewish immigration was not imposed only because of the wish to reconcile with the Arabs, or not only because of the absorption capabilities of Palestine, but also because of the demand of the perfect society to reach "complete and autonomous economic social and political life". Thus the utopian society comes first, before the lives of the members of the nation. Buber remained consistent after independence. In a meeting of intellectuals with Ben Gurion, "Martin Buber expressed his anxiety that the massive immigration which is flooding the country (of

Holocaust survivors) brings to its shores peoples who are just immigrants and who lack ideology. While this time he was ready to accept them, he was worried from the dilution of the old element which he called the 'semolina' by the new element" (Shapira, 1997, p. 119; Ohana, 2003, pp. 72-9). Here testified Ernst Simon:

> … In March 1953, … he continued to follow this line more vigorously, and emphasized that by the way that Zionism was realized, its soul was almost distorted, though it was not its (that is Zionism's) fault but rather that of the Holocaust. Instead of a slow selective flow required for a strong basis, a flow of pioneering enthusiasm, came the push of the masses running away from their destroyer, and this great reality made possible the creation of the Jewish State with the consent and the approval of the rest of the world. The prospect of the creation of the state abolished the possibility of the establishment of something, which will be greater and steadier. Instead of people who build their lives with cooperation of the peoples of the Near East, a state was established through successful war with its neighbors, a state which had looked and is looked by them as predatory. (Simon, 1973, p. 36).

The expression concerning Zionism, whose "soul was almost distorted, though it was not its fault …" should be noted: Zionism is not a mass movement, or a movement for national self-determination, but rather a transcendental being, separated from the masses, which has "a soul" of its own. One should have asked Buber what is greater and more moral than a country that gives shelter to the masses, running away from their destroyer.

Collectivism, Ethnocentrism and Chauvinism

Contrary to the sharp distinction which Jacob Talmon (1952) had drawn between political messianism, on one hand, and liberal democracy, on the other, there had probably been no movement of national self-determination, or an independent nation, which had not included messianic elements, even religious ones, in its national ethos. There had always been a messianic element in the French republicanism expressed by the wish to spread the ideas of the French revolution, and the forefathers of the American nation had considered themselves as successors of the Ancient Hebrews and America as "New Jerusalem" and God's messenger, who was supposed to lead the rest of the world towards freedom or salvation (Bellah, 1970, 168-188). Yet, unlike the New Zionist Myth, both the American and the French messianic discourses included the ideas of the republicanism: the notion of the sovereignty of the people, the idea that the prime aim of the State is to serve the people and the sanctity of human rights.

The New Zionist Myth was not republican: it did not recognize the existence of a concrete territorial people, on one hand, and was essentially collectivist, on the other hand. It did not see the Israeli state as an instrument for securing the rights and the welfare of its people, at least not in a foreseeable future, or not until the transcendental mission is accomplished. It rejected the notion that the nation is free to choose its policies by its democratic institutions and demanded that its members would subordinate themselves to the myth's transcendental ideals. It did not acknowledge the right of national self-determination of the individual Jews. The obligation to serve the ideals of the myth had been casted upon all those who were considered Jews, without any considerations for their own will, even if they considered themselves and were considered members of other nations.

Nevertheless, it is important to see that sometimes, especially when new nations are concerned, there is a need for a collective effort, at least in the short run, which comes at the expense of the rights and welfare of the nation and its members (Diamond 1993). Thus, the collectivist approach that had characterized Israel in the first decades after independence was not unique. Yet, the New Zionist Myth had turned what might have been provisional into eternal. Paradoxically, regimes which base themselves upon messianism are not interested in the fulfillment of their vision (which, anyway, cannot be fulfilled), because it would deprive them of their legitimacy. Thus, though the Soviet Union had become officially a classless society, the 'withering away of the state', or of the Dictatorship of the Proletariat, had been postponed indefinitely, until the completion of the world revolution. Similarly, the subordination of Israel to the myth of "the ingathering of the exiles and salvation" had given the Israeli regime a legitimization and justified the denial of the rights of the Israeli nation and the Israeli individual as long as there was one person who was considered a Jew and who lived outside of Israel, or until the goal of the perfect society was reached. Indeed, while Ben Gurion spoke about contemporary Israel as the beginning of redemption, he postponed the coming of the messiah, or its completion, to a time indefinitely in the future:

> I say: the messiah has not yet come, and I don't wish him to come … when you find the address of the messiah in the phonebook – he is no longer the messiah; The greatness of the messiah is that his address is not known, and that he could not be reached and it is not known what car he drives and whether he drives a car, or rides a donkey or fly by the wings of the eagles. Yet, we need the messiah – the one who is not coming. (Keren, 1988, pp. 85-86).

The introduction of the New Zionist Myth in the nineteen fifties meant that from the point of view of the state and the ruling elite the Jewish religion and Jewish tradition had turned into the prime source of national values. Yet, alongside with the notions of vocation, salvation and the abnormality of the Jewish existence and of Israel, chauvinist and ethno-centrist motifs also appeared, as a result of the politicization of the religious discourse that defined the relations between Jews and gentiles. As Liebman and Don Yehiya (1983, p. 62) note this "New Civil Religion" was:

... the most ethno-centric of all civil religions. It affirms all
Jewish history and culture and gives special emphasis to the
isolation of Jews and hostility of Gentiles. The characteristic
slogan of this period is the biblical phrase "a people that dwells
alone" or the rabbinic metaphor "Esau hates Jacob". It is,
needless to say, a civil religion especially well suited to masses
who are familiar with and attached to traditional symbols but
unsophisticated concerning their explicit meaning.

Indeed, Zionism had always acknowledged both the abnormality of the
Jewish existence, on one hand, and the hostile attitude of the gentiles to
the Jews, on the other. Yet, alongside this recognition was the desire for
normalization and the hope that it would lead eventually to the disappearance
of anti-Semitism. "The New Zionist Myth" or "The New Civil Religion",
considered the abnormality of Israel as "normal", and anti-Semitism as an
unchangeable element in the character of the gentiles.

As noted above, the New Zionist Myth originated within the secular
socialist elite. So it seems that from its inception, the leadership did not
believe in the myth and considered it only as a means for mobilization. As
Liebman (1984, p. 140) notes:

At the heart of these conceptions ... lie the seeds of an
ethnocentric and chauvinist view of Judaism and the Jewish
people. Neither the founders of Israel nor the early religious
Zionists shared this view. But Israeli leaders inculcated this view
through the mass media, school curricula, army educational
programs and elitist rhetoric. Why did Israel's cultural and
political elite pay lip service to conceptions and beliefs which
were really not their own? ... Part of the answer stemmed
from fears that first arose in the 1950s, that the alternative was
a loss of Jewish identity, an absence of national consensus, a
weakening of collectivist values among the population and a

consequent weakening of resistance to perceived Arab threats. The other part of the answer, as already suggested, lies in the misunderstanding and misinterpretation of elitist values by population groups such as the Orientals and the young.

Liebman's analysis is, (though he probably did not mean it to be), a severe indictment against the ruling elite, that had tried to deliver a myth to the masses – that they themselves did not believe. As Liebman emphasized, it was mainly those groups who were more rooted in the Jewish tradition, (such as new immigrants from the Middle Eastern countries and the religious Zionists), who absorbed the message of the ruling elite. Both groups played a minor role in Israeli politics until the nineteen seventies. The Mizrachim, or the Israeli Jews of Middle Eastern origin, had been the weakest segment within the Israeli Jewish society and politically under-represented; while the religious Zionists circles, who were economically better off than the Mizrachim, still lived at the margins of the Israeli Jewish Society. Though, unlike the Mizrachim, the religious Zionists were in fact represented, sometimes over-represented; this was because "the political arrangements in Israeli society dictated their presence, and not because Israel's real leaders or Israeli insiders had any regard for their opinions" (Liebman, 1987, p. 134). Another group that had absorbed the New Zionist Myth, was the youth, who are always weak, being subordinated to the indoctrination of State-education.

In the recent decades there had been a substantial weakening of the "New Civil Religion" introduced in the nineteen fifties among the Israel secular elite (Liebman, 1999, pp. 80 – 83). Martin Buber had already envisaged this problem in the fifties when he said it would be very difficult to preserve the notion of the utopian society that was rooted in the Jewish religion among the secular Israelis (Luz, 1999, pp. 201 – 201). After the 1973 War all these groups mentioned above – Mizrachim, Religious Zionists and Youth –

intended to demand their legitimization in the name of those "Jewish" values vs. the secular Ashkenazi elite who appeared weak or unable to carry on the burden.

Enter God – Religious Zionism and Israeli Messianism

> How is it that the movement for concrete redemption in our time, including the settlement and conquest of the Land [of Israel] and the abandonment and abolition of exilic existence, did not originate with the religious? How is it that some religious spokesmen even withheld their support for Zionism and the movement for redemption? ... They failed to recognize that it was not that we mortals were forcing the End, but rather that the Master of the House, the Lord of the Universe, was forcing our hand; that it was not human voices that broke down the wall separating us from our land, but the voice of the living God calling upon us to "Go up!" (Ravitzky, 1996, p. 79)

The above declaration was made by Rabbi Zvi Yehudah Ha-Cohen Kook (1891-1981), whom Ravitzky calls "the mentor of the 'redemptionist' religious-Zionist camp, during the decades following the establishment of the State of Israel". According to Ravitzky this declaration "sums up concisely and eloquently the way this camp reacted to the ultra-Orthodox theological criticism of Zionism" (ibid.)

Indeed, the ultra-Orthodox camp rejected Zionism from its inception exactly because it identified it with (false) messianism. Yet, the criticism of Zvi Yehuda Kook was directed also at the so-called religious Zionists for failing to understand the redemptionist aspect of Zionism. Thus, what Zvi Yehuda Kook was offering here was not revolutionary only for the so-called 'ultra-Orthodox', but also for the so-called of 'religious Zionists'. For, as noted above, not only that the forefathers of the Mizrahi, the Zionist religious party, were not redemptionists, but they were actually anti-redemptionists, and their leaders had enthusiastically adopted the Herzlian slogan that "Zionism has nothing to do with religion". During the years this original anti-redemptionist position of the Mizrahi had somewhat faded away and some of its members even become redemptionists – no doubt also because of the increase of the redemptionist element in Zionism after the death of Herzl. In addition, after the establishment of Israel, there was still a big gap between having a neutral or even sympathizing attitude towards redemptionism and adopting a full fledge redemptionist outlook.

Indeed, "religious Zionism", in the proper sense, had not developed within the Zionist movement. Rabbi Reines had casted the Mizrahi as a party of religious Zionists, and not as a party of a special kind of Zionism. The forefather of "Religious Zionism", Zvi Yehuda Kook's father – Avraham Yitzhak Ha-Cohen Kook, was not a Zionist, in the sense that he was not a member of the Mizrahi or of the Zionist movement. Indeed, as Ravitzky notes, Rabbi Kook's teachings had to wait a full generation after his death, in 1935, before they could win popularity within the religious-Zionist camp. And there should be no doubt that the road of his teachings to the heart of this camp had been paved – to a large extent – by the messianic secular discourse of the Ben Gurionist state.

It is not the place here to explore the teachings of Rabbi Avraham Kook, in detail. What is important for our discussion is the rather surprising, (or perhaps not so surprising,) similarity between his religious messianism, on one hand, and the Zionist secular messianism that originated with Ahad Ha'am, and developed in the nineteen fifties, on the other. While both messianisms had been developed independently, their similarity stemmed mainly from their common Jewish messianic background and the influence of romanticist nationalism and philosophy of the nineteen century. These two worldviews of Jewish messianism, or using Ehud Luz phrasing, these two "parallels", eventually met in the nineteen seventies in the image and form of *Gush Emunim*.

Rabbi Avraham Kook, like Ahad Ha'am, was not a member of the Zionist movement. What made him hostile towards Herzl's Political Zionism was exactly what had made Ahad Ha'am hostile to it – its non-redemptionist worldview and its supposed "neutrality" on the question of culture, which was expressed by the famous slogan "Zionism has nothing to do with religion" (Ravitzky, 1996, p. 95). Thus, unlike the traditional ultra-Orthodox criticism of Zionism, as a false redemptionism, or perhaps as a logical outcome of this criticism, Avraham Kook's position was that the only possible Zionism was the redemptionist one. In a sense, Rabbi Avraham Kook was a "Spiritual Zionist" or a "cultural nationalist". His Zionism was meant primarily to solve the problem of Judaism, rather than that of the Jews (though as a religious person he considered both to be the same). However, since he was religious, and in fact ultra-Orthodox, he identified Judaism (and eventually Zionism) with the (ultra-Orthodox) religion (Aran, 2013, pp. 139 – 150). Thus, the difference between Ahad Ha'am's Spiritual Zionism, on one hand, and Avraham Kook's Religious Zionism, on the other, was that the former, was predominantly secular, and was trying to secularize the Jewish religion; while the latter, being religious, was trying to "religionalize nationalism" (Aran, 2013, p. 148).

While Rabbi Avraham Kook's starting point of view could have not made him, or any religious Jew, a member of the Zionist movement, he developed a theory that legitimized (and even made it mandatory) for the religious Jews to participate in the "Zionist Project". Avineri notes three central elements in the teachings of Kook concerning the relation between traditional Judaism and Zionism: (1) "Bestowing essentially religious meaning to the centrality of the terrestrial, and not merely heavenly, Land of Israel". (2) "The development of a dialectical perception about the relationship between Jewish religion and secular Zionist praxis;" and (3) Conferring universal significance to the Jewish renaissance within the framework of a religious philosophy (Avineri, 1981, p. 189).

The location of the Land of Israel had always been central in the Jewish tradition. Yet, even though immigrating and settling in *Eretz Yisrael* had been considered as one of the decrees that should obligate every Jew; that was so, within the framework of the acceptance of Judaism as a Diaspora religion. In other words, the connection between the Jews and the Land of Israel had remained spiritual rather than concrete. Rabbi Kook, however, had elevated making *aliya* – the immigration and physically settling in Palestine – into a prime, if not *the prime*, tenet of Judaism:

> A Jew cannot be as devoted and true to his own ideas, sentiments and imagination in the Diaspora as he can in *Eretz Yisrael* Revelations of the Holy, of whatever degree, are relatively pure in *Eretz Yisrael*; outside it, they are mixed with dross and much impurity. (Avineri, 1981, p. 190).

Nevertheless, though, as Avineri (1981, p. 191) notes, "what Rabbi Kook is attempting here is a radical religious attack on the whole religious tradition of accommodating oneself to the life of the Diaspora", the settlement of *Eretz Yisrael* served Kook also to legitimize Judaism in the Diaspora:

> A valid strengthening of Judaism in the Diaspora can come only from a deepened attachment to *Eretz Yisrael*. The hope of the return to the Holy Land is the continuing source of the distinctive nature of Judaism. The hope for the Redemption is the force, which sustains Judaism in the Diaspora; the Judaism of *Eretz Yisrael* is the very Redemption… (Avineri, 1981, p. 191).

Indeed, what we can see here, in a nutshell, is the notion of the "spiritual center". The settlement in the Land of Israel is supposed to become a religious, spiritual center for the entire diaspora, as it had been in the days of the *Sanhedrin* (Ravitzky, 1996, pp. 85 – 93). In other words, nationalism, or more precisely the fusion of religion and nationality, had opened a new possibility for connecting the Jews to the Land of Israel. Unlike the Jewish tradition, which had demanded the concrete settlement in the land, by each and every Jew – and this created a gap between the *Torah* and the notion of Diaspora Judaism, – seeing Judaism as a (religious) nation, or as a collective, enabled the nation to be connected to the Land of Israel, even if only a portion of it would actually settle there; more so, if this portion would assume the (religious) leadership of the Jewish nation. Thus, though Rabbi Kook's redemptionist worldview considered the total ingathering of the exiles at the end of the process, his immediate purpose was not only to legitimize Zionism and the beginning of redemption, but also to legitimize Judaism as a Diaspora nation.

As such, while Diaspora Judaism's connection with the Land of Israel was "spiritual", Rabbi Kook gave it concrete meaning. It is the actual settlement of the Land of Israel (by part of the nation), which paved the way for the redemption, on one hand, and the unity of the Jewish people as a Diaspora nation, on the other. Again, the resemblance of Rabbi Kook's philosophy to that of Ahad Ha'am is striking. Yet, the resemblance does not end here. While Rabbi Kook indeed gave a concrete meaning to the decree of the settlement of the Land of Israel, he did not necessarily give it a political meaning, which meant that the Jewish settlement in Palestine was not necessarily meant to be a State. Like Ahad Ha'am, Rabbi Kook considered earthly politics as corrupted and unworthy of Jews. Rabbi Kook gives an interesting justification for the Diaspora:

> We left the political arena [and went into exile] under duress
> but also with a certain inner willingness, until that happy
> time when a polity could be governed without wickedness

> or barbarism. The delay has been necessary. We have been disgusted with the terrible iniquities of ruling during the evil ages. Now the time has come, is very near, when a world will be refined and we shall be able to prepare ourselves [for our polity] … It is not for Jacob to engage in government as long as it entails bloodshed, as long as it requires a knack of wickedness. (Ravitzky, 1996, p. 120).

According to Ravitzky, for Rabbi Kook: "the political restoration of Israel depends on a moral transformation of global proportions, that the Jewish return to history is conditional on the elimination of all the corruptions of worldly politics" (Ravitzky, 1996, p. 120). Consequently, Ravitzky concludes that it is doubtful whether "in Kook's view a Jewish return to history and politics, in the world as we know it, is feasible", as "a social life and political sovereignty will immediately bring out the anomie in their hearts, and ancient corruptions will be revived" (Ibid., p. 123). Avineri notes that this pitfall made Rabbi Kook skeptical whether a Jewish State is desirable at all: If a Jewish State were to be established in a yet unredeemed world, in order to survive, such a State would have to behave like a wolf among wolves, (which would make it unsuitable for the purpose of redemption). Alternatively, only in a redeemed world could a weak "spiritual" nation like the Jewish nation find among the other "material" nations the good will, needed for the complete restoration of its homeland (Avineri, 1981, pp. 195-6).

The resemblance of Rabbi Kook's message to Buber, Kohn, and for that matter, to Ahad Ha'am, is striking. Like Buber, Rabbi Kook thinks politics is not suitable for the Jews, as it corrupts them and leads to what Kohn calls "the distortion of the image". Furthermore, it seems that, at least in the short run, Rabbi Kook was aiming to create something similar to Ahad Ha'am's "Spiritual Center". The other, perhaps less pleasant notion, would be to grant the Jewish

State, – once it is established – a status of a "Divine State" and "the pedestal of God's throne in this world" (Ravitzky, 1996, p. 83), and an active role in the purification of world politics:

> Once the Lord's people are established on their land in some definite way, they will turn their attention to the [geo] political realm, to purify it of its dross, to cleansing the blood from its mouth and the abominations from between its teeth (Ravitzky," 1996, p. 121).

Yet, the problem was that the actual settlement of Jews in the Land of Israel had been carried out by secular Jews, and by an apparently secular Jewish movement. Here is the second element in the teachings of Rabbi Kook pointed out by Avineri: "The development of a dialectical perception about the relationship between Jewish religion and secular Zionist praxis". According to Rabbi Kook, though the pioneers who had come to settle in Palestine disowned their religious heritage and considered themselves motivated by secular causes, such as nationalism and socialism, they were a part of a cosmic design of God, which was meant to bring about the redemption. Unknowingly, those pioneers were serving as tools in the hand of the divine, and in this sense *were* divine. As Avineri (1981, p. 193) notes: the resemblance between this theory and Hegel's theory of the "Cunning of Reason" is remarkable. The role of "Religious Zionism," so it seems, was to penetrate the secular cloak of national and socialist ideas and discover the true religious redemptionist essence of Zionism. The religious public should not separate itself from the pioneers, but draw them nearer, and eventually they will recognize that they are a part of God's divine scheme and return to (Orthodox) Judaism as well (Avineri, 1981, p. 193; Aran, 2013, pp. 128-133). Thus, though the sanctification of Zionists stems also from the conviction that in the future they will return to (Orthodox) Judaism, it existed unconditionally also in the present: those who were loyal to the land, were also loyal to God (Aran, 2013, p. 150).

Though considered the founding father of the redemptionist camp, the teachings of Rabbi Kook had to wait for a full generation after his death (in 1935), before they became popular within the Religious-Zionist camp – after the 1967 war. Most of the commentators pointed out the labor of his son and the circles around him in laying the groundwork for this development (Ravitzky, 1996, p. 123; Aran, 2013, pp. 178-191). Yet, there is no doubt that an important work in this respect had already been done by the Ben Gurionist State. Those religious youth who enthusiastically adopted Rabbi Kook's messianism grew up in post-independence Israel and were a product of the Israeli education system.

Religious messianism, under Zvi Yehuda Kook, acquired a different form than under his father. In fact, one can say that Zvi Yehuda had done to his father's teachings what Ben Gurion had done to Ahad Ha'am's, which was to politicize them. As noted above, Rabbi Avraham Kook's messianism was mitigated by his political quietism. However, in the presence of a Jewish State and a Jewish sovereignty, the entering of the Jews into politics could not have waited any longer for the utopian general redemption. The holiness which had been bestowed upon Zionism had also to be transferred to the Jewish State and what seemed to be a modest "beginning of redemption" on a long road to salvation in the image of the establishment of a small Jewish community in Palestine, had turned out to a full fledged universal redemptionist process, in which the Israeli State had an active leading role.

Indeed, the language of the leaders of *Gush Emunim* in the 1970s seemed as if it was lifted from the 1950s. Like Ben Gurion and Buber in the 1950s, Rabbi Yehuda Amital from Gush Etzion Yeshiva spoke after the Six Days War on the need for "another Zionism":

> There is also another Zionism, which is Zionism of salvation, whose forerunner and great interpreter was Rabbi Kook .... This Zionism had not come to solve the problem of the Jews by the establishment of a Jewish State, but is used as an instrument by the providence to prepare Israel for redemption. (Rubinstein, 1997, p. 139).

Amital saw his Zionism as based on the realization of the End of Days prophecies, including that of universal salvation. *Gush Emunim's* messianism contained universal elements, as did the messianic ideas of the '50s. As has been noted above, one of Rabbi Avraham Kook's main ideas was the notion that Jews entering politics was conditioned by the purification of politics, which, eventually would take place in a much more advanced stage of the redemptionist process. While for Rabbi Kook this condition awaited fulfilment in some undefined future, now, since the Jews had already become political, they had to conduct "pure" politics, on one hand, and actually assume a leading role in the purification of universal politics, on the other. In the words of one of the disciples of Zvi Yehuda, Rabbi Eliezer Waldman, Dean of the Kiryat Arba Yeshiva, during the war in Lebanon:

> When the [Lebanon] war broke out, there were those who claimed we had not come to impose order on Lebanon but rather to save the Galilee. But we pointed out that it is Israel's task to bring order into the world. This statement incensed many learned Jews ... but we must not recoil or shrink from this responsibility. ... Who is going to bring order into the world? Those who submit to evil? The great powers, which are themselves suffused with wickedness or give in to it? The people of Israel is the only one which is prepared to bring order . . . The situation of crime and injustice . . . will continue until we make order. (Ravitzky, 1996, p. 84).

The conception of peace among the disciples of Rabbi Zvi Yehuda Kook also reminds one of that of Ben Gurion (i.e., the End of Days peace). Many of his disciples, which were the leaders of *Gush Emunim*, considered the peace treaties with Egypt not only a betrayal of the idea of the integrity of the Land of Israel, but also of the integrity of the Jewish idea of peace. Rabbi Ya'akov Ariel protested:

> What is being done today is a mockery of the word peace. The true peace for which we aim and to which we must educate [our people] is a peace based on the unification of the human race around one Torah ... [The present] peace is not the peace of the Bible ... It is not for this "peace" that a Jew lifts his eyes in prayer. True peace entails a spiritual revolution ... The idea of peace includes the absolute dominion of the Lord. A peace that lacks the element of a common faith and a single [shared] idea is not a true peace or a stable one. (Ravitzky, 1996, pp. 140 -141).

The subjugation of Israel to the idea of "world peace", or to "End of Days peace", means that the wars of Israel are nothing but wars for this peace. Writes Rabbi Zvi Tau, a leading spiritual leader of *Gush Emunim*:

> From the perspective of faith we see the Divine hand spread over us, and especially for our wars. It leads us to recognize the righteousness of our actions and our wars and their indispensability, not only for us but for all the nations! The wars of Israel are essentially wars against war, for whoever rises against Israel rises against the light of God in the world, which is the supernal peace. (Ravitzky, pp. 83-84).

Contemporary Left-wing Messianism

The messianic discourse is by no means limited to the religious right-wing of contemporary Israeli political arena, and appears also in so called Israeli left-wing or liberal circles. This discourse includes the elements discussed above: the subordination of Israel to the "Jewish vocation" which meant the creation of the "perfect society" guided by the universal morality of the prophecies, on one hand, and the spread of these universal ideas for the sake of humanity, on the other.

These messianic ideas, similar to those of Ben Gurion and Buber, appear also in the words of one of Israel leading sociologists, Shmuel Eisenstadt, who describes the Israeli society as one "whose destiny is to carry the burden of a certain realization of the Jewish civilization". (2002, pp. 372-373):

> …The best way to understand this experience is to see the Jews not only as an ethnic or religious group, nation or "people", though they are entitled to all these adjectives, but as a carriers of civilization … only the one who looks at this experience in civilizational terms, in the terms of an overall vision which engulfs all the efforts to rebuild new life according to ontological vision, could cope with the greatest riddle of this experience: its continuity in spite of the destruction, the exile, the loss of political independence and the absence of territorial continuity. (Eisenstadt, 2002, pp. 372-373).

The idea that the vocation of Israel and its legitimization are anchored in the realization of universal ideas is common. For example, the words of the famous historian Saul Friedlander, are clearly written under Buberian influence:

> I say to myself that the Jewish State is maybe a stage in the way of a people whose special destiny comes to symbolize the appropriate search - with a constant hesitation yet without rest – of the entire humanity. (Shaked, 1988, p. 59).

Also Shulamit Aloni considers Israel as a means for the realization of cosmopolitan ideas. In an interview with Ben Ezer (1974), Aloni expressed her opinion on the teachings of George Steiner. Steiner, a professor of comparative literature in Oxford and Cambridge, is a cosmopolitan who considers the nation-state an anachronism. He especially rejects Zionism and the Jewish State because they harm the Jewish special qualities and the true vocation of the Jews, which, according to him, could be realized only in the Diaspora. There, where they are "guests" among the nations, they are the vanguard of a moral and cultural awakening, the prophets of a deeper and more sublime humanity (Sagiv, 2002). Aloni responds to Steiner's criticism of Zionism and says:

> My argument with Steiner is not with his cosmopolitan ethical thinking – with which I agree. But I think that a more tenable, stronger, more convincing point of departure for the battle he proposes and for the Jewish role he envisages – is one in which I have a sovereign State of my own. (Ben Ezer, 1974, p. 37).

Thus, Steiner and Aloni share the same starting point, which is the need to realize the "Jewish vocation". Also both identify the "Jewish vocation" with "cosmopolitan ethical ideas". Yet, while Steiner sticks to the more traditional notion of the Jewish vocation, Aloni thinks that the Israeli State could realize it better. The idea that Israel should set as an example to humanity as a continuation to the notion of the Jewish vocation in the Diaspora is expressed also by Avraham Burg:

> Judaism has always lived an unresolved tension between absolute universalism and high-walled isolationism. The will and natural tendency to dwell in isolation were undermined through history by individuals who broke out and changed the world – Karl Marx, Leon Trotsky, Sigmund Freud, Heinrich Heine, Moses Mendelssohn, Abraham Joshua Heschel, and members of the civil rights movement in the United States. This is just a short and very partial list. Can the State of Israel best herself to the level of these individuals

and serve the world as a collective of universalistic Jews? Entirely diverse but mutually inspiring? Can Israel help the world free itself from its hostility block and blaze new trails to the venue of peacemaking, reconciliation and acceptance? (Burg, 2008, p. 218).

Again, we can see here the shift from the more traditional notion of the "Jewish vocation," which was personal (represented by the list of Jewish personalities which Burg includes) to its collective "Zionist" interpretation.

One peculiar branch of this "left" messianism is that espoused by Yeshayahu Leibowitz. The latter, though religious and even Orthodox, had been usually classified as "left" and even "liberal". As we have seen above, in Leibowitz's teaching the messianic idea of the realization of the halachic State replaces that of the "perfect society" (See above, pp. 108-111). True, Leibowitz considered the Rabbi Kooks' sanctification of Zionism and the present Israeli State as idol worship. Yet, eventually Kook and Leibowitz did not differ in as much as the final goal is concerned, that is the creation of an halachic State. For Leibowitz, the implementation of the halachic State turned out to be an eternal task:

> … this is a struggle for years or generations or hundreds of years, and even eternal, because it is possible that the Torah could not be realized: Precisely because it is divine it is unrealizable by human beings, and all the meaning of its realization is the constant human struggle for its realization.

The messianic motives here are clear: the subjugation of Israelis to a transcendental idea, which is not connected to their earthly materialist interests. Leibowitz had repeatedly emphasized that he "abhor[s] and despise[s]" the idea that "the Torah and Mitzvot should be maintained for the sake of the interests of the Jewish people" (Leibowitz, 1992, p. 54).

Another element is the notion of the eternal struggle; a reminder of Ben Gurion words quoted above that the messiah we need is the one who is not coming.

The examination of Shimon Peres' ideas of the "New Middle East" reveals the same motives. Like Ben Gurion, whom Peres considers as his teacher, the motive of redemption is central. The object of redemption is not just the Jewish people, but of all mankind:

> We are facing a new genesis. Judaism could play a role in this renovation of man and his world. In the history of the Jewish nation, which from its birth had turned its face to the future and its Golden Age has not yet arrived there has been a hidden message, that no numerical variables set the spiritual power…
> (Peres, 1998, p.11).

Here it is important to emphasis that the demand that the nation-state will also consider the overall human interest is certainly a necessary condition for the development of normal national identity. Yet in the Israeli case this demand becomes in many cases a condition for legitimization. Thus, Gershon Shaked reacts to the words of Saul Friedlander quoted above: "It is obvious that the State in itself is not satisfactory for him and deserves a legitimization only if it will fulfill a universal mission; that is, a "Jewish vocation". Shaked considers Friedlander as representing an elite in the Israeli society:

> There is something in the words of Friedlander of the intellectual superiority of a European intellectual elite, which is ready to accept the narrow and insecure borders of Israel only by being compensated of the loss of the European wide-existence ranges by the qualities of the perfect society … in as much as the State could boast in its cultural and social achievements, it is proper

to identify with it. Yet, when its value decrease in the moral and cultural market it should be renounced both inwardly and outwardly (ibid., p. 63).

Indeed, Shaked emphasizes the elitist elements of this approach:

> Friedlander continues in his ideas those of the intellectual elite which had established "Brit Shalom" and wanted to create here a sort of pacific island in the see of hatred, the one which had dreamt to realize the Zionist vision without violence and with a positive affinity to the inhabitants of the country – utopists who wanted to fight for a Jewish place under the sun yet to avoid that this struggle will cast upon them moral deficiencies. Yet, the less attractive side of all this matter is that this group had turned later on into one which asks to remain liberal, European and leftist in the middle east in order to be accepted in all the political saloons and all the elites of western society (ibid., pp. 64 – 65).

Another peculiar branch of contemporary Israeli messianism is the current so called "post-Zionism", which has been discussed extensively in this book. Its messianic discourse is usually overlooked because, as in many other cases of modern messianism, it has been cloaked by the usage of the naturalist language of the social sciences, on one hand, and by its struggle against the messianic discourse of the Jewish State, on the other. Yet, the post-Zionist message is clearly messianic, that is the establishment of a non-national State, probably the first in modern time. While this messianic demand could be attributed also to the influence of universal ideas, there is no doubt that they have found a fertile soil in the Jewish State. If we see post-Zionism also as a special discourse of Jewish-Zionist messiaism, then it becomes understandable why it demands that Israelis will be the first ones to shed their nationality in a predominantly national world.

$$\mathcal{C} \Diamond \mathcal{C}$$

Conclusion
Towards an Israeli National Consciousness

In recent years, I have presented the ideas put forward in this book to audiences across the country. The response has always been interested, and sometimes even enthusiastic. The audiences, even those that disagreed, could appreciate how these novel ideas challenged the prevailing Israeli ethos. To date, there have been two principal suggestions for the solution of Israel's identity crisis: one, which is called "Zionist", suggests that the solution to the crisis lay in the establishment of a "Jewish and Democratic State". The response in this book is that the notion of a Jewish and Democratic State is an oxymoron. In other words, it is possible to speak about an Israel, which would be both Jewish and democratic only if it would be the State of the Israeli nation. In this case, Israel would be Jewish as France is Catholic and Britain is English.

The second proposition on the agenda is the so called "post-Zionist" concept, which suggests to solve the identity crisis by turning Israel into a "citizens' state". On this idea, my book is also unequivocal: The post-Zionist's citizen's state is a creature, which could not be found anywhere. In other words, Israel will become a citizens' state when it will be a republic.

The idea of the Israeli Nation is sometimes rejected as "utopian". The concept "utopia", which usually means an "ideal society", was taken from the title of the book by Thomas Moore, written in 1516. The word utopia is composed of two Greek words: *ou*, which means "no", and *topos* which means "place", thus utopia means no-place, consequently when we call a plan utopian we mean that it could not be implemented anywhere. This book demonstrates that the nation-state is not utopian, at least in the sense that this is the accepted model for the contemporary State, and there are many countries in which this model prevails, and many other countries aspiring to this model. I hope that my book will lead to the acknowledgment that this model did not contradict the original purposes of the Zionist movement, and that the underlying ideas were appreciated by the forefathers of Zionism when they talked about the normalization of the Jewish existence. Consequently the concept of the "Jewish State", as we know it today, has been to a large extent a post-independence creation. There will be those who would say that the demand to establish Israel as a nation-state is utopian, as there is no Israeli nation, and there are no conditions for its creation. It is my hope that this book shows that the Israeli nation exists, at least as a socio-cultural entity, or that the necessary conditions for its creation exist: a strong state, on one hand, and a rich and stable Hebrew culture which supports a modern industrial society, on the other. What is needed is a change of consciousness: to acknowledge the existence of the nation and to complement this acknowledgment with a constitutional institutionalization of the Israeli nation as customary among the family of democratic nations. Alternatively, the assertion that the existence of an Israeli nation-state, or an attempt to create one, is utopian means that the Jews, unlike other peoples, need special arrangements, as what is good for the latter is not good for the former. Consequently, the true utopia is not Israel, which recognizes its own nation, but rather Israel of today is the "utopia", it is indeed a "no-place".

The separation between nationality and religion will not necessarily solve the problems of Israel, as every democracy has problems: socio-economic cleavages, tensions between ethnic groups and discrimination of minorities. All democracies are debating how to accommodate multiculturalism within the nation-state. In Israel, there are additional problems of security and survival, which are not simple. Yet, the establishment of Israel as a normal nation-state will give us the framework, which is a precondition for the solution of these problems and will enable us also to be helped by the experience of other nation-states. The present "Jewish State" not only constitutes a framework within which the problems of Israel could not be solved, but is also the prime source for Israel's problems, including those which are not usually considered as related to identity. Thus, in Israel the "Jewish State" is the main source for the socio-economic gaps: the poorest sectors in the Israeli society are the Arab and the ultra-Orthodox. Their deprivation is not "social", but rather "political" and stems directly from the ideologies and practices of the Jewish State.

The phenomenon of both the Arab and the ultra-Orthodox sectors is rather unique. Usually traditional communities find it difficult to maintain traditional way of life within modern nations. The modern industrial society is a powerful "melting pot", and Israel has proven itself as such, as during the six decades of its existence it has managed to create a Hebrew nation from people who arose from "seventy languages". The existence of both sectors, and especially their constant growth during the years of independence, testify to the fact that this sectarianism is molded and encouraged by the political system, i.e., by the Jewish State. The latter, so it seems, incubates and perpetuates a constantly growing numbers of "citizens" who are either resentful or indifferent to it. The marginalization of both sectors, the Arabs and the ultra-Orthodox, create a heavy burden on the Israeli economy and welfare state. Recently the Governor of the Israeli Central Bank, Karnit Flug, explained the recent decrease in the national growth rate by the shortage of high-quality working power, which she attributed to the growth of the Arab sector, the ultra-Orthodox sector, and the number of elderly people. The Governor warned that unless appropriate measures, such as improved education and "working habits", will be taken, the constant growth of these two sectors, which by the year of 2060 will constitute 50% of the population, will continue to slow down the economy and the rate of national growth.[26]

Complementary to the burden upon the economy of both sectors is the burden upon the welfare system.

As the marginalization of both sectors is more political than social, to the extent that welfare budgets are allocated to these sectors they are directed towards their maintenance and perpetuation rather than to the improvement of their socio-economic status. In other words, if one of the incentives of a welfare policy is the wish to alleviate the poorest sections of society of their deprived position in the hope that once they will get out of this deprived situation they will also contribute to the national economy, this incentive does not exist in this case. On the contrary, not only that the money invested will not change the socio-economy status of members of both sectors and make them more "productive" for the economy, but actually will lead to a further growth of these sectors and thus increase the burden laid upon the welfare state. This gives the State more reasons for not wanting to invest in both sectors. There is no doubt that this ambivalence of the State towards the poorest sections of the Israeli society prevents the emergence of a universal welfare policy in Israel and consequently reflects also upon all Israelis.

Thus, the integration of both sectors, the Arab and the ultra-Orthodox, is not just desired from political and moral reasons, but also from economic reasons. There is not need to elaborate much further how the Jewish State perpetuates what has been known here as the "Arab Sector", and how acknowledging the existence of an Israeli nation could improve the socio-economic situation of Israelis of Arab origin.

The incorporation of the ultra-Orthodox in the national life is also an Israeli interest of the utmost importance. The isolation of the ultra-Orthodox in the Israel is usually conceived as an expression of their will. But here also the practices of the Jewish State encourage this isolation and even desire it. The ultra-Orthodox sector is not a "natural" social cleavage, but rather is largely maintained by the State. The Israelis usually consider this as the outcome of coalition politics, yet the Jewish State perpetuates the ultra-Orthodox isolation and considers it a part of the Jewish character of the State, a character which the secular elite, so it seems, is unable to supply. In addition, in the absence of an Israeli identity, which is common to the various ethnic and religious groups, the identities which are created here create a "zero sum game", which means that they are not "complementary identities" but rather "antithetical" or "polarized" identities. When there is a common national identity, it can serve as a common denominator for the various particular identities. Thus, the African-American identity and the Jewish-American identity are molded through the American identity also as complementary rather than confrontational. In the language of political science we refer to this phenomenon as "cross-cutting cleavages".

In Israel the situation is different, as in the absence of a common national identity the various ethnic and religious identities tend to mold as confrontational, or as "overlapping cleavages". This increases the tendency of the various groups to define themselves also through the negation of the other and for this a clear distinction between the groups is required, which is supplied by the sectarianism of the Israeli society. Complementary to this is the fact that the struggles between the secular and the religious tend to be an overall cultural war. In as far as the Israeli secular elites are concerned this had led to the absence of a "republican attitude" towards the lowest classes of society: the absence of compassion towards them, on one hand, and the absence of a republican desire to "redeem" them, on the other.

Indeed, it is the Israeli secular elite who especially want an Israeli identity. Religious communities could draw their identity from the religion and the tradition, resources that are not available to the Israeli secular. Consequently, the latter find it difficult to provide a positive dimension to their national identity, thus they are enforced to define themselves negatively: they are not

"Arabs", and they are not "Orthodox" (or, for that matter, not "settlers"). For this they need these groups to be clearly separated and isolated and any kind of integration or the blurring of the borders between the groups constitutes a threat to their identity.

It is, then, the Israeli secular elite which first seeks an Israeli national identity. Within the framework of the fusion of religion and nationality this elite finds itself in a "cognitive dissonance". As national identity is necessary for the modern person, the Israelis need it as other peoples do. Yet, under the conditions of the fusion of religion and nationality the main national "material" around either comes from religion or constitutes an interpretation of religion. Here one can mention the answer which a famous Israeli rabbi and ultra-Orthodox leader, Chazon Ish, gave to the question that Ben Gurion posed to him: how the religious and the irreligious will live together in Israel? Chazon Ish likened the situation to a narrow road where two wagons are passing moving in opposite directions, one is loaded and the other is empty: the empty wagon, meaning the secular, should make way for the loaded wagon, meaning the religious.

Seeing the secular as "empty" might seem outrageous, but in the absence of Israeli national consciousness, there is a measure of truth in the words of Chazon Ish. As individuals, the wagon of the secular, as sons and daughters of modernity and the Enlightenment, is probably loaded no less than that of Chazon Ish. Yet, when it comes to collective identity, in the absence of Israeli consciousness, Chazon Ish has a clear advantage. Indeed, even if religion is different from nationality, it is sill communal, it socializes, and, in the case of Judaism could be a source for values and sense of belonging to a particular group. Within the existing fusion of religion and nationality the main substance from which the secular could load their national wagon is in the Chazon Ish's wagon. It would be of no avail for them to try and create "secular Judaism" or to go to the "Jewish

Bookshelf" (*aron hasfarim hayehudi*). This is not because it is impossible to create "secular Judaism" or "humanist Judaism", but because those Israelis who run to find rescue in the "Jewish Bookshelf" are not really looking for a different Jewish identity, but rather for a national identity.

In other words, they are not motivated by the feeling that they are Jews and by the desire to find out the meaning of their Judaism, but rather by the deficit in national identity and the wish to fill it using the "Jewish Bookshelf". Yet this attempt looks artificial. Indeed, the "Jewish Bookshelf" and Judaism in general could be a source for Israeli national identity (or other national identities) for those whom Judaism constitutes a central component of their being, whether as a religion, or as a culture (and it is important to stress that the "Jewish Bookshelf" could be a source for national identity, not necessarily Israeli. Thus, an American Jew could find in Judaism sources for his American national identity). Yet, the "Jewish Bookshelf" could not serve those who were called, perhaps mistakenly, "Hebrew-speaking Gentiles" for whom Judaism is only marginal and because of the fusion of religion and nationality approach it to try to draw from it their national identity. Their national identity (the one which they do not recognize), their being Israeli or Hebrew, is not a product of their Judaism; on the contrary, their Judaism is to a large extent a product of their being Israeli or Hebrew. In other words, more than they are Jews from home, they are Jews form the fact that their Israeliness is saturated with Judaism. For these secular Jews the way to national identity does not pass through the "Jewish Bookshelf". Rather, it is possible that one day, a national Israeli consciousness would lead them, as Israelis, to the "Jewish Bookshelf". This consciousness is bound to be based also on other ingredients as accepted among other nations: country, language, sovereignty, constitution, democracy, history, common destiny and so on. The language of nationalism is "natural" to the modern man, and the fact that more and more Israelis express their nationalism through the wagon of Chazon Ish or a new interpretation of it, indicates perhaps more than anything else that the emancipation of the national Jew is far from being completed. When a national Israeli consciousness will exist, the wagon of Chazon Ish would be only one of other loaded wagons from which Israeli nationalism would draw.

An Israeli national consciousness is also needed upon which to base the legitimization of Israel among Israelis as well as within the international community. It seems as if there is not one State on earth whose legitimacy is frequently doubted and debated as much as Israel. Israel is not conceived as legitimate like other democratic nations in the west, and more than that; tyrannical regimes, among them those who are our enemies, are less frequently demanded to defend their legitimacy. Why is it that the legitimacy of Israel is still on the international agenda? There is no doubt that we have here, among other factors, the continuation of classical anti-Semitism. The latter had become politically incorrect after the Holocaust, yet it found its contemporary expression through anti-Israel platforms. One of the classical expressions of anti-Semitism was "the double standard", that is the tendency to judge Israel according to measures, which are different from those applied to other nations. Yet, it should be noted that the application of the "double standard" to the Jews does not always stem from anti-Semitism, but also from seeing the Jews as "unique" in the positive way and as those who should act differently and become an example in the international arena. Here the notion of the uniqueness of the "Jewish State" as it is accepted today in Israel, and to some degree among members of the international community, complement and reinforce one another, in the same manner that the image of the Jew among the Gentiles, and the Jewish self-image in the Diaspora had reinforced one another.

To the extent that States need external legitimization, this was based upon the principle of national self-determination over the last two centuries.

States justify their existence, and their right to act, by claiming that they are expressing the right of nations to self-determination, that they are seeking to advance the survival and interests of their nations. Apparently, Israel seems to do the same, as it claims that it expresses the right of the "Jewish People" for self-determination. Yet, to the extent the Jews are indeed "people", they are certainly not "people" of the political type, which means they do not constitute a nation as they belong willingly to different nations. Thus, the framework within which the Israelis try to legitimize Israel could not be based on the existence of a concrete nation. They turn to morality, history, and God to look for legitimization and by this they are constantly confusing the elements, which constitute a nation and what legitimizes it. To be sure, all those elements exist to various degrees in other nationalisms alongside the republican elements, yet what is unique in the Israeli case is the centrality of those elements and the rudimentary character of the republican element.

All this leads also to confusion between what had constituted the nation, on one hand, and that which legitimizes it, on the other. The Bible constitutes us, if only because it is the source of our national language, but it is not our "kushan" (Bill of Sale) for Palestine. Relating ourselves to the ancient Hebrews had no doubt served as a constituting element of Israel, yet it cannot legitimize our sovereignty over the country. We are sovereign over our land for the same reasons that France is sovereign over its land, which is from the mere existence of the nation. Also the Holocaust and the persecution of the Jews had been a prime cause in the constitution of Israel, yet this history does not legitimize us or our actions. The suggestion often heard that the Holocaust provides the legitimization of Israel is the ultimate expression of the abnormality of Israel. As it means that the self-determination of the Jews had become legitimate only after a catastrophe in which the vast majority of the potential sons and daughters of the nation had been exterminated. If Britain has the right to exist on its soil without having a Holocaust in its past, so does Israel. Alternatively seeing the Holocaust as the source of legitimization for Israel means that Israel is not accepted as a nation, but rather as an artificial entity given by the gentiles to the Jews as a "compensation" for killing them. This approach invites all kinds of "moral calculations" – do the wrongs suffered by the Jews justify inflicting wrongs on the Palestinians? Why do the Palestinians have to suffer because of the wrongs that the European had inflicted upon the Jews? And all kinds of questions, which are not normally asked regarding other conflicts. One injustice could not justify another, and it is not clear why the wrongs which had been inflicted upon the Jews in Europe justified the wrongs which the Israelis are accused of inflicting upon the Arabs.[27] If one wrongdoing could indeed justify another, then the wrongs committed in the Holocaust were of such magnitude that they should allow us to do anything. Yet, all this is nonsense, the roots of which are found in viewing Israel as a moral-religious fighting community. We are a nation, and as such it is our right and our duty to do whatever is necessary for our survival. Our message to the international community should be the opposite; the meaning of normalization is that we do not need special justifications to act.

Seeing history as the source for the legitimization of Israel is one cause for the fierce debate concerning the history of Israel. The attack of most of the "New Historians" on the "official" version of the Israeli history conceal the wish for the delegitimization of Israel, as well as the defenders of the "official" version (and probably the version itself) conceals the wish to legitimize Israel. Thus, it had become common to speak about the "Original Sin" concerning the establishment of Israel: the "deportation" and the "disinheritance" of the Palestinians. Yet, in as much as history cannot legitimize a nation, it cannot delegitimize it. In almost every nation's past, there are difficult events. Yet, these do not cast doubts on its right to self-determination. The fate of the Indians, slavery and the involvement of the

United States in various wars which cost the lives of millions, have evoked criticism against the United States, but never resulted in doubting the right of America to exist, and moreover, have not carried with it the kind of moral calculations which are constantly present in the case of Israel. So, too, France, whose national history from the time of the French Revolution is full of bloody wars costing the lives of untold numbers of its own people and of other peoples. Had anyone drawn the "moral account" of the French Nation? In modern history, there is probably only one case of revocation of the right of national self-determination of a nation because of its past: Germany post-World War II. And even here, when Germany was ultimate reunited, this was done with the agreement and the blessing of the international community. If the right of Germany for self-determination is recognized -- despite its past -- so should be the right of the Israeli nation. There is no "original sin" in the establishment of Israel and in the fact that it was "created by colonialism" and that considerable part of its population, including the elite, which established it, had come from Europe. The United States, Canada, and Australia are also nations created by colonialism and peopled by European immigrants. Sovereignty is not granted to natives, but rather to nation-states. Had sovereignty been granted according to native-ness, then today's France would not have been legitimate, as notwithstanding the myth of the French Nation, France's natives in the 19th century were not French. More than that, most of the States of the third-world, and those which, surround us had been a product of colonialism, which had drawn their borders and created and armed their tyrannical regimes. Israel's advantage over these regimes is obvious: Israel is still a democracy governed by consent and not by a military or other dictatorship.

Our 'Original Sin' was not in our War of Independence, when we fought and triumphed over those who wished to trample our right to self-determination. To the extent that this term can be used, our 'Original Sin' was the establishment of the "Jewish State", instead of the Israeli republic. As far as the Palestinians who sit in our midst are concerned, our "Original Sin" is the fact that we had not incorporated them into our national life ever since Independence. The debate which rages concerning the "settlements" in the West Bank conceals the fact that inasmuch as there are differences in the perspective of international and other law between Jewish settlements across the Green Line and those within the Greek line, they have in common one substantive factor: their being "Jewish settlements". The "settlement" in the Biblical sense meant a place where 'the other' had no place. In this sense, there is no difference between Elkana and the kibbutz, or between Ofra and Tel Aviv: all are Jewish settlements.

The purpose of Political Zionism was not the establishment of Jewish settlements, but rather of Jewish sovereignty. To a certain extent "resettlement" symbolizes the opposite of sovereignty: the sovereign does not need "to resettle" as it owns the land. As the sovereign is the nation, the ownership which sovereignty grants is collective or national, and thus should be distinguished from private ownership. Jewish (that is Israeli) sovereignty in Palestine does not entail Jewish private ownership of the land. Similarly, since the existence of "natives" in a certain territory does not entail their being sovereign in this territory, so the existence of "Jewish" individuals in a certain territory does not make it "Jewish" or "Israeli", as the fate of Yamit and Gush Katif had demonstrated. Sovereignty is granted to nation-states and, if in the pre-independence times the establishment of Jewish settlements had seemed necessary for achieving Jewish sovereignty, then, after independence and after achieving Jewish sovereignty, Tel Aviv should stop being a Jewish settlement and become a multirigious and multiracial city, one of the expressions of the sovereignty of the Israeli nation-state. The strengthening of Israel's sovereignty should be achieved by the strengthening of the Israeli nation-state and democracy, among other things, by the incorporation of the "native element" into the nation. Our problem is not that we arose from "seventy languages", but rather that we have refused and are still refusing to accept the seventy-first "native" nation. We should not be afraid of democracy, as democracy and nationalism complement one another, and the most successful nations are also the most democratic ones. The democratic nation is a source of power and pride and it will endow us with the national self-confidence, which is so common among democratic nations.

Bibliography

Adler, C., & Kahana, R. (1975). *Israel - A Society in the Making: A Sociological Analysis of Sources.* Jerusalem: Akademon [Hebrew].

Agassi, J. (1999). *Liberal Nationalism for Israel: Towards an Israeli National Identity.* Jerusalem and New York: Gefen.

Agassi, J. (2014, January 1). There is an Israeli National Identity. *Haaretz* [Hebrew].

Agassi, J., Buber-Agassi, J., & Berent, M. (1991). *Who is an Israeli?* Rehovot: Kivunim [Hebrew].

Agbaria, A. K. & Mustafa, M. (2011). Two States for Three Peoples: The 'Palestinian-Israeli' in the Future Vision Documents of the Palestinians in Israel. *Ethnic and Racial Studies, 35*(4), pp. 718-736.

Ahad Ha'am (1947). *The Writings of Ahad Ha'am.* Tel Aviv: Dvir [Hebrew].

Ake, C. (1997). Dangerous Liaisons: The Interface of Globalization and Democracy. In A. Hadenius (Ed.) *Democracy's Victory and Crisis*, pp. 282 – 296. Cambridge: Cambridge University Press.

Akzin, B. (1966a). Notes on the Draft of the Constitution for Israel. In B. Akzin, *Sugiot be-mishpat u-ve-medinaut*, pp.151-159. Jerusalem: Magnes [Hebrew].

Akzin, B. (1966b). A Proposition for the Constitution of the State of Israel. In B. Akzin, *Sugiot Be-mishpat u-ve-medinaut.* Jerusalem: Magnes [Hebrew].

Akzin, B. (1966c). The Declaration of the Establishment of the State of Israel. In B. Akzin, *Sugiyot be-mishpat u-ve-medinaut*, pp.128-143. Jerusalem: Magnes [Hebrew].

Akzin, B. (1980). *Nations and States.* Tel Aviv: Am Oved [Hebrew]

Almog, S. (1982). *Zionism and History.* Jerusalem: Magnes [Hebrew].

Aloni, S. (1987). From Birth to Death. *Politika*, 17, pp. 1-13 [Hebrew].

Anderson, B. (1991). *Imagined Communities.* New York and London: Verso.

Aran, G., & Hassner, R. (2013). Religious Violence in Judaism: Past and Present. *Terrorism and Political Violence*, 25(3), pp. 355-405.

Arian, A. (1998). *The Second Republic: Politics in Israel.* Chatham, N.J.: Chatham House Publishers.

Avineri, S. (1981). *The Making of Modern Zionism: The Intellectual Origin of the Jewish State.* New York: Basic Books.

Avineri, S. (1994). Zionism and the Jewish Religious Tradition: The Dialectics of Redemption and Secularization, in S. Almog, J. Reinharz & A. Shapira (Eds.), *Zionism and Religion*, pp. 1-12. Jerusalem: Shazar Center [Hebrew].

Avineri, S. (1998). "National Minorities in Democratic Nation-States". In E. Rekhess (Ed.) *The Arabs in Israeli Politics: Dilemmas of Identity*, pp. 117-124. Tel Aviv: Dayan Center, University of Tel Aviv [Hebrew].

Barak, A. (1994). *Judicial Discretion part 3.* Jerusalem: Nevo [Hebrew].

Barak, A. (2004) *A Judge in a Democracy.* Haifa: University of Haifa [Hebrew].

Barak, A., & Spanic, T. (Eds.). (1990). *In Memoriam of Uri Yadin.* Tel Aviv: Bursi [Hebrew].

Bareli, A. & Kedar, N. (2011). *Israeli Republicanism.* Jerusalem: The Israeli Democracy Institute [Hebrew].

Bartal, I. (1987). *Cossack and Bedouin: Land and People in Jewish Nationalism.* Tel Aviv: Am Oved [Hebrew].

Barzilai, G. (2000). "Fantasies of Liberal Jurisprudence: State Law, Politics, and the Israeli Arab-Palestinian Community". *Israel Law Review,* 34, pp. 425 – 451.

Bechor, G. (1996). *Constitution for Israel: Story of a Struggle.* Or Yehuda: Maa'riv Publications.

Beeri, Y. (1992). *The Importance of a Name.* Tel Aviv: Yaron Golan [Hebrew].

Bellah, R. (1970). Civil Religion in America. In R. Bellah (Ed.), *Beyond Belief: Essays on Religion in a Post-Traditional World*, pp. 168-189. New York: Harper & Row.

Bellamy, R. (1996). The Political Form of the Constitution: The Separation of Powers, Rights and Representative Democracy. In R. Bellamy & D. Castiglione (Eds.), *Constitutionalism in Transformation: European and Theoretical Perspectives,* pp. 24-44. Oxford: Blackwell.

Ben Ezer, E. (1974). *Unease in Zion.* New York: Quadrangle.

Ben Gurion, D. (1931). *We and Our Neighbours.* Tel Aviv: Davar [Hebrew].

Ben Gurion, D. (1957). Concepts and Values. *Hazut 3*, pp. 7-11 [Hebrew].

Ben Gurion, D. (1969). *The Renewed State of Israel.* Tel Aviv: Am Oved [Hebrew].

Ben Israel, H. (1966). "Theories of Nationalism and their Application to Zionism". In P. Ginossar & A. Bareli (Eds.), *Zionism: A Contemporary Controversy*, pp. 203-222. Sde Boker: Ben Gurion Institute, Ben Gurion University [Hebrew].

Ben Israel, H. (2000). Zionism and European Nationalism. In A. Shapira, J. Reinharz & J. Harris (Eds.), *The Age of Zionism*, pp. 19 – 36. *Jerusalem: Shazar Center* [Hebrew].

Ben Israel, H. (2002). National identity of the scholar and the study of nationalism. *Academia*, 11, pp. 13 – 17 [Hebrew].

Ben Israel, H. (2003). Zionism and European nationalisms. *Israel Studies*, 8(1), pp. 91-104.

Ben Israel, H. (2004). *In the Name of the Nation: Studies in Nationalism and Zionism.* Sde Boker: The Ben Gurion Research Institute [Hebrew].

Ben-Rafael, E. (2001). *Jewish Identities* (with Y. Gorni & S. Ratsaby). Sde Boker: The Ben Gurion Research Institute [Hebrew].

Ben-Rafael, E. (2002). *Jewish Identities: Fifty Intellectuals Answer Ben Gurion*, Leyden and Boston: Brill.

Ben-Rafael, E. & Ben-Chaiml, L. (2006). *Jewish Identities in an Era of Multiple Modernities.* Raanana: Open University [Hebrew].

Benner, E. (1997). Nationality Without Nationalism. *Journal of Political Ideologies*, 2(2), pp. 190-206.

Benyamini, E. (1990). *States to the Jews: Uganda Birobijan and 34 Additional Programs.* Tel Aviv: Hakibutz Hameuchad.

Benziman, U. & Mansour, A. (1992). *Subtenants: Israeli Arabs, their Status and Policy towards Them.* Jerusalem: Keter [Hebrew].

Berent, M. (2000). Sovereignty: Ancient and Modern. *Polis*, 17(1-2), pp. 2-34.

Berent, M. (2009). *A Nation Like All Nations: Towards the Establishment of an Israeli Republic.* Jerusalem: Carmel [Hebrew].

Berent, M. (2010). The Ethnic Democracy Debate: How Unique is Israel?", *Nations and Nationalism*, 16 (4), pp. 657–674.

Bilby, K. W. (1950). *New Star in the Near East.* New York: Doubleday.

Bishara, A. (1993). On the Question of the Palestinian Minority in Israel. *Theory and Criticism 3*, pp. 7-20 [Hebrew].

Bishara, A. (1995). "The Crisis of the Arab Leadership – Where is the Future Generation". In E. Reches & T. Yanges (Eds.), *Arab Politics in Israel at a Crossroad.* Tel Aviv: Moshe Dayan Center, Tel Aviv University [Hebrew].

Breuilly, J. (2005). Dating the Nation: How Old is an Old Nation? In A. Ichijo & G. Uzelac (eds.), *When is the Nation?* pp. 15-39. London and New York: Routledge.

Brieman, S. (1950). "The Debate between Lilienblum and Ahad Ha'am and Dubnov", *Shivat Zion 1*, pp. 138-168 [Hebrew].

Brinker, M. (1987). *Brenner's Jewishness.* Jerusalem: The Israeli National Academy for Sciences [Hebrew].

Brinker, M. (1997, October 21). Varieties of Post-Zionism. *Haaretz* [Hebrew].

Brinker, M. (2000). "A Democratic State – Form and Substance". In Y. David (Ed.), *The State of Israel: Between Judaism and Democracy*, pp. 77- 92. Jerusalem: The Israel Democracy Institute [Hebrew].

Brubaker, R. (1992). *Citizenship and Nationhood in France and Germany.* Cambridge Massachusetts: Harvard University Press.

Brubaker, R. (1996). *Nationalism Reaffirmed: Nationhood and the National Question in the New Europe*, Cambridge: Cambridge University Press.

Brubaker, R. (1998). "Myths and Misconceptions in the Study of Nationalism". In J. Hall (Ed.) *The State of the Nation: Ernest Gellner and the Theory of Nationalism.* pp. 272-306. Cambridge: Cambridge University Press.

Brubaker, R. (2001). "The Return of Assimilation? Changing Perspectives on Immigration and its Sequels in France, Germany, and the United States". *Ethnic and Racial Studies*, 24(4), pp. 531-548.

Brunner J. & Peled Y. (1998). "On Autonomy, Capabilities and Democracy: A Critique of Liberal Multiculturalism." In M. Mautner, A. Sagi & R. Shamir (Eds.), *Multiculturalism in a Democratic and Jewish State*, pp. 107-132. Tel Aviv: Ramot Press [Hebrew].

Buber, M. (1961). *Israel and the World: Essays in the Time of Crisis.* Jerusalem: The Zionist Library [Hebrew].

Buber, M. (1984). *Between a People and their Land.* Jerusalem: Schocken [Hebrew].

Buber, M. (1988). *A Land for Two Peoples.* Jerusalem: Schocken [Hebrew].

Burg, A. (2008). *The Holocaust is Over; We Must Rise from its Ashes.* New York: Palgrave Macmillan.

Canovan, M. (1991). "Republicanism". In Vervon Bogdanor (Ed.) *The Blackwell Encyclopedia of Political Science*, pp. 434-435. Oxford: Blackwell.

Canovan, M. (2000). "Patriotism is not enough". *British Journal of Political Science*, 30(3), pp. 413-432.

Charbit, D. (2008). "Israel as a Multicultural State: Prospects and Risks". In S. Ozacky-Lazar, & M. Kabha (Eds.), *Between Vision and Reality: The Vision Papers of the Arabs in Israel, 2006-2007*, pp. 49-62. Jerusalem: The Citizens' Accord Forum between Jews and Arabs in Israel [Hebrew].

Chlenov, M. (2003). "Characteristics of the Ethnic and Religious Identity of Russian Jews. *The Jews of the Former Soviet Union in Israel and in the Diaspora*, pp. 20-21, 254-273 [Hebrew].

Cobban, A. (1969). *The Nation-State and National Self-Determination*, London: Collins.

Cohen, A. (1998). *Hatalit Vehadegel.* Jerusalem: Yad Ben Zvi [Hebrew].

Cohen, A. (2006). *Non-Jewish Jews in Israel.* Jerusalem: Keter [Hebrew]

Cohen, C. (1991). *Hamishpat.* Jerusalem: The Bialik Institute [Hebrew].

Cohen, E. (1995). "Israel as a Post-Zionist Society". In R. S. Wistrich & D. Ohana (Eds.), *The Shaping of Israeli Identity: Myth, Memory and Trauma.* London: Frank Cass.

Connor, W. (1972). "Nation Building or Nation Destroying?" *World Politics*, 24(3), pp. 319-355.

Crossman, R. H.S. (1947). *Palestine Mission.* New York: Harper.

Crossman, R. H. S. (1960). *A Nation Reborn.* London: H. Hamilton.

Danette-Light, P. (1998). *The Role of the Military in Social Stratification and Mobility in American Society* (Doctoral Dissertation). http://scholar.lib.vt.edu/theses/available/etd-71198-13614/unrestricted/danette3.pdf

Deutsch, K. & Foltz, W. J. (Eds.). (1966). *Nation Building*, New York: Atherton Press.

Diamond, L. (1993). "Three Paradoxes of Femocracy". In L. Diamond and M. Plattner (Eds.), *The Global Resurgence of Democracy*, pp. 111-124. Baltimore, Maryland: Johns Hopkins University Press.

Diatchkove, S. (2005). Ethnic Democracy in Latvia. In S. Smooha & P. Järve (Eds.), *The Fate of Ethnic Democracy in Post-Communist Europe*, pp. 81-114. Budapest: European Center for Minority Issues, Open Society Institute.

Dinstein, Y. (1971). *The International Law and the State*. Tel Aviv: Schocken [Hebrew].

Don Yehiya, E. (1983). "Ideology and Politics in Religious Zionism: The Zionist Theory of Rabbi Reines and the Politics of the Mizrahi Party under his Leadership". *Hatzionut*, 8, pp. 103-146 [Hebrew].

Don Yehiya, E. (1994). "The Book and the Sword: The Nationalist Yeshivot and Political Radicalism in Israel". In M. Marty & S. Appleby (Eds.), *Accounting for Fundamentalism: The Dynamic Character of Movements*, pp. 262-300. Chicago: The University of Chicago Press.

Don Yehiya, E. (1999). *Religion and Political Accommodation in Israel*. Jerusalem: The Floerheimer Institute for Policy Studies.

Don-Yehiya, E., & Susser, B. (1999). "Democracy versus Nationalism: Israel as an Exceptional Case". *Tarbut Demokratit*: pp. 9-22 [Hebrew].

Dotan, S. (1992). *The Struggle for Eretz Yisrael*. Tel Aviv: Ministry of Defense [Hebrew].

Downs, A. (1991). "Social Values and Democracy". In K. R. Monroe (Ed.), *The Economic Approach to Politics*, pp. 143-170. New York: Harper Collins.

Dowty, A. (1999). "Is Israel Democratic? Substance and Semantics in the Ethnic Democracy Debate". *Israel Studies*, 4(2), pp. 1-15.

Drori, Z. (2012). "The Gap between the Yarmulke and the Beret: How is the IDF coping with Religionization?" In R. Gal (Ed.), *Between the Yarmulke and the Beret: Religion, Politics and the Military in Israel*, pp. 115-150. Modan: Ben Shemen [Hebrew].

Eisenstadt, S. N. (1999). *Fundamentalism, Sectarianism, and Revolution: The Jacobin Dimension of Modernity*. Cambridge, Cambridge University Press.

Eisenstadt, S. N. (2002). *Jewish Civilization*. Sde Boker: Ben Gurion Institute [Hebrew].

Elboim-Dror, R. (1999). "Herzl as a Proto-'Post-Zionist'?" In G. Shimoni and R. S. Wistrich (Eds.), *Theodor Herzl: Visionary of the Jewish State*, pp. 240-264. Jerusalem: Magnes Press.

Eliav, M. (1987). The Mizrahi Faction and the Vote on the 'Uganda Program'. *HaTzionut*, 12, pp. 85-98 [Hebrew].

Elon, A. (1975). *Herzl.* London : Weidenfeld and Nicolson

Elroi, G. (2011). *Seeking a Homeland: The Jewish Territorial Organization and its Struggle with the Zionist Movement 1905-1925.* Sde Boker: Ben Gurion Institute [Hebrew].

Esman, M.J. (1988). "Ethnic Politics: How Unique is the Middle East?" In M.J. Esman & I. Rabinovich (Eds.), *Ethnicity, Pluralism and the State in the Middle East* (pp. 271 -287). Ithaca, New York: Cornell University Press, pp. 271-287.

Even-Zohar, I. (1980). "The Emergence and Crystallization of a Native Local Hebrew Culture in Palestine". *Kathedra,* pp. 165-189 [Hebrew].

Evron, B. (2002). *A National Reckoning.* Or Yehuda: Dvir [Hebrew].

Franklin, J. H. (1978). *John Locke and the Theory of Sovereignty,* Cambridge: Cambridge University Press.

Friedman, Y. (1971). "The Attitude of the Jamʿiyyat al-ʿulamā-ʾi Hind to the Indian National Movement and to the Establishment of Pakistan". *Asian and African Studies,* 7, pp. 57-180.

Friedrich K. J. (1949). On the Constitution of Israel. *Molad* 2(10), pp. 203-207 [Hebrew].

Fukuyama, F. (Ed.) (2006). *Nation Building: Beyond Afghanistan and Iraq.* Baltimore: John Hopkins University Press.

Gans, C. (2006). *From Richard Wagner to the Right of Return: Philosophical Analysis of Israeli Public Affairs.* Tel Aviv: Am Oved [Hebrew].

Gans, C. (2008). *A Just Zionism: On the Morality of the Jewish State.* New York: Oxford University Press [Hebrew].

Gans, C. (2011). *A Political Theory for the Jewish People: Three Zionist Narratives.* Haifa: Haifa University Press [Hebrew].

Gavison, R. (2001). "Zionism in Israel? In the Aftermath of the Kaadan Case". *Mimshal u-mishpat,* 6, pp. 25-52 [Hebrew].

Gavison, R. (2002). "The Law of Return: Changes are Needed in Principle". *The Jews of the Former Soviet Union in Israel and in the Diaspora,* pp. 20-21, 34-39 [Hebrew].

Glazer, N. & Moynihan D. P. (1970). *Beyond the Melting Pot.* Cambridge: MIT Press.

Gellner, E. (1983). *Nations and Nationalism.* Oxford: Blackwell.

Gellner, E. (1993). *Nations and Nationalism* (Hebrew Edition). Tel Aviv: Open University [Hebrew].

Gellner, E. (1994a). *Encounters with Nationalism*. Oxford: Blackwell.

Gellner, E. (1994b). *Conditions of Liberty: Civil Society and Its Rivals*. London: Hamish Hamilton.

Gellner, E. (1996). "Do Nations Have Navels?" *Nations and Nationalism*, 2(3), pp. 366-370.

Ghanem, A., & Mustafa, M. (2008). "The Future Vision as a Collective Program for the Palestinians in Israel". In S. Ozacky-Lazar, & M. Kabha (Eds.), *Between Vision and Reality: The Vision Papers of the Arabs in Israel, 2006-2007*, pp. 83-96. Jerusalem: The Citizens' Accord Forum between Jews and Arabs in Israel [Hebrew].

Ghanem, A., Rouhana N., & Yiftachel O. (1998). "Questioning 'Ethnic Democracy': A response to Sammy Smooha". *Israel Studies*, 3(2), pp. 253-267.

Goldstein, Y. (1991). *Between Political and Practical Zionism: The Beginnings of Zionism in Russia*. Jerusalem: Magnes [Hebrew].

Gorni, Y. (1985). *The Arab Question and the Jewish Problem*. Tel Aviv: Am Oved [Hebrew].

Gorni, Y. (1987). *Zionism and the Arabs, 1882-1948: A Study of Ideology* [English translation by Chaya Galai]. Oxford: Oxford University Press.

Gorni, Y. (1990). *The Search for National Identity*. Tel Aviv – Am Oved [Hebrew].

Gorni, Y. (1993). *Policy and Imagination: Federal Ideas in Zionist Political Thought 1917–1948*. Jerusalem: Yad Ben Zvi [Hebrew].

Gorni, Y. (1994). *The State of Israel in Jewish Public Thought: The Quest for Collective Identity*. Houndmills, U.K.: Macmillan.

Gorni, Y. (1999). "Reflections on the Jewish Present-Past". *Gesher*, pp. 45, 15-22 [Hebrew].

Govrin, N. (1985). *The Brenner Affair*. Jerusalem: Yad Ben Zvi [Hebrew].

Gutmann, E., & Dror, Y. (Eds.), (1967). *The Government of the State of Israel: A Collection of Sources*. Jerusalem: The Hebrew University [Hebrew].

Habermas, J. (1998). Citizenship and National Identity. In J. Habermas, *Between Facts and Norms*. Cambridge Mass: MIT Press.

Haeri, N. (2000). "Form and ideology: Arabic sociolinguistics and beyond". *Annual Review of Anthropology*, 29, pp. 61-87.

Hazony, Y. (2000). Did Herzl Want a Jewish State? *Azure*, 9, pp. 37-73.

Heizner, Z. (2000). "If You Will It, It Is No Dream". *Psi'fas*. Tel Aviv: Open University.

Hermann, T. & Newman, D. (1990). "The Dove and the Skullcap: Secular and Religious Divergence in the Israeli Peace Camp". In C. Liebman (ed.), *Conflict and Accommodation between Jews in Israel* (New York: Avi Chai).

Herzl, T. (1988). *The Jewish State*. New York: Dover.

Herzl, T. (1961). *The Writings of Herzl*. Jerusalem: The Zionist Library [Hebrew].

Hinsley, F.H. (1986). *Sovereignty* (2nd edition). Cambridge: Cambridge University Press.

Hobsbawm, E. (1990). *Nations and Nationalism Since 1780: Programme, Myth, Reality.* Cambridge: Cambridge University Press, 1990.

Holtzman, A. (1993). "Literature and National Revival: Between Berdichevsky and Ben Gurion". *Iyunim Bitkumat Yisrael*, 3, pp. 191-204 [Hebrew].

Huntington, S. P. (1993). The Clash of Civilizations? *Foreign Affairs*, 72(3), pp. 22-49.

Hutchinson, J. (1994). *Modern Nationalism*. London: Fontana Press.

Jamal, A. (2008). "Future Visions and Current Dilemmas: On the Political Ethos of the Palestinian Citizens of Israel". In S. Ozacky-Lazar, & M. Kabha (Eds.), *Between Vision and Reality: The Vision Papers of the Arabs in Israel, 2006-2007* pp. 13-35. Jerusalem: The Citizens' Accord Forum between Jews and Arabs in Israel [Hebrew].

Järve, P. (2000). "Ethnic Democracy and Estonia: Application of Smooha's Model". *ECMI Working Paper* 7, Flensburg, Germany: European Center for Minority Issues.

Järve, P. (2005). "Re-independent Estonia". In S. Smooha & P. Järve (eds.), *The Fate of Ethnic Democracy in Post-Communist Europe*, pp. 61-80. Budapest: European Center for Minority Issues, Open Society Institute.

Johnson, K. R. (1998). "The Immigration Laws and Domestic Race Relations: A 'Magic Mirror' into the heart of darkness". *Indiana Law Journal*, 73, pp. 1111-1159.

Kamir, O. (2000). "The Declaration of Independence has Two Faces: The Zionist Declaration and the Democratic Declaration", *Iyunei Mishpat*, 23(1), pp. 473-538 [Hebrew].

Kaniuk, Y. (1987). A Cruel Crossroads. *Politica*, 17, pp. 2-8 [Hebrew]

Kaplan, E. (2005). "A Rebel with a Cause: Hillel Kook, Begin and Jabotinsky's Ideological Legacy". *Israel Studies 10*(3), pp. 87-103.

Karayanni, M. (2006). "Jewish and Democratic Ricochets". *Mishpat Umimshal 9*, pp. 461-496 [Hebrew].

Karlibach, E. (1946). *The Anglo-American Committee of Inquiry on Jewish Problems in Palestine and Europe.* Tel Aviv: Leinman.

Karsh, E. (1997). *Fabricating Israeli History: The 'New Historians'.* London: Frank Cass.

Katz, J. (1983) *Jewish Nationalism: Essays and Studies.* Jerusalem: The Zionist Library [Hebrew].

Kaufmann, Y. (1961). *Gola ve'Nechar* vol 2. Tel Aviv: Dvir [Hebrew].

Kaufmann, Y. (1965). *Selected National Writings: Chapters in the Criticism of National Thought.* Jerusalem: The Zionist Library [Hebrew].

Kedar, A., & Yiftachel, O. (2006). Land Regime and Social Relations in Israel. In H. de Soto and F. Cheneval (Eds.), *Swiss Human Right Book* vol. 1, pp. 129-146, Zurich: Ruffer & Rub Publishing House.

Kedar, N. (2007). Jewish Republicanism. *Journal of Israeli History*, 26 (2), pp. 179 – 99.

Kedar, N. (2009). *Mamlakhtiut.* Jerusalem: Yad Ben Zvi [Hebrew].

Kedar, N. (2013). "Ben Gurion Opposition to a Written Constitution". *Journal of Modern Jewish Studies, 12*(1), pp. 1-16.

Keren, M. (1988). *Ben Gurion and the Intellectuals.* Sde Boker: Ben Gurion Institute [Hebrew].

Kimmerling, B. (1994). Religion, Nationalism and Democracy in Israel". *Z'manim*, pp. 50 – 51, 116-140 [Hebrew].

Kimmerling, B. (1997). The Test of the Burning Children. *Z'manim*, pp. 60, 87-88 [Hebrew].

Kimmerling, B. (2001). *The End of Ashkenazi Hegemony.* Jerusalem: Keter [Hebrew].

Kohn, L. (1948). *A Constitution for Israel, Draft and Explanatory Statement*. Tel Aviv: Mo'etset Ha'medina [Hebrew].

Kolatt, I. (1994). Religion, Society and State During the Period of the National Home. in S. Almog, J. Reinharz & A. Shapira (Eds.), *Zionism and Religion*. pp. 329-371. Jerusalem: Shazar Center [Hebrew].

Kolatt, I. (1996). "Was the Yishuv the Realization of Jewish Nationalism?" In J. Reinharz, Y. Salmon, & G. Shimoni (Eds.), *Jewish Nationalism and Politics - New Perspectives*, pp. 225-252. Jerusalem: Shazar Center [Hebrew].

Kook, H. & Merlin, S. (1975, April 18). "A Proposition for National Debate". *Haaretz*. [Hebrew].

Kook, R. (2002). *The Logic of Democratic Exclusions: African Americans in the United States and Palestinians Citizens in Israel*. Lanham Maryland: Lexington Books.

Kukathas, C. (1992). "Are There Any Cultural Rights? *Political Theory*, 20, pp. 105-139.

Kurzweil, B. (1955). "Judaism as a Manifestation of a National Biological Will: Critical Notes on Ahad Ha'am's Theory of Continuity". *Luach Haaretz*, pp. 144-170 [Hebrew].

Kuzio, T. (2001). "'Nationalizing States' or 'Nation-Building'? A Critical Review of the Theoretical Literature and Empirical Evidence." *Nations and Nationalism, 7* (2), pp. 135-154.

Kymlicka, W. (1989). *Liberalism, Community and Culture*. Oxford: Oxford University Press.

Kymlicka, W. (1995). *Multicultural Citizenship*. Oxford: Oxford University Press.

Lahav, P. (1998). "Personal and Collective Identity: Judaism and Modernity in the *Shalit* Case." In M. Mautner, A. Sagi, & R. Shamir (Eds.), *Multiculturalism in a Democratic and Jewish State*, pp. 279-299. Tel Aviv: Ramot Press [Hebrew].

Laitin, D. (1996a). National Revival and Competitive Assimilation in Estonia. *Post-Soviet Affairs*, 12(1), pp. 25-39.

Laitin, D. (1996b). "Language and Nationalism in the Post-Soviet Republics". *Post-Soviet Affairs*, 12(1), pp. 4-24.

Laitin, D. (2003). "Three Models of Integration and the Estonian/Russian Reality". *Journal of Baltic Studies*, 34(2), pp. 197-223.

Laitin, D. (2007). *Nations, States and Violence*. Oxford: Oxford University Press.

Lasker, M. (2006). *Israel and Jewish Immigration from North Africa 1948-1970*. Sde Boker: Ben Gurion Institute [Hebrew].

Lavsky, H. (1990). *Before Catastrophe – The Distinctive Path of German Zionism 1918-1932*. Jerusalem: Magnes Press [Hebrew].

Lavsky, H. (2002). "Nationalism between Theory and Praxis: Hans Kohn and Zionism," *Zion* 57(2), pp. 189-212 [Hebrew].

Lebel, U., & Luvish-Omer, S. (2012). "'To go back to what we have been before': The Yarmulke as a Conservative Opposition to a Post-Modern Army. In R. Gal (Ed.), Between the Yarmulke and the Beret: Religion, Politics and the Military in Israel, pp. 151-204. Modan: Ben Shemen [Hebrew].

Leibowitz, Y. (1976). *Judaism, Jewish People and the State of Israel*. Tel Aviv: Schocken [Hebrew].

Leibowitz, Y. (1992). *People, Land, State*. Jerusalem: Keter [Hebrew].

Levy, Y. (2007) *From the 'People's Army' to the 'Army of the Peripheries'*. Jerusalem: Carmel [Hebrew].

Levy, Y. (Forthcoming). *The Divine Commander: The Theocratization of the Israeli Military*. Tel Aviv: Am Oved and Sapir Academic College [Hebrew].

Liebman, C. S. (1987). "The Religious Component in Israeli ultra-Nationalism". *The Jerusalem Quarterly*, 41 (Winter), pp. 127 – 144.

Liebman, C. S. (1988). "Conceptions of 'State of Israel' in Israeli Society". *The Jerusalem Quarterly*, 47 (Summer), pp. 95-107.

Liebman, C. S. (1997a). Prospects for Jewish Secularism. *Alpayim*, 14, pp. 97-115 [Hebrew].

Liebman, (1997b). "Reconceptualizing the Culture Conflict Among the Israeli Jews". *Israel Studies*, 2(2), pp. 172-189.

Liebman, C. S. (1999). Religion, Democracy and the Dilemma of the Social Order. *Tarbut Democratit*, 1, pp. 71-83. [Hebrew].

Liebman, C. S., & and Cohen, S. M (1990). *Two Worlds of Judaism*. New Haven and London: Yale University Press.

Liebman, C. S., & Don Yehiya, E. (1983). "The Dilemma of Reconciling Traditional Culture and Contemporary Needs: Civil Religion in Israel". *Comparative Politics*, 16, pp. 53 – 56.

Lijphart, A. (1968). *The Politics of Accommodation*. Berkeley: University of California Press.

Lijphart, A. (1977). *Democracy in Plural Societies*. New Haven CT: Yale University Press.

Linz, J., & Stepan, A. (1996). *Problems of Democratic Transition and Consolidation: Southern Europe, South America, and Post-Communist Europe*. Baltimore and London: John Hopkins University Press.

Linz, J., Stepan, A., & Yadav, Y. (2004). "'Nation State' or 'State Nation': Conceptual Reflections and Some Spanish, Belgian and Indian Data". United Nations Development Programme, Human Development Report Office, Background Paper for HDR.

Lissak, M. (2002). Introduction. *The Jews of the Former Soviet Union in Israel and in the Diaspora*, pp. 20-21, 24-29 [Hebrew].

Lissak, M. & Horowitz D. (1990). *Troubles in Utopia: The Overburdened Polity of Israel*. Tel-Aviv: Am Oved [Hebrew].

Livne, N. (2001, September 20). "The Rise and Fall of Post-Zionism". *Haaretz* [Hebrew].

Luz, E. (1988). *Parallels Meet: Religion and Nationalism in the Early Zionist Movement (1882 – 1904)*. Philadelphia: The Jewish Publication Society.

Luz, E. (2003). *Wrestling with an Angel: Power, Morality, Jewish Identity* (Michael Swirsky, trans.) New Haven: Yale University Press.

Machiavelli, N. (1965). *The Prince* (translated by Christian E. Dermond). New York: Airmont Publishing Company.

Maor, Y. (1986). *The Zionist Movement in Russia*. Jerusalem: Magnes [Hebrew].

Marbry, T. (2013). Arab Di-Nationalism. *The Levantine Review*, 2(1), pp. 27-53.

Margalit, A., & Halbertal, M. (1998). "Liberalism and the Right to Culture". In M. Mautner, A. Sagi & R. Shamir (Eds.), *Multiculturalism in a Democratic and Jewish State*, pp. 93-106. Tel Aviv: Ramot [Hebrew].

Margolin, R. (Ed.). (1999). *Symposium: The State of Israel as a Jewish and Democratic State*. Jerusalem: World Union of Jewish Studies [Hebrew].

Masalha, S. (27 Sptember 2010). "Arabs, Speak Hebrew!" *Ha'aretz*.

Michman, D. (1997). *Post-Zionism and the Holocaust*. Ramat Gan: Bar Ilan University [Hebrew].

Mill, J.S. (2010). *On Liberty and Other Essays*. Digiread.com.

Miller, O. (2004). "'*Canaanite*' Tendencies and Opposition Amongst *Etzel* and *Herut* Movements". *Iyunim Bitkumat Israel* 14 (2004), pp. 153–90 [Hebrew].

Moller-Okin, S. (1998). "Feminism and Multiculturalism: Some Tensions". *Ethics* 108(4), pp. 661-684.

Naor, A. (2004). "Ze'ev Jabotinsky's Draft Constitution for the Jewish State in *Eretz Yisrael*". in A. Bareli & P. Ginosar (Eds.), *A Man in the Storm – Essays and Studies by Ze'ev Jabotinsky*, pp. 51-92. Sde Boker: Ben Gurion Institute [Hebrew].

Negbi, M. (1987). *Above the Law: The Crisis of the Rule of Law in Israel*. Tel Aviv: Am Oved [Hebrew].

Netanyau, B. (2003). *The Five Forefathers of Zionism*. Tel Aviv: Yediot Achronot [Hebrew].

Neuberger, B. (1997a). *Politics and Government in the State of Israel*. Tel Aviv: Open University [Hebrew].

Neuberger, B. (1997b). *Religion and Democracy in Israel*. Jerusalem: The Floerheimer Institute for Policy Studies.

Neuberger, B. (2003). "Israel – A Liberal Democracy with Four Flaws". In Y. David (Ed.), *The State of Israel: Between Judaism and Democracy* pp. 361-370. Jerusalem: The Israel Democracy Institute.

Nordau, M. (1937). *To His People*. Tel Aviv: Hotza'ah Medinit [Hebrew].

Ohana, D. (2003). *Messianism and Mamlachtiut – Ben Gurion and the Intellectuals between Political Vision and Political Theology*. Sde-Boker: Ben Gurion Institute [Hebrew].

Pappe, I. (1995). "The New History of Zionism: The Academic and the Public Confrontation". *Kivunim*, 45, pp. 39-47 [Hebrew].

Pawel, E. (1989). *The Labyrinth of Exile: A Life of Theodor Herzl*. New York: Farrar, Straus & Giroux.

Peled, Y. (1993). "Strangers in Utopia: The Civic Status of Israel's Palestinian Citizens", *Theory and Criticism*, 3, pp. 21-35 [Hebrew].

Peled, Y., & Shafir, G. (2005). *Being Israeli: The Dynamic of Multiple Citizenship*. Tel Aviv: Tel Aviv University [Hebrew].

Peres, S. (1998). *The New Genesis*. Tel Aviv: Zemora Bitan [Hebrew].

Pettai, V. (1996). "The Games of Ethno-Politics in Latvia". *Post-Soviet Affairs*, 12(1), pp. 40-50.

Pettit, P. (1999). *Republicanism: A Theory of Freedom and Government*. Oxford: Oxford University Press.

Pettit, P. (2003). Republicanism. In Edward N. Zalta (Ed.), *The Stanford Encyclopedia of Philosophy*. Retrieved from <http://plato.stanford.edu/archives/spr2003/entries/republicanism/>.

Pinsker, Y.L. (1951). *Auto-Emancipation*. Jerusalem: The Zionist Library [Hebrew].

Plamenatz, J. (1976). "Two Types of Nationalism". In E. Kamenka (Ed.), *Nationalism, The Nature and Evolution of an Idea*. London: E. Arnold.

Rabinowicz, O. (1958). *Herzl: Architect of the Balfour Declaration*. New York: Herzl Press.

Rachlevsky S. (1988). Messiah's Donkey. Tel Aviv: Miscal.

Ram, U. (1996). "Memory and Identity: The Sociology of the Historians' Debate in Israel". *Theory and Criticism*, 8, pp. 9 – 32 [Hebrew].

Ram, U. (2006). *The Time of the Post: Nationalism and the Politics of Knowledge in Israel*. Tel Aviv: Resling [Hebrew].

Ratzabi S. (1988). "The Jewish State in Buber's Political Thinking 1942-1965". In A. Shapira (Ed.), *Independence: The First Fifty Years*, pp. 195-214. Jerusalem: Shazar Center [Hebrew].

Ratzabi, S. (1999). "Martin Buber and the Jewish State". In M. Bar-On (Ed.), *The Challenge of Sovereignty*, pp. 133-147. Jerusalem: Yad Ben Zvi [Hebrew].

Ravitzky, A. (1996). *Messianism, Zionism and Jewish Religious Radicalism* (Translated by Michael Swirsky and Jonathan Chipman). Chicago: The University of Chicago Press.

Raun, T. (1997). "Estonia: Independence redefined". In I. Bremmer & R. Taras (Eds.), *New States New Politics: Building the Post-Soviet Nations*. Cambridge: Cambridge University Press.

Ravitzky, A. (1997). *Religious and Secular Jews in Israel: A Kulturkampf?* Jerusalem: The Israeli Democracy Institute [Hebrew].

Refael, G. (1983). "The Cultural Question in the First Congresses". In A. Shapira (Ed.), *The Religious Trend in Zionism*, pp. 39 – 54. Tel-Aviv: Am Oved [Hebrew].

Reinharz, J. (2000). "Zionism as a Jewish Identity". In J. Reinharz, A. Shapira & J. Harris (Eds.), *The Era of Political Zionism*, pp. 45-63. Jerusalem: Shazar Center [Hebrew].

Reiter, I. (1995). "Between a 'Jewish State' and a 'Citizens' State': The Status of the Arabs in Israel in the Peace Era". *Hamizrach Hachadash*, 37, pp.45-60 [Hebrew].

Reiter, I. (2008). "Nakba and Revival: A Zionist – Jewish Perspective on the Vision Documents of the Arabs in Israel". In S. Ozacky-Lazar, & M. Kabha (Eds.), *Between Vision and Reality: The Vision Papers of the Arabs in Israel, 2006-2007*, pp. 140-158. Jerusalem: The Citizens' Accord Forum between Jews and Arabs in Israel [Hebrew].

Resnick, P. (1997). *Twenty-First Century Democracy*. Montreal: McGill-Queen's University. Rotenstreich, N. (1962). *Questions in Philosophy*. Tel Aviv: Dvir.

Rozen-Zvi, A. (2001). "A Jewish and Democratic State: Spiritual Parenthood, Alienation and Symbiosis – Can we Square the Circle". *Iyunei Mishpat*, 19(3), pp. 479-519 [Hebrew].

Rubinstein A. (1996). *The Constitutional Law of the State of Israel* (Fifth Edition with B. Medina) Jerusalem and Tel Aviv: Schocken [Hebrew].

Rubinstein, A. (1997). *From Herzl to Gush Emunim and Back*. Tel Aviv: Schocken.

Sachar, H. M. (1977). *A History of Israel: From the Rise of Zionism to Our Time*, Oxford: Blackwell.

Sagiv, A. (2002). "George Steiner's Jewish Problem". *Azure*, 12, pp. 133-157.

Salameh, F. (2011). "Does Anyone Speak Arabic?" *Middle East Quarterly*, Fall, pp. 47- 60.

Salmon, Y. (1996). "Religion and Nationalism in Early Zionism". In J. Reinharz, Y. Salmon & G. Shimoni (Eds.), *Jewish Nationalism and Politics – New Perspectives*. pp. 115-140. Jerusalem: The Shazar Center [Hebrew].

Salmon, Y. (1999). Herzl and Orthodox Jewry. In G. Shimoni, & R. S. Wistrich (Eds.), *Theodor Herzl: Visionary of the Jewish State*. pp. 294-307. Jerusalem: Magnes.

Sand, S. (2008). *The Invention of the Jewish People*. Tel Aviv: Resling [Hebrew].

Sand, S. (2009). *The Invention of the Jewish People*. New York: Verso

Sandel, M. J. (1996). *Democracy's Discontent: America in Search of a Public Philosophy*. Cambridge Massachusetts: Harvard University Press.

Segev, T. (1966, April 3). The First Post-Zionist. *Haaretz* [Hebrew].

Segev, T. (2001). *The New Zionists*. Jerusalem: Keter [Hebrew].

Shachar, Y. (1991). "The Diaries of Uri Yadin". *Iyunei Mishpat*, 16(3), pp. 537-557 [Hebrew].

Shachar, Y. (2003). The First Drafts of the Declaration of Independence. *Iyunei Mishpat*, 26, pp. 523-600 [Hebrew].

Shafir, G., & Peled Y. (2002). *Being Israeli: The Dynamic of Multiple Citizenship*. Cambridge. Cambridge University Press.

Shaked, G. (1988). "There is No Other Place: On Literature and Society". Tel Aviv: Hakibbutz Hameuchad [Hebrew].

Shapira, A. (1997). *New Jews Old Jews*. Tel Aviv: Am Oved [Hebrew].

Shapira, A. (2000). "Agreement on the Limits of Disagreement". In J.E. David (Ed.), *The State of Israel: Between Judaism and Democracy*, pp. 17-32. Jerusalem: Israel Institute for Democracy [Hebrew].

Shapira, A. (2003). "Whatever became of 'negative exile'". *Alpaim*. 25, pp. 9-54. [Hebrew].

Shapiro, Y. (1977). *The Democracy in Israel*. Ramat Gan: Masada [Hebrew].

Shapiro, Y. (1996). *A Society Captured by Politicians*. Tel Aviv: Syfriat Poalim [Hebrew].

Shavit, Y. (1984). *From Hebrew to Canaanite - From Radical Zionism to Anti-Zionism*. Tel Aviv: Domino [Hebrew].

Shavit, Y. (1992). "Messianism, Utopianism and Pessimism in the 1950th: Notes on the Criticism of Ben Gurion's State". *Iyunim Be'tkumat Yisrael*, 2, pp. 56-78 [Hebrew].

Shimoni, G. (1995). *The Zionist Ideology*. Hanover: Brandeis University Press.

Shimoni, G. (1999). "The Ideological Debate after the Establishment of the State". In M. Bar On (Ed.), *The Challenge of Sovereignty*, pp. 104-132. Jerusalem: Yad Ben Zvi [Hebrew].

Shimoni, G. (2000). "The Theory and Practice of 'Shlilat Hagalut' Reconsidered". In J. Reinharz, A. Shapira & J. Harris (Eds.), *The Era of Political Zionism*, pp. 45-63. Jerusalem: Shazar Center [Hebrew].

Simon, A. E. (1973). *The Line of Demarcation: Nationalism, Zionism and the Jewish Arab Conflict in Martin Buber's Theory and Action*. Givat Haviva: Hotsa'a Medinit [Hebrew].

Skinner, Q. (1988). *Liberty Before Liberalism*. Cambridge: Cambridge University Press.

Skinner, Q. (2002). "Classical Liberty and the Coming of the English Civil War". In Martin Van Gelderen & Quentin Skinner (Eds.), *Republicanism: A Shared European Heritage 2*. Cambridge: Cambridge University Press.

Smith, A. D. (1986). *The Ethnic Origin of Nationalism*. Oxford: Blackwell.

Smith, A. D. (1991). *National Identity*. Harmondsworth: Penguin Books.

Smith, A. D. (1995a). Zionism and Diaspora Nationalism. *Israel Affairs* 2(2), pp. 1-19.

Smith, A. D. (1995b. Gastronomy or Geology? The Role of Nationalism in the Reconstruction of Nations. *Nations and Nationalism*, 1(1), pp. 3-23.

Smith, A. D. (1996a). Nations and their Past. *Nations and Nationalism*, 2(3), pp. 359-363.

Smith, A. D. (1996b). "Memory and Modernity: Reflections on Ernest Gellner Theory of Nationalism". *Nations and Nationalism*, 2(3), pp. 371-388.

Smith, A. D. (1996c). *Nations and Nationalism in a Global Era*. Cambridge: Cambridge University Press.

Smith, G., Law, V., Wilson, A., Bohr, A., & Allworth, E. (1998). *Nation-Building in the Post-Soviet Boarder Lands: The Politics of National Identities*. Cambridge: Cambridge University Press.

Smooha, S. (1990). "Minority Status in Ethnic Democracy: The Status of the Arab Minority in Israel". *Ethnic and Racial Studies*, 13(3), pp. 389-413.

Smooha, S. (1997). Ethnic Democracy: Israel as an Archetype. *Israel Studies*, 2(2), pp. 198-241.

Smooha, S. (2000). "The Regime of the State of Israel: Civil Democracy, Non-Democracy, or Ethnic Democracy?" *Sociologia Yisraelit*, 2(2), pp. 565 – 630 [Hebrew].

Smooha, S. (2001a). "Arab-Jewish Relations in Israel as a Jewish and Democratic State". In E. Yaar and Z. Shavit (Eds.), *Trends in Israeli Society*, pp. 231-363. Tel Aviv: The Open University [Hebrew].

Smooha, S. (2001b). The Model of Ethnic Democracy. ECMI Working Paper 13. Flensburg, Germany: European Center for Minority Issues.

Smooha, S. (2002). "The Model of Ethnic Democracy: Israel as a Jewish and Democratic State", *Nations and Nationalism*, 8(4), pp. 475-503.

Smooha, S. (2002a). Types of Democracy and Modes of Conflict Management in Ethnically Divided Societies. *Nations and Nationalism*, 8(4), pp. 423-431.

Smooha, S., & Järve P., (Eds.). (2005). *The Fate of Ethnic Democracy in Post-Communist Europe.* Budapest: European Center for Minority Issues, Open Society Institute.

Stepan, A. (1998). "Modern Multinational Democracies: Transcending a Gellnerian Oxymoron". In John A. Hall (Ed.), *The State of the Nation: Ernest Gellner and the Theory of Nationalism*, pp. 219-239. Cambridge: Cambridge University Press.

Stepan, A. (2000). "Religion, Democracy, and the 'Twin Tolerations'". *Journal of Democracy*, 11(4), pp. 37-57.

Stepan, A. (2002). "Multi-Nationalism, Democracy and 'Asymmetrical Federalism' with Some Tenatative Comparative Reflections on Burma". *Technical Advisory Network of Burma Working Paper.* Retrieved from http://burmalibrary.org/ docs4/TAN-WP02-02- AStepan-Multinationalism.pdf

Talmon, J. L. (1952). *The Origin of Totalitarian Democracy.* London: Secker & Warburg.

Tamir, Y. (1993). *Liberal Nationalism.* Princeton, New Jersey: Princeton University Press.

Taylor, C. (1998). "The Dynamics of Democratic Exclusion". *The Journal of Democracy*, 9(4), pp. 143-156.

Tedeschi, G. (1962). "Who is a Jew?" *Hapraklit*, 19, p. 101 [Hebrew].

Van Duin, P. (2001). "Is National Mobilization in Slovakia on the Decline? A Contribution to the debate on Determinants and Manifestations of Ethnic Nationalism". *Slovak Foreign Policy Affairs*, Spring, pp. 121-128.

Viroli, M. (1995). *For Love of Country: An Essay on Patriotism and Nationalism*, Oxford: Clarendon Press.

Vital, D. (1982). *Zionism: The formative years.* Oxford: Clarendon.

Vital, D. (1984). The Afflictions of the Jews and the Afflictions of Zionism. *Hatzionut*, 9, pp. 9-19, [Hebrew].

Walker, A., & Wood, E. (2000). The Parliamentary Oath. Research Paper 00/17, Parliament and Constitution Center, House of Commons Library.

Warhaftig, Z. (1988). *A Constitution for Israel – Religion and State*. Jerusalem: Mesillot [Hebrew].

Weiler, G. (1976). *Jewish Theocracy*. Tel Aviv: Am Oved [Hebrew].

Wolitz, S. (1991, February 20). "The American Jew is American First". *The Jerusalem Post*.

Yakobson, A., & Rubinstein, A. (2009). *Israel and the Family of Nations: The Jewish Nation-State and Human Rights*. London and New York: Routledge.

Yehoshua, A. B. (1980). *In Praise of Normalcy: Five Essays on Zionism*. Jerusalem: Schocken [Hebrew].

Yehoshua, A. B. (1988, December 6). 'A Monologue' (part 1). *Ha'aretz* [Hebrew]. (1989, January 6) 'A Monologue' (Part 2). *Ha'aretz* [Hebrew].

Yehoshua, A. B. (2002). "The Law Needs to be Changed". *The Jews of the Former Soviet Union in Israel and in the Diaspora,* pp. 20-21, 46-50 [Hebrew].

Yiftachel, O. (1992). The Concept of Ethnic Democracy and its Applicability to the Case of Israel. *Ethnic and Racial Studies*, 15(1), pp. 125-136.

Yiftachel, O. (1999). "Ethnocracy: The Politics of Judaizing Israel/Palestine". *Constellations*, 6(3), pp. 364-390.

Yiftachel, O. (2006 December 6). "The Example of Slovakia". *Haaretz* [Hebrew].

Zidon, A. (1954). *The Knesset*. Jerusalem: Achiasaf [Hebrew].

Zertal I. (1997). *Shulamit Aloni: Lo Yechola Acheret*. Ramat Gan: Hed Arzi [Hebrew].

Zur, Y. (2001). *Between Orthodoxy and Zionism: Religious Zionism and its Opposition (Germany 1896 – 1914)*. Ramat Gan: Bar Ilan University [Hebrew].

$$\text{ᘓ} \Diamond \text{ᘔ}$$

Endnotes

1   Besides Agassi's book mentioned above, which contains a short biography
    of Hillel Kook, see also David S. Wyman, *The Abandonment of the Jews:
    America and the Holocaust 1941-1945* (New York: Pantheon Books, 1984).
    David S. Wyman and Rafael Medoff, *A Race against Death: Peter Bergson,
    America and the Holocaust* (New York, New Press, 2002). Lewis Rapoport,
    Shake Heaven and Earth: Peter Bergson and the Stuggle to Rescue the Jews of Europe
    (Jerusalem, Gefen, 1999).

2   Every citizen has a registered nationality at the Population Registry.
    The Jewish and the Arab nationalities are the two main recognized
    nationalities. In fact, the Israeli Population Registry recognizes some
    144 nationalities (see pp. 86- 88).

3   The religious *Mechina* (plural: *Mechinot*) is intended for graduates of a
    Yeshiva high school or a religious high school, and prepares them for
    service in the Israel Defense Forces.

4   As published on Ynet on 26.3.01

5   For the relation between Hillel Kook and Canaanism see also Miller, 2004.

6   International Constitutional Law (ICL) http://www.oefre.unibe.ch/law/icl.

7   Yet in other rullings the High Court declared the Hebrew language as the
    "principle" or "first" language of the State. (Karayanni, 2006, pp. 465-470).

8   Unless suggested otherwise all the quotations of the constitutions of the
    various countries are taken from the International Constitutional Law (ICL)
    http://www.oefre.unibe.ch/law/icl/

9   See International Constitutional Law (ICL), http://www.oefre.unibe.ch/law/icl

10 http://www.greekembassy.org.uk/pages_en/citizenships.html

11 *"Yesh Gvul"* ("There is a limit!") is an Israeli peace group campaigning against
    the occupation by backing soldiers who refuse duties of a repressive or
    aggressive nature.

12 This is not entirely accurate, for Bellah stresses that this civil religion precludes atheists and members of non-monotheist religions.

13 Liebman and Don Yehiya also distinguish an additional intermediate approach, "selective", which prevailed for a short time after independence.

14 "It is a people that shall dwell alone, and shall not be reckoned among the nations" (*Bamidbar* 23:9).

15 http://www.unhchr.ch/html/menu3/b/o_reduce.htm

16 The second document, *An Equal Constitution for All: On the Constitution and the Collective Rights of Arab Citizens in Israel,* by Dr. Yousef Taysir Jabaree, was published by the Mossawa Center. The third document *The Democratic Constitution,* was published by Adalah, the Legal Center for Arab inority Rights in Israel. The fourth, *The Haifa Declaration,* was published by Mada al Carmel, the Haifa-based Center for Applied Social research, headed by Prof. Nadim Rouhana (Rekhess, 2008, pp. 12-13). In the following, when I refer to the 'Vision Document' (in singular) I mean the one produced by The National Committee for the Heads of the Arab Local Authorities in Israel. Similarly most of the quotations are taken from this document, unless specified otherwise. However, the general analysis refers to the four documents.

17 Paragraph 2 of the Law of Citizenship was amended in 1980. According to Rubinstein, the purpose of the amendment was "to give to those who were born in Israel, whose father and mother are Israeli, Israeli citizenship by birth, and not by Return, as it had been before the amendment (Rubinstein, 1996, p. 878).

18 One of the committees established by Kook in the United States was *The Committee for a Jewish Army of Stateless and Palestinian Jews* the phrasing was meant to emphasize that the committee had no interest to mobilize American Jews to this Jewish Army (Agassi, 1993, p. 135).

19 The five attacking "nations" were Egypt, Transjordan, Syria, Lebanon and Iraq, helped also by forces from Yemen and Saudi Arabia. The overall population of these seven countries was approximately 30 millions.

20 Unless otherwise specified all constitutional drafts are taken from http://huka.gov.il/wiki/index.php/%D7%94%D7%A6%D7%A2%D7%95%D7%AA_%D7%97%D7%95%D7%A7%D7%94_%D7%91%D7%A2%D7%91%D7%A8

21 There are some differences between the English version of the draft (which was originally composed in English) and the Hebrew one. The text that is most relevant to our case is that in the Hebrew version the phrase "to rebuild our commonwealth" appears as "to rebuild our state". It seems that the words "state" and "commonwealth" are used as synonyms.

22 http://en.idi.org.il/projects/constitution-and-democratic-principles/constitution-by-consensus

23 The English translation of the declaration is taken from the Knesset official site http://www.knesset.gov.il/docs/eng/megilat_eng.htm. However, I have changed the wording in one place, where I replaced term "soveriegn Jewish people" with the term "sovereign Hebrew people" which appeared in the Hebrew original.

24 Nevertheless, this formulation did not appear in the Law of Return 1950, and was entered into the Law of Citizenship in 1952.

25 http://www.mfa.gov.il/mfa/foreignpolicy/peace/guide/pages/un%20general%20assembly%20resolution%20181.asp

26 Ynet 17.2.14 http://www.ynet.co.il/articles/0,7340,L-4489161,00.html

27 The latest in this genre is Chaim Gans' *A Political Theroy for the Jewish People: Three Zionist Narratives* (University of Haifa Press, 2013). Gans uses the three elements dicussed above: the principle of self determination, the Holocaust and the Historical connection of the Jews to Palestine, to assess the moral calculation of Israel and to reach the conclusion that Israel is justified only within the 1967 borders.

INDEX

www.ingramcontent.com/pod-product-compliance
Lightning Source LLC
Chambersburg PA
CBHW062152270326
41930CB00009B/1508